Jasmin Mahadevan

CROSS-CULTURAL MANAGEMENT

A Contemporary Approach

Sara Miller McCune founded SAGE Publishing in 1965 to support the dissemination of usable knowledge and educate a global community. SAGE publishes more than 1000 journals and over 800 new books each year, spanning a wide range of subject areas. Our growing selection of library products includes archives, data, case studies and video. SAGE remains majority owned by our founder and after her lifetime will become owned by a charitable trust that secures the company's continued independence.

Los Angeles | London | New Delhi | Singapore | Washington DC | Melbourne

Jasmin Mahadevan

CROSS-CULTURAL MANAGEMENT

A Contemporary Approach

⊗SAGE

Los Angeles | London | New Delhi
Singapore | Washington DC | Melbourne

ⓢSAGE

Los Angeles | London | New Delhi
Singapore | Washington DC | Melbourne

SAGE Publications Ltd
1 Oliver's Yard
55 City Road
London EC1Y 1SP

SAGE Publications Inc.
2455 Teller Road
Thousand Oaks, California 91320

SAGE Publications India Pvt Ltd
Unit No 323-333, Third Floor, F-Block
International Trade Tower Nehru Place
New Delhi – 110 019

SAGE Publications Asia-Pacific Pte Ltd
3 Church Street
#10-04 Samsung Hub
Singapore 049483

Editor: Matthew Waters
Editorial assistant: Charlotte Hanson
Production editor: Sarah Cooke
Copyeditor: Christine Bitten
Proofreader: Neil Dowden
Indexer: Elizabeth Ball
Marketing manager: Lucia Sweet
Cover design: Francis Kenney
Typeset by: C&M Digitals (P) Ltd, Chennai, India
Printed in the UK

© Jasmin Mahadevan 2023

Apart from any fair dealing for the purposes of research, private study, or criticism or review, as permitted under the Copyright, Designs and Patents Act, 1988, this publication may not be reproduced, stored or transmitted in any form, or by any means, without the prior permission in writing of the publisher, or in the case of reprographic reproduction, in accordance with the terms of licences issued by the Copyright Licensing Agency. Enquiries concerning reproduction outside those terms should be sent to the publisher.

Library of Congress Control Number: 2022944533

British Library Cataloguing in Publication data

A catalogue record for this book is available from the British Library

ISBN 978-1-5264-5923-7
ISBN 978-1-5264-5924-4 (pbk)

At SAGE we take sustainability seriously. Most of our products are printed in the UK using responsibly sourced papers and boards. When we print overseas we ensure sustainable papers are used as measured by the PREPS grading system. We undertake an annual audit to monitor our sustainability.

To Fredrik, Io and Peer

Contents

Acknowledgements — ix
About the Author — x
Figures and Tables — xi
What This Book Is About And Why It Is Useful — xv
Praise for This Book — xvii

PART I   CCM Underpinnings — **1**

1 Cross-Cultural Management in a Changing World — 3

2 From National Culture to Global Virtual Teams:
   Focus points of cross-cultural management studies — 39

3 Identities of the Cross-Cultural Manager — 67

PART II   CCM Perspectives — **101**

4 Contemporary Cross-Cultural Management Paradigms:
   How to assess and manage a cross-cultural situation — 103

5 Functionalist Cross-Cultural Management: How does CCM work? — 134

6 Interpretive Cross-Cultural Management: What does CCM mean? — 165

7 Critical Cross-Cultural Management: Whom does CCM serve, and
   how does this happen? — 198

PART III   CCM Applications — **237**

8 CCM and International Business — 239

9	CCM and Organization	276
10	CCM, and Technology and Social Media	318

PART IV CCM Skillset 355

11	Developing Your Cross-Cultural Management Competencies	357
12	Designing Your Cross-Cultural Management Research	401

Index 428

Acknowledgements

I wish to thank all students, fellow academics, practitioners, colleagues and friends with whom I could exchange my thoughts, and develop and refine the content of this book. At Sage, I am very grateful to my editor, Matthew Waters, to editorial assistants Jasleen Kaur and Charlotte Hanson, to copy editor Christine Bitten, to project editor Sarah Cooke, and to the rest of the Sage team, and to the five anonymous reviewers commissioned by Sage. Further thanks go to research assistants Iuliana Ancuța Ilie, Annabelle Stärkle and Larissa Dausien, and to student assistants Jasmin Kensington and Alexander Philipp.

Jasmin Mahadevan, Pforzheim, Germany, January 2023

About the Author

Jasmin Mahadevan is Professor of International and Cross-Cultural Management at Pforzheim University, Germany. She has experienced cross-cultural management as a researcher, as an intercultural trainer and consultant, and as an academic. She is also the author of the *Very Short, Fairly Interesting and Reasonably Cheap Book about Cross-Cultural Management* (Sage, 2017), and the main editor of *Cases in Critical Cross-Cultural Management: An Intersectional Approach to Culture* (with Henriett Primecz and Laurence Romani, Taylor & Francis/Routledge, 2020).

Figures and Tables

Figures

1.1	The changing realities of cross-cultural management	8
1.2	Sectors of the contemporary cross-cultural management environment	10
1.3	The cross-cultural management triangle	16
1.4	Building the cross-cultural management pyramid	19
1.5	Culture streamlines groups of people	24
1.6	Two culturally learned perspectives on good management	25
1.7	Cultural glasses	26
1.8	Culture as a backpack	28
1.9	Culture as an iceberg	29
1.10	N-cultural individuals in contemporary cross-cultural management	30
1.11	Cross-cultural management as a process of mutual learning and growth	31
2.1	Two initial interests of cross-cultural management studies	42
2.2	Multiple nested cultures in cross-cultural management	44
2.3	Cultural complexity and multiple cultures	46
2.4	Cultural complexity, and power and identity	48
2.5	A framework for a team-based cross-cultural management	56
3.1	The ongoing formation of the cross-cultural manager's identity	70
3.2	Monocultural identities in cross-cultural management	72
3.3	Third and bicultural identity work in cross-cultural management	77
3.4	An inside-out view on biculturalism in cross-cultural management	83
3.5	Developing a sense of rooted cosmopolitanism in cross-cultural management	85
3.6	Cross-cultural management as collective identity work: An integrative model	93
4.1	Cross-cultural management paradigms in relation to each other	111
4.2	Culture as an iceberg: The symbolic meaning perspective	119

5.1	Space bubbles (proxemics) according to Hall	144
5.2	Switzerland, France and Vietnam in terms of Hall's cultural dimensions	149
6.1	The perspectivity of reality and the positionality of CCM: What is an elephant, and from which position does one 'manage' or 'study' it?	166
6.2	Interpretive cross-cultural management as approximating emic meanings	168
6.3	How culture emerges from an interpretive perspective	173
6.4	Culture as an iceberg: the symbolic meaning perspective	174
6.5	Meaning-making in context	178
6.6	The circle of intercultural interactions	181
6.7	Assumptions about cross-cultural reality and their consequences	188
6.8	Another cross-cultural map of project Alpha	189
6.9	Circle of cross-cultural interaction	191
7.1	The everyday power of A and B	203
7.2	A exercises power over B	203
7.3	B's power to resist A's power over	204
7.4	A dominates B	204
7.5	A power kaleidoscope	206
7.6	Discourse	207
7.7	Hegemonic discourse	208
7.8	Capital and field – an overview	211
7.9	Cross-cultural management as circuits of power (simplified model)	216
7.10	The creative potential of power	225
III.0	Culture in today's business, organizations and management (simplified)	238
8.1	Typology of multinational companies and its CCM implications	249
8.2	Corporate philosophies and required managerial mindsets	252
8.3	Contemporary corporate internationalization: An overview	255
8.4	Modes of market entry and cultivation, and associated risks and opportunities	256
8.5	IKEA's internationalization path	261
8.6	Responsibility, ethics and sustainability in international business	264
9.1	How organization happens and becomes permanent	280
9.2	Mechanistic and organic organizational designs	285
9.3	Organizational networks	292
9.4	Organizations, stakeholder networks and the environment	294
9.5	BCG matrix as a metaphorical image	299
9.6	Metaphors of organization and their link to CCM paradigms	300
9.7	Knowledge as an iceberg	307
9.8	SECI Spiral	308
9.9	The contours of organization, including culture	314

10.1	Organizational transformation and the environment	325
10.2	Production technology in the manufacturing organization: Three types	328
10.3	Long-linked technologies	330
10.4	Mediating technologies	331
10.5	Intensive technologies	333
10.6	Organizational technologies in relation to task variability and analysability	336
11.1	Intercultural learning in context	359
11.2	How to build earthquake-resistant and ecologically friendly bridges	367
11.3	Cross-cultural management as a process of individual growth	370
11.4	Culture as backpack, glasses, iceberg and water	374
11.5	Need to integrate deep emic meanings into the interaction	375
11.6	An integrative cycle of intercultural interaction	376
11.7	Cultural norms – the intra-cultural view	379
11.8	Cultural norms – the cross-cultural view	379
11.9	Managerial growth via experiential intercultural learning	382
11.10	Stages of intercultural learning	384
11.11	Culture shock (U-curve)	386
11.12	Reverse culture shock (W-curve)	388
11.13	Multiple cross-cultural adjustments instead of single culture shocks	390
11.14	(Re-)packing your cultural backpack to enlarge your managerial repertoire	394
12.1	Facets of culture	406
12.2	Emics and etics: A combined approach	414

Tables

1.1	Cross-cultural management – then and now	14
3.1	Identities in CCM	87
3.2	Myself as a cross-cultural manager – a SWOT analysis	96
4.1	Three key cross-cultural management questions and the paradigms underlying them	108
4.2	GLOBE leadership styles	117
4.3	GLOBE leadership styles for China and the Netherlands	117
4.4	Meaning-mapping Ewoud's and Tian's perspective	120
5.1	The cultural dimensions of Kluckhohn and Strodtbeck	140
5.2	Overview of high- and low-context orientation	148
5.3	Summary of Hall's cultural dimensions	148

5.4	The cultural dimensions by Hofstede	151
5.5	The cultural dimensions by Trompenaars and Hampden-Turner	154
5.6	Cross-cultural dimensions according to GLOBE	157
6.1	Mapping objective and subjective culture	190
8.1	Chinese and Pakistani perspectives on international business cooperation	241
8.2	Types of companies and cross-cultural management requirements	251
8.3	A strategic stakeholder analysis (application of phronēsis)	268
9.1	Organization and cultural dimensions	284
9.2	Key decisions of organization	286
9.3	Metaphors of organization	302
10.1	GLOBE leadership styles	329
10.2	Organizational technologies and their cross-cultural management implications	334
10.3	Organizational technologies in relation to cultural dimensions	338
12.1	Individual-level indicators of collectivism and individualism	411
12.2	Horizontal and vertical collectivism and individualism and their indicators	412
12.3	How to design your cross-cultural management research – a structured summary	419

What This Book Is About and Why It Is Useful

This textbook is about the contours and requirements of contemporary cross-cultural management (CCM). Part I provides an overview of what characterizes contemporary CCM and makes it different and unique, Part II discusses the perspectives which underpin contemporary CCM, and Part III details the contexts to which contemporary CCM knowledge and skills need to be applied. Bringing this content to the point, Part IV outlines key CCM skillsets. Readers will familiarize themselves with key aspects of contemporary CCM, such as paradigms, organization, technology, international business and cross-cultural management competencies.

This book stems from the insight that classic CCM concepts and tools, while still useful, need to be adapted to the contemporary world. This is a world wherein an increasing number of people cross and bridge multiple cultures, wherein technology and social media create new, virtual cultural spheres, and wherein organizations and teams are globally exposed. What differentiates this book is thus firstly doing full justice to the contemporary conditions and requirements of today's and tomorrow's CCM.

Secondly, this book does not only report on the status quo of today's cross-cultural management. Rather, it tries to consider how CCM *should* be configured to do the multiplicity of perspectives, identities and experiences justice.

Thirdly, this book makes theory 'practical' via employing problem-based and experiential learning techniques. Each chapter's content is exemplified and brought to life via an Opening Case, and readers complete activities associated with this case. At the end of each chapter, the Opening Case is reflected upon, and a Closing Activity initiates the next learning loop and puts the learning into its wider context.

Via integrating the aforementioned elements, this book is able (1) to take a wider lens and also more meta-level perspective on CCM as is normally done, (2) to link CCM to the multiple people, tasks-at-hand and fields shaping its contours, and, at the same time, (3) to examine the details and the specific situations by which CCM is formed today.

What is unique to the readers' learning experience are (1) the problem-based and experiential learning focus, (2) the multi-paradigmatic learning process employed, (3) the full consideration of the contemporary CCM conditions to which this learning shall be applied and (4) the acknowledgement of the contemporary cross-cultural manager's multiple identities.

Lecturers will find useful cases, applications, theory and examples in this book, researchers will encounter a variety of potentially novel perspectives on their field, and practitioners can view their daily business in a new light. Together, these aspects make this first textbook on a contemporary cross-cultural management highly useful for teachers, researchers, students and practitioners alike.

Praise for This Book

'Jasmin Mahadevan has again brought to life cross-cultural management scholarship in its contemporary setting, its importance to everyday corporate life, building on her already impressive body of work. No student, academic or manager can afford to ignore this thoughtful, critical and highly practical work.'

Professor Terence Jackson, Middlesex University Business School London, UK, and Editor-in-Chief of *The International Journal of Cross Cultural Management*

'Professor Mahadevan brings a multi-paradigmatic approach to explain in accessible language the role of culture in a world of ethnic diversity, migration, and technological interconnectedness. This book is a timely and much-needed addition to cross-cultural management education. It is a must-read for anyone interested in International Business.'

Luciara Nardon, Professor of International Business, Carleton University, Canada

'Increasing workplace diversity resulting from migration and global talent mobility necessitates that cross-cultural management consider differences that go beyond language, dress, customs, and traditions. I am delighted to see a cross-cultural management book that is devoted to an examination of equity and inclusion across culturally diverse individuals. I applaud Jasmin Mahadevan for bringing a critical lens to issues related to power and identities in cross-cultural management.'

Professor Eddy Ng, Queen's University, Canada, and Editor-in-Chief of *Equality, Diversity and Inclusion: An International Journal*

'In this book, Jasmin Mahadevan combines her vast research and significant pedagogical expertise to provide an up-to-date textbook, explaining theories from the most basic level to ones that deal with the most complicated and controversial issues of our globalized world. For this reason, the book is suitable for students learning about cross-cultural management for the first time, while also addressing more advanced issues, which would be of interest to graduate students and researchers. Ultimately, it is the authors' unique critical approach that contributes to a ground-breaking and highly useful resource, which will no doubt become a standard text in years to come.'

Professor Henriett Primecz, Corvinus University Budapest, Hungary, and Johannes-Kepler University, Linz, Austria

PART I
CCM UNDERPINNINGS

This section provides you with the conceptual groundwork of a contemporary CCM.

Chapter 1 highlights the changing locations, the changing business environment, and the changing technological and organizational contexts that shaped contemporary CCM in its present contours. The chapter provides you with an in-depth understanding of the conditions under which present and potentially future CCM takes place, and how these are different from 'classic' CCM, as conceptualized in the past.

Chapter 2 introduces key focus points of CCM studies, and how they have developed over time. It provides you with ideas of how to assess and identify culture and enables you to understand the requirements for a successful cross-cultural management under contemporary conditions.

Chapter 3 focuses on the changing identities of the cross-cultural manager, and on how the identity of the cross-cultural manager is relevant to CCM as a collective task. Via this chapter, you become oriented in CCM in terms of your own cultural identity in relation to the cultural identities of others. This way, you can better assess your own strengths and weaknesses, and become aware of your learning path in CCM.

Cross-Cultural Management in a Changing World

1

Learning Objectives

After reading this chapter, you should:

- be able to outline the contours and challenges of cross-cultural management today
- be able to differentiate contemporary cross-cultural management from more 'classic' approaches to CCM.

Introduction

Cross-cultural management (CCM) focuses on investigating and managing the interrelations between culture and management, or organizations. The purpose of this initial chapter is to outline the contours of a contemporary CCM, and thus to provide an introduction to themes covered in subsequent chapters of this book, such as the concept of culture, the interrelations between CCM and international business, organizations and technology, or questions of how to develop your cross-cultural management skillset.

CCM evolved in the USA after World War II, and its first focus lay on how differences in national cultures impact on management and organizations. Since then, however, CCM realities have changed: the international business environment has evolved, corporate internationalization has become more complex, and technological advancements have enabled new and virtual cross-cultural workplaces. Also, people are more mobile and interconnected than they used to be, and many societies are characterized by internal heterogeneity. Therefore, 'classic' CCM concepts (such as 'culture') had to be adjusted to new realities and new situations became relevant to CCM. Out of this stems a more contemporary CCM upon which this book focuses.

Two features differentiate contemporary CCM from early CCM studies ('classic CCM'). First, cultures interrelate in more complex and differentiated ways with management and organizations, and most individuals' lives today evolve around more than one culture. This requires that a contemporary CCM moves beyond the classic CCM focus on national cultures when going abroad and to consider cross-cultural interactions 'at home' and in virtual and technologized settings. Second, cultural differences are seen less as an obstacle to be overcome and more as a resource to be utilized. Out of this follows the goal of figuring out how to create complementarities and synergies across multiple cultural differences in management and organizations.

Contemporary CCM does not mean that a more 'classic' CCM is outdated - it simply requires that academics and practitioners use classic CCM theories and methods from a more contemporary angle, and that they readjust their ideas of what constitutes culture and relevant cultural differences in CCM, and of how these should be conceptualized, studied and managed. The Opening Case of this chapter is a first illustration of these ideas.

Towards a Contemporary CCM

Opening Case

Let's say you are about to start your job as a corporate manager, and let's now think of two possibilities.

Scenario A is that you are going abroad to another country which you are unfamiliar with (let's assume that English is the business language of this country and that you, having been educated as an international manager, are capable of doing your job in the English language). Your task is to manage suppliers there, and you don't know anything about them besides them being locals to this country.

Scenario B is that you will manage global supplier relations or similar interactions across distance and via virtual channels, in a city within your own country and in English language. You will manage a local team of people who, as is evident from their corporate profiles, are diverse in terms of nationality, ethnicity, race, religion, gender and age.

Spotlight: Intercultural Competencies

Intercultural competencies, also referred to as **cross-cultural** or **intercultural management competencies** (Maznevski, 2020), are a key requirement and measuring rod of a successful CCM. A prominent definition describes intercultural competency as the ability to influence a cross-cultural management **context** in a way that is 'effective and appropriate' (Spitzberg and Changnon, 2009). 'Effectively' refers to reaching one's goals, 'appropriately' requires that one takes the needs of others and other contextual requirements into account. Any interculturally competent CCM practice can thus never be sheer dominance, for this would characterize an approach that is merely effective but not appropriate, and therefore fails to achieve complementarity and to utilize synergies. Therefore, CCM is always a collective task, especially in a culturally complex and '**n-cultural**' world.

Intercultural competency The ability to influence a CCM context effectively and appropriately

Context The boundary conditions and/or influencing factors of a situation which can help explain it

N-cultural The understanding that several cultures shape contemporary management and organization, to be identified and 'numbered' by the cross-cultural manager

Context refers to the boundary conditions or influencing factors of a situation; context is what the situation, or what people think, feel and do, is 'connected' to, and it can help explain the situation. The notion of context implies there is no universal rule of 'how to act appropriately and effectively' in CCM. Rather, CCM rules are context-dependent. Intercultural competency thus requires that cross-cultural managers need to carefully observe the situation, and to also reflect upon how they feel, act and interpret it, and then choose an appropriate and effective strategy *in context*, which takes the specificity of the situation, its boundary conditions and the people involved into account.

STUDENT ACTIVITY 1.1

What Makes a Situation Cross-Cultural?

Please consider scenarios A and B of the Opening Case. Think about what you have already learned about culture so far and answer the following questions:

1. How and in which aspects are Scenario A and Scenario B cross-cultural?
2. Which challenges do you expect in Scenario A and in Scenario B, respectively?
3. How do the intercultural interactions that characterize Scenario A and Scenario B, respectively, differ from each other? What does this imply for the intercultural competencies which you are required to develop, or, in other words: How shall you (develop the knowledge and skills to) act effectively and appropriately in each scenario? (see Spotlight: Intercultural Competencies)
4. Which scenario do you consider to be more representative of a contemporary CCM, and why?

Take notes and keep them for your further reading of this section.

The Changing Realities of Cross-Cultural Management

Both scenarios of the Opening Case are 'cross-cultural', as both describe a situation wherein multiple – and potentially divergent – cultural elements (e.g. rules and regulations, individual life experiences, physical locations) come together. In Scenario A, the cross-cultural dimension emerges from a change in location (a move to another country) and the meeting of two different national cultures (the overseas manager – i.e. you – and the local suppliers), at which the investigation of which cultures matter stops. In Scenario B, the cross-cultural dimension emerges from the virtual interactions between people from multiple cultures and in multiple locations, without any physical movement.

In this sense, Scenario A is representative of a more 'classic' CCM – as it developed after the end of World War II until and including the 1990s – and its three implicit core assumptions regarding culture and cross-cultural differences:

- First, the idea of classic CCM is that cross-cultural experiences are mainly triggered by physical movements ('going abroad'). For example, a prominent theme of classic CCM is expatriate management, **expatriates** being those who move to another country for job purposes.

> **Expatriate** Person moving to another country for job purposes (often sent overseas by companies for a specified duration of several years)

- Out of this follows the classic CCM assumption that cross-cultural differences are mainly experienced on country-level, in the sense of going to or meeting people from *another country*, and further investigated mainly in mono-dimensional ways.
- From this perspective, individuals and organizations need to proceed from the assumption of definable cultural units with clear demarcation lines. For example, companies are asked to offer **intercultural training** activities to familiarize managers with a thus defined 'overseas culture' for which they need to prepare and which is classified and experienced as 'foreign'.

> **Intercultural training** Human resource development activity to prepare for cultural differences, mainly at country level. Sometimes critiqued as being paternalistic (because the other culture is understood as 'difficult' or even 'problematic')

Conversely, Scenario B describes a more contemporary CCM reality:

- Here, people experience cross-cultural situations 'at home', and information and communications technology (ICT) enables virtual and real-time cooperation across distance.
- This perspective considers that many countries are characterized by societal heterogeneity and cultural diversity, that national borders are more permeable, and that people are increasingly mobile. This implies multi-dimensional cross-cultural situations which are devoid of clear and dualistic cultural

demarcation lines. Rather, cross-cultural managers thus need to ask: 'Which cultures are relevant to the situation, and how?' Secondly, these situations are 'fuzzy' in the sense that there is no single and absolute 'logical' explanation. Rather, cross-cultural managers need to apply 'fuzzy logic' by building and testing plausible hypotheses on the situation which can never be 'absolutely right' or definite.

- Cultural demarcation lines are thus less clear, and managers experience more complex inner-national cultural environments and higher inner-societal diversity at work, and even if they do not move physically, they are still largely exposed to 'the world'. For example, they might be asked to do their job in English language and to manage a global team virtually, in a country where English is not normally spoken and without ever moving abroad.

Figure 1.1 visualizes these changing realities of CCM.

Classic CCM → Shifting / broadened / more complex understanding → **Contemporary CCM**

Often involves physical movement
→ *full access points to single cultures*

ICT enables people to stay in one location and connects them across multiple locations
→ geographic and temporal dispersion, *partial access points to multiple cultures*

Culture is experienced on country-level

Culture is experienced on individual-level

Local environment is assumed to be culturally homogeneous

Local environment is assumed to be culturally diverse

CCM is an *individual* task

CCM is a *collective* task

Cultural differences are seen as an *obstacle* to be overcome

Cultural diversity is seen as an *opportunity* for the team

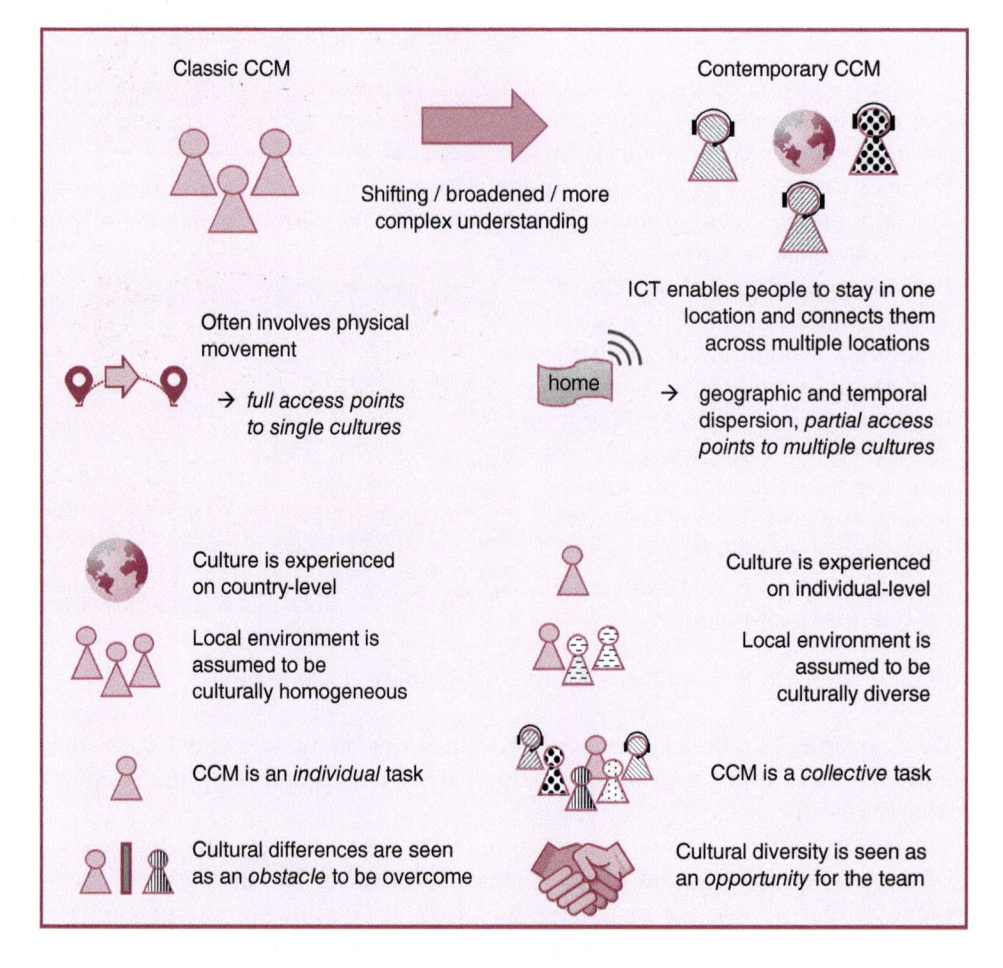

Figure 1.1 **The changing realities of cross-cultural management**

Link to Practice: The World and Cultural Identity of Generation Z

Those born between approximately the 1990s and 2010 are referred to as Generation Z (Gen Z), or 'post-millennials'. Their world is different to the environment encountered by previous generations (Benitez-Márquez et al., 2022), and the characteristics of Generation Z thus exemplify ongoing intergenerational cultural change (Schroth, 2019). For example, Generation Z has 'grown up with technology literally at their fingertips' (Evans-Reber, 2021), and even higher and different exposure to technology compared to the first 'digital natives', the so-called Millennials (born between 1981 and 1995).

As Schroth (2019) points out, every generation has its doubts about a younger generation's culture and technologies. However, for achieving corporate integration and success, it is essential to understand the 'behaviour and distinct needs that a new generation has in the workplace' (Schroth, 2019: 5).

What distinguishes Generation Z at the workplace are characteristics such as: being highly ambitious and self-confident, accepting one's circumstances, being realistic but also entrepreneurial and flexible, being aware and informed about the world, being financially conscious and oriented towards ethical consumption, and valuing freedom of expression and open-mindedness (Benitez-Márquez et al., 2022). The influencing factors proposed for these specific generational characteristics are: the global financial crisis, political uncertainty, climate change, the aftermath of 9/11, globalization effects such as the opportunity of free movement and the same currency within the European Union, and, last but not least, the COVID-19 pandemic (Benitez-Márquez et al., 2022; Evans-Reber, 2021; Hoffower, 2021; Schroth, 2019). The combination of these factors led to Generation Z's high adaptability in a flexible world of work (Hoffower, 2021) but also made them more prone to suffer from depression or anxiety (Schroth, 2019).

In the workplace, Generation Z is likely to switch jobs more frequently (always searching for the best opportunity), to place high value on work–life balance (Evans-Reber, 2021), and to prefer a multidisciplinary and global focus. They desire to make a direct contribution and want the outcome of their actions to be visible. They value honesty in leaders and enjoy open dialogues and have a strong desire to have their ideas listened to and to be valued for their opinion. Their focus lies on values-based careers (Evans-Reber, 2021), for example, when selecting employers based on their ethical commitment and global citizenship (Macwhinney and Betts, 2022). At the

(Continued)

> same time, Generation Z 'values salary less than every other generation' (Macwhinney and Betts, 2022).
>
> For older generations, these new preferences might come as a 'culture shock' (Schroth, 2019). For example, compared to the Millennials, Generation Z is likely to make bolder demands for change at work and to take more risks (Hoffower, 2021); from the perspective of Generation Z, flexibility of work (regarding hours, place and other aspects) is a prerequisite of work, not a perk, and they are likely to demand such conditions from their employer (ibid.). If the needs of Generation Z are not met at work, they are also more likely to quit, which implies that attracting Generation Z employees and keeping them engaged becomes harder and requires a change in corporate mindsets (Mawhinney and Betts, 2022).
>
> It remains to be seen how those born after 2011 – Generation Alpha – will further contribute to cultural change at work, based on the different environment in which they grew up and which then again shaped their 'ideas and ways of how to do things' in novel and distinct generational ways.

Several factors have contributed to how the contours of CCM have changed over the last decades. These effects will be highlighted in the subsequent chapters of this book.

Figure 1.2 Sectors of the contemporary cross-cultural management environment

First, *technology* is a major factor in this development. Technological advances – for example in ICT – have facilitated new modes of communication and co-operation and have enabled collaboration across distance. Equipment and hardware, such as laptops and smartphones, have provided people and organizations with new ways of work. Consequently, cross-cultural differences also manifest virtually and at home, not only 'abroad' or overseas. Therefore, it has become more difficult to establish where one culture 'ends' and another one 'begins'. Also, people have only limited information and exposure to those members of other cultures whom they interact with. This is why Chapter 10 of this book views CCM from a social media and technology perspective.

Secondly, the contours of *international business* are fuzzier than they used to be. Most governments have opened their markets at least partly to the outside world, and institutions such as the World Trade Organization (WTO) aim at establishing rules of the game for all. Companies are increasingly exposed to international markets, and the international business environment is more integrated and more easily accessible, yet also more complex, than used to be the case. Therefore, companies nowadays assess each part of their business operations for its international or global potential, and it might well be that some corporate units operate internationally, while other units are fully local. Some companies, the so-called 'born globals', even start their operations with a global outlook and sell their products and services worldwide. Chapter 8 provides an overview of the contemporary international business world and its interrelations with CCM.

Organizations and teams are now embedded in both local and global networks with customers, suppliers and partners. For example, supply chains are now coordinated on a global level, products are marketed across single locations, and value chains span multiple organizational units. Chapter 9 introduces the organizational dimension and analyses CCM in relation to its organizational boundary conditions, and for the purpose of managing cross-functional, often global teams.

Societies have always been internally heterogeneous, but nowadays more and more different groups of people make it into the managerial sphere in most societies. *People* (actors) are also increasingly mobile for a variety of reasons. For example, people study and work abroad, others migrate voluntarily and even others are part of refugee movements and forced migration. Both developments mutually reinforce the heterogeneity of cross-cultural management actors and change the logic of when a situation is or becomes 'cross-cultural' – it is not that people need to travel 'overseas' or 'to another culture' to deliberately seek out cross-cultural experiences. Rather, these cross-cultural experiences are always there because a diverse group meets at the managerial sphere. This makes management and work at least partially 'cross-cultural' at any given locality. Out of this, more opportunities for all, but also higher potential for conflict between interest groups might arise. Consequently, societies and organizations in many countries implement diversity, equity and inclusion policies in order to redress imbalances. Chapter 3 focuses on the identities of the cross-cultural manager and how they have changed over time.

> **Global North** Denomination for the richer and more industrialized countries, which are mainly located in the northern hemisphere. From a critical perspective, also a questionable term as the current status quo is assumed to be rooted in historic inequalities such as colonialism and imperialism (which made certain regions 'richer')

> **Global South** Denomination for the poorer and less industrialized countries, which are mainly located in the southern hemisphere. From a critical perspective, also a questionable term as the current status quo is assumed to be rooted in historic inequalities such as colonialism and imperialism (which made certain regions 'poorer')

The mixture of these factors then change and impact the *configurations of power* that underlie and shape contemporary CCM contexts. For example, it has been argued that technology has a democratizing effect in the sense that it reduces the costs, e.g. of information, education, knowledge and so on, in particular in those countries of the **Global South** which were previously understood as 'less developed' or 'developing' by the **Global North**. On the other hand, it has been said that some organizations, such as powerful multinationals, or even countries, namely those with the highest political and economic power, have increased their power on a global scale. From yet another perspective, new actors – such as emerging countries (for example, China) or members of minority groups – claim their place in CCM and need to be considered as relevant. Chapter 7 of this book provides you with the toolset for conducting a detailed and differentiated analysis of the interrelations between power and CCM.

Together, actors, locations, technology, the power configurations and the organizational context, and the international business (IB) environment shape the contours of contemporary CCM (Figure 1.2). As a successful cross-cultural manager in the contemporary world, you will need to analyse them in light of each other, as well as separately, and to engage in processes of cross-cultural interaction, conflict management, mediation and negotiation to build complementarities and synergies across difference together with others.

STUDENT ACTIVITY 1.2

The Changing Realities of CCM

This activity can be done in two ways:

Option 1: Identify and talk to a person who worked internationally to at least some extent during or even prior to the 1990s. Ask them: How has working internationally changed since then?

Option 2: You realize that you do not know anyone who worked internationally to at least some extent during or even prior to the 1990s. Ask yourself: Why is this the case?

For both options, consider sub-questions such as:

- Was management in general, and international management in particular, in the 1990s (and earlier) characterized by diversity and inclusion? To what extent (not)?
- Could you fathom yourself to be a (cross-cultural) manager in the 1990s (and earlier), and why (not)? What are the (critical) implications of this insight?
- What did culture 'mean' during the 1990s (and earlier)? How much was known about 'other cultures' and to what degree was one exposed to them?
- Where did cross-cultural interactions take place in the 1990s (and earlier), and what was their impact, and on whom?
- How has the international exposure of companies changed since then? To what extent were customers, partners, suppliers, markets, etc. global during these days?
- By means of which technologies was work organized? What did it mean to communicate across distance? How long did it take to organize a certain activity on an international or global level? What was the speed of information, and of transport and travel?
- Were teams local or global? How did people communicate with people elsewhere? Would it have been possible to form global or virtual teams (if not, what made it impossible)?
- What were the existing power relations in international business (IB) in the 1990s? How has the IB environment changed since then?

(Continued)

> Organize your findings by means of the following table:
>
> **Table 1.1** Cross-cultural management – then and now
>
> | CCM | Past | Present |
> |---|---|---|
> | Actors (people) | | |
> | Locations | | |
> | IB environment | | |
> | Organizational context | | |
> | Technologies | | |
> | Power relations | | |
>
> *Source*: own table
>
> Exchange your findings with fellow students.

What Is Management, and How Is It Cross-Cultural?

The Cambridge academic content dictionary refers to **management** as controlling or organizing something (business, employees) and, more generally, as being in charge and using or dealing with something in a way that is effective. Management, thus broadly defined, requires some sort of recognized authority; it involves a variety of responsibilities, such as strategy, leadership, delegation, motivation, physical and social organizational design, and decision-making, for which hard and soft skills need to come together as integrated professional skills. It is also based on the idea that managers will be measured against certain standards or goals (management needs to be effective).

Management (the people tasked with) 'controlling or organizing something' (effectively)

Cross-cultural Involving conditions, requirements, considerations, tasks, experiences and/or actions 'across cultures'

Management is **cross-cultural** if it involves conditions, requirements, considerations, tasks, experiences and/or actions 'across cultures'. Cultures might influence, for example, communication, decision-making, motivation, negotiation, leadership, expectations and behaviour in multicultural teams.

Cross-cultural management is not limited to those whose job description is 'management'. For example, technicians need to install machines across cultures and need to manage the knowledge transfer. Computer experts solve technical problems for corporate units across the globe – they need to manage customer problems across cultures. Medical doctors might send their MRT scans to an offshore site abroad for an overnight analysis to be discussed with a local patient – they manage a cross-cultural workflow. A company might offshore their legal, customer service or tax accounting department to a low-cost site elsewhere – they organize across cultures. As these examples suggest, a significant number of corporate roles and professions involve a strong cross-cultural component if one considers how workflows, organizational units, people or technology are managed and organized effectively.

STUDENT ACTIVITY 1.3

Experiencing Other Cultures

Please think of scenarios which can make you experience 'other cultures' without physical movement to another country and which involve 'cultures' other than national cultures. Write them down and clearly state how these scenarios involve a component 'across cultures'. Also explain what it is that needs to be 'managed' here, beyond a narrow view on management and as involving other professions, such as engineering or healthcare. Define management and cross-cultural in the aforementioned sense.

Managing the cross-cultural management triangle

Literally, **cross-cultural management** (CCM) refers (solely) to managing *across* cultures. Yet, most CCM studies also consider the next step, namely managerial advice regarding how to deal with, and potentially integrate, these differences, for example via creating new intercultural (literally, between cultural) solutions. In several other, non-English language academic traditions, such as France, Spain and Germany, the term

Cross-cultural management (literally) management across cultures (but also) the whole of CCM as a discipline or academic field

CCM Underpinnings

> **Intercultural management** (literally) management between cultures (but also) the whole of CCM as a discipline in several, non-English language, academic traditions

intercultural management – and not cross-cultural management – has been chosen to cover the whole of the discipline: *gestion interculturelle* (France), *administración intercultural* (Spain), *interkulturelles Management* (Germany), with slightly different connotations in the sense that the focus is more on the interactional process between representatives of different cultures, rather than on the comparison between two distinct cultures. Regardless of the term chosen, CCM as a discipline always involves both elements: managing 'across' and 'between' cultures.

Successful CCM requires both hard skills (e.g. knowledge about cultures and methods of how to analyse and interpret them) and soft skills (e.g. how to deal with cross-cultural conflict), personal abilities (e.g. reflexivity) and interpersonal competencies (e.g. communication). Chapters 11 and 12 consider both aspects, i.e. how to build the required CCM competencies and how to conduct fitting CCM research – both go hand in hand when it comes to the skillset of the cross-cultural manager.

For acquiring such a combined professional CCM skillset, it is not enough just to study other cultures. Rather, managers need to reflect upon their own cultural orientation and seek to enlarge their managerial repertoire. In simple terms, every journey to the cultural unknown begins within oneself. For example, you alone will know what you experience as different and how you judge this difference, if you know what is familiar to you. Questions of identity and identification are thus relevant: the life experiences which you bring to CCM, and how you access it and journey through it, matter for how you manage within, across and between cultures.

CCM as a discipline can thus be conceptualized as involving three sides of a triangle. Figure 1.3 visualizes this idea.

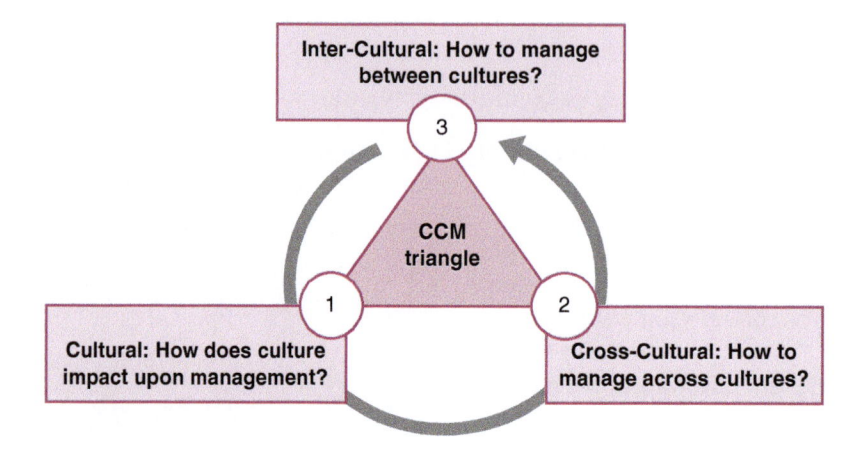

Figure 1.3 The cross-cultural management triangle

The cultural perspective focuses on how culture impacts on and interrelates with management. For example, what are the common habits, attitudes, expectations and ways of how to make sense of a situation that unites and separates people at work? Who shares which perspective, with whom and in which situation? Which influencing factor is causing such similarities and differences? Analysing their own cultural backpack thus enables managers to become more aware of who they are, what they have learned to experience as 'normal', and with whom they share their expectations and experiences of 'normality'. The first side of the cross-cultural management triangle is thus about training your abilities to identify culture in a situation and to recognize when a situation becomes or is experienced as 'cross-cultural'; namely, when expectations of 'normality' are not met from your own perspective and/or the perspective of others.

The cross-cultural perspective provides managers with tools that help them to build first hypotheses as to what exactly makes people's cultural orientation similar or different in relation to each other. For example, every person is only an individual in relation to others, but where do people draw the line? How much should 'we' be part of the 'I', and how exactly does the right ratio of 'We-ness/One-ness' feel and look like in a certain situation or regarding a certain task? The answer to the universal human question 'how much "we" should be in the "I"?' differs vastly, and the cross-cultural management insight is that this is not only because every person has a different personality, but also because they have been infused with different blueprints of what is 'normal' on a collective level. As social animals, humans learn different cultural perspectives from others throughout their lives, and they then use their past experiences as potential blueprints for future situations. Humans are thus not only products of, but also producers of, culture.

The tools that investigate and measure the relative differences in people's specific cultural blueprints to universal social questions are called cultural dimensions or cultural value orientations. The (expected degree of) individualism and (expected degree of) collectivism (Triandis, 1995) is a prominent example of a cultural value orientation.

Cultural dimensions are thus a measuring rod for the differences that might occur across groups of people. They are helpful to make cross-cultural managers aware that any experience or reality of 'difference' is never just merely a personal choice or conscious nuisance on behalf of the other person. Rather, it is evidence of a larger and patterned social process of which no human being can ever be free; all humans are individual entities embedded in social groups, and no individual or group can ever be without a blueprint of how to integrate both conditions. The second side of the CCM triangle is thus about familiarizing yourself with those concepts that help you address cross-cultural differences as both universal (a human condition) and specific (a cultural condition), and to develop your managerial strategy and practice from there.

The intercultural perspective is about what to do about the thus identified cross-cultural differences and move beyond them. How can one identify and manage cross-cultural conflict? Which conflicts are negative, for example, because they lead to mistrust and a lack of coherence, and which ones are positive, for example, because a diversity of thoughts and ideas spurs a group's or organization's innovativeness? Which cross-cultural differences should be retained and which ones should be integrated, and how can one mediate and bridge the latter ones? In order to do so, which interpersonal skills are required, and what are promising strategies for becoming more culturally versatile?

The third side of the cross-cultural management triangle is thus about the conclusions to draw from the investigation of one's own cultural backpack and the careful assessment of the cross-cultural differences as impacting upon a situation. It is also about how to develop the required hard skills (knowledge) and soft skills (interpersonal, communicative and self-reflexive skills), and about how these skills are to be polished and refined by experience and a learning mindset.

Building the cross-cultural management pyramid

In the contemporary world, there are multiple cultures at any given location, and many people cross many cultures routinely over the course of a day (see Figure 1.1). Therefore, culture is much more than just 'country culture' or 'societal culture', and its demarcation lines are tricky to identify in a globalized and interconnected world. Any person who is, let's say, somehow 'Brazilian' in their idea of how to lead a team, and thus different to another person promoting a 'Swedish' idea of team leadership in the same organization, might also be similar with regard to other cultures which they might share. These are, for example:

- Generational culture: management scholars have convincingly argued that leadership patterns have changed in similar directions across the globe
- Gender culture: sociologists have argued that there might be archetypical gender-specific patterns of leadership
- Professional culture: the curriculum of renowned MBA-programmes is fairly similar in countries all over the globe
- Organizational culture: the 'Swedish' and the 'Brazilian' work in the same organization, and this means that their respective actions take place within this shared framework which steers and sometimes constrains individual choices.

Consequently, international management scholar Martha Maznevski (2020) has stated that CCM needs to consider increasingly 'n-cultural individuals' in interaction, 'n' being the placeholder for any given number of whole numbers. When interacting with others, you will thus never know which (and how many) cultures you encounter and which (and how many) cultural orientations you yourself bring to the interaction – this is to be 'puzzled with' and to be deduced from the situation.

A key aspect to a successful contemporary cross-cultural management is thus to constantly test and refine one's hypotheses as to *which culture* is relevant to the situation, and *how exactly*. From this perspective, the assessment of cultural differences arises from the process of dealing with people's similarities and differences, and their relatedness and separateness in a situation – it is not that 'being Brazilian' or 'being Swedish' determines how people behave. One can also never be sure that it is 'country culture' – or any other of the 'n' cultures in interaction – which are the relevant cultural demarcation line; it could also be generation, gender, profession, organization, or any potential combination of all of them, to name but a few. Classic CCM would assume that these 'other cultures' are mere 'subcultures' which must be less impactful than country or society culture. However, this idea comes from a managerial world wherein cross-cultural means movement across countries; with modern ICT technology and people's mobility, this has changed. Or, as Martha Maznevski (2020) put it: 'the next CCM frontier is inward-bound'. This statement is insightful in two ways:

- Firstly, it means that managers do not need to go elsewhere to find themselves in a cross-cultural situation; rather, they need to look at any given situation as culturally complex (n-cultural) and cross-cultural.
- Secondly, it demands that each individual manager – you and me! – look inwardly to figure out which cultural orientations they bring to the situation.

This way, cross-cultural managers move the CCM triangle to higher levels – they build a pyramid from it (Figure 1.4).

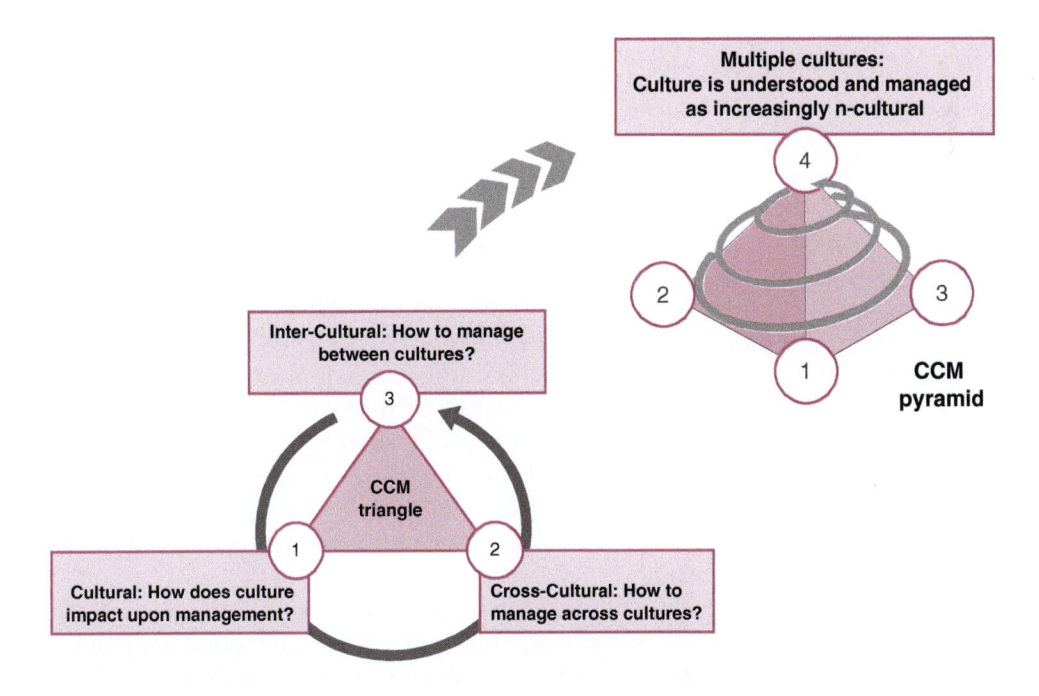

Figure 1.4 Building the cross-cultural management pyramid

With this, it is meant that the more you investigate people's similarities and differences, and their relatedness and separateness in a situation (including yourself), the more you refine your categories of culture and cross-cultural differences. As a result, you develop the ability to experience more and more complex things in context. For example, you might initially think of yourself as a 'German' interacting with 'the Chinese' (to give but two examples), but if you engage in cross-cultural interactions and reflect upon your experiences across all sides of the CCM triangle, you might then find out that you are, let's say, also influenced by generational, gender, ethnic, professional, regional, local and many more cultures, and will also start viewing your counterpart in these more differentiated and n-cultural ways. Rather than seeing just 'the Chinese', you will now see more, and more individualized and contextualized cultures, in the other person, and you will also think about your own cultural identifications in such ways. You thus move your cross-cultural management skills 'up the ladder' (Figure 1.4).

The process of refining your cross-cultural categories involves a dialectical and binary process – you try out, and argue for and against cultural hypotheses which come in pairs. The initial categories which people tend to apply to a situation are national or societal cultures such as 'English', 'French' or 'Spanish' – they assume that these categories influence people's intentions and behaviour. However, beyond these initial categories, there are more cultural categories which are equally relevant. Thus, if the initial cultural hypothesis (country culture influences people) is too general, other cultural categories need to be tested upon the situation. For example, are they doing X/Am I doing X because they are/I am, for example, a village person (as opposed to 'city person')? By trying out alternatives, managers train themselves in thinking in smaller, more contextualized cultural categories. From this perspective, the ability to identify oneself and another person more specifically than merely as a representative of a certain national culture signifies a higher level of cross-cultural competencies.

When engaging in this process, it is important to keep in mind that binaries such as 'French versus English', 'village versus city person', 'older versus younger generation' or 'well-travelled versus local' are mere hypotheses; they are plausible ideas about how certain cultural categories might impact upon a situation, not a given reality. Therefore, categories of cultural difference, if used as hypotheses to be tested, ultimately lead beyond dichotomist ideas such as 'they' versus 'we'; you will see that people are not only different, but also related in multiple ways. For the cross-cultural manager, analysing people's relatedness and differences in relation to each other is an essential prerequisite for establishing common ground, for motivating people towards shared goals and for aligning the preferred ways of doing things for reaching these goals.

What is essential to building cross-cultural competencies, is, of course, the *motivation* to engage in this strenuous, sometimes scary and often frustrating process, yet with potentially highly rewarding results and a great view from atop.

CCM in a Changing World

Also, there are entry requirements in terms of knowledge and skills. For example, in most CCM contexts, a certain proficiency in English language is a key communicative requirement – without it, even the first step of the process might be out of reach, even though the rest of your skillset might be very fitting to the task.

STUDENT ACTIVITY 1.4

What Motivates Me to Manage Across Cultures?

Please consider who you are. Which motivations do you bring to cross-cultural management, and why do you expect CCM to be a rewarding activity or task?

- Answer spontaneously, without much thought, within 15 minutes, and write your ideas down.
- Form groups of three students and exchange ideas with each other.
- Each student should then write down three takeaways from the exercise.

Keep your notes for the further reading of this chapter.

Link to Practice: Erasmus +

Erasmus + is an exchange programme within the European Union (EU) that aims to foster the competencies and skills described in this chapter via the exchange of youths, students, lecturers and others. As the European Commission (EC, 2022a) describes the rationale:

> European citizens need to be better equipped with the knowledge, skills and competences needed in a dynamically changing society that is increasingly mobile, multicultural and digital. Spending time in another country to study, to learn and to work should become the standard, and the opportunity to learn two other languages in addition to one's mother tongue should be offered to everyone.

(Continued)

> To this end, the programme (EC, 2022a) offers:
>
> > High quality, inclusive education and training, as well as informal and non-formal learning, ultimately equip young people and participants of all ages with the qualifications and skills needed for their meaningful participation in democratic society, intercultural understanding and successful transition in the labour market.
>
> In the programme, eight levels of competencies and skills according to the thus defined European Qualification Framework (EQF) are described, and a bachelor student should seek to achieve levels 5 or 6 via studying abroad (EC, 2022b). More information on the EQF, also useful for a quick self-check, can be found online (EU, 2022).

What Managers Do in Terms of Culture

Culture as 'the way in which we normally do things around here' (Deal and Kennedy, 1982) is probably the most accessible definition of culture, and this is also why this book proceeds from it. Like any other profession, management involves 'ideas and ways of how to normally do things': it is thus a cultural activity.

Still, management is often not perceived as cultural. Rather, those studying and practising management tend to assume that the managerial 'ways of doing things' which they have learned, believe in and practise is just 'normal' and 'natural' to all those who are 'good managers'. However, what managers *actually* believe in is the culture of management which they have learned: a certain socially learned 'measuring rod' for judging a situation, and a 'blueprint' of how to deal with it.

One can therefore understand culture as the ubiquitous second layer to what managers experience, expect and do. If not reflected upon, culture thus leads to managerial myopia and the categorical rejection of alternative ways of doing things as inferior or simply 'bad management'. The key to successful cross-cultural management is to make this second layer visible to oneself and others, and to draw conclusions on how to improve upon a situation from there.

> **Culture** The ways in which we normally do things around here – but not there (initial working definition)

Culture as 'the ways of how to normally do things around here' thus automatically implies that there is more than one culture: how people do things 'around here' might not be the same as how people do things 'around there'. Any single management style is thus only *one* potential version of how things might be normally done.

For example, it might be that people have learned that 'good managers' are those who take charge and make decisions for the team. Or it might be that people have learned that 'good managers' do exactly the opposite and involve the team in decision-making. Depending on the cultural perspective taken, the same exact behaviour can thus come to mean 'good' or 'bad' management.

Out of this follows that no selective 'way of doing things' of any group of people can ever involve the complete picture – they have just made a specific culture choice out of much richer cultural possibilities. Thus, the more perspectives enter that management, the more possibilities of how things might be done will be explored – a powerful argument in favour of **cultural diversity**.

> **Cultural diversity** Multiple cultures which contribute to a system, task or situation

The social dimension of culture: How a certain variation is selected as 'normal'

How do cultural differences come into being? One starting point is the realization that people only encounter and adopt *certain*, not all, ideas and ways of doing things. This process of selective adoption (see Figure 1.5) is called **enculturation.**

Enculturation – e.g. into a certain professional role, into an organizational culture, into a societal cultural environment – makes groups of people similar to each other but also different to other groups of people which have not been subjected to the same enculturation process.

> **Enculturation** The social process by which people learn culture and become an accepted member of a cultural group

The cross-cultural dimension of culture: When different 'normalities' meet

Culture as a process of selective adoption implies that whatever you assume to be 'good management' and what you learn about it from others can never be the objectively 'best' way of doing things. Other groups of people could

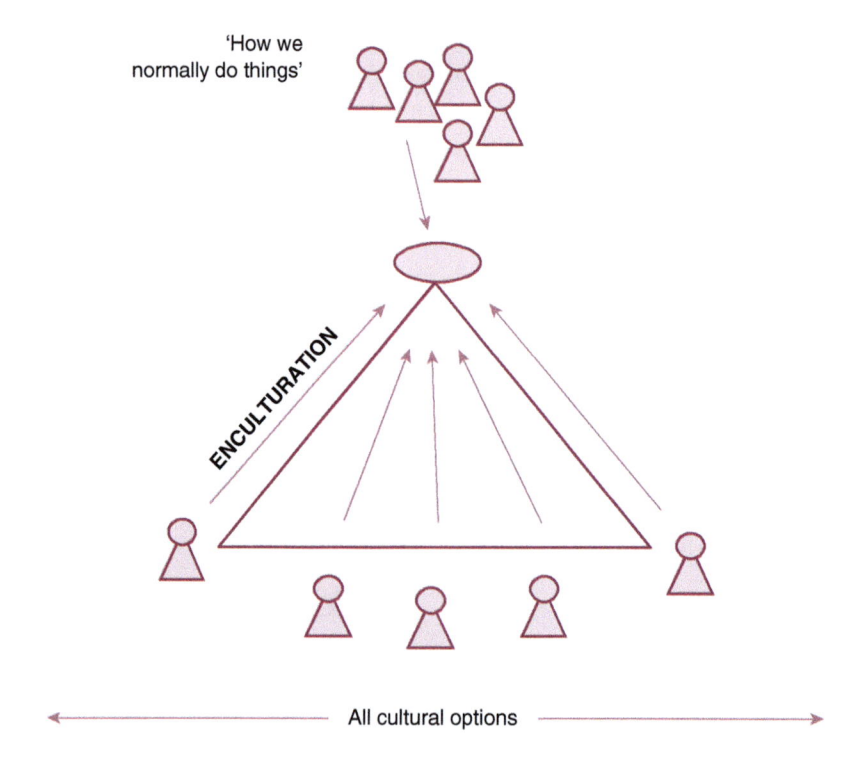

Figure 1.5 Culture streamlines groups of people

have – and have – chosen otherwise, and it is culture that makes the difference. Out of this realization should follow a certain humbleness and humility, for if everyone has learned certain cultural blueprints for 'good management', they also have lost access to all other possibilities (see Figure 1.6). Whatever a person culturally believes to 'know' about 'good management' (and life in general) is thus complemented with an immensely rich fundus of what they do not know.

Cross-cultural management is the art and practice of discovering, of trying out and of making use of these hidden alternatives. Out of this follows that CCM in the contemporary world *must* be a collective task because what I don't know, I can neither recognize nor apply to a situation – therefore, I need to involve, seek out and learn from those to whom these hidden alternatives are not lost.

Cultural group A

Cultural group B

'This is good management'

'This is good management'

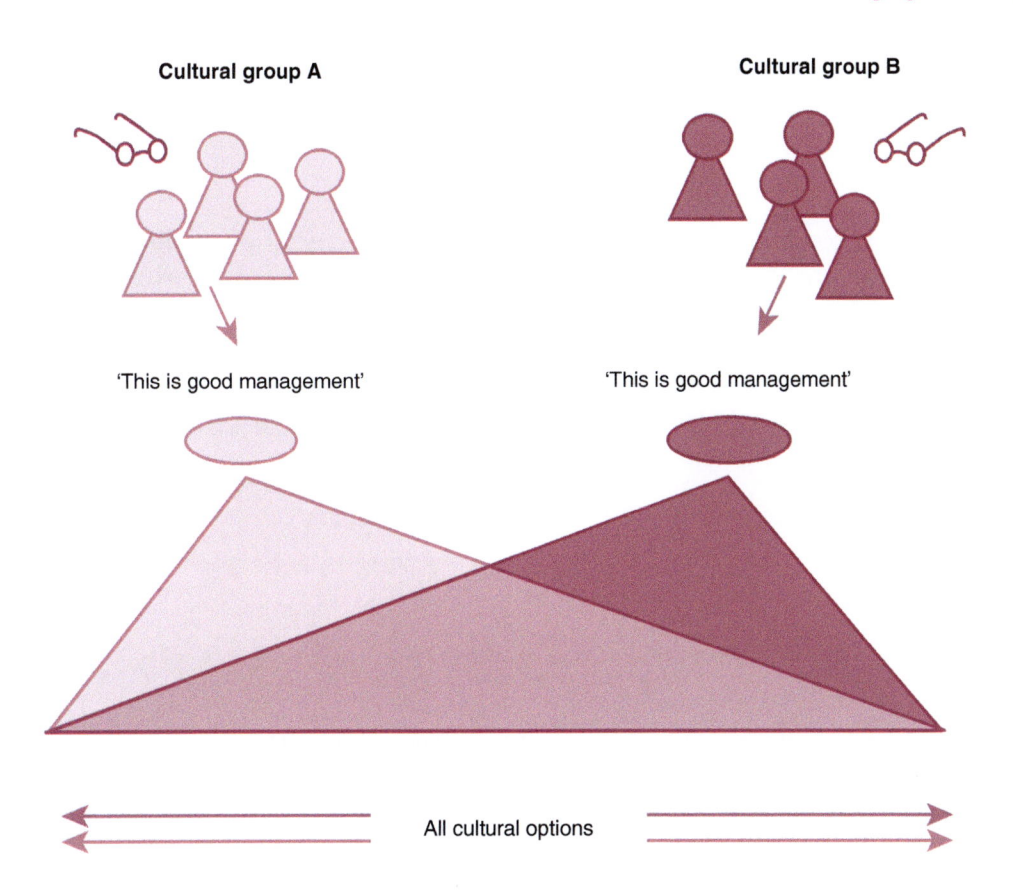

All cultural options

Figure 1.6 Two culturally learned perspectives on good management

STUDENT ACTIVITY 1.5

How Did It Happen that I Access CCM in This and Not in Another Way?

Consider your notes from Student Activity 1.4 and think about yourself as a social being, as a person who has acquired specific cultural glasses via others (e.g., parents, friends, teachers, fellow students) and via the

(Continued)

conditions into which you were born and have lived (e.g. family ties, time and place of birth, income conditions, gender, ability and opportunity to travel).

- Now consider how is what you bring to CCM and what you expect from it 'cultural', that is learned via others, and shared only with certain, but not all people? Think about how to answer this question in depth and take your time.
- Form groups of three students and exchange ideas with each other.
- Each of you should then write down three takeaway ideas from the exercise.

Keep your notes for the further reading of this chapter.

Metaphors of Culture

Metaphors of culture enable managers to become aware of culture's imprint on themselves and others. Metaphors are pictures or images that are easily accessible and malleable, but nonetheless transport complex ideas and knowledge. Metaphors include, for example:

- *Cultural glasses.* When you manage across cultures, you just have to remember that you are wearing them, and that others do so as well, and that your respective glasses are tinted in slightly different colours. This implies that it is also easy to add aspects to a metaphor. A metaphor thus enables you to move your CCM competencies 'up the ladder' – to use to another metaphorical image.

Figure 1.7 Cultural glasses

- Culture as the '*software of the mind*' (Hofstede, 1980). While reality might be objective, culture has provided us with the specific programming (or 'code') which we run against this reality.
- Culture as an *onion*. Culture has also been compared to an onion (Hofstede, 1980) – when you learn another culture or wish to become aware of the imprint which culture has on you, you need to peel away layer by layer.

- Culture as an *identity tree*. There is also the suggestion that we all have cultural 'identity trees'; that is, the roots upon which we build our lives, the branches we grow, the buds and flowers which blossom, and the sky to which we wish to reach out.
- Culture as *ocean and waves*. Culture can also be seen metaphorically as an ocean (Fang, 2015); that is, the water is permanent whereas the individual wave wanders. This image thus explains how culture is paradoxical in the sense that it always exists, yet also changes its configurations and that each single culture ('ocean') encompasses an infinite number of variations ('waves').

STUDENT ACTIVITY 1.6

Metaphors of Culture

Work together in groups of students.

- Come up with more images, visualizations and metaphors of culture. Explain in one to two sentences which aspect of culture is captured by this image (see previous explanation on the 'ocean' metaphor).
- Discuss which metaphors fit Scenarios A and B of the Opening Case the best. Do you need different metaphors for each case, and, if (not), why is this so?
- Present in class.

Culture as a backpack

The idea of *culture as a backpack* (Figure 1.8), another metaphor of culture, visualizes this idea of culture as something that is 'carried around' by individuals. It highlights how people and culture are mutually constitutive; that is, people's previous cultural experiences influence how they experience and interpret current situations. This then guides their actions in current situations, and provides them with cultural blueprints of how to deal with future situations. For example, people create business cultures while at the same time being influenced by the business cultures in existence, and, this way, they configure and re-configure the interrelations between 'old' and 'new' cultural elements. When doing so, they make their own choices of how they relate to the cultures already in existence.

CCM Underpinnings

Figure 1.8 **Culture as a backpack**

> ### STUDENT ACTIVITY 1.7
>
> **Culture as a Backpack**
>
> Consider the two scenarios of the Opening Case. What will the people who meet in Scenario A and in Scenario B, respectively, have in common? How will their backpacks differ? When and how did they pack these commonalities and differences into their respective backpacks, and who packed them (themselves or others)? Do they have a choice of what to unpack and when, or is how they do things merely 'instinctive'?

Culture as an iceberg

The idea of *culture as an iceberg* (Figure 1.9) visualizes that there is always more to culture than people are aware of; that is, some aspects of culture simply are 'below the surface', both to ourselves and to others.

Invisible parts of culture are, for example, meaning, knowledge, feelings, sensations, motivations, aspirations, interpretations and values. These provide people with ideas of what a certain situation means and how it should be interpreted. They also motivate people's practices and structure the actions by which people wish to influence a situation.

Visible parts of culture are, for example, language, facial expression, body language, behaviour, how people carry, clothe and generally present themselves towards others, and the material and technological products of human existence. Some theories also include nature and the environment, which might be a point,

Figure 1.9 **Culture as an iceberg**

because the people's culture is influenced by the possibilities of their surroundings. For example, it seems logical that climate influences the patterns of how people dress or live, or that space influences how buildings are normally constructed. However, culture is always acquired and learned – it is not a 'natural' phenomenon.

> ### STUDENT ACTIVITY 1.8
>
> ### Culture as an Iceberg
>
> Revisit the two scenarios of the Opening Case. For each, visualize culture by means of an iceberg. Which elements of culture will be visible to others in each case, which ones will be hidden? Try to find as many elements of culture as you can and map them as 'below' or 'above' the surface.

Challenges of Cross-Cultural Management Today

As John Hendry (2013) points out, management is never fully predictable as a large portion of it requires managers to 'cope with things' in the sense of unexpected situations, challenges or requirements. Culture and cross-cultural differences are one dimension of how management involves unpredictable and inexplicable elements that need to be coped with as they arise. Each CCM situation involves unique configurations of culture and cross-cultural differences, as Scenarios A and B of the Opening Case exemplify.

The idea of 'culture as the way in which we normally do things around here' automatically implies that how things are done 'around here' are not the same as how they are done 'around there'. Consequently, cross-cultural differences across these demarcation lines emerge and are experienced.

The tricky aspect of a contemporary CCM (Scenario B) is to define 'here' and 'there'. In a more classic CCM environment (Scenario A), the borders and demarcation lines between distinct cultures are more easily identified, and there are also fewer 'cultures' involved. Conversely, Scenario B is characterized by multiple, overlapping cultures in the sense of 'how to normally do things' which n-cultural individuals bring to the situation (Figure 1.10).

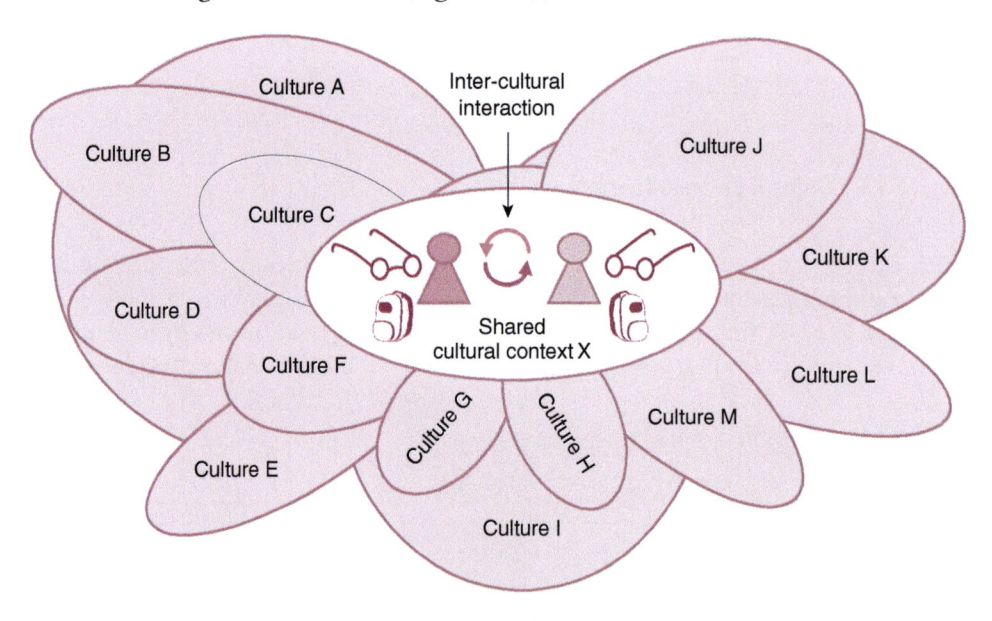

Figure 1.10 **N-cultural individuals in contemporary cross-cultural management**

STUDENT ACTIVITY 1.9

My N-Cultural Self

Who are you? Name all the cultures of which you are a part and that you might identify with. Remember, culture is every 'way of how to normally do things' which you might share with others in a certain context or sphere of life. For example, there is yoga culture, soccer culture, vegan culture and many more, but also student culture, managerial culture, societal culture, family culture and so on.

Compile a visualization of how they overlap and interrelate to form your 'n-cultural self'.

Next, exchange with a fellow student and discuss the similarities and differences of your respective 'n-cultural self' visualization. For a specific cultural sphere, such as being a student, create a visualization of your 'n-cultural selves' that involves both of you (see Figure 1.10). Discuss and reflect on which cultures you share and which ones are different across the two of you.

When and how is cross-cultural management successful?

A successful cross-cultural management facilitates understanding where there previously was none; it bridges and spans boundaries, and it translates and integrates between previously divergent perspectives.

It is thus not the initial cross-cultural differences that count, but the processes of intercultural creation that emerge between and across people. The goal is achieved when those involved move beyond the initial cross-cultural differences of a situation and succeed in building new shared ways of doing things (Figure 1.11). On both interpersonal and larger organizational levels, this goal is difficult to achieve.

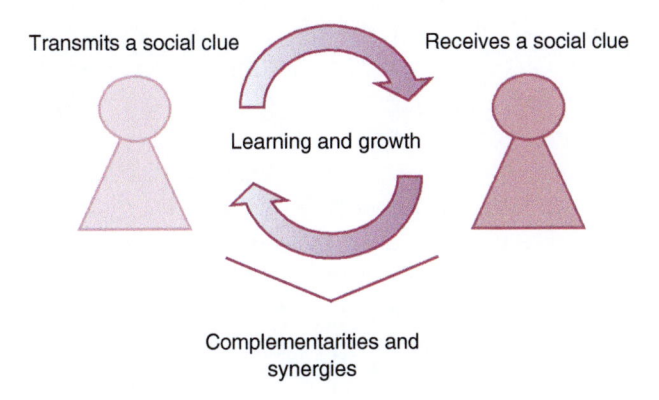

Figure 1.11 Cross-cultural management as a process of mutual learning and growth

Link to Practice: Corporate–Startup Partnerships

Large corporations ('corporates') and small, innovative technological start-up companies ('startups') are characterized by radically different organizational cultures (Boscher, 2022), and none of them can transform their 'ways of doing things' (Sharma, 2016). Whereas corporates have 'been around' for a (relatively) long time and have thus developed hierarchies, startups are young organizations with a strong vision and a dynamic, 'flat' work culture. Whereas corporates rely on stable processes and well-defined roles, startups are goal-focused and driven. Also, from a corporate perspective, innovation is 'anything that is new' whereas, from a startup perspective, innovation is what is 'disruptive and game changing' (Boscher, 2022; Sharma, 2016).

When working together with a startup, corporates might face difficulties such as the 'not invented here' syndrome (that is, the neglect or devaluation of knowledge from outside of their own corporate world), fear of failure and dependency, or regarding the startups' resources or technological maturity as insufficient. From the startups' perspective, it is difficult to bear long-lasting negotiations, extended response times, slow working speeds and extensive processes (see Mohammed, 2014).

Nonetheless, as Miteva (2021) suggests, both need each other in order to survive. For example, as startups usually take more risks and operate in a more agile manner, they are able to disrupt innovation and develop the next 'big product' ('high risk high reward'). Corporates have a responsibility regarding their employees and even though they are (economically) much bigger than a startup, they usually will not invest large sums for exploring disruptive innovation, as it comes with high risks. Corporates are usually good in economies of scale or have a market presence which is exactly what startups need. This is why the two entities complement each other and need each other to create and foster innovation. From a market perspective, startups also may utilize their reference costumers to leverage new investments and grow bigger.

Main risks include the startup being 'swallowed' by the corporate, or corporate structures and processes 'strangling' the startup, suffocating their innovative drive (Grosse, 2016). However, there are also examples that illustrate the potential opportunities of corporate–startup partnerships, such as the one of Aurora and Toyota on robot–taxi development (Goldstein, 2021).

CCM in a Changing World

Chapter Summary

Cross-cultural management investigates and manages the interrelations between culture and management or organizations. As a discipline, CCM has emerged from the need to understand what people experience when they go abroad or overseas (Scenario A). Yet, as Scenario B of the Opening Case suggests, the three assumptions of classic CCM – predominance of cultural differences on national level, physical movement across countries and clear-cut demarcation lines between presumably distinct national cultures – do not characterize a vast bulk of people's contemporary cross-cultural experiences.

People's cross-cultural exposure has changed from long-term expatriation to single cultures to multiple, often virtual, touchpoints with many cultures. Companies have successfully internationalized their operations and now need to acknowledge both inner-country diversity and cross-national homogeneity. Technology has facilitated new ways of working together across multiple cultures and enables new organizational contexts such as global virtual teams.

Many contemporary CCM contexts are thus both global and local; they are simultaneously characterized by multiple connections and differences. Individuals are increasingly n-cultural. Often, it is technology which provides the 'glue' across all these partly distinct and partly overlapping cultural spheres.

Still, identifying and overcoming differences between cultures, with its two steps of managing 'across' and 'between' cultures remain key focus points of CCM. The contemporary idea is to utilize difference in a positive way, and then to make difference a resource – and not an obstacle – to how individuals, organizations and societies work together. The student activities in this chapter allowed you to glimpse and gather information on these conditions of a contemporary CCM.

Key Points

- Contemporary CCM is different from, and more complex than, classic CCM.
- Culture is 'the way of how we normally do things around here (but not there)'.
- Every culturally learned way of doing things is limited by what has not been learned.
- Individuals in contemporary CCM are increasingly n-cultural.
- Cultural diversity, if utilized for achieving synergies and complementarities, is beneficial to people, societies and organizations.
- Contemporary CCM is a collective task that needs to consider all sides of the CCM triangle.
- Cross-cultural managers need to move their cross-cultural competencies 'up the ladder', and to refine their cultural categories by building the CCM pyramid.
- Metaphors of culture make culture tangible.

Review Questions

1. What are the three core assumptions of a classic CCM?
2. Which assumptions are part of a contemporary, but not of a classic, CCM?
3. Which sectors of the CCM environment have triggered changes that brought about the much wider focus of a contemporary CCM? Give an example for each sector.
4. What are the properties and purposes of culture?
5. What is meant with 'n-cultural individuals', and how is this relevant for CCM?
6. What are the elements and required processes that constitute the cross-cultural management triangle?
7. How is the cross-cultural management pyramid different from and more than the cross-cultural management triangle?
8. What is the link between cultural perspectivity and utilizing the benefits of diversity?
9. What is meant by 'contemporary CCM is a collective task', and what does this imply for the interculturally competent actions of the individual manager?
10. Why is it a power-sensitive and context-dependent task to turn cross-cultural differences into synergies and complementarities?

Opening Case Revisited

In Scenario A of the Opening Case, a manager is sent overseas and will most likely experience cross-cultural differences at a country level. In Scenario B, a manager stays at home and will most likely experience cross-cultural difference on an individual level. What differs is thus the trigger for their cross-cultural exposure (physical movement versus virtual interaction), and their access point to it (moving to another country versus interacting with team members). What the managers in both scenarios have in common is the professional knowledge of 'how to normally do things in supply chain management' and a certain global orientation (doing their job using the English language), and this is what they potentially also share with others in the situation. However, because there is also inner-societal diversity, managers in both scenarios cannot be sure that commonalities will be all-encompassing. Neither may they assume that national culture is the most relevant cultural demarcation line when managers from different countries meet. As a result, they are required to *'puzzle with culture in context'*: to pay attention to the situation, to reflect upon themselves and others in interaction, to acquire knowledge and skills, and to engage in processes of intercultural learning. However, they are also not in sole control of the cultural context upon which they wish to improve.

Closing Activity

With the knowledge of this chapter, reconsider Scenario A and B of the Opening Case. For each scenario:

- Identify three key strategies: What would you do in order to be successful as a cross-cultural manager?
- Check your strategies: Are they interculturally competent (appropriate and effective)? Why and how (not)? What, if anything, needs to be improved?
- Check yourself: Which skills and knowledge do you personally need to implement these interculturally competent strategies? Is this realistic?
- Exchange with a fellow student and choose the best possible (= the most interculturally competent) strategy for each scenario that is also realistic in terms of what will be required by you.
- Together, identify detrimental contextual factors for each scenario. Which contextual factors might thwart the interculturally competent and feasible best practice strategy chosen and what, if anything, can you do to overcome them? Do you need to choose your strategy, and, if so, how and why?

If asked for by your lecturer, present your work process and its outcome in class.

Further Reading

The Sage Handbook of Contemporary Cross-Cultural Management (Szkudlarek et al., 2020) outlines many aspects of a contemporary CCM as envisaged in this book. It is particularly helpful to read the introductory chapter 'Setting the stage' (Adler and Aycan, pp. 1–17), which highlights the requirements of a successful CCM in the 21st century, and the chapter on intercultural competencies by Maznevski (pp. 536–545) which is entitled 'Developing intercultural management competencies: The next frontier is inward bound' and in which the author argues for a CCM 'at home' and as involving n-cultural individuals.

The idea of International Business as a field that wishes to build synergies and complementarities, rather than haggling over differences and obstacles, has been put forward by Stahl and Tung (2015), and Stahl et al. (2016). The idea has been taken over by several CCM scholars, including Barmeyer et al. (2021), who label it 'constructive interculturality'. Some CCM scholars, e.g. Primecz et al. (2016), have cautioned against an overly optimistic integrative approach that neglects the power inequalities and restrictions of the wider contemporary CCM context. This chapter has tried to integrate these considerations.

For required intercultural competencies, see Deardorff (2009), and for a comprehensive introduction to CCM in its wider international business context, have a look at Schneider et al. (2014). Hendry (2013) is a good source for refining your managerial knowledge, prior to making it 'cross-cultural' (his chapter on CCM is very basic, though).

References

Barmeyer, C., Bausch, M. and Mayrhofer, U. (2021) *Constructive Intercultural Management: Integrating Cultural Differences Successfully*. Cheltenham/Northampton: Edward Elgar.

Benitez-Márquez, M.D., Sánchez-Teba, E.M., Bermúdez-González, G. and Núñez-Rydman, S. (2022) 'Generation Z within the workforce and in the workplace: A bibliometric analysis', *Frontiers in Psychology*, 1 February. Available at: https://doi.org/10.3389/fpsyg.2021.736820 [last accessed 31 July 2022].

Boscher, P. (2022) 'Cultural differences between tech startups and corporates', *42.digital*, 29 September. Available at: http://forty-two.digital/de/cultural-differences-between-tech-startups-and-corporates.html [last accessed 31 July 2022].

Cambridge Dictionary (n.d.) *Management*. Available at: https://dictionary.cambridge.org/de/worterbuch/englisch/management [last accessed 1 September 2020].

Deal, T.E. and Kennedy, A.A. (1982) *Corporate Culture: The Rites and Rituals of Corporate Life*. Boston: Addison-Wesley.

Deardorff, D.K. (ed.) (2009) *The Sage Handbook of Intercultural Competence*. Thousand Oaks: Sage.

EC (European Commission) (2022a) *Part A: General Information about the Erasmus + Programme*. Available at: https://erasmus-plus.ec.europa.eu/programme-guide/part-a [last accessed 31 July 2022].

EC (European Commission) (2022b) *Studying Abroad*. Available at: https://erasmus-plus.ec.europa.eu/opportunities/individuals/students/studying-abroad [last accessed 31 July 2022].

EU (European Union) (2022) *Description of the Eight EQF Levels*. Available at: https://europa.eu/europass/en/description-eight-eqf-levels [last accessed 31 July 2022].

Evans-Reber, K. (2021) 'How to meet Gen Z's workplace expectations', *Forbes Human Resources Council*, 1 November. Available at: www.forbes.com/sites/forbeshumanresourcescouncil/2021/11/10/how-to-meet-gen-zs-workplace-expectations/?sh=10a7ba1974ff [last accessed 31 July 2022].

Fang, T. (2015) 'From "Onion" to "Ocean": Paradox and change in national cultures', *International Studies of Management and Organization*, 35(4): 71–90.

Goldstein, M. (2021) '5 powerful corporate–startup partnerships in 2021', LinkedIn, 17 March. Available at: www.linkedin.com/pulse/5-powerful-corporate-startup-partnerships-2021-michael-goldstein/ [last accessed 31 July 2022].

Grosse, P. (2016) '18 reasons why as many as 50% of business partnerships fail within the first 2–3 years', LinkedIn, 29 November. Available at: www.linkedin.com/pulse/18-reasons-why-many-50-business-partnerships-fail-within-grosse/ [last accessed 31 July 2022].

Hendry, J. (2013) *Management: A Very Short Introduction*. Oxford: Oxford University Press.

Hoffower, H. (2021) 'Gen Z and millennials actually want the same things at work. But Gen Z has the upper hand', *Business Insider*, 6 November. Available at: www.businessinsider.com/millennials-versus-gen-z-workplace-trends-flexibility-work-life-balance-2021-11 [last accessed 31 July 2022].

Hofstede, G. (1980) *Culture's Consequences: International Differences in Work Related Values*. Beverly Hills: Sage.

Macwhinney, T. and Betts, K. (2022) 'Understanding Generation Z in the workplace: New employee engagement tactics for changing demographics', *Deloitte Insights Magazine*. Available at: www2.deloitte.com/us/en/pages/consumer-business/articles/understanding-generation-z-in-the-workplace.html [last accessed 31 July 2022].

Maznevski, M.L. (2020) 'Developing intercultural management competencies: The next frontier is inward bound', in B. Szkudlarek, L. Romani, D.V. Caprar and J. Osland (eds), *The Sage Handbook of Contemporary Cross-Cultural Management*. London: Sage. pp. 536–544.

Miteva, S. (2021) 'Corporate startup collaboration: The key to innovation', *Valuer*, 22 June. Available at: www.valuer.ai/blog/why-business-collaboration-between-startups-and-corporations-is-key-to-innovation [last accessed 31 July 2022].

Mohammed, A. (2014) 'Startup–corporate partnerships 2/3: Why are there so few?', *Wamda*, 30 December. Available at: www.wamda.com/2014/12/why-more-corporate-startup-partnerships [last accessed 31 July 2022].

Primecz, H., Mahadevan, J. and Romani, L. (2016) 'Why is cross-cultural management blind to power relations? Investigating ethnicity, language, gender and religion in power-laden contexts', *International Journal of Cross-Cultural Management*, 16(2): 127–136.

Schneider, S.C., Barsoux, J.-L. and Stahl, G.K. (2014) *Managing Across Cultures*. Harlow: Pearson Education (1st edn, 2003).

Schroth, H. (2019) 'Are you ready for Gen Z in the workplace?', *California Management Review*, 61(3): 5–18.

Spitzberg, B.H. and Changnon, G. (2009) 'Conceptualizing intercultural competence', in D.K. Deardorff (ed.), *The Sage Handbook of Intercultural Competence*. Thousand Oaks: Sage. pp. 2–52.

Sharma, B. (2016) 'Why corporates cannot adopt the startup culture', *Yourstory*, 30 November. Available at: https://yourstory.com/2016/11/corporates-and-startup-culture/amp [last accessed 31 July 2022].

Stahl, G.K. and Tung, R.L. (2015) 'Towards a more balanced treatment of culture in international business studies: The need for positive cross-cultural scholarship', *Journal of International Business Studies*, 46(4): 391–414.

Stahl, G.K., Tung, R.L., Kostova, T. and Zellmer-Bruhn, M. (2016) 'Widening the lens: Rethinking distance, diversity, and foreignness in international business research through positive organizational scholarship', *Journal of International Business Studies*, 47(6): 621–630.

Szkudlarek, B., Romani, L., Caprar, D.V. and Osland, J. (eds) (2020) *The Sage Handbook of Contemporary Cross-Cultural Management*. London: Sage.

Triandis, H.C. (1995) *Individualism & Collectivism*. Oxford: Westview Press.

From National Culture to Global Virtual Teams 2

Focus points of cross-cultural management studies

Learning Objectives

After having read this chapter, you should:

- know how CCM and its key focus points have developed over time
- understand how the conceptualization of culture's impact has evolved from mono-schematic and mono-directional to multi-level and multi-directional
- be aware that a more contemporary approach to CCM involves multiple nested cultures, cultural complexity, and identity- and power-related factors
- be able to differentiate culture into macro, meso and micro levels
- understand cultural complexity and cultural flows and what they involve
- have a first understanding of the requirements of a CCM beyond national cultures
- be aware that global and local virtual teams and (distributed and shared) global and local leadership are key focus points of CCM today
- understand how the COVID-19 pandemic has further promoted the shift towards a more virtual and technologized CCM of the future.

Reading Requirement

- You should have read Chapter 1 of this book

Introduction

CCM is a young discipline; it started to emerge in the USA only after World War II, and scholars locate its beginnings as a distinct academic 'field' as late as the 1980s (Thomas, 2020). However, in this short period of time, some fundamental disciplinary advances have been made. This chapter traces the development of CCM studies from the focus on national comparison to ideas of cultural complexity and cultural flows, and from a focus on the individual manager to a more collaborative understanding of the shared leadership required for global and virtual teams. After having read this chapter, you should have a more differentiated understanding of how culture interrelates with management. Being able to locate culture more precisely enables you to act more adequately and effectively in the role of the cross-cultural manager.

Opening Case

An Oil Refinery is an Oil Refinery is an Oil Refinery…

An oil refinery processes crude oil into heavy oil, light oil and petroleum gas. Its operation requires a certain hardware, certain operational procedures and safety regulations, and certain people with the required skills and competencies. The safety requirements and the operational procedures of an oil refinery, as well as the required properties of the end products, can be defined and evaluated against objective and universal criteria.

STUDENT ACTIVITY 2.1

Is the Oil-refining Business Culture-free or Culture-bound?

Consider the example of the oil refinery.

- Will the oil refinery be operated similarly or in the same way in each country? Why (not)?

- Which aspects of the operations do you expect to be universal to all cultural contexts (culture-free) and which do you expect to be culture-bound (contingent upon the country from which they emerge)?
- What would be the best possible combination of culture-free and culture-bound elements when it comes to operating an oil refinery successfully?

Answer in writing. If need be, familiarize yourself with the oil-refining business more (see online sources in Link to Practice box below).

Link to Practice: Oil Refining, and Worldwide Production and Demand

Oil refining, also referred to as the 'downstream' process of the business, involves a variety of processes, depending on which end product one seeks to produce. The goal of this complex process is 'straightforward: to take crude oil, which is virtually unusable in its natural state, and transform it into petroleum products used for a variety of purposes such as heating homes, fuelling vehicles and making petrochemical plastics' (Library of Congress, 2022). As of 2022, the two countries on the globe with the highest consumption rates of raw oil are the USA and the China (World Population Review, 2022). Consumption and production are distributed unequally across the globe, with the top ten consuming countries accounting for approximately 60 per cent of the world's total oil consumption (ibid.). In 2021, the three largest producers of raw oil were the USA (20 per cent of world total), Saudi Arabia (11 per cent) and Russia (11 per cent) (US Energy Information Administration, 2022). Due to this global imbalance, events such as the Russian military invasion of Ukraine on 24 February 2022 thus have market-distorting effects and tend to affect both the availability and the price of crude and refined oil. Countries also try to avoid or at least reduce their dependency on foreign energy sources to remain politically and economically independent: if crude oil is less available or more expensive, countries might invest in alternative energy sources more (McKinsey, 2022).

From National Culture to Multiple Nested Cultures

Culture is part of any business interaction. The tricky thing, however, is to locate culture: from where does it emerge, and how does it relate to management and organization? Over time, CCM studies have come up with more and more differentiated answers to these questions. As a first step, this required a move from solely considering national culture to the insight that there are (sub-)cultures within cultures. From this perspective, you enter one 'culture' only to find that it comprises multiple, smaller cultures, each of which comprises multiple, smaller cultures, and so on and so forth. This is referred to as the 'multiple nested cultures' perspective,

Two initial interests of CCM studies

In the 1960s and 1970s, the main purpose of studies within the area of what later became known as 'Cross-Cultural Management' was to show that culture (in the sense of **macro-culture**) had *any impact at all* on management and organization. Early studies highlighted, for example, that managerial values, attitudes, behaviour, etc. (**micro-culture**) differed across countries. Thus, the first idea of CCM was to show that *there is macro in the micro* (culture impacts on management, e.g. US-American managers differ from Brazilian managers *because of culture*). The underlying idea was that individuals are, indeed, representatives of national cultures. Out of this followed the need to specify culture's impact on management, in order to enable comparisons. This led to the more differentiated question of: *How much macro is in the micro?* (e.g. how 'US-American' *are* managers' values, and how does US-American management style differ from Brazilian management style, for example in business meetings?). Figure 2.1 visualizes these two initial interests of CCM studies.

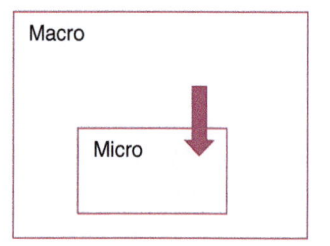

Macro-culture   'Large' levels of culture, such as nations or societies

Micro-culture   'Small' levels of culture, such as individuals, groups and teams

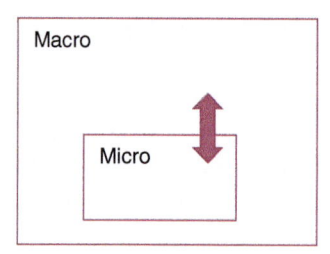

Figure 2.1   **Two initial interests of cross-cultural management studies**

STUDENT ACTIVITY 2.2

How Much Macro Is in the Micro?

Consider the example of the oil refinery. Now, imagine that the oil refinery is located either in Venezuela or in South Korea.

- Do some research on the internet. What information can you find about how the oil refining business works in each of the two countries? Don't forget to note your sources and to consider whether you find the sources reliable and of adequate academic standard.
- Also, try to find sources about what characterizes a typical management style in Venezuela and in South Korea. Again, don't forget to note your sources and to consider whether you find the sources reliable and of adequate academic standard. If you find that the sources are stereotypical, then discard them as insufficient.
- Afterwards, reflect upon both sets of sources and answer the question: How 'Venezuelan' and 'South Korean', respectively, do you expect an oil refinery to be operated in each country? Or, in other words: To what extent do you expect differences in macro-societal culture to play a role in how oil refineries are operated in different countries? Discuss your answers with fellow students.

A focus on multiple nested cultures

When methodological advances in the social sciences started to inform CCM, scholars began to acknowledge that culture as a group-related phenomenon is not a one-way process (see Thomas, 2020). Rather, it became apparent that individuals are influenced by their group identifications (cultures) but they also influence groups (cultures) in return. The next step in the development of CCM studies was thus to view people and culture as mutually constitutive.

For example, in 1986, Nancy Adler examined the interrelations between culture, management and organizations. She stressed the need to acknowledge organizational context as an intermediate cultural level (**meso-culture**), and to investigate how meso-cultural levels mediate between macro- and micro-cultures. Out of this insight emerged new questions such as: How much

> **Meso-culture** Intermediate ('middle') levels of culture (such as companies and organizations) that mediate between 'large' macro-cultures (countries, societies) and 'small' micro-cultures (e.g. teams)

macro is in the meso? (e.g. how 'French' *is* this organization?), or How much meso is in the micro? (e.g. to what extent is the management style in a certain company influenced by national culture and to what extent is it specific to this organization?). Relevant meso-cultures are, for example, the company which you work at, the industry wherein this company is located, or the university you are a student of, and the study programme which you pursue.

> **Nested cultures** Several levels of culture within each other, e.g. macro, meso, micro

The new idea was thus that multiple **'nested' cultures** were to be considered by CCM, and macro, meso and micro are a simplified approximation of this idea. Out of this, a new question emerged: *How do nested cultures (macro, meso, micro) interrelate?* Formulating and investigating this question can help cross-cultural managers understand how exactly multiple cultural levels come together in specific ways to shape specific situations (Figure 2.2).

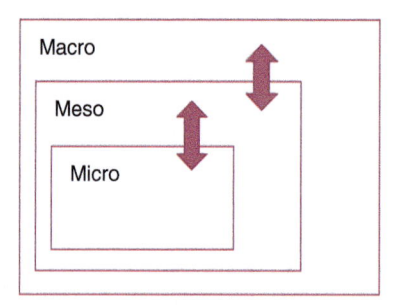

Figure 2.2 Multiple nested cultures in cross-cultural management

STUDENT ACTIVITY 2.3

Multiple Nested Cultures in an Oil Refinery

Re-consider the example of the oil-refinery business. Assume that there are two oil refineries, one in Venezuela and one in South Korea. Now imagine different departments and professional groups in each oil refinery, such as:

- Financial control
- Sourcing
- Engineering and operations
- Marketing
- Public relations
- Logistics and delivery

Focus Points of CCM Studies   45

Consider:

- What motivations and professional values will be important to the head of each department? What will be their respective core interests in the oil refinery?
- How will each head of department define 'excellent operations' differently? How will they also train their staff differently?
- Which interests do the different departments and professional groups share across departments?

Now, re-consider what you have previously identified as typical Venezuelan and South Korean influences, respectively, on each oil refinery's 'culture' in the sense of 'how to normally do things around here'.

- How might the influence of certain professional and departmental demands be integrated with a potential influence of Venezuelan and South Korean culture, as well as with certain universal requirements of the oil refining business?

Discuss with fellow students.

Cultural Complexity as a Framework for CCM Studies

Adding to the idea of multiple nested cultures, the term **cultural complexity** (Sackmann, 1997) acknowledges that people routinely cross many cultures over the course of a day, thus developing multiple, contextualized identities (**cultural identities**) (see Figure 2.3). These identities are then 'switched' on and off in specific situations, often instinctively. Relevant cultural levels to be considered are, for example, macro-cultures (supra-national, national or societal cultures), meso-cultures (such as regional, organizational or inner-organizational cultures), micro-cultures

Cultural complexity   The idea that individuals are part of many cultures and switch between multiple collective identities (cultures) in context

Cultural identities   The group affiliations (cultures) with which an individual identifies and/or is identified with in a certain context. Also referred to as social identities

> **Virtual cultures** Shared cultural identifications and/or practices which are mediated via new technologies and are not bound to a specific physical location

(such as team cultures), or **virtual and global cultures** that run across macro, meso and micro levels. Supra-national cultures are, for example, regions characterized by shared cultural roots such as 'Latin America' or 'Greater China' that cross national borders. National and societal cultures are often used interchangeably, but they are not necessarily identical. For example, Canadian (national) culture might be differentiated into two Anglo-Canadian and Franco-Canadian (societal) cultures.

Relevant group identity?

Macro: greater regional, national, societal, regional cultures

Meso: multiple organizational factors (e.g. department, function, profession)

Micro: individuals and teams

Global and virtual cultures; cultural flows

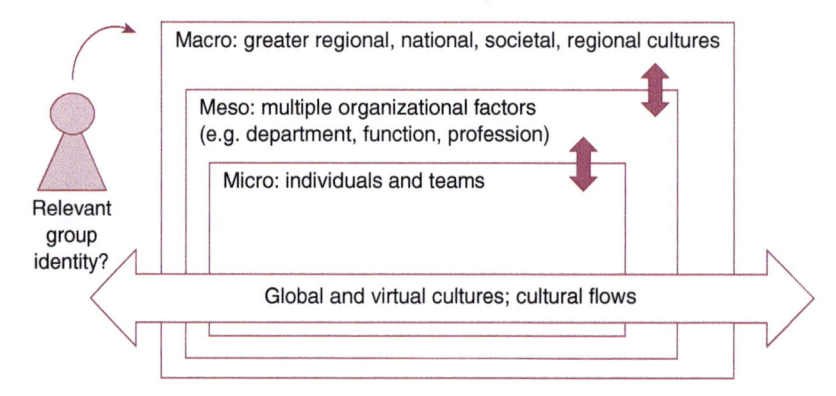

Figure 2.3 Cultural complexity and multiple cultures

Source: adapted from Sackmann (1997: 3)

The model of cultural complexity implies that people who enter or interact in a cultural context automatically relate themselves to available group identities. For example, financial control might try to lower the safety margins of the oil refining process, because cost considerations come first. It is at this point that the head of the engineering department is likely to switch their 'engineering identity' on and defend the need for higher safety standards. Group identities are thus not 'fixed' but emerge from the context and from how others position themselves, and they are more or less salient.

Salience refers to the (psychological) understanding that cultures and identities are not static but are switched 'on' and 'off', depending on influencing factors such as situational context, personal interests, organizational circumstances and wider boundary conditions. To identify and, thus, manage relevant difference, managers therefore need to carefully assess the situation to find out which cultural or social identities become salient and for whom, and under which conditions.

The idea of cultural complexity furthermore shows how contemporary CCM involves multiple cultural fault lines, all of which have the potential to turn a situation into a 'cross-cultural' one. For example, supply chain management involves universal disciplinary theories such as the '*bull-whip effect*'. This model describes that, if customer demand varies slightly, this variation will increase along the supply chain the further away one moves from the customer, and thus enables managers to better manage their supplies. Students in many countries learn this model, and, subsequently, apply it at work: it is part of a **global professional culture** across distinct macro- and meso-cultures. Likewise, the process of oil refining needs to meet certain technological requirements which are universal and part of the global education and knowledge-base of process engineers.

> **Global cultures** Unifying cultural identifications and/or practices across the globe

> **Professional cultures** Shared work-related identifications and practices that are (thought of as) specific to a certain profession

STUDENT ACTIVITY 2.4

Switching Cultural Identities On and Off

Re-consider your insights from Student Activity 2.3 on the different professional identities in the oil refinery business in South Korea *or* Venezuela (for this activity, country culture is less relevant). Now, re-imagine the interests and professional values of each of the following departments:

- Financial control
- Sourcing
- Engineering and operations
- Marketing
- Public relations
- Logistics and delivery

Consider:

- What needs to happen so that departmental identity becomes the most salient for the respective head of department? At which point will a person behave like 'head of department X' and focus on representing their department's needs?
- Construct a scenario in which the respective departmental identity is likely to be compromised by another departmental identity or by a combination of meso-level factors as outlined in the cultural complexity model (Figure 2.3). Also consider what people might be 'afraid of' in that scenario.

Discuss with fellow students.

Power and identity as relevant to cross-cultural management

The idea of cultural complexity might also involve power-related and **identity-related** factors (my own wording). Power-related factors are, for example, tenure, organizational status and hierarchy. Identity-related factors are elements such as age, religion, gender. As this list suggests, power and identity-related factors intersect. For example, imagine that you are a 20-year-old intern amongst a group of male engineers in their mid-fifties. Here, age might play a role. If you are also the only woman, non-binary or transgender person on the team, then gender might become relevant as well.

> **Identity** Sense and characteristics of self in relation to others

The same argument might be made for other identity-related factors such as ethnicity, religion, national identity, ability or sexual orientation. The picture might change again, if your own power position were different, for example, if you were the manager of the team (hierarchy), had a long period of experience on the job (tenure), or were delegated to the team from a more prestigious organizational unit. Figure 2.4 adds such power-related and identity-related factors to the model of cultural complexity.

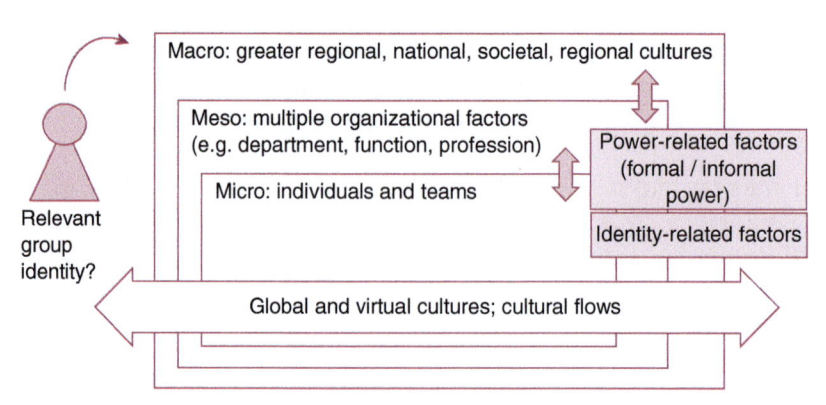

Figure 2.4 Cultural complexity, and power and identity

Source: adapted from Sackmann (1997: 3)

STUDENT ACTIVITY 2.5

Being Myself (or Another) in a Culturally Complex Context

This is a two steps task for which you need your previous notes on the oil-refinery activities.

Focus Points of CCM Studies 49

First, consider your actual identity characteristics, such as gender and gender identity, age, profession, country of origin and residence, ability, ethnicity, religion, fluency in English language. Now, assume, that you will be employed as the head of a department at the oil refinery in Venezuela and South Korea, respectively. Assume that the corporate language is English, and that you are new on the job and to the company. Based on who you are:

- What will your actual power and identity position in the company be?
- Will it be comparably easy or difficult for you to influence organizational culture and to put through your professional and departmental interests?
- Visualize this with the help of Figure 2.4 (cultural complexity).

Group with another student who is different in terms of their identity characteristics.

- Exchange your findings.
- Together, reflect upon the difference which it makes to be 'yourself' (and not another) in CCM. Do you find this situation 'fair'?
- What does the situation tell you about power in CCM? Is power clear inequalities and majority dominance, or is there also the power to change and resist, and the power of the cultural outsider or underdog?

Discuss in class, if required.

Link to Practice: Multicultural and Inclusive Leadership

Studies on national diversity (e.g. Lu et al., 2021) suggest that multicultural experiences make leaders more effective, in particular when the team is culturally diverse as well. They find a greater communicative versatility, and also a greater versatility in leadership style for those with more multicultural experiences. As Soo (2012) states: 'Multicultural leadership involves deep immersion within different cultures to understand their values and specific context.' Transferred to the idea of cultural complexity, this then implies the

(Continued)

relevance of considering which cultural contexts shape one's identity, in order to utilize all of them for a better work performance.

A related concept is leadership diversity or inclusive leadership. Inclusive leadership recognizes and utilizes the potential of a diverse workforce and customer base. It requires leadership diversity, which is established via recruiting and promoting individuals who are diverse in terms of nationality, culture, gender, gender identity, age, ethnicity, race, ability, etc. As the 'business case for diversity' proposes, the advantages of inclusive leadership – beyond inclusiveness generally being a 'moral' or 'human' obligation – are innovativeness, agility, being nearer to customers and markets, and generally less corporate 'blind-spots' (Bourke, 2016). Furthermore, employees (who are also diverse) seek representation in their leaders; they might trust them more and be more engaged when feeling represented (ibid.). Still, many industries – such as the oil, gas and mining extracting industry – have a long way to go in terms of diversity and inclusiveness (The Advocates for Human Rights, 2019), with potentially negative consequences for market share, employee satisfaction and organizational learning.

CCM Beyond National Cultures

In 2002, Margaret Phillips and Sonja Sackmann (based on Boyacigiller et al., 2003) gave further advice for how to 'manage in an era of multiple cultures'. They asked managers to focus on synergies instead of conflict, and invited CCM researchers to move beyond concepts of national cultural distinctness. From this perspective, CCM should investigate how people *create* cultural similarities and differences via their interactions, not on how cultural differences *define* the situation. Rather than being mere 'victims of culture', individuals are thus thought of also as potential 'creators' of cultural differences and how they interpret the situation also influences the situation.

STUDENT ACTIVITY 2.6

Managing in an Era of Multiple Cultures

Read the seminal article by Sonja Sackmann and Margaret Phillips on 'Managing in an era of multiple cultures' (https://gbr.pepperdine.edu/2010/08/managing-in-an-era-of-multiple-cultures/), and answer the following questions:

Focus Points of CCM Studies 51

1. In a nutshell, what is the key message of this text?
2. What is new about 'managing in an era of multiple cultures' when you relate it back to 'classic' CCM (Chapter 1) and the prior focus points of CCM studies?
3. What are the new skills required in order to 'manage in an era of multiple cultures'?
4. How can cross-cultural managers find synergies instead of conflict in CCM?
5. What does this text add to your understanding of culture's imprint onto the Venezuelan and South Korean oil refineries (see previous student activities)?

Cultural flows and the interconnectedness of CCM

Linked to a CCM beyond national cultures is the insight that culture is not static but rather flows across distinct locations (see Figures 2.3 and 2.4), and that this flow is not limited by 'national cultural containers'. It could be, for example, that cultural objects, practices and technologies cross national borders and distinct cultural locations or that actual people migrate and move and thus carry culture 'with them'. An example for this phenomenon would be the cuisine in any given country as it always involves a variety that is at least partly due to cultural flows.

Cultural flows connect various places and individuals, and in the process, cultural practices and cultural meanings travel and change. Cultural flows are thus linked to a variety of cultural practices, such as translation.

> **Cultural flows** Connections between people, ideas, practices, objects and/or technologies across distinct 'cultures'

This means that people do not only translate between languages but also that they make sense out of new cultural influences. For example, cricket, formerly an

English gentlemen's activity, became a mass event, after it had travelled to India (Appadurai, 1995). Likewise, Disney theme parks have travelled from the USA to, for example, Japan and France. Yet, Mickey 'means' different things at these different locations, local customers expect different things and make sense of the same 'Disney universe' differently, and as a result these Disney theme parks differ from each other (Brannen, 2004).

Cultural flows are often bi- or even multi-directional. They often involve global media and how they are interpreted differently at different locations (Abu-Lughod, 1997). For example, Indian Bollywood movies are inspired by Hollywood movies, yet, at the same time, they also serve to paint a picture of 'India' to a diverse audience worldwide. One can also look at the same cultural flow at different points in time or across different cultural groups to see how its meaning changes. For CCM, the implication is that it is part of the managerial task to reflect upon cultural flows, and how they influence certain groups of people at certain locations and are in return influenced by them. For example, every corporate strategy is also a cultural flow.

STUDENT ACTIVITY 2.7

Cultural Flows as an Asset for CCM Practice

This activity enables you to imagine yourself in terms of cultural flows, and to also connect to other cultural locations by means of these cultural flows.

- First, find as many aspects in your life as possible which are only possible because of cultural flows. Consider, for example, objects, technology, cuisine, activities, practices, behaviour, ideas, aspirations. Focus on as many cultural contexts as possible, such as work, university, leisure activities, circle of friends. You have ten minutes to compile a list of all items. Afterwards, compare your list with at least three other students to generate more ideas, and then spend another five minutes to extend your own individual list.
- Next, reflect upon your findings. Have you found more or less than expected? Take notes.
- Finally, imagine that you introduce yourself as new department head at the oil refinery in South Korea or Venezuela. You should choose the department which is closest to your own professional education. You should choose the country to which you can make the stronger connections based on the cultural flows which are on your list. Now, write a short introductory statement of who you are and what you will contribute to the department and the company which makes use of connecting cultural flows the most.

- Give this speech in class or in front of fellow students. Make it an act but don't overstress the argument and take the act seriously.
- Reflect upon the exercise and its outcome. What have you learned about yourself and who you could be, and about culture in the contemporary world in general?

Link to Practice: The Port of Rotterdam

The Port of Rotterdam, located in the Netherlands and first opened in the 14th century, is the largest seaport in Europe. In 2018, it handled 469 million tons of sea freight and generated seven per cent of the Dutch gross domestic product. Approximately 30,000 maritime and 105,000 inland waterway vessels dock there each year (for all statistics, see Marvest, 2022). For logistics, the port uses an Internet of Things, that is, a sophisticated sensor network that provides accurate and up-to-date data for planning and management of shipping (Port of Rotterdam, 2019). The Port of Rotterdam employs 180,000 people, amounting to approximately 19 per cent of the total workforce of the region (Port of Rotterdam, 2022), and 320,000 people live on port premises (Marvest, 2022). These features make the Port of Rotterdam the perfect example of an interconnected workspace that is both global and local and characterized by multiple cultures and cultural flows. Crude and refined oil are part of the port's operations.

CCM Beyond Locations and Individuals

Another feature of contemporary CCM is that it is increasingly team-based which then poses new challenges to cross-cultural managers in the role of 'global leaders'. Both intersecting developments will be outlined.

The increasing relevance of global and virtual teams

A team is usually defined as a group of at least three people working towards a common goal or desired end-state. A team is virtual if it uses information and communications technology (**ICT**) to collaborate, communicate and achieve its goals, and in the contemporary world, this is often the case. If ICT is

ICT Information and communications technology

> **(Global) virtual teams** Teams collaborating across multiple cultures and locations supported by ICT

employed on a global level, one speaks of a **global virtual team.** Often, the demarcation lines between virtual and global virtual teams are not clear-cut; in reality, global and virtual elements intersect in most teams (Gibson et al., 2014).

Team-based organizing, that is building business operations and whole companies out of teams, is a recent trend in international business (Zander et al., 2015). Because team-based organizing is less hierarchical and static than older organizational forms, it helps companies to react quickly towards a changing and complex environment, and to utilize the benefits of cultural diversity. However, team-based organizing also brings about increased communication and coordination costs (Drogendijk et al., 2015). These may be reduced by appropriate (cross-cultural) management and leadership.

Team **performance**, often defined as the best possible combination of ability, motivation and opportunity, is the measuring rod for evaluating how well teams, also global virtual teams, are configured. To maximize performance, people's ability and motivation need to be utilized and developed, and they need to be given the opportunity to use both. Again, this underscores the need for appropriate and effective CCM in such contexts.

> **Performance** A function of ability, motivation and opportunity, to be maximized, for example, by appropriate and effective CCM

How to differentiate between global and virtual teams?

Contemporary teams come in many forms. Many teams are not only virtual, but also global, whereas others are virtual and local. In some, task interdependence is high, whereas in others, collaboration is only loosely organized. To figure out which conditions are relevant to the cross-cultural manager, the three categories teamness, virtualness and globalness (Martins and Schilpzand, 2011) are helpful:

- Teamness refers to the degree to which tasks are interdependent, to which team members are mutually accountable for each other's work and to which the team is identifiable as such.
- Virtualness refers to the degree to which technology, such as information and communications technology (ICT), is required and used in the team.
- Globalness refers to the degree to which the team involves multiple national cultures, locations and time-zones.

Three main factors influence teams which are characterized by at least some virtualness and globalness. These are: **dispersion** (the distance effect), **diversity** (the culture effect) and **power** effects (Maznevski, 2012). Dispersion and diversity can be both beneficial and harmful to teams, depending on how they are configured and moderated. For example, time lags (a distance effect) enable global teams to work longer hours per day, yet also complicate communication. Divergent approaches to work (a cultural effect) might result in more viewpoints on the same matter, thus contributing to the innovative potential of global teams, yet might also lead to mutual distrust.

Diversity and dispersion effects are often experienced simultaneously, but need to be sorted out in order to create the conditions for utilizing their benefits. For example, difficulties in communication might originate from the need to communicate across distance, yet are often ascribed to different cultures. Therefore, it is relevant to precisely define what impacts negatively upon the team, and then to manage the root cause of the problem.

Power in global virtual teams can be many things. It can be the power of hierarchy or the power of knowledge. It can be the power to give commands or the power to resist these demands. Generally speaking, power refers to an imbalance of sorts which is also harmful in its effects. For example, when knowledge is not shared across locations or when the largest sub-team or the cultural majority dominate remote sub-teams or minority members, such power imbalances impact upon the team's ability to utilize abilities and motivation, and to present people with suitable opportunities to perform.

> **Diversity, dispersion, power** Three major influencers of how (well) global virtual teams perform

What is relevant here is that virtual teams in general, and global virtual teams in particular, cannot be managed by means of a clear 'prescription'. Rather, managers need to assess a team's characteristics (its virtualness, globalness and teamness), and then to moderate diversity, dispersion and power effects in such a way that these effects play out positively, not negatively (diversity and dispersion), or not at all (power effects).

A key task is the management of positive and negative convergent and divergent processes (Jonsen and Gehrke, 2014). Convergent processes bring the team together, divergent processes bring it apart; both can be positive and negative, depending on their configuration. For example, high diversity can be negative to the team because it increases the likeliness of conflict (a negative divergent process). However, if the team invests in building trustful relationships and understanding each other's divergent approaches better via communication (a positive convergent process), then diversity plays out. 'Different ways of how to normally do things' (a divergent process), coupled with task-related trust (a positive convergent process), can then facilitate higher innovativeness (a positive divergent process).

CCM Underpinnings

Managing (partly or fully) global virtual teams also requires that managers accommodate themselves to alternative ways of doing things, even if they do not (yet) understand how and what they could be useful for. Basically, that means to venture out of one's comfort zone. For example, low diversity (similarities in personal traits among team members) makes communication easy, yet also tends to result in complacency and group-think (a negative convergent process); it feels 'easy' but it does not deliver novel ideas. Consequently, innovativeness – as a positive divergent process – is negatively impacted upon and might be reduced. Therefore, in a team with low diversity, managers need to constantly introduce elements of 'difference' in order to mediate the negative effects of low diversity on innovativeness. By doing so, they may differentiate between personal and task-related trust. Personal trust is what holds a non-diverse team together instantaneously – people are similar, and thus they trust in each other. However, this trust is not backed up by how people do their job – this would be task-related trust, and it is the kind of trust that needs to be built in a diverse team. Therefore, 'being similar to each other' is not a requirement for, but rather an obstacle to, high-performing teams. If team members understand this and start focusing on task-related trust instead, more diverse approaches to work can be explored without fear.

Further factors to be considered are the degree of task interdependence, configuration aspects such as the number of team members per location, leadership roles and organizational context, e.g. how the organization 'ticks' in terms of culture (Maznevski, 2012). These factors can be linked back to the three influencing factors distance, diversity and dispersion. For example, low task interdependence might be managed by a clear hierarchy whereas high task interdependence requires mutual adjustment and a more collaborative leadership style.

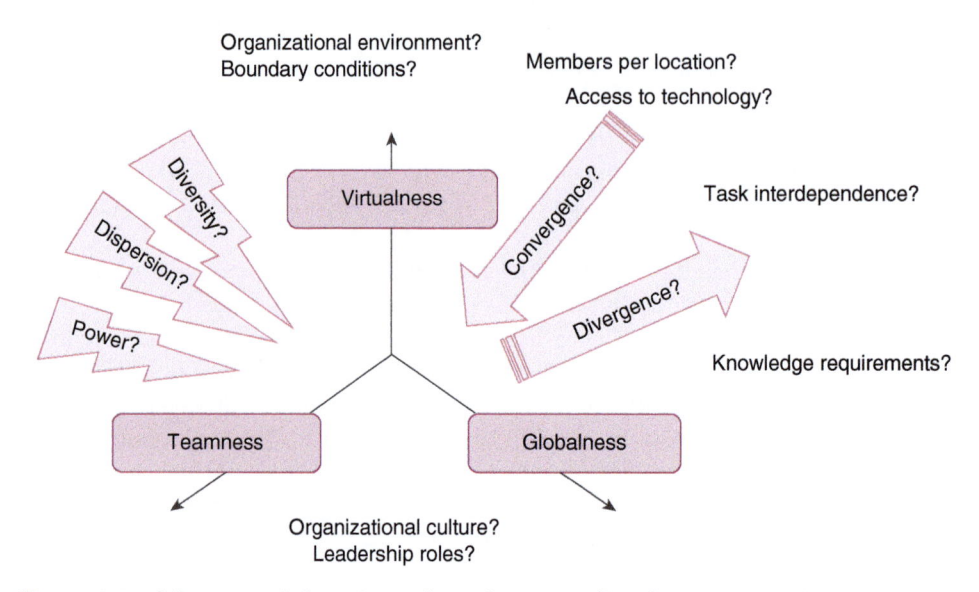

Figure 2.5 A framework for a team-based cross-cultural management

Source: adapted from Jonsen and Gehrke (2014); Martins and Schilpzand (2011); Maznevski (2012)

From cross-cultural management to global leadership

Global leadership as another key focus point of CCM studies evolved in the 1990s when companies started to face the international business environment on a global level (see Bird and Mendenhall, 2016). They were dealing with multiple locations, cultures and languages, they were configured by means of global value chains, and they were facing multiple technological, political, economic, etc. environments. Out of this emerged the need for 'global leaders', that is individuals who were not only able to bridge and span boundaries between *specific* cultures, but individuals who were able to deal with difference and diversity *in general*. Furthermore, the idea of a 'global' leadership involves a virtual component as it also refers to the need to lead a diverse and dispersed team or organization.

It has been argued that global leaders must possess a global mindset, which, according to Javidan (2010), includes:

- intellectual capital – understood as having global business skills, cognitive complexity and the outlook of a citizen of the world
- psychological capital – understood as a passion for diversity, a quest for adventure and self-assurance
- social capital – understood as intercultural empathy, having interpersonal impact and diplomacy

Another concept that has been proposed as a requirement for global leadership success is global dexterity (Molinsky, 2013), understood as 'the ability to smoothly and successfully adapt how you act in a foreign setting – so that you are effective and appropriate in that setting without feeling that you are losing yourself in the process' (p. ix).

These ideas of leadership are rooted in the assumption that leadership is a quality inherent to individuals, the 'leader'. However, the question is whether leadership can be located within individuals. Can one be a leader without followers? As Mary Parker Follett (Fox, 1968) states, leadership is inherently social in that in order to be or become a leader, others have to accept this leadership. Therefore, leadership emerges between people, and those being led have as much part in it as those 'leading'. Additionally, there is the organizational context, such as corporate strategy on international markets, to be considered (Kedia and Mukherji, 1999). All of this makes global leadership a team-, group- or organization-wide responsibility.

Some argue that leadership is more or something entirely different than management. For example, there is idea ascribed to Drucker (2001) that managers are routine administrators (they do things right) whereas leaders are those with a strategic outlook (they do the right things). What seems clear is that management has become more challenging and complex beyond the routine administration that might have characterized early and mid-20th-century bureaucracies. Therefore, John Hendry (2013) suggests that every managerial work involves three components, namely routine administration, troubleshooting and leadership. Troubleshooting – the need for and ability to 'clean-up messes' – has become more relevant as the corporate environment and internal configurations have become more complex and require frequent, often unforeseen changes. Under such circumstances, leadership, as the quality to inspire people and motivate them to aligned action towards a common goal, involves less the setting of direction and being infallible ('doing the right things') but rather integration between different perspectives and the building and maintaining of internal and external networks. For this, contemporary (global or cross-cultural) leaders need to span boundaries and act as bridge-builders between cultures, locations, organizational units and network partners.

Ultimately, it depends on perspective whether one speaks about cross-cultural management or about global leadership. One could well argue that a contemporary approach to CCM always involves a global leadership component. At the same time, leadership in CCM is also more than merely 'global' because it is culturally complex and encompasses local or virtual contexts as well. Most managers at work experience a component that is cross-cultural, international and/or global. For most of them, it is not enough anymore to do things 'right' (routine administration). Rather, they also need to figure out what the 'right things' to be done could be, to clean up unforeseen messes, and to engage others in common purposes. However, and this is tricky about global leadership or CCM, no single person has the complete picture about what needs to be done and what it would take to get there without deviation.

Therefore, the focus on the individual global leader that characterizes leadership theory before and slightly after the turn of the millennium has been replaced with a more collaborative approach to global leadership; it is not the individual leader who matters but rather how leadership is shared amongst a diverse and often dispersed group of people. From a contemporary CCM perspective, this seems reasonable. If the goal is to capitalize upon differences via complementarities and synergies, then multiple individuals need to contribute to make this feasible. However, as Zander et al. (2015) point out, shared leadership might not be accepted by all and not be suitable for all tasks, and a challenge to it is the lack of a clear line of authority on which the leader can rely.

For establishing team-based and shared leadership, Zander et al. (2015) find that organizations need more openness towards linguistic and cultural differences, to accumulate the ability to build and maintain social networks. and to develop effective practices of communication and knowledge-diffusion in light of higher obstacles to both. These recommendations then provide the link between global leadership and virtual teams in contemporary CCM.

STUDENT ACTIVITY 2.8

Virtual and Team-Based Organizing in CCM

In today's world, corporate operations are often steered by means of technology. For example, in order to refine oil, one needs to employ interconnected software and machinery that manages and supervises the process. Key elements of the task are:

- the smooth running of operations
- the monitoring of the process
- the prevention of/quick reaction in case of malfunction.

Form a team of four to six students. Based on your notes from the previous student activities, imagine that you are part of the control centre crew for any of the two oil refineries. Assign on-site roles to half of the team, and remote roles to the other half of the team. When you assign roles make sure that you don't assign a 'single leader'. What you face is a highly interdependent, knowledge-based task – you cannot structure it by means of hierarchy. Rather, you need to develop a collaborative approach to team processes beyond simple descriptions that involves every team member. In your discussion, consider questions such as:

- How will you make sure that the team uses every person's abilities to the best possible level, that the team capitalizes upon every person's motivation (and also maintain it), and each person is given the opportunity to perform admirably?
- How much teamness, virtualness and globalness (if any) does your team need?
- What are likely dispersion, diversity and power effects in your team and how do you plan to manage them so that they play out positively, not negatively?
- What is the ideal ratio between convergent and divergent processes in the team?
- How shall leadership be shared among the team members?
- How often and for what purposes does your team need to meet on-site?
- Which organizational culture and structures does your team need to perform well?
- ...

Bring in your actual personality, abilities and motivation when considering these and further questions on how to configure your team for maximum performance.

The road ahead: Where is culture?

Since the 1990s, CCM beyond national cultures has become increasingly relevant. Cultural complexity has increased, and technology has enabled people and organizations to collaborate across distance on a global level. Out of the decreasing relevance of national boundaries, new CCM demands emerged. They are associated with new requirements, such as managing cultural flows, global leadership and virtual team collaboration.

For the future of CCM, it is likely that the interconnectedness of global and local, and virtual and non-virtual is going to increase, with new cross-cultural workplaces emerging. For example, the recent COVID-19 pandemic (see Spotlight) spurred further turns towards remote and virtual work, and to work-from-home settings, thus profoundly impacting upon the locations of culture in CCM. For example, due to a COVID-induced need for social distancing to contain the spread of infection, people who were actually close by started to work remotely. They then experienced a dispersion effect at work, they needed to use technology, and – because they did not experience the same organizational meso-culture in their respective remote work settings – they also brought in cultural diversity beyond national cultures. Many people simultaneously experienced their home environment and were exposed to multiple cultures, often beyond mere local levels.

As a next and prospective future development, it is thus to be expected that (virtual) technology is going to play an even larger role regarding the location of culture in CCM, and that more people than before will find themselves in teams which are at least partly virtual and cross-cultural – even 'at home' – and that the boundaries between the 'local' and the 'cross-cultural' and 'global' will blur even further for more people.

Spotlight: The COVID-19 Pandemic

On 31 December 2019, health authorities in Wuhan, China, announced 27 pneumonia cases of an unknown cause (ECDC, 2020). A new coronavirus was soon identified causing symptoms such as breathing difficulties, fever and dry cough. Three months later, on 11 March, some 118,000 cases were reported in 114 countries, and the World Health Organization (WHO) assessed COVID-19 to be a global pandemic (WHO, 2020). In September 2020, there were no less than 26,000,000 cases worldwide and over 860,000 people had lost their lives (CSSE, 2020).

COVID-19 changed the world as people knew it in unexpected ways. For example, cities and afterwards entire countries had been locked down, flights had been suspended, economic activity had been reduced, cultural and sport events had been postponed, social distancing and the use of masks had been imposed. For example, in the German state of Baden-Württemberg, a maximum of five persons were allowed to meet in private spaces during Easter time (*The Local*, 2020). Thus, in many countries, family gatherings were reduced to a minimum and religious celebrations, such as Easter, Ramadan or Passover, took place online.

> In May 2020, it was forecasted that the European economy would fall by 7.5 per cent, the impact of COVID-19 on the economy being even deeper than that of the financial crisis of 2009 (EC, 2020). As the European Commission stated:
>
> > the lockdowns implemented in most Member States and globally, reduce supply as many non-essential activities are suspended, delivery of inputs is disrupted, and workers are unavailable due to sickness, quarantine or because they have to take care of relatives and children whose schools are closed. (EC, 2020: ix)
>
> The COVID-19 pandemic also impacted on education and access to it. In many countries, primary and sometimes even secondary schools were closed. Even though universities were quick to move from on-campus to remote courses, this did not result in equal access to education for all; for example, the resources of the average university in a high-income country are far above the resources of the average university in a low-income country. Likewise, internet accessibility differs across countries, and even within high-income countries, students with less financial resources might lack the tools to access online courses.
>
> In terms of the locations of culture, the COVID-19 pandemic initiated a boom in remote work. In the words of market analyst Saikat Chatterjee: 'We're being forced into the world's largest work-from-home experiment and, so far, it hasn't been easy for a lot of organizations to implement' (Wiles, 2020). Leaving aside the fact that some jobs cannot be done from home (e.g. working on a farm), there are other factors to be considered, too: technology and infrastructure, work–life balance and caring commitments (e.g. parents with kids at home), the implications of home-office for corporate culture, trusting employees, etc. The present and future consequences of this global educational and socio-economic 'experiment' are thus far-reaching, moving contemporary CCM even further away from its 'classic' foundations.

Chapter Summary

As the field of CCM evolved after World War II in North America and parts of Western Europe, its disciplinary focus points changed from identifying culture in management and national comparison to a more differentiated understanding of multiple nested cultures and identity dynamics in culturally complex contexts. Particularly, cultural diversity 'at home' and cultural flows beyond national cultures have become increasingly relevant to CCM studies, as have dispersed and virtual work environments that are mediated by technology. Cross-cultural managers are asked to consider how power- and identity-related aspects are intertwined with CCM, and to develop their skills beyond single cultures and physical locations of culture. Furthermore, team-based organizing has become a recent trend, with the need to develop shared and more collaborative approaches to global leadership. Out of all these developments it follows that cross-cultural managers need to train themselves in a multi-level and differentiated approach to culture. Another change is related to the cultural identities of the cross-cultural manager themselves. This development and its CCM implications will be outlined in Chapter 3.

Key Points

- The focus points of CCM studies have changed over time towards a more sophisticated, multi-directional and multi-level conceptualization of culture and its interrelation with business, management and organizations.
- Culture and management are mutually constitutive on multiple, nested levels, involving macro-, meso-, micro, global and virtual levels.
- Cultural flows, and virtual and global cultures connect people and organizations across multiple locations.
- People today cross multiple cultures over the course of a day and switch multiple cultural identities on and off.
- Cultures are intertwined with identity- and power-related factors.
- Global and local virtual teams and global and local leadership are key challenges of a contemporary CCM.
- Leadership in CCM, in particular when employed in more team-based organizations, needs to be shared and distributed.
- CCM in the future is likely to be more virtual, more delocalized, more culturally complex and more technologized. The COVID-19 pandemic has further accelerated this transformation.

Review Questions

1. What are the major advances in culture's impact on management and how is it currently conceptualized by CCM studies?
2. What are macro-, meso-, micro-, global and virtual cultures, and how are they relevant for present and future CCM theory and practice?
3. What is meant by 'managing in an era of multiple cultures' (see Student Activity 2.6)? What are the implications for present and future CCM theory and practice?
4. What is meant by cultural complexity, and how is the concept relevant to present and future cross-cultural managers today?

5. Why are identity- and power-related factors to be considered by present and future cross-cultural managers?
6. What is team-based organizing, and how is it relevant to present and future CCM theory and practice?
7. What are the main characteristics, influencing factors, moderators and performance factors of global and non-global virtual teams?
8. What is global leadership and how is it related to present and future CCM theory and practice?
9. What is meant by shared and distributed leadership and how is it relevant to present and future cross-cultural managers?
10. What are the recent trends associated with CCM, which changes are likely to occur, and which factors have triggered or contributed to these trends?

Opening Case Revisited

The Opening Case is an almost perfect example of a culturally complex context in which multiple cultures come together and in which multiple identities might be switched on and off by the individual, depending on the contextual factors and wider circumstances. The activities of this chapter walked you through this context. If you wish to deepen your learning, choose and analyse another contemporary CCM context in these terms.

Closing Activity

Revisit the oil refinery of the Opening Case with the full knowledge of this chapter. Imagine that you need to compile a report on how to manage cultural complexity and to train employees in utilizing the benefits of cultural diversity for the highest standard of operations. This report is to be delivered to the plant's management (managing director and department heads). Consider questions such as:

- Which knowledge and CCM concepts need to be in your report? Which culture-bound and culture-free factors need to be considered?
- What would you recommend to the oil refinery's management? For example, What do they need to pay attention to and reflect upon? Which principles should guide them when doing things?
- What is relevant about management's and employees' skills development? Who should be hired and retained?
- To what extent will people (who?) work on-site or remotely? How much team-based organizing is required? How to find the best possible configuration here?
- …

Work together in groups of students. The report can be a maximum of five written pages with visuals or ten presentation slides.

Further Reading

There is no single story of how CCM studies have conceptualized culture. This chapter offers some suggestions. Further options are provided by Boyacigiller et al. (2003) who look at the CCM conceptualization of culture from a more international management-oriented perspective. Bird and Mendenhall's (2016) overview on Global Leadership focuses on the development of this sub-field and how it might replace the notion of 'cross-cultural management'. Appadurai's (1995) 'Playing with modernity' is a study of cultural flows; it traces how Indian cricket has been transformed from an upper-class English gentlemen's activity into an Indian mass phenomenon with very different conventions and rules. Zander et al.'s (2015) conceptualization of team-based organizing gives you an idea of the CCM requirements of the future.

References

Abu-Lughod, L. (1997) 'The interpretation of culture(s) after television', *Representations*, 59: 109–134.

Adler, N.J. (1986) *International Dimensions of Organizational Behavior*. Boston: Kent Publishing.

Appadurai, A. (1995) 'Playing with modernity: The decolonization of Indian cricket', in C. Breckenridge (ed.), *Consuming Modernity – Public Culture in a South Asian World*. Minneapolis: University of Minnesota Press. pp. 23–48.

Bird, A. and Mendenhall, M.E. (2016) 'From cross-cultural management to global leadership: Evolution and adaptation', *Journal of World Business*, 51(1): 115–126.

Bourke, J. (2016) 'The six signature traits of inclusive leadership', Deloitte Insights, 14 April. Available at: www2.deloitte.com/us/en/insights/topics/talent/six-signature-traits-of-inclusive-leadership.html [last accessed 31 July 2022].

Boyacigiller, N., Kleinberg, J., Phillips, M. and Sackmann, S. (2003) 'Conceptualizing culture: Elucidating the streams of research in International Cross-Cultural Management', in B. Punnett and O. Shenkar (eds), *Handbook for International Management Research*. Ann Arbor, MI: University of Michigan Press. pp. 99–167.

Brannen, M.Y. (2004) 'When Mickey loses face: Recontextualization, semantic fit and the semiotics of foreignness', *Academy of Management Review*, 29(4): 593–616.

CSSE (2020) COVID-19 Dashboard by the Center for Systems Science and Engineering (CSSE) at Johns Hopkins University (JHU). Available at: https://gisanddata.maps.arcgis.com/apps/opsdashboard/index.html#/bda7594740fd40299423467b48e9ecf6 [last accessed 3 September 2020].

Drogendijk, R., van Tulder, R. and Verbeke, A. (2015) 'Introduction: Three organizational challenges for multinational enterprises', in R. van Tulder, A. Verbeke and R. Drogendijk (eds), *The Future of Global Organizing. Progress in International Business Research*. Bingley: Emerald Group Publishing Limited. pp. 3–21.

Drucker, P.F. (2001) *Essential Drucker: 'The Pre-Eminent Management Thinker of our Time'. Selections from the Management Works of Peter F. Drucker*. Abingdon: Taylor & Francis.

ECDC (2020) Event background COVID-19. Available at: www.ecdc.europa.eu/en/novel-coronavirus/event-background-2019 [last accessed 3 September 2020].

EC (2020) European Economic Forecast. Spring 2020, Institutional Paper 125. Available at: https://ec.europa.eu/info/sites/info/files/economy-finance/ip125_en.pdf [last accessed 4 September 2020].

Fox, E.M. (1968) Mary Parker Follett: The enduring contribution, *Public Administration Review*, 28(6): 520–529.

Gibson, C.B., Huang, L., Kirkman, B.L. and Shapiro, D.L. (2014) 'Where global and virtual meet: The value of examining the intersection of these elements in twenty-first-century team', *The Annual Review of Organizational Psychology and Organizational Behavior*, 1(1): 217–244.

Hendry, J. (2013) *Management: A Very Short Introduction*. Oxford: Oxford University Press.

Javidan, M. (2010) 'Bringing the global mindset to leadership', *Harvard Business Review*. Available at: https://hbr.org/2010/05/bringing-the-global-mindset-to [last accessed 16 July 2020].

Jonsen, K. and Gehrke. B. (2014) 'Global team collaboration', in B. Gehrke and M.-T. Claes (eds), *Global Leadership Practices – A Cross-Cultural Management Perspective*. London: Palgrave Macmillan. pp. 118–131.

Kedia, B.L. and Mukherji, A. (1999) 'Global managers: Developing a mindset for global competitiveness', *Journal of World Business*, 24(3): 230–251.

Library of Congress (2022) 'Downstream: Refining and marketing', in *Oil and Gas Industry: A Research Guide*. Available at: https://guides.loc.gov/oil-and-gas-industry/downstream [last accessed 31 July 2022].

Lu, J.G., Swaab, R.I. and Galinsky, A.D. (2021) 'Global leaders for global teams: Leaders with multicultural experiences communicate and lead more effectively, especially in multinational teams', *Organization Science*, 33(4). Available at: https://doi.org/10.1287/orsc.2021.1480.

Martins, L.L. and Schilpzand, M.C. (2011) 'Global virtual teams: Key developments, research gaps, and future directions', in A. Joshi, H. Liao and J.J. Martocchio (eds), *Research in Personnel and Human Resources Management*. Bingley: Emerald Group Publishing Limited. pp. 1–72.

Marvest (2022) 'The port of Rotterdam', *Marvest*. Available at: www.marvest.de/en/magazine/ships/the-port-of-rotterdam/ [last accessed 31 July 2022].

Maznevski, M.L. (2012) 'State of the art: Global teams', in M.C. Gertsen, A.-M. Søderberg and M. Zølner (eds), *Global Collaboration: Intercultural Experiences and Learning*. London: Palgrave Macmillan. pp. 187–206.

McKinsey (2022) 'Snapshot of global oil supply and demand: May 2022', McKinsey & Company, 16 September. Available at: www.mckinsey.com/industries/oil-and-gas/our-insights/petroleum-blog/snapshot-of-global-oil-supply-and-demand [last accessed 31 July 2022].

Molinsky, A. (2013) *Global Dexterity*. Boston: Harvard Business Review Press.

Philipps, M. and Sackmann, S. (2002) 'Managing in an era of multiple cultures', *Graziadio Business Report*, 5(4), Pepperdine Business School. Available at: https://gbr.pepperdine.edu/2010/08/managing-in-an-era-of-multiple-cultures/ [last accessed 1 December 2021].

Port of Rotterdam (2019) *Digitisation: Port of Rotterdam Puts Internet of Things Platform into Operation*, press release. Available at: www.portofrotterdam.com/en/news-and-press-releases/port-rotterdam-puts-internet-things-platform-operation [last accessed 31 July 2022].

Port of Rotterdam (2022) *Working and Learning*. Available at: www.portofrotterdam.com/en/building-port/working-and-learning [last accessed 31 July 2022].

Sackmann, S.A. (1997) 'Introduction', in S.A. Sackmann (ed.), *Cultural Complexity in Organizations: Inherent Contrasts and Contradictions*. Thousand Oaks: Sage. pp. 1–13.

Soo, J. (2012) 'Multicultural leadership starts from within', *Harvard Business Review*, 17 January. Available at: https://hbr.org/2012/01/multicultural-leadership-starts-fr [last accessed 31 July 2022].

The Advocates for Human Rights (2019) 'Promoting gender diversity and inclusion in the oil, gas and mining extractive industries – Am women's human rights report (January 2019)'. Available at: https://www.theadvocatesforhumanrights.org/Res/promoting_gender_diversity_and_inclusion_in_the_oil_gas_and_mining_extractive_industries.pdf [last accessed 01 November 2022].

The Local (2020) 'Coronavirus: What is (and isn't) allowed over Easter weekend in Germany', *The Local*, 8 April. Available at: www.thelocal.de/20200408/coronavirus-what-travel-is-and-isnt-allowed-over-easter-weekend-in-germany [last accessed 4 September 2020].

Thomas, D.C. (2020) 'Reflexive chapter: Some thoughts on cross-cultural management research', in B. Szkudlarek, L. Romani, D.V. Caprar and J.S. Osland (eds), *The Sage Handbook of Contemporary Cross-Cultural Management*. London: Sage. pp. 393–405.

US Energy Information Administration (2022) What Countries are the Top Producers and Consumers of Oil? Available at: www.eia.gov/tools/faqs/faq.php?id=709&t=6 [last accessed 31 July 2022].

Wiles, J. (2020) 'With Coronavirus in mind, is your organization ready for remote work?', *Gartner*, 23 July. Available at: www.gartner.com/smarterwithgartner/with-coronavirus-in-mind-are-you-ready-for-remote-work/ [last accessed 4 September 2020].

WHO (2020) WHO Director-General's Opening Remarks at the Media Briefing on COVID-19 – 11 March 2020. Available at: www.who.int/dg/speeches/detail/who-director-general-s-opening-remarks-at-the-media-briefing-on-covid-19---11-march-2020 [last accessed 3 September 2020].

World Population Review (2022) 'Oil consumption per country', *World Population Review*. Available at: https://worldpopulationreview.com/country-rankings/oil-consumption-by-country [last accessed 31 July 2022].

Zander, L., Butler, C.L., Mockaitis, A.I., Herbert, K., Lauring, J., Mäkelä, K., Paunova, M., Umans, T. and Zetting, P. (2015) 'Team-based global organizations: The future of global organizing', in R. van Tulder, A. Verbeke and R. Drogendijk (eds), *The Future of Global Organizing. Progress in International Business Research*. Bingley: Emerald Group Publishing Limited. pp. 227–243.

Identities of the Cross-Cultural Manager

3

Learning Objectives

After reading this chapter, you should:

- be able to differentiate between monocultural and bicultural identity formation processes, and how they are relevant to the competencies of the cross-cultural manager
- have a differentiated understanding of identities in CCM, including identities beyond national cultures such as halfie, hyphenated and third cultural identities, marginal and fringe identities, and cosmopolitan and global nomad identities
- be able to assess your own and others' identities in relation to their strengths and weaknesses, and opportunities and risks for CCM
- know how mobility and identity are intertwined in contemporary CCM
- have encountered first strategies for developing a sense of rooted cosmopolitanism in CCM
- be able to understand why and how cross-cultural managers need to engage in collective identity work in order to utilize the benefits of multiple identities.

Reading Requirement

- You should have read Chapter 2 of this book.

Introduction

In contemporary CCM, multiple cultural identities meet. **Identity** refers to a sense of self which people develop in relation to others. Classic CCM has differentiated between three different identities: monocultural, bicultural and third cultural. Since then, the concept of culture has become more differentiated in CCM studies, to involve multiple cultures, cultural complexity and many social groups (see Chapter 2). In the process, the concept of cultural identity in CCM studies has become more differentiated and inclusive, and is now central to it (Brannen, 2020). Identity is relevant to CCM because the way in which people experience themselves in relation to others impacts upon how they master the role of the cross-cultural manager and partially shapes the perspective from which they approach CCM theory and practice.

This chapter outlines the changing identities of the cross-cultural manager and their relevance for CCM. After having read this chapter, you should have a better understanding of how identity formation processes and CCM are interlinked, be able to assess your own strengths and weaknesses in the role of a cross-cultural manager, and be able to seek out cultural identities which might complement your own perspective on CCM.

> **Identity** People's sense of self in relation to others

Opening Case

Elif's Story

German industrial engineer Elif (pseudonym) is in her mid-twenties. Her grandparents came to Southwest Germany as work migrants in the early 1960s (the so-called guest workers, Gastarbeiter) and were employed as workers in the automotive industry. Her parents work as technicians for a car manufacturer. Elif speaks Turkish well, but not with full fluency, and there is a Turkish accent in her English. She says: 'I am German – but my family and a part of me are Turkish, and this is how it should be. These are my strengths.'

In her studies, Elif specialized in International Technical Sales. She made that decision after an internship of six months in the sales department of a Chinese automotive company. She says: 'Working with Chinese customers was just fun. I realized that I am good at this. And I did not even know that I had it in me. My boss was enthusiastic, as were the customers.'

After another year of studies, a second internship in the USA followed, and, again, her boss praised her skills at work. It was at this point that Elif decided: 'I want to work across cultures.'

CCM and Identity

Over the last decades, the focus of CCM studies shifted from macro to micro, and from singular cultures to cultural complexity and multiple, sometimes virtual and global, cultures. In the process, CCM studies also diversified their image of the cross-cultural manager's cultural identity (Brannen et al., 2004; Brannen, 2020), also in relation to old and new forms of global mobility (McNulty and Brewster, 2020). Building upon a short introduction to the concept of identity, this section details these developments.

Identity and identification: Who I am in relation to others

The formation of identity (understood as people's sense of self in relation to others) involves two interrelated processes, namely 'Who am I?/How do I see myself?' (identification) and 'Who are you?/How do others see me?' (recognition). Out of this, individual options for belonging emerge. Both processes are mutually constitutive; one cannot successfully identify as a member of a certain group without being recognized as such, and vice versa. Or, in other words, people function as 'identity mirrors' for each other, and identity formation involves a process of trying to make sense of oneself in the eyes of others. Rather than 'having' an identity, people thus 'try out' identities, in order to figure out where and how they might socially fit. For example, Elif (in the Opening Case) 'tries on' the role of the 'International Technical Sales manager', and she experiences that she is recognized positively in this role by others. As a result, it becomes an option for belonging to her. Other aspects of her identity, for example, the question of whether she is or might be 'German' or 'Turkish', or a combination of both, are subject to the same processes. Figure 3.1 visualizes identity formation in these terms.

It is relevant to note that people don't try out every potential identity. For example, in Elif's case, alternative identity facets, such as gender and age, are not salient at this point. Therefore, as the concept of cultural complexity (Chapter 2) suggests, some identity facets come to the foreground, in relation to other people, under certain circumstances and in relation to certain kinds of boundary conditions.

CCM Underpinnings

Identification: How I see myself ↔ Recognition: How others see me

↓

Options for belonging: Who can I successfully claim to be?

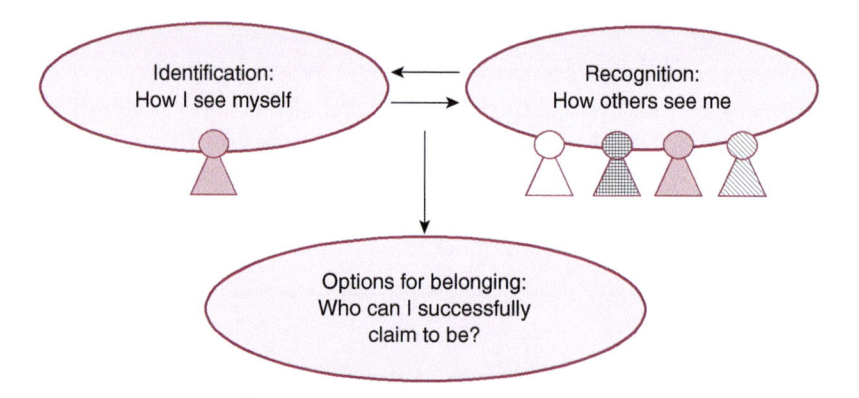

Figure 3.1 The ongoing formation of the cross-cultural manager's identity

---

STUDENT ACTIVITY 3.1

Cultural Complexity as a Framework for CCM Studies

Read the section on cultural complexity as a framework for CCM studies in Chapter 2 and the seminal article by Sonja Sackmann and Margaret Phillips on 'managing in an era of multiple cultures' (https://gbr.pepperdine.edu/2010/08/managing-in-an-era-of-multiple-cultures/). Note key elements of how to manage under the conditions of cultural complexity and multiple cultures. Next, answer the following questions:

- How is the situation which Elif faces at work culturally complex and characterized by multiple cultures?
- How is her identity formation representative of a culturally complex world and of the condition of multiple cultures?

The initial assumption: The monocultural expatriate or student sojourner

The classic image of the internationally mobile manager in CCM studies is the so-called **expatriate**. These are individuals who are sent abroad by their companies, who stay abroad for an extended period of time – usually two to three years – and who then return home (thus becoming a **repatriate**). Another classic image is the internationally mobile student who studies abroad for a semester or two. The difference is that the internationally mobile student tends to move individually and for a shorter period of time, whereas the managerial expatriate tends to relocate with spouse and/or family for longer.

Together, both groups are referred to as **sojourners**. The assumption is that, via exposing themselves to the culture of other countries, they will gather cross-cultural experiences and become more cross-culturally competent. Elif fits both concepts, however, there is also more to her identity, and these other facets are lost if one only considers her as a 'German' international technical sales manager. In the words of German sociologist Aladin El-Mafaalani (2020), she is 'German-plus' on the international arena, and it is this 'plus' which makes her skillset worth investigating.

> **Expatriate** Here: employee sent overseas or abroad by their company for a prolonged period of time and afterwards returning to their home country

> **Repatriate** Here: employee returning from an expatriation period overseas or abroad to their previous corporate location

> **Sojourner** Here: a person who goes to another country for a period of time to achieve a certain goal and who will go back as soon as this purpose is achieved

STUDENT ACTIVITY 3.2

Expatriation and Repatriation

Imagine that you study or work abroad for, let's say, a year.

- During expatriation: Which challenges do you expect? What do you hope for? What will you learn? How will you make sure that you acquire this learning? Which worst-case and best-case scenarios are on your mind?
- During repatriation: Which challenges will you face upon your return? What do you hope for? What will you learn? How will you make sure that you acquire this learning? Which worst-case and best-case scenarios are on your mind?

> After answering these questions, complete the following sentence: 'Going abroad will have been worth it, if …'
>
> Exchange your sentence with as many fellow students as possible and write down another person's sentence which you find to be the most insightful.

Monocultural identities in CCM

In classic CCM studies, with its focus on differences between macro-cultures, expatriates have been traditionally thought of as monocultural, or, put another way, as people with a single-country history. This then implies that cross-cultural managers, when being in their home country environment, don't experience themselves as different from others, and are also not perceived as different by others. The result is an almost automatic and largely unquestioned belonging for all those who reside in the same country (Figure 3.2).

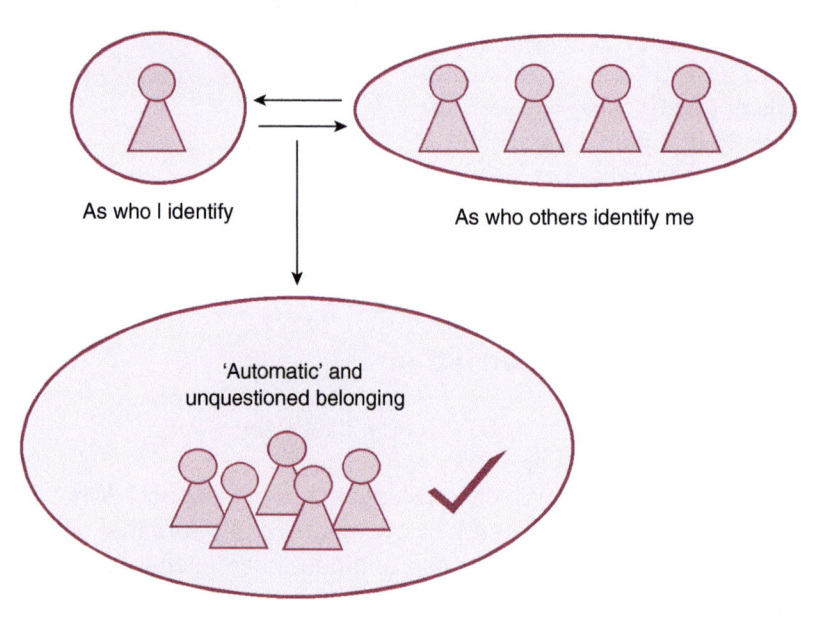

Figure 3.2 Monocultural identities in cross-cultural management

If one presumes the monocultural identity of the cross-cultural manager, then managers will need to go outside of their home country to experience identity challenges. For example, if a US-American manager is relocated to, let's say, Mexico, the assumption is that they will experience cross-cultural differences because they bring 'American culture' to people who live a 'Mexican culture' which is different. For managing 'over there', the US-American manager thus needs to change their style to a more 'Mexican' version of 'how to manage'. However, Elif enters CCM with history that is already 'international', even prior to her working in international management; it is not that clear anymore which cultural differences she might experience when going abroad.

Elif's identity thus exemplifies a paradigmatic shift in CCM studies. The presumed 'US-American' manager might be of Mexican descent as well, they might have had interactions with descendants from Mexico, or they might have been trained or been exposed to a global managerial culture. Likewise, the people whom they meet in Mexico are also more than 'just Mexican'. To figure out what might happen in such a scenario, CCM studies therefore started to understand 'expatriation' in much wider terms, for example, as involving migration and mobility beyond work, and to also focus on what happens after repatriation (McNulty and Brewster, 2020).

Pause and Reflect: Have Cross-Cultural Managers Ever Been Monocultural?

Early CCM studies have thought of the cross-cultural manager as **monocultural** in the sense of being representative of distinct national cultures. Also, early research, for example into expatriates' or students' experiences abroad, seemed to confirm that they experienced cultural difference and 'culture shock' abroad. However, empirically, this might be rooted in other factors than national culture. For example, as sociologists have pointed out, the managerial class in most developed countries has become more diverse over the last decades. Half a century ago, many managers shared other group identity characteristics beyond being from the same country. The stereotype was that they were male, within the same age-group, from middle- or upper-class backgrounds, and married with children and a wife at home or in part-time work. Who can say whether it was national culture that united them or all these other identity facets? Therefore, it could be that the wrong influencing factor (national culture) was tested upon people's experiences, and that it is gender, age, ethnicity, class, ability, religious background or lifestyle which united the presumably monocultural cross-cultural managers of classic CCM.

Monoculturality The quality of being monocultural, i.e., being oneself in relation to a single culture

STUDENT ACTIVITY 3.3

My Expatriate Self

Consider yourself in terms of national culture. Is your history national (single country) or international (between or as involving at least two countries). How [English/French/Chinese/Brazilian/etc.] do you expect yourself to be when being abroad or overseas for a longer period of time? Why? Take notes and discuss with fellow students. Note any additional insights gained from the discussion.

Bicultural and third cultural identities as a CCM asset

Identities beyond single countries became an interest of CCM studies because of the insight that the learning associated with their formation is transferable to CCM. Or, in other words, what people need to do in order to form identities beyond single countries is what cross-cultural managers need to learn to succeed. The process began with investigating two distinct identities, namely bicultural individuals and 'third culture kids'.

> **Biculturality** The quality of being bicultural, i.e. being oneself in relation to a combination of two cultures

Bicultural individuals (Brannen and Thomas, 2010) are those growing up between two macro-cultures, e.g. because their parents originate from different countries. It is expected, for example, that they are bilingual and generally competent (defined as behaving appropriately and effectively) in two cultures. Brannen and Thomas (2010) define the degree of a person's biculturalism as the degree to which they have access to different 'cultural schemes'. **Cultural schemes** are mental models or cultural blueprints which the person can utilize. The higher the variety, the higher the cross-cultural versatility. It is assumed

> **Cultural schemes** Mental models that, if internalized by and accessible to a person, can be utilized for better results in (cross-)cultural situations

that many bicultural competencies are culture-general, not culture-specific, and thus transferable across cultures and therefore biculturalism, if utilized, might be an asset for CCM in general. For example, Elif seems to possess the general quality of being able to interact well with customers across cultures.

Third culture kids (Pollock and Van Reken, 1999) are children of internationally mobile parents, e.g. diplomats or international managers, who spent their childhood in one or more countries (host cultures), mostly outside of their parents' home country (home culture). They experienced several host cultures, and combined 'home' and 'host' culture in new, often unforeseen ways. Thus, they developed third culture configurations which are the result of the creative combination of different cultural influences which they engage in at different stages of their lives. These third culture configurations are different from their parents' cultural identifications and identities, and they might even differ across siblings who have experienced different cultural environments at different age levels or who simply experienced different identity formation processes in similar environments. Again, what they have achieved by selecting from distinct cultural identities is part of the cross-cultural manager's task, for example when having to build a team from members of many cultures. While not being a 'third culture kid' in the classic sense, Elif of the Opening Case nonetheless seems to be able to build connections across difference, for example, when interacting with Chinese or US-American customers – a third culture skill.

> **Third culture** A novel combination of two different cultural influences A and B which involves a creative combination of selected elements as well as unforeseen elements beyond A and B

Monocultural identity formation on the one hand, and bicultural and third cultural identity formation on the other hand, differ regarding their access points to cross-cultural learning in relevant ways.

Firstly, monocultural identities evolve 'inside' or 'in the middle' of a single culture. Thus, the first experience of being 'outside' of culture tends to emerge somewhere else. Consequently, in such an identity formation process, the existence of cultural differences and the need to deal with 'being a cultural outsider' is mainly triggered by 'going abroad' or 'overseas'. Conversely, a bicultural or third cultural person has already experienced being 'outside' of more than one culture. Therefore, such an identity formation process involves an awareness that cultural differences exist, also 'at home'. Thus, when going abroad, a bicultural or third cultural person will most likely recognize the situation as familiar. Elif, for example, seems to fit in both in China and in the USA, despite never having been to either country before.

Secondly, bicultural or third cultural identity formation processes are often not self-chosen. Others initiate these identity processes because the bicultural or third cultural individual does not automatically 'fit' in their eyes. For example, one must imagine that Elif, with a Turkish name and a Turkish accent in her spoken English (yet with clearly non-native Turkish language skills), is puzzling to others. She is not automatically identifiable as 'Turkish', yet, because of her Turkish name and her Turkish accent when speaking English, she is not immediately identified as 'German' either.

> **Identity work**   Process of 'trying to make oneself fit' and reflecting upon to which extent this fit is desirable, triggered by an experience of one's identity being incongruent to a situation or people's expectations

> **Identity negotiation**   Process by which people reconcile incongruences in identity

In contrast to monocultural identities, bi and third cultural identities thus require **identity work**. For a potentially bicultural or third cultural person, the challenge often is that others tend to identify them in singular, monocultural terms. Bi and third cultural identity is thus not an automatic process of belonging but requires conscious effort. What emerged as Elif's sense of self is thus a process of negotiating herself, others and the circumstances in such a way that the result 'made sense' to her and, potentially, others (**identity negotiation**). The benefit of this largely involuntary process is that bicultural and third cultural individuals are often exposed to more triggers for cross-cultural learning. Conversely, those who identify and are recognized as monocultural belong quasi-automatically (Figure 3.2). Therefore, in-depth identity work might not be triggered equally, unless they consciously seek out experiences that allow them to self-identify in alternative terms.

The difference between the bicultural and third cultural identity experience is that it is often easier for the bicultural individual to 'choose' one of the two national cultures as their own, often the one in which they have grown up; they might feel that they *could* fit in in a single culture if others let them belong. For example, Elif could choose to identify as 'German only' if others accept this claim. Conversely, a third cultural person often has difficulties to identify with any of these cultures, because none of them feels like 'their own'. They have a higher likelihood to feel that they don't fit in anywhere.

Figure 3.3 visualizes third cultural and bicultural identity work. The starting point is an individual with potentially three options of self: third culture, bicultural or either of the two monocultures A and B. In Elif's case, the options would be 'a new combination of various influences', 'Turkish-German' or either 'German' or 'Turkish'.

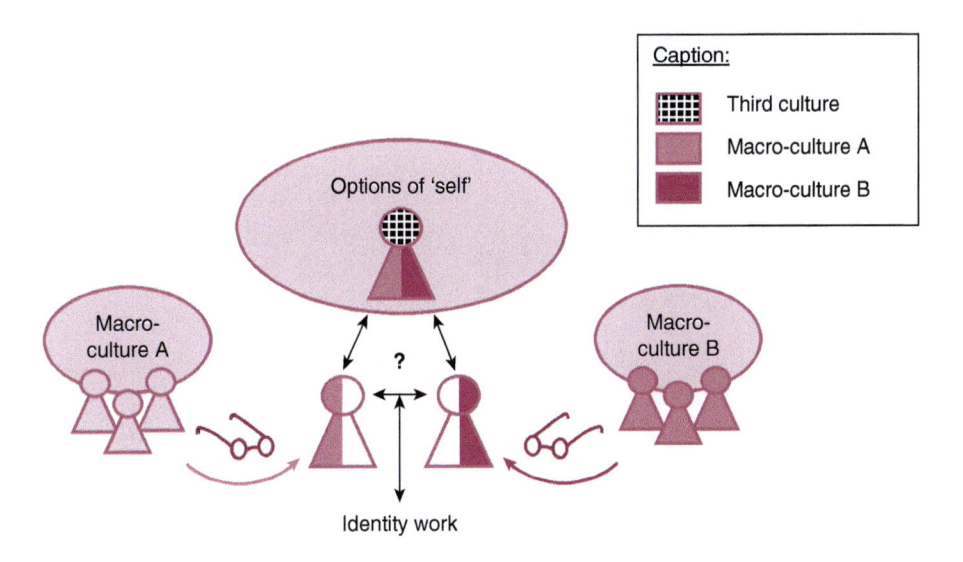

Figure 3.3 Third and bicultural identity work in cross-cultural management

STUDENT ACTIVITY 3.4

Cultural Identities in Relation to Each Other

Individually, consider yourself in terms of monocultural, bicultural and third cultural identities. Which of these three terms fits to how you experience your own identity? Why, and how so? Give examples.

Next, form groups of three to four students, ideally with one or two students who identify as monocultural and two students who identify as bicultural or multicultural. Discuss the advantages and disadvantages of each of the identities for CCM, in a respectful and non-violent manner. Take away at least one strength from every alternative identity that you wish to develop yourself.

High and low bicultural identity integration

If one considers the benefits of identities for CCM, the story is not as simple as 'bicultural is better' and 'monocultural' is worse. For example, individuals between cultures may experience high or low **bicultural identity integration** (BII, see Brannen and Thomas, 2010). Depending on how they relate to their identity work trigger points, they might or might not make use of their bridging and boundary-spanning potential.

> **Bicultural identity integration (BII)** Degree to which bicultural individuals experience two cultural schemes which are accessible to them as incongruent (low BII) or complementary (high BII)

- High BII means that a (potentially bicultural) individual perceives their dual identities as complementary, often because such complementarity is not challenged by others.
- Low BII means that the individual perceives their dual identities as being in constant conflict which each other, often because these identities are perceived as conflicting in the eyes of others.

Both low and high BII can potentially result in high CCM competencies:

- If BII is low, then the experience of conflict might spur reflexivity and the creation of new, innovative solutions – a clear asset to a successful CCM. However, it might also lead to the individual to stop pursuing their biculturalism actively, for example because one of the two cultural identities is less accepted by others, and rather settle for one identity, namely the one that is more accepted by others. If this is the case, then the benefits of biculturalism are not utilized as CCM resources.
- If BII is high, then the individual experiences high appreciation of their bicultural identity by others and develops a sense of cultural richness. This is similar to a monocultural person perceiving themselves as 'whole' and as belonging 'automatically'. However, due to the lack of conflict, the potentially bicultural individual then might not develop conscious biculturalism in the sense of being aware of multiple cultural schemes.

Elif's case therefore provides an example of an individual with high BII – to her, all facets of her identity contribute to her strengths. She does not feel forced to separate her identity into a 'German' (e.g. at work) and a 'Turkish' one (e.g. at home), and, thus, she does not lose access to all cultural schemes she might have been potentially exposed to. On the other hand, due to the lack of identity conflict, she might not be fully aware of *why* exactly she is successful in International Technical Sales – she simply notes that she is.

STUDENT ACTIVITY 3.5

Identity Work in CCM

Choose version 1) or 2) of this activity, as befits you.

1. If you have previously identified as bicultural, which conditions characterize your experience of self more – low or high BII? How can you deal with this condition in order to develop it into higher cross-cultural management competencies?
2. If you have previously identified as monocultural, imagine that you are outside of your home country for a longer period of time and are now exposed to another country culture. The host country culture seems:

    i. fundamentally different to your home country culture
    ii. complementary to your home country culture

   Consider both scenarios. Which one would you prefer and why? How can you deal with each of these scenarios in such a way that you develop the experience into higher cross-cultural management competencies?

For both versions, reflect upon this individually, only share what you wish to share with others.

CCM, and Mobility and Migration

For several reasons, such as the ones in Elif's case, people today are highly mobile: They move to another country for education, work or other purposes. Some are the descendants of mobile individuals, others flee their country for various reasons, such as war.

STUDENT ACTIVITY 3.6

Faces of Contemporary Mobility

Why are people today globally mobile? Find as many different reasons and terms that contribute to contemporary global mobility as you can. Define each term that you find.

From mobility to migration

> **Migration** The movement of people from one country or region towards other countries or regions with the purpose to settle there for a longer period of time

Classic CCM, with its idea of the monocultural expatriate, has used the term 'mobility' over the alternative term 'migration'. However, recently, this perspective has changed, and **migration**, including refugee movements, has now become an interest of CCM studies. Migration (see Spotlight) is relevant to CCM because it has changed and still changes the 'faces' of the representatives of different countries who meet at work.

Spotlight: Migration

If you ever thought, after watching the news, that migration is a new phenomenon or a challenge to our present-day societies, rest assured that migration has been around for almost the entire human history. It just continues today with people leaving their countries of origin and regions in search of better employment prospects (sometimes it's not even about a better job, but just about a job), safer places for living (either because of natural disasters or armed conflicts and political instability), education and training opportunities, reunification with their families, or just as a lifestyle act (O'Reilly, 2014).

In the Global South, contemporary migration is considered the main driver of population growth and mitigates the decline in the working age population (United Nations, 2017). Nonetheless, migration often does not enjoy a positive image. Rather, it is linked to fears of losing one's jobs in the receiving countries and regions, concerns about the (un)willingness of migrants to integrate, or doubts in migrants' loyalty to the receiving country. Central to this negative idea of migration are the notions of nation-states, borders and 'foreignness' (as a dominant concept that challenges the belonging of certain groups). If belonging is based on a homogeneous concept of national identity, then individuals are 'made foreigners' (in the aforementioned sense) once they have crossed the border to another country (Bartram et al., 2014).

Migration has many faces. For example, migrants often compete for slots for those countries that have put admission policies in place. Canadian and

American migration policies, for example, encourage the migration of highly skilled workers, and the European Union (EU) hopes to attract professionals from outside the EU with its Blue Card programme. At the same time, gaining a highly skilled worker ('brain gain') in one place can be considered a loss in another place. The countries of origin of the highly skilled speak of 'brain drain' and, in spite of remittances and the chance that these highly skilled might return, brain drain is said to produce more losers than winners (Docquier, 2014).

On the other end of the scale, low-skilled migrant workers meet seasonal labour needs, for example in agriculture or tourism, and even though it might seem that seasonal worker programmes are beneficial for both low-skilled individuals and their employers (maybe the consumer should also be considered here), they are often characterized by precarious conditions and migrants' exploitation (Brickenstein, 2015; Corrado, 2017). Migration is therefore a complex phenomenon and one can gauge the consequences for all those involved only by considering all its stakeholders from multiple angles, be they states, institutions, societies, companies, policy makers or individuals.

Hidden bicultural potentials in CCM

A major influencing factor in how and whether people explore and develop their potential biculturality are dominant ideas of what constitutes successful internationality. For example, literally, an expatriate is simply a person who is 'outside of their country' for longer. The same is true for a **migrant** or a **refugee**. Based on this insight, contemporary CCM has widened their understanding of which and whose international experiences should be studied and considered, beyond a narrow definition of expatriation.

Migrant An unprecise category for a person who moves their place of residence/centre of life for more than a year

Refugee An unprecise category for a forced migrant

To overcome a potentially narrow conceptualization of the internationally mobile class, several CCM scholars have started to include formerly marginalized and fringe identities (Guttormsen and Lauring, 2018), such as migrants and their descendants, ethnic minority groups and refugees. These groups, too, start their identity work from an expatriate, third cultural or bicultural perspective and might thus bring relevant assets to CCM. Nonetheless, the same assets might be interpreted differently: For example (to give two random examples), if a university-educated, white English manager is bilingual in French and English because of their British–French parentage, this is considered to be an elite and favourable CCM identity, which is not often challenged by others. However, if the same manager is a university-educated black Cameroonian, the same potential CCM assets might not be looked upon as equally favourable. For CCM studies, it thus became important to reflect upon which experiences are perceived as 'favourably international' and to become more inclusive in that sense. Elif's case exemplifies this insight: She is not 'bicultural' in the sense of classic CCM – but nonetheless develops a bicultural identity which is highly integrated. The following section details this insight.

STUDENT ACTIVITY 3.7

The CCM Asset of Being 'Marginal'

Construct two stereotypical images in your mind:

- one image of perceived positive international mobility: an expatriate
- one image of perceived negative international mobility: a refugee

Who are they? Where do they come from? What were there life experiences so far?
  Remarks:

- Assume that both hold a relevant university degree.
- Be aware that you are being asked to stereotype. Therefore, be careful to reflect upon these stereotypes as well. Where did you encounter them? Do you actually believe in them or are you aware of the fact that they are exaggerations of the fact?

Now, answer the question:

- What has the refugee experienced that could potentially make them an excellent cross-cultural manager?

Finally, reflect upon the task. What can you do so that these stereotypes don't blind you in recognizing the CCM skills of others and hinder your own learning process?

Halfie and hyphenated selves in CCM

Migration has changed the faces of those who are considered to be 'bicultural'. Alternative terms that have been suggested for the phenomenon described by the term 'biculturalism' are *halfies* and *hyphenated selves*. The critique is that the term 'biculturalism' presupposes that national cultures still matter over alternative identifications, and that it is a presumed 'monocultural majority' who defines national identity. Also, biculturalism involves a narrow approach towards what makes a person 'bicultural' (in the positive sense), namely internationally mobile parents or at least one internationally mobile parent in the classic sense, but *not* a history or lived experience of migration or taking refuge. The idea behind the alternative terms 'halfie' and 'hyphenated self' is thus not to force elite ideas of national culture onto other people. Rather than perceiving individuals beyond single cultures as being 'caught between (national) cultures', one should rather let them self-identify as a new combination of influences in whatever ways they choose. They could call themselves halfie, for example, or refer to themselves by means of a hyphenated term such as Asian-American, Turkish-German or Kenyan-Indian. Such an 'inside-out' view on biculturalism is depicted in Figure 3.4.

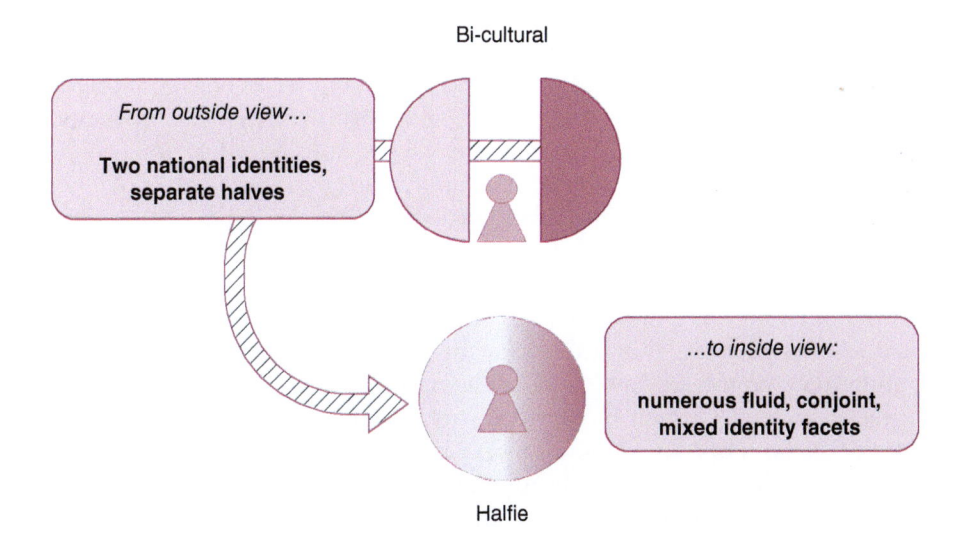

Figure 3.4 An inside-out view on biculturalism in cross-cultural management

The inside-out view makes it clearer what is actually meant by biculturalism as a positive resource for CCM; namely, the cultural versatility of a person who has grown up beyond single cultural identifications and thus might be more able to bridge difference and span boundaries in CCM. These abilities can be developed via lived experiences of classic biculturalism in the narrow sense, or via lived experiences of migration and taking refuge, and neither of them should be considered to be more valuable than any other.

Combining cosmopolitanism and (multi-)cultural rootedness in CCM

Mobility and migration are linked to the formation of the cross-cultural manager's identity because they influence the degree of rootedness which a person experiences in relation to their identity.

Local and global are in constant interaction when forming identities in CCM. For example, there is the term *global nomad* which refers to a person who has grown up in a variety of cultures (such as third culture kids). Global nomads of the third culture kid variety engage or have engaged in-depth with a variety of cultures, yet still cannot root themselves in any of them. The term global nomad can also refer to perpetual backpackers or internationally mobile managers who are constantly on the move (and thus not rooted) but are exposed to culture only superficially, in the context of tourism or in hotel and meeting rooms.

On the other hand, international life experiences can also lead to the formation of a *cosmopolitan identity* – people who perceive themselves as citizens of the globe and who interact well in spheres beyond national culture, such as international diplomacy or global management and leadership. They engage more deeply with a variety of cultures than the global nomad; however, this elite cosmopolitan sphere (overview in Lee, 2014; see Figure 3.5) is not accessible for everyone – accessing it often requires money and/or family background, for example, when it comes to receiving the kind of international education that enables them to enter this sphere. Also, cosmopolitanism might lack deep rootedness, albeit less than global nomads.

On the other end of the global–local scale, there are those people who develop a *local identity* because they can't look back onto a history of mobility and/or migration, for example because they grow up and live in, and identify with a single locality, such as a region or city. The strength of this identity is the rootedness which the global nomad and the cosmopolitan elite identity lack. They engage on a very deep level with a certain locality and they can still link themselves to the non-international and potentially monocultural people there.

The art of CCM thus also involves the question of how to develop a sense of *rooted cosmopolitanism* (see Figure 3.5). This concept requires combining globally nomadic experiences and the aim to develop a cosmopolitan identity for the best global performance *and* the required degree of rootedness to translate the requirements of the global and cross-cultural sphere to single locations and local identities.

Identities of the Cross-Cultural Manager

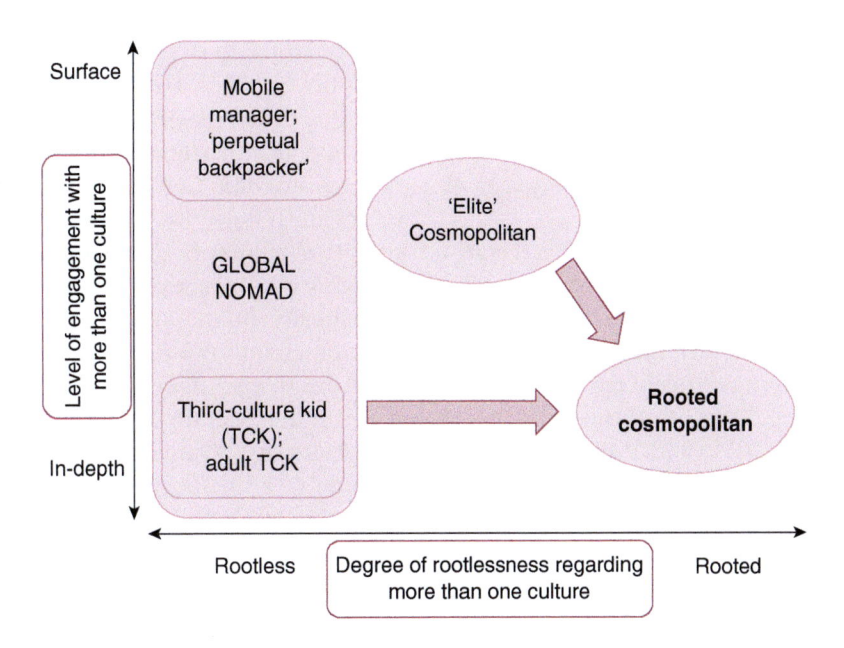

Figure 3.5 Developing a sense of rooted cosmopolitanism in cross-cultural management

Source: adapted from Lee (2014: 97)

As Figure 3.5 shows, there are different ways towards this goal of rooted cosmopolitanism in CCM. The local identity is not part of the picture, because they need to multiply their sense of rootedness first, from a single culture towards the sphere of multiple cultures. Depending on the individual and the circumstances, this might require more engagement with cultural diversity at home or to seek cross-cultural experiences abroad. The other suggested paths of development are depicted in Figure 3.5. Out of this idea comes the idea that it is the complementarity of diverse identities and identity formation processes in CCM which is the most beneficial to management, organizations and business.

The future of identity and mobility in CCM

CCM, like any business activity, is rooted in the idea of **meritocracy**. Meritocracy means that promotion and reward at work should be merit-based (however defined); i.e. people should have earned their place in management

> **Meritocracy** A system in which people receive status or rewards based on how they perform and what they achieve

> **Privilege** An (identity) advantage not personally earned by a person

and organizations. However, if some identities seem to be a 'better fit' to a certain position such as management, then identity privilege gets in the way of a meritocratic CCM. **Privilege** refers to an advantage not earned by a person; you can think of it as a head-start advantage, even before the actual race has begun. If a certain identity is presupposed in such ways, this might result in disadvantage for other identities which do not automatically 'fit' the image.

Examples for such identities in CCM are those of migrants and refugees (Roy et al., 2020). They have been referred to as *marginal* or *fringe identities* (Guttormsen and Lauring, 2018), and the danger is that their unique identity resources are not utilized for CCM (ibid.). For example, if one speaks of a 'German' manager, it is often implied that the manager is 'ethnic German' (and not, let's say, Turkish-German). On a second level, you can also ask yourself whether the normalized picture of this implicitly ethnic German manager is 'male' or 'female', whether they are able-bodied or not, and so on – more layers of potential identity privilege and disadvantage.

Does this mean that CCM is a constant clash between identities which only some can win? To the contrary:

- Because humans are products and producers of culture, power effects concerning identity are never absolute. For example, more people than ever migrate or grow up bicultural or as third culture kids. This alone changes the privilege–disadvantage ratio between monocultural and bicultural/third cultural identities.
- Secondly, people can choose (within boundaries) who they wish to be. Identity is not fixed, and people might develop their sense of self and their abilities throughout their lives. From a cross-cultural perspective, being assigned an identity beyond what is considered 'mainstream' exposes people to new cross-cultural learning triggers. Likewise, a person who is assigned a 'monocultural identity' might explore those identity facets which do not fit this picture and, thus, engage in cross-cultural learning as well.
- Furthermore, *any* managerial identity is privileged compared to groups such as unqualified low-cost workers who might not have the ability and opportunity (agency) to self-define.
- Finally, there is the argument that the perception of migration and identity conflict is more negative than its reality (El-Mafaalani, 2020). Increasing diversity at work also increases competition, for example, for jobs. Therefore, it is logical that increased opportunity for more groups of people and the successful decline of privilege is perceived as more conflicting than the lack thereof. As German sociologist Aladin El-Mafaalani (2020) thus argues, increased conflict at work proves higher inclusiveness: the more people sitting down at the managerial table, the more discussion (and thus conflict) about 'how to do things' and by whom.

Elif's story is thus also an example for how social class has become permeable and how management (one hopes) is characterized by fewer social closure mechanisms than before. A **closure mechanism** refers to the social phenomenon of 'not getting into' a certain sphere or job because those already there 'shut the door'. In the case of Elif, she has entered the sphere of management in just two generations. As a woman, she has enrolled in a study programme which used to be considered a 'male' choice, at least in Germany.

> **Closure mechanism** (Social or cultural) ways in which (identity) privilege is retained

Of course, it is open to debate whether this is true equality for all or whether some might still have more privilege concerning the status at work which they can achieve. For example, it seems more likely that one enters the sphere of top management if someone in one's social circle is already there and can provide advice. Therefore, the most likely answer to the question of whether it has been harder for Elif to attend university and enter the sphere of management than others is yes, but she has experienced more equal opportunities than the generations of her parents and grandparents – and she also expects the world to be like this and is thus not satisfied with a lesser seat at the table anymore. Of course, there are also groups not yet included, so Elif's story is also not representative for all potential identities of the cross-cultural manager.

Table 3.1 summarizes the previous identity considerations and their relevance for CCM.

Table 3.1 Identities in CCM

Identity type	Source texts (if any)	Explanation	Example	CCM implications
Mono-cultural	None (assumed to be the 'default' identity by Classic CCM)	A person who is identified as the member of the ethnic/racial majority in their country and who also identifies in terms of (majority) national culture	(Caucasian) American, (Ethnic German) German	• Grows up in the cultural middle • How they perceive themselves in terms of national identity is how others perceive them • Assumes that their identity is representative of national identity • Experiences few triggers for looking at themselves from the outside • Experiences 'culture shock' abroad • Identity work is sought by themselves

(Continued)

Table 3.1 (Continued)

Identity type	Source texts (if any)	Explanation	Example	CCM implications
Bi-cultural	Brannen and Thomas (2010); Brannen (2020)	A person born to parents from two different countries who lives in one of these countries. A person born to parents originating from another country	Descendant of Indian immigrants in Britain	• Grows up between national cultures • How they identify themselves is not how others identify them • Needs to engage in identity work to reconcile both perspectives • Identity work is triggered by others • Is aware that national culture is not homogeneous and that their identity is not representative of most people's idea of this national identity • Opportunity for CCM
Halfie	Abu-Lughod (1991)	An alternative term for 'bicultural' from the 'inside-out'	Anyone who identifies as 'whole' when 'between' cultures	• Same as above, but with a focus on the individual ability and need to develop an integrated identity beyond national cultural labels. • Opportunity for CCM
Hyphenated	Schütz (1944); Fine and Sirin (2007)	A person identifying and being identified in terms of two conjoint identities. Also: a term that moves beyond 'bicultural' (e.g. Muslim Kenyan-Indian)	Muslim American', Kenyan-Indian	• Same as bicultural, but with a focus on how a person's identity involves a 'double consciousness' (DuBois, 1903) • Opportunity for CCM
Marginal or Fringe	Park (1928); Guttormsen and Lauring (2018)	Identities which the majority considers to be at the fringe of the expected identity, which are also often not equally included (marginalized).	Refugees, racial or other minorities	• Same as bicultural but with critical implications: Because certain identities are placed at the margins, the potential of these (often halfie and hyphenated) identities is not utilized • Missed opportunity for CCM

Identity type	Source texts (if any)	Explanation	Example	CCM implications
Third cultural	Pollock and Van Reken (1999)	A person growing upon in one or several countries which are not the countries of origin of their parents and who develops a 'third' cultural orientation.	Children of diplomats	• Grows up beyond national cultures • Is partially exposed to any of them • Identifies beyond national cultures • Identity work is part of who they are • Difficulties to identify with and root themselves in any local culture • Partial opportunity for CCM
Global normad	McCaig (1996); Kannisto (2016)	A person who lives a permanently mobile, location-independent life and/or whose identity formation has been influenced by global mobility in such a way that they cannot identify with a single local culture anymore.	Former children of mobile parents, perpetual backpackers, internationally mobile managers	• Same as above
Cosmopolitan	Vertovec and Cohen (2002)	A person who identifies as a citizen of the world, not as member of any local culture(s).	Diplomats, top managers	• Identity develops across multiple locations and cultures • This can, but must not, result in a lack of rootedness • Cosmopolitanism integrates diverse identities • Opportunity for CCM

Link to Practice: 'What's wrong with asking: "Where are you from?"' (Ravishankar, 2020)

Companies nowadays try to promote an inclusive workplace for all identities. However, it is often the simple things that turn out to be problematic

(Continued)

in practice. For example, asking a person 'where are you from?' seems like a simple question; however, the question can indicate something else. For example, when people who look different to the majority of that place by a member of that majority, it implies that they do not (fully) belong. In a certain context, the question thus feels like alienation, for example, if an ethnic majority native English language speaker couples it with (a rather surprised): 'Your English is very good! (Where are you from?)' (Ravishankar, 2020). There is thus a fine line between curiosity and microaggression. **Microaggression** refers to interpersonal behaviour by means of which people are discriminated against, excluded or 'put in their places' in subtle ways (Sue et al., 2007).

> **Microaggression** Subtle ways in which identity privilege and disadvantage are reproduced in interpersonal interactions

Unlike overt discrimination (which is generally frowned upon), microaggression is difficult to detect and even more difficult to respond to (Eschmann et al., 2020). However, it is still problematic because it reproduces identity **privilege** and disadvantage. For example, how will Elif feel when being congratulated for 'speaking excellent German' (or when being asked where she is from) by a male, ethnic German manager at headquarters? Can this statement ever be 'innocent', even if the manager (who speaks and acts from a position of power and, potentially, also privilege) 'meant well'? Furthermore, why should Elif have to 'deal with' this question and negotiate her identity (whereas some others, e.g. the person asking it, might not have to do so)? To ponder such questions in order to figure out the fine line between curiosity and microaggression, and to act accordingly, is thus part of today's CCM challenge.

STUDENT ACTIVITY 3.8

The Future of Identity and Mobility in CCM

The world is changing, and so are people's identities within it. Therefore, consider identity and mobility in CCM:

- What will happen if even more people migrate, and if societies become even more heterogeneous?
- How would the situation change to the better if there is more equality of opportunity in more societies, and if no one is given a head-start anymore?
- However, concerning the risks, who could be the majority, who will be the new marginalized, and how, if at all, could your own privilege–disadvantage ratio change in the process?
- What is the role of CCM in overcoming these old and new inequalities? How can you personally contribute and what could it personally cost you (and are you willing to give up these privileges)?

Reflect upon these questions and, when ready, discuss them with fellow students.

Identity Work in Contemporary CCM: An Integrative Model

Biculturalism, third culture identifications or rooted cosmopolitanism, just like CCM competencies in general, are mainly acquired and developed; they require adequate experiences which are to be reflected upon, and the will and motivation to rethink oneself and to learn from others. These skills can be acquired by previously 'monocultural' individuals as well, for example, when studying or moving abroad or when constantly seeking out new trigger points for cross-cultural learning 'at home'.

The starting point of this learning process is the insight that, under the conditions of cultural complexity and multiple cultures, there can be no identity formation which is merely 'monocultural'. For example, a German or French student without any family history of migration might not fully understand the identity challenges faced by a fellow German or French student of Turkish or Algerian descent. However, if they consider how they are the first in their family to attend university, they can relate to how it feels to be perceived as 'lacking key skills or resources' in the eyes of those for whom attending university is 'normal', and the kind of identity work it takes to move beyond it. In difference, they find relatedness, and in relatedness, they find difference.

Therefore, from a more contemporary perspective, the world is not divided into monocultural and rooted people on the one hand, and bi-, multi- or third cultural, or cosmopolitan and culturally nomadic people on the other hand, because culture is more than just national culture. Rather, everyone may pursue more than one option of how to relate themselves to a combination of multiple cultures.

It is true that some people might *think* of themselves as monocultural when considering themselves only in terms of country culture. Nonetheless, they could still investigate their own lives as involving more than one culture and focus on developing the potential assets of their third or bicultural selves, such as what they have learned from being the first in their family to go to university, and how this experience can be transferred into general techniques for utilizing the benefits of cross-cultural differences.

At the same time, those who are exposed to two or more macro-cultures are not automatically bicultural. If they shy away from the hardship of identity work, alternative cultural schemes become inaccessible to them. Therefore, developing CCM skills is about exploring the identity implications of one's experiences to the fullest (and to seek out experiences that trigger learning in the first place), even though one could get by with investing less effort.

What makes the difference in achieving cross-cultural management competencies are thus (1) the degree to which a person is seeking out and exploring the identity development triggers available to them, and (2) the amount and quality of identity work they are willing to engage in.

This does not imply that cross-cultural managers need to change the whole of 'who they are' just because they live in a culturally complex world. Rather, the logic is inverse. If managers (1) consider themselves as more than just 'monocultural' and (2) consciously engage with cross-cultural differences from there, they will (3) discover more options of who they might be and where they might belong, which they can then (4) utilize for their future CCM practice. Via considering how they are related and different to each other, they may then pursue the best possible combination of a cosmopolitan rootedness and a deep engagement with multiple cultures – a collective task for *all* involved in CCM today. Figure 3.6 summarizes these ideas.

Chapter Summary

Identity is relevant to CCM, because how a person lives the role of the cross-cultural manager is informed by their identity formation processes. From a classic CCM perspective, cultural identity is related to macro-cultures and becomes relevant when people encounter other national cultural environments or interact with representatives of other macro-cultures. Therefore, the first identity focus point of classic CCM studies was the presumably monocultural expatriate or student sojourner.

Identities of the Cross-Cultural Manager 93

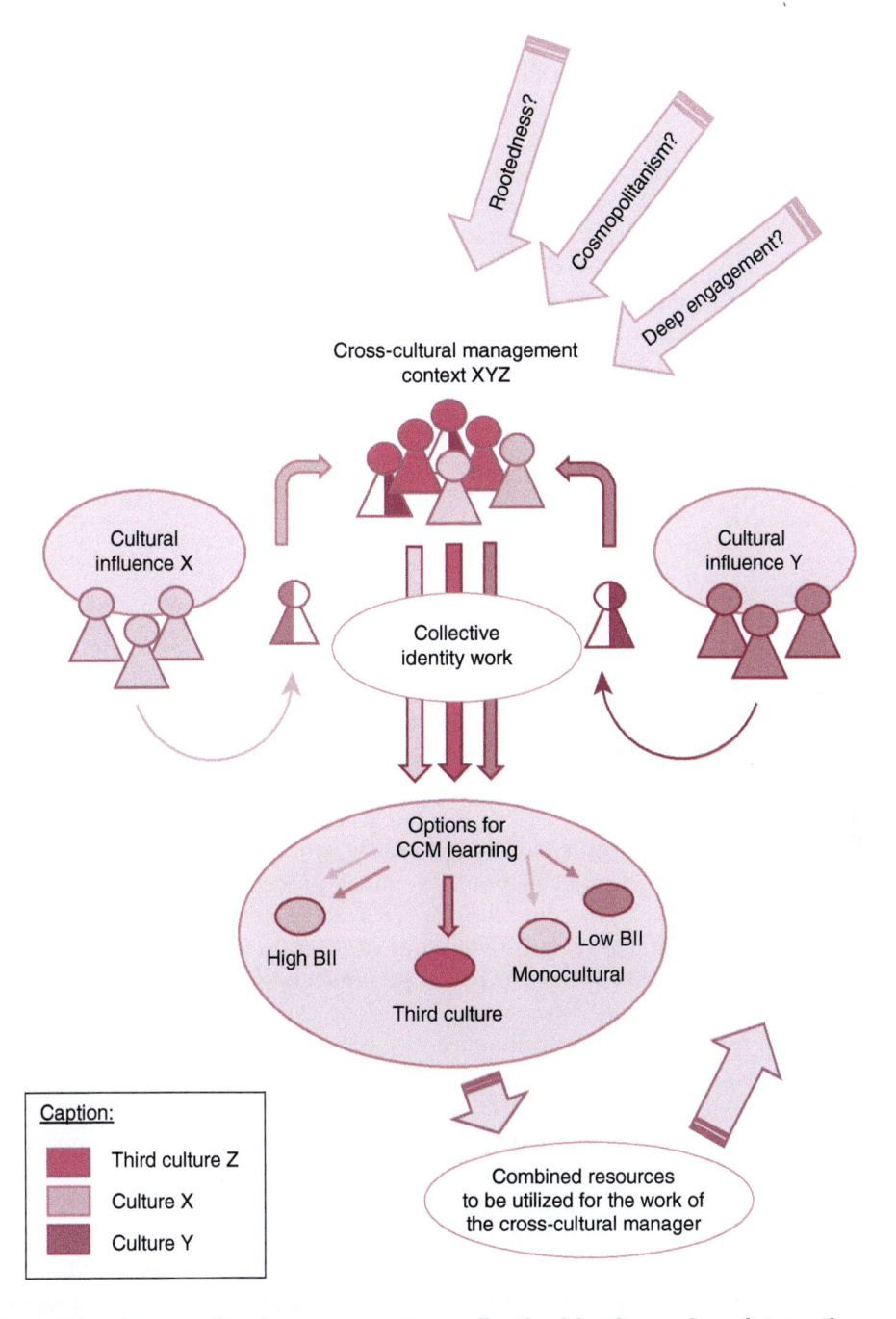

Figure 3.6 Cross-cultural management as collective identity work: an integrative model

From a more contemporary perspective, any group-related (social) identity formation process is also cultural. Therefore, CCM studies began to embrace the concept of cultural identity under the conditions of cultural complexity and multiple cultures. As a first step, the experiences of bicultural individuals and third culture kids were considered as relevant to CCM. It was considered how the skills which a bicultural or third cultural life experience requires (such as the ability to 'switch' between cultural identifications, to establish connections across opposing viewpoints, to find synergy in differences or to combine cultural influences in novel and creative ways) largely equal the required skills of the expatriate cross-cultural manager. Afterwards, CCM studies moved from mobility in the narrow, elite sense to also include migration and refugee movements, as well as the experiences of the descendants of migrants. Developing a sense of rooted cosmopolitanism and the need for deep engagement with multiple cultures became the contemporary requirement for CCM, understood as the collective identity work of individuals who are different and related at the same time.

Key Points

- Under contemporary CCM conditions, the cross-cultural manager's identity options have diversified and include bicultural and third cultural identities, halfie and hyphenated identities, marginal and fringe identities, and cosmopolitan and global nomad identities.
- Mobility in the wider sense and as involving migration and cultural flows has contributed to the diversification of the cross-cultural manager's identity.
- Monocultural and bicultural identity formation processes are relevant to the competencies of the cross-cultural manager in different ways.
- The inside-out view on bicultural identities enables the cross-cultural manager to identify the benefits and resources of identities beyond national cultures.
- Each identity formation process involves strengths and weaknesses, and is associated with certain opportunities and threats to be utilized and overcome, respectively.
- Various identities may complement each other.
- Cross-cultural managers need to engage in collective identity work in order to utilize the benefits of multiple identities.
- Be able to assess your own and others' identities in relation to their strengths and weaknesses, and opportunities and risks for CCM.
- Know how mobility and identity are intertwined in contemporary CCM.
- Have encountered first strategies for developing a sense of rooted cosmopolitanism in CCM.

Review Questions

1. How does monocultural, bicultural and third identity formation differ?
2. What is meant by high and low bicultural identity integration (BII), and how is either of them relevant to CCM?
3. What is meant by an 'inside-out' view on biculturalism and why and how is this viewpoint relevant for present and future CCM and for the cross-cultural manager's skills development?
4. What is meant by 'majority' and 'fringe' or 'marginal' identities, and how are they relevant to CCM?
5. What is meant by rooted cosmopolitanism, and why and how should cross-cultural managers develop a sense of rooted cosmopolitanism?
6. What are the dangers of a globally nomadic identity, and how can these be overcome?
7. How can the contribution of all of the aforementioned identities create complementarities and synergies for CCM?
8. What is meant by CCM as 'collective identity work'? What are its challenges and opportunities? What is required for putting this idea into practice?
9. How are mobility and migration different and related? Are they the same concept? (Why/why not?)
10. How are mobility (in the wider sense) and identity intertwined under contemporary CCM conditions?

Closing Activity

1. *Step 1: Myself as a cross-cultural manager*

    'Who you are' and how a person develops their sense of self and which concepts they use to self-define is relevant to how they master the role of the cross-cultural manager. With this in mind, reconsider the identities of the cross-cultural manager.

    i. Who do you identify as/are you identified? Is the experience congruent or are you identified as someone you are not?
    ii. Which identity concepts could you use to understand your own identity formation processes?

Next, place yourself in the role of a cross-cultural manager. Consider your own strengths (S) and weaknesses (W) in relation to being a cross-cultural manager. Which tasks and responsibilities of the cross-cultural manager, and which CCM situations will be an opportunity (O) for you because your internal strengths fit to the external situation, and which ones will be an identity threat (T) or challenge for you because you will find yourself in a situation which exposes your weaknesses?

Visualize this as follows:

Table 3.2 **Myself as a cross-cultural manager – a SWOT analysis**

S – internal strengths	W – internal weaknesses
What are the strengths of your identity experiences?	What are the weaknesses of your identity experience?
e.g. unique resources / learning triggers, know-how...	e.g. lack of resources / learning triggers, lack of know-how...
O – external opportunities	**T – external threats**
What identity opportunities do you see for yourself in the role of the cross-cultural manager?	What identity threats do you see for yourself in the role of the cross-cultural manager?
e.g. situations which bring to light your strengths, tasks you can handle well, ...	e.g. situations which expose your weaknesses, tasks you cannot handle well, ...

The task is to relate what you bring to the role of the cross-cultural manager (internal strengths and weaknesses) to potential configurations of the role of the cross-cultural manager (external opportunities or threats). For this, you need to think about the multiple configurations of the role of the cross-cultural manager, based on what you already know about CCM. For example, are you better suited to virtual CCM or to going abroad for a long period of time? Which professional focus and CCM activities suit you best, and why is this so?

2. *Step 2: Identities in CCM – a collective SWOT analysis*

    Pair with another student. Compare your visualizations, exchange with each other and then visualize your insights in a combined SWOT analysis for the both of you. Figure out how your combined identities might utilize more opportunities in CCM than any of the single identities and also whether the combined identities might prevent or neutralize certain identity threats to the single identities.

3. *Step 3*

    If you find that your strengths and weaknesses do not complement each other sufficiently, seek out another student whose identity experiences can. Repeat the exercise in the new team. Repeat these steps, if required, until all of you are fully satisfied with the strengths and weaknesses of your cross-cultural management team.

4. *Step 4*

    Exchange across teams.

Further Reading

Part V of *The Sage Handbook of Contemporary Cross-Cultural Management* (Szkudlarek et al., 2020) focuses on global mobility in the wider context of contemporary CCM. You will find chapters on global migration trends (Lee et al., 2020), the changing context of expatriation (McNulty and Brewster, 2020), and also on refugees and their relevance for CCM studies (Roy et al., 2020). Guo and Al Ariss (2015) reflect upon the need to re-consider theories and research on international migrants. Brannen (2020) provides an overview of how cultural identities have been and are presently conceptualized by CCM studies. Brannen and Thomas (2010) is an introductory source on bicultural individuals. Maznevski (2013) details on options of how to develop your CCM competencies via learning from experience. Appiah (1997) considers the concept of rooted cosmopolitanism and how it is linked to patriotism and nationalism.

References

Abu-Lughod, L. (1991) 'Writing against culture', in R. Fox (ed.), *Recapturing Anthropology: Working in the Present*. Santa Fe: School of American Research Press. pp. 117–135.

Appiah, K.A. (1997) 'Cosmopolitan patriots', *Critical Inquiry*, 23(3): 617–639. Available at: https://appiah.net/wp-content/uploads/2010/10/Cosmopolitan-Patriots.-Critical-Inquiry-23.3.-1997.pdf [last accessed 1 February 2022].

Bartram, D., Poros, M.V. and Monforte, P. (2014) *Key Concepts in Migration*. London: SAGE.

Brannen, M.Y. (2020) 'Cross-cultural management and cultural identity: Past perspectives and present prerequisites', in B. Szkudlarek, L. Romani, D.V. Caprar and J.S. Osland (eds), *The Sage Handbook of Contemporary Cross-Cultural Management*. London: Sage. pp. 233–297.

Brannen, M.Y. and Thomas, D.C. (2010) 'Bicultural individuals in organizations: Implications and opportunity', *International Journal of Cross Cultural Management*, 10(1): 5–16.

Brannen, M.Y., Goméz, C., Peterson, M.F., Romani, L., Sagiv, L. and Wu, P.-C. (2004) 'People in global organizations: Culture, personality and social dynamics', in H.W. Lane, M.L. Maznevski, M.E. Mendenhall and J. McNett (eds), *Handbook of Global Management: A Guide to Managing Complexity*. Oxford: Blackwell Publishing. pp. 26–54.

Brickenstein, C. (2015) 'Impact assessment of seasonal labor migration in Australia and New Zeeland: A win-win situation?', *Asian and Pacific Migration Journal*, 24(1): 107–129.

Corrado, A. (2017) Migrant Crop Pickers in Italy and Spain, Heinrich-Böll-Stiftung. Available at: www.boell.de/en/2017/06/30/migrant-crop-pickers-italy-and-spain [last accessed 23 June 2020].

Docquier, F. (2014) The Brain Drain from Developing Countries. Available at: https://wol.iza.org/uploads/articles/31/pdfs/brain-drain-from-developing-countries.pdf [last accessed 23 June 2020].

Du Bois, W.E.B. (1903) *The Souls of Black Folk*. New York: Penguin.

El-Mafaalani, A. (2020) *Das Integrationsparadox: warum gelungene Integration zu mehr Konflikten führt*. Köln: Kiepenheuer & Witsch. 1st edn, 2018.

Eschmann, R., Groshek, J., Chanderdatt, R., Chang, K. and Whyte, M. (2020) 'Making a microaggression: Using big data and qualitative analysis to map the reproduction and disruption of microaggressions through social media', *Social Media + Society*, 8(4) (online first). Available at: https://journals.sagepub.com/doi/epub/10.1177/2056305120975716 [Last accessed 01 November 2022].

Fine, M. and Sirin, S.R (2007) 'Theorizing hyphenated selves: Researching youth development in and across contentious political contexts', *Social and Personality Psychology Compass*, 1 : 16–38.

Guo, C. and Al Ariss, A. (2015) 'Human resource management of international migrants: Current theories and future research`, *International Journal of Human Resource Management*, 26(10): 1287–1297.

Guttormsen, D.S.A. and Lauring, J. (2018) 'Fringe voices in cross-cultural management research: Silenced and neglected?', *International Studies of Management and Organization*, 48(3): 239–246.

Kannisto, P. (2016) *Global Nomads and Extreme Mobilities*. Farnham: Ashgate.

Lee, E.S., Nguyen, D.C. and Szkudlarek, B. (2020) 'Global migration and cross-cultural management: Understanding the past, moving towards the future', in B. Szkudlarek, L. Romani, D.V. Caprar and J.S. Osland (eds), *The Sage Handbook of Contemporary Cross-Cultural Management*. London: Sage. pp. 408–423.

Lee, H-J. (2014) 'Identities in the global world of work', in B. Gehrke and M.-T. Claes (eds), *Global Leadership Practices – A Cross-Cultural Management Perspective*. London: Palgrave Macmillan. pp. 85–101.

Maznevski, M. (2013) 'Comments on the interview: Best approaches and practices to increase cultural awareness and prepare managers for working in a culturally diverse environment', *Academy of Management Learning and Education*, 12(3): 509–511.

McCaig, N. (1996) 'Understanding global nomads', in C.D. Smith (ed.), *Strangers at Home*. New York: Aletheia Publications. pp. 99–120.

McNulty, Y. and Brewster, C. (2020) 'The changing context of expatriation and its impact on cross-cultural management', in B. Szkudlarek, L. Romani, D.V. Caprar and J.S. Osland (eds), *The Sage Handbook of Contemporary Cross-Cultural Management*. London: Sage. pp. 424–438.

O'Reilly, K. (2014) 'What is lifestyle migration?', *bpb*, 19 December. Available at: www.bpb.de/gesellschaft/migration/kurzdossiers/198255/what-is-lifestyle-migration [last accessed 23 June 2020).

Park, R.E. (1928) 'Human migration and the marginal man', *American Journal of Sociology*, 33(6): 881–893.

Pollock, D. and Van Reken, R. (1999) *Third Culture Kids: The Experience of Growing Up Among Worlds*. London: Nicholas Brealey.

Ravishankar, R.A. (2020) 'What's wrong with asking "Where are you from?"', *Harvard Business Review*, 22 October. Available at: https://hbr.org/2020/10/whats-wrong-with-asking-where-are-you-from [last accessed 31 July 2022].

Roy, P.A., Szkudlarek, B. and Caprar, D.V. (2020) 'Refugees and cross-cultural management studies', in B. Szkudlarek, L. Romani, D.V. Caprar and J.S. Osland (eds), *The Sage Handbook of Contemporary Cross-Cultural Management*. London: Sage. pp. 452–464.

Schütz, A. (1944) 'The stranger: An essay in social psychology', *American Journal of Sociology*, 49(6): 499–507.

Sue, D.W., Capodilupo, C.M., Torino, G.C., Bucceri, J.M., Holder, A.M.B., Nadal, K.L. and Esquilin, M. (2007) 'Racial microaggressions in everyday life: Implications for clinical practice', *American Psychologist*, 62(4): 271-286.

Szkudlarek, B., Romani, L., Caprar, D.V., and Osland, J.S. (eds) (2020) *The Sage Handbook of Contemporary Cross-Cultural Management*. London: Sage.

United Nations (2017) *Migration and Population Change – Drivers and Impacts*. Available at: www.un.org/en/development/desa/population/migration/publications/populationfacts/docs/MigrationPopFacts20178.pdf [last accessed 23 June 2020].

Vertovec, S. and Cohen, R. (eds) (2002) *Conceiving Cosmopolitanism: Theory, Context and Practice*. Oxford: Oxford University Press.

PART II
CCM PERSPECTIVES

Part I has introduced the underpinnings of contemporary CCM in relation to the CCM environment and current developments, in relation to culture and in relation to the identities of the cross-cultural manager.

Part II provides you with the knowledge and tools of how to assess and manage a cross-cultural situation the most appropriately and effectively.

Chapter 4 introduces three major angles, so-called paradigms, from which to conceptualize and manage a cross-cultural situation. Paradigms, such as the functionalist, interpretive and critical perspective, underlie contemporary CCM theory and practice. They are characterized by three key questions: How does CCM work? What does CCM mean? Whom does CCM serve (and how does this happen)? Together, these questions enable you to understand the multiplicity of the tools available to the cross-cultural manager and researcher. The chapter also provides initial insights into which tool to use (or which tool not to use) for which purpose.

Chapters 5 to 7 are dedicated to these perspectives in detail. The discussion of three interrelated questions further develops your abilities to assess and manage a cross-cultural situation. These are:

1. How does CCM work? This is a question to be answered by *functionalist CCM* (Chapter 5). The underlying idea is that there is one best way to manage across large cultural units, such as nations and societies. Thus, the task of the cross-cultural manager is to gather and analyse objective and reliable data. The focus is on *national and societal macro-cultures*.
2. What does CCM mean? This is a question to be answered by *interpretive CCM* (Chapter 6). The underlying idea is that cultures and cross-cultural differences are subjective, and that there is an inherent perspectivity to CCM. Thus, the task of the cross-cultural manager/researcher is to learn culture from the insider's perspective, mainly by means of qualitative methods, and to reflect upon their own subjectivity. The focus is on *cultural interactions in context*.
3. Whom does CCM serve? This is a question to be answered by *critical CCM* (Chapter 7), and its power-sensitive methods. The purpose is to critique 'how CCM works' and 'what CCM means', and to come up with fairer or more responsible and inclusive ways of 'how CCM *should* work' and 'what CCM *should* mean'. Three angles are central to it, namely *critiques of meanings, of structures and functions, and of history*. The role of the cross-cultural manager/researcher is one of a person who *cares* and who wishes to change cross-cultural management to the better.

The purpose of this second part of this book is to provide you with multiple tools for contemporary CCM, and also to help you make decisions of how (or how not) to use them in your own CCM practice. This understanding builds upon your previous knowledge of CCM in a changing world (Chapter 1), and the configurations of culture and identity therein (Chapters 2 and 3).

Contemporary Cross-Cultural Management Paradigms

How to assess and manage a cross-cultural situation

Learning Objectives

After reading this chapter, you should:

- be aware of major paradigms in CCM studies, and their characteristics, contrasts and connections
- have developed an initial understanding of CCM as a multi-paradigmatic practice
- have gained first insights into interplay as a specific multi-paradigmatic practice.

Introduction

The previous chapters have considered the contemporary contexts in which cross-cultural managers experience and identify with culture. This chapter concerns itself with what researchers and managers 'see' in the situation when looking upon it, namely with CCM paradigms.

A **paradigm** is an assumption, rule or principle that people within a certain school or discipline accept as true (Schultz and Hatch, 1996). Managers or researchers tend to approach their job or object of study in line within the paradigms they assume to be 'true' (Hatch, with Cunliffe, 2006). For example, construction engineers don't prove gravity anew when constructing something – they just work within the assumption that gravity exists, and they apply Newton's law of gravity in their work without questioning it. In cross-cultural management theory and practice, multiple paradigms exist.

> **Paradigm** An assumption, rule or principle that people within a certain school or discipline accept as true

Paradigms are something to be used in practice. You can best think of CCM paradigms as hammers and screwdrivers in a carpenter's toolkit, and of yourself, a student of CCM, as a future carpenter wishing to learn this craft.

This chapter introduces you to three CCM paradigms – functionalist, interpretive and critical (differentiated into three focus points: history, meaning and function). The idea behind this **multi-paradigmatic** approach is that paradigm awareness leads to more conscious and informed choices in CCM. Simply speaking, paradigm awareness makes it more likely that you will use a screwdriver – and not a hammer – when the CCM challenge at hand is fastening a screw. The underlying discussion of whether, and if so, how, paradigms shall be combined is called the *paradigms debate* in management and organization studies (see In a Nutshell below).

> **Multi-paradigmatic** Building theories and applying methods across multiple paradigms

This chapter is based on the assumption that it is, indeed, possible to combine paradigms. The specific multi-paradigmatic method upon which this chapter is built is called **interplay** (Romani et al., 2011; Schultz and Hatch, 1996). It requires researchers and managers to move back and forth between paradigms, considering their connections and contrasts. This way, they 'zig-zag' towards their goal. Interplay as a multi-paradigmatic practice increases a researcher's or manager's ability to analyse a situation and, thus, to act effectively and adequately across cultures.[1]

> **Interplay** A specific practice of moving back and forth between paradigms. This practice considers paradigms, and their contrasts and connections, in light of each other

---

1 Other methods of a multi-paradigmatic approach are: keeping paradigms in mind simultaneously (simultaneous approach) or employing them one after the other (sequential approach) (Schultz and Hatch, 1996).

Contemporary CCM Paradigms

In a Nutshell: The Paradigms Debate

Since the 1970s, management and organization studies have engaged in a paradigms debate. Its roots lie in the social sciences, mainly sociology. Gibson Burrell and Gareth Morgan (1979) proposed a sociologically informed matrix of how to classify paradigms. Other scholars (e.g. Deetz, 1996) built further paradigm delineations, introducing ideas from other disciplines such as communication studies (Deetz, 1992) or anthropology (Moore and Mahadevan, 2020), recently also within CCM studies (Romani et al., 2018a, 2020b). In this process, the possibilities and benefits, as well as specific methods of multi-paradigmatic research, have been discussed (overview in Schultz and Hatch, 1996), also regarding CCM studies (Lowe et al., 2007; Romani et al., 2011) and CCM practice (Mahadevan, 2013). The five major paradigms which are the most frequently considered by CCM studies, and which are also covered in this chapter, are functionalist or positivist, interpretive, postmodern, postcolonial and critical.

Opening Case

'Is there anything you'd like to say?'

'I can't work this way. Whenever I ask them: "Is there anything you'd like to say?" – there is just nothing, nothing!' With these slightly exasperated words, Ewoud removes his headset, ending the web meeting with China.

Ewoud (35, male, Dutch by nationality and ethnicity) is employed as Global Key Account for Customer Relationship Management (CRM) at the headquarters of a multinational Dutch company (Bedrijf) in Rotterdam. Usually, he is also the one to train local staff at Bedrijf's sites in different countries in the company's approach to CRM. For a few months, his new challenge has been in training local staff in Nanjing, China. Ewoud has met the team, seven people in total, including the local CR manager Tian (34, male, from China) twice, at the Chinese site. In regular intervals, he invites them to participate in web-workshops regarding Bedrijf's global CRM policies and practices. The idea behind this corporate approach is that, this way, Ewoud will not only introduce global CRM to local staff but will also make sure that local ideas and requirements contribute to Bedrijf's global way of doing things.

The company prides itself in being an involving employer, and in offering a culture and climate wherein everyone can participate, feel at home and

(Continued)

is truly 'equal'. These are also the values which should stand behind how customer relationships are built, in whatever country, because these are the values Bedrijf stands for. The company is prepared to listen to and to include local needs, if need be.

Ewoud's approach is: As global as possible, and as local as necessary. However, with the Chinese staff, in particular with Tian, he has a problem: They do their work well, but they never voice anything when he asks for feedback in the web-based workshops. Instead, Tian sends him formal reports on behalf of the whole team via e-mail which, to Ewoud, is very frustrating, because it is the purpose of the web-based workshops that new ideas are discussed freely and openly by everyone, including all local team members.

To his co-worker Koen (32, male, Dutch by ethnicity and nationality), Ewoud says:

> 'I suppose, it's in their culture: They are just not used to participating, and they want strong managers who take care of them at work. You know this, we learned that in the culture training for China. But I still don't get it: I mean, who does not *want* to contribute? But they seem to be *so* stuck in all this ancient cultural stuff, it's like, much more than we here in Holland ever were, with global trade and multiculturalism, and all. Or is it Communist Party rule, and the fear of stepping out of line? – I truly don't know. It's like all these ethnic minorities in their own *wijken* [city districts]: they stick to their culture for generations, they never meet anyone else, and they just don't *want* to integrate. And now I need to invest all this additional work to develop them into the right direction, just to get things done. But that's not *my* responsibility, actually, they also need to do *their* part of the job. I mean: Why on earth are they working for a multinational company, if all they want is sticking to their own way of doing things, and *not participate*? I should not even have to ask them whether they want to say something. If they care about what we are doing here, they should just say what needs to be said, for the common goal. And Tian should understand that what he is doing really *is* management from the middle-ages, to control his team like that, and to prevent them from participating!'

Koen considers this and then says with a shrug:

> 'Well..., maybe you don't need to develop them: who says that the Dutch way is better than the Chinese one? Also, I am wondering: how *do* Chinese participate or give feedback to their managers? – There *must* be a Chinese way of doing this, maybe it's just that you don't see it yet.'

Paradigmapping CCM

Like many other fields of interest, CCM studies (as a whole – not as related to every individual scholar) is **multi-paradigmatic**. Its major strands are functionalist, interpretive and critical CCM.[2]

Paradigms influence disciplinary research and practice on three levels, namely **ontology** (what is reality, and how can we understand our existence?), **epistemology** (what is knowledge, and how can we obtain it?), and **methodology** and **methods** (how can I study this reality?).

Methodology refers to the system of the methods used to obtain knowledge; you can think of it as 'methods' on a higher level. Methodology does not provide immediate solutions; it thus differs from method. For example, an experiment is a specific method, and the ways in which it was carried out is the methodology. This way, methodology provides the link between epistemology and method.

Ontology Assumptions about reality and human existence

Epistemology Assumptions about knowledge and how to obtain it

Methodology The system of the methods used in a particular area or field of study

Method A way of gaining what is considered to be knowledge, within held assumptions regarding reality and human existence

---

2 Teaching note: There are different conceptualizations of paradigms in management and organization studies. The perspectives which are most frequently considered are positivism (also referred to as functionalism or objectivism), interpretivism, postmodernism, critical management studies and postcolonialism (e.g. Alvesson and Deetz, 2000; Deetz, 1992; Jack and Westwood, 2009; Primecz et al., 2009; Romani et al., 2014). The bottom line of all paradigm delineations is that positivism (or functionalism or objectivism), interpretivism and critical approaches are three fundamentally different paradigms to be considered (based on Burrell and Morgan, 1979), and this is also the differentiation prevalent in CCM studies (Romani et al., 2018a, 2018b, 2020b) and related disciplines such as International Human Resource Management studies (Mahadevan and Schmitz, 2020; Primecz, 2020). Alternatively, some overviews depart from Deetz (1996) and consider postmodernism as a separate, fourth, paradigm (e.g. Romani et al., 2014). Most CCM paradigm delineations subsume postcolonialism under the critical paradigm (e.g. Romani et al., 2014), yet some consider it to be a distinct, fifth, paradigm (Romani et al., 2018b, 2020b). Whatever delineation chosen, the ways in which the content of the five approaches is described are fairly similar. Most delineations also agree that the critical approach – regardless of whether it is considered as emerging from a single paradigm or from multiple critical paradigms – involves a variety of perspectives. In this chapter, the basic differentiation of 'critical with regard to meaning' and 'critical with regard to structure' (see Figure 4.1) is put forward. Further differentiations regarding '*how* to be critical' are subsumed under this paradigm. They will be further discussed in Chapter 7, which is dedicated exclusively to Critical CCM, and which presents postmodernism, postcolonial and subaltern studies, and critical theory as three interrelated, yet distinct approaches within the Critical CCM paradigm.

Paradigms also have implications for how to understand the cross-cultural researcher's and manager's role. Table 4.1 depicts these aspects for the three major CCM paradigms – functional, interpretive and critical.

Table 4.1   Three key CCM questions and the paradigms underlying them

Key question	Underlying paradigm	Idea about reality	Manager/researcher role
How does CCM work?	Functionalist (*also:* positivist, objectivist)[3]	Reality exists objectively	Describe and analyse objective CCM facts; find the best way to manage across cultures; *detached manager/researcher*
What does CCM mean?	Interpretive	Reality is subjective (perspective matters)	Uncover inside meanings; consider differences in meaning when managing across cultures; *involved manager/researcher*
Whom does CCM serve?	Critical	(Objective/ subjective) reality suffers from power-inequalities	Uncover and consider power-effects, and how they 'happen'; change CCM to the better; *manager/researcher who 'cares'*

Depending on the paradigmatic angle from which cross-cultural managers look at the Opening Case, they will thus see different aspects in the situation, and they will also choose different actions to improve upon it.

Three paradigmatic angles for managing across cultures

Functionalist CCM assumes that reality exists objectively, and that it is the cross-cultural manager's and researcher's task to describe and analyse the facts of this reality from a detached perspective. Functionalism can be traced back to the natural sciences (Comte, 1907) and the idea that the social sciences should employ the same 'scientific' methods for higher validity (based on Durkheim, see Swingewood, 1991). Based on these assumptions, functionalist research tends to employ quantitative methods and is concerned with questions of internal and external validity and academic rigour (Comte, 1907). For the Opening Case, this implies that Ewoud should gather reliable facts of Chinese culture to gain insights into the objective reasons for the behaviour of the Chinese team (for tools of functionalist CCM, see Chapter 5). This way, he can identify the best way to manage across cultures.

---

3 In line with Burrell and Morgan (1979), and in contrast to, for example, Deetz (1996), I have chosen the term functionalism, instead of positivism or objectivism, because functionalism focuses more on the goal of a certain discipline or practice, and less on theory. Simply speaking, positivism and objectivism are different terms for the world-views (ontology) that underpin the functionalist idea to study 'how things work' (epistemology). Within the debate about what constitutes positivism, the two major perspectives are those by Comte (1907), which is more applicable to the natural sciences, and the one by Durkheim (see Swingewood, 1991), which is the application of Comte's ideas to the social sciences.

Interpretive CCM maintains that there can be no objective reality that is 'true' for all people, including the researcher/manager (reality is subjective). Rather, people 'make sense' of the world. Because groups of people have learned to view the world differently, the meaning which these groups give to the same situation or phenomenon will inevitably differ (Schwartz-Shea and Yanow, 2012). Meanings are 'below the surface' of culture; one cannot observe them from the outside. Therefore, one has to be a cultural insider to understand what reality *means* to a group of people. Conversely, a cultural outsider is likely to misinterpret the insufficient visible cultural clues which are 'above the surface' (Spencer-Oatley and Franklin, 2009).

From this viewpoint, Ewoud needs to accept that there are culturally different ways of asking for and giving feedback. For example, a behaviour which, from his culture-specific perspective, expresses 'a lack of participation' could well mean 'participation' from another cultural perspective which eludes him. To solve the situation, Ewoud thus needs to become aware of his own ('Dutch') and of the Chinese team's divergent ideas of feedback, and to find ways to design a 'way of doing things' that 'makes sense' to both cultural groups involved. For this, he should employ interpretive and qualitative methods (for tools of an interpretive CCM, see Chapter 6).

Pause and Reflect: When CCM is 'Grue' – Functionalist and Interpretive Implications

Interpretivism maintains that groups of people have learned different categories via which they structure their ideas and experiences of the world. For example, some languages differentiate between the colours 'green' and 'blue', others know a single cover term for both colours. The ratio between the two types of languages is reported to be about equal (Kay et al., 2009). Comparative linguists have thus devised the term 'grue' (from 'green' and 'blue') to name the cover term which is non-existent in English language (Berlin and Kay, 1969). Perception and language are two aspects of culture. Interpretivism then implies that the respective colours only exist if people perceive and name them as such. This is in contrast to the objectivist worldview upon which functionalism rests. Functionalist researchers would, for example, aim at devising a universally applicable measurement scale for colours which differentiates colours based on a valid scientific standard (e.g. a spectral analysis of sunlight). So, what do you believe – are there 'real' colours, or are colours what people have learned to name and perceive?

Power is a key element of the analysis in neither functionalism nor interpretivism, but it is central to *critical CCM*. From a critical perspective, the social world is seen as a constant imbalance between opposing forces, and whatever 'reality' emerges is assumed to often be a product of power struggles. Depending on the critical perspective taken, power effects are investigated with regard to meaning and/or with regard to function and structure (see Figure 4.1). The researcher/manager is part of these power struggles and might even produce them (power and meaning does not exist *per se*, but 'happens').

Bedrijf's headquarters are in the Netherlands, and Ewoud is based there, and Dutch. This means that he is advantaged over Tian and the Chinese team as Ewoud is closer to the centre of corporate power. He also is part of the dominant cultural group in the company, and, in addition, he is formally in charge. These structural and meaning-related power inequalities advantage Ewoud (and Koen) over Tian and the Chinese team.

Power inequalities do not *have to* result in negative effects (headquarters are *always* more powerful than the subsidiary site). Still, a critical CCM requires that Ewoud needs to check for power inequalities, just to make sure; headquarters' power has to be exercised, and he has to make responsible choices. He should thus reflect upon the power structures wherein he works and his own position within them. This way, he can be more certain that he *really* supports a participative approach and does not just perpetuate hidden power structures and dominant meaning, such as the corporate idea of what constitutes 'participation'. In summary, the critical CCM perspective asks Ewoud to consider that power – and not cultural differences of any kind – is the problem to be addressed (for power sensitive and critical CCM tools, see Chapter 7).

Pause and Reflect: When CCM is 'Grue' (Part 2) – Critical Implications

About half of the languages in the world differentiate between 'green' and 'blue', and the other half knows a cover term for both colours which has been translated as 'grue' to the English language (Berlin and Kay, 1969; Kay et al., 2009). Furthermore, 'grue' is assumed to be a pre-stage to the development of further differentiation of colour perceptions (Kay et al., 2009).

From a critical CCM perspective, there are power effects associated with these ideas. For example, some economies are more powerful than others. What if 'green' and 'blue' are found in most of the more powerful economies, and 'grue' involves only the less powerful ones? In the global marketplace, this would imply that the needs of those perceiving 'grue' are neglected more because they have less economic buying power. Or, to critique theory itself, could it be that the idea of 'grue' being a less advanced stage of colour perception (Kay et al., 2009) is already an example for how the perception scheme of 'green' and 'blue' dominates the world?

Paradigms in light of each other

Based on the previous considerations, Figure 4.1 visualizes the three major CCM paradigms – functional, interpretive and critical – in relation to each other. Critical CCM is further differentiated based on what is critiqued: function (critically

Contemporary CCM Paradigms

functionalist), meaning (critically interpretive) or history (which requires a combination of the previous two). These are the three major aspects by which a critical CCM wishes to identify negative power effects and to achieve change to the better. Conversely, interpretive and functionalist CCM are interested in identifying and maintaining balance.

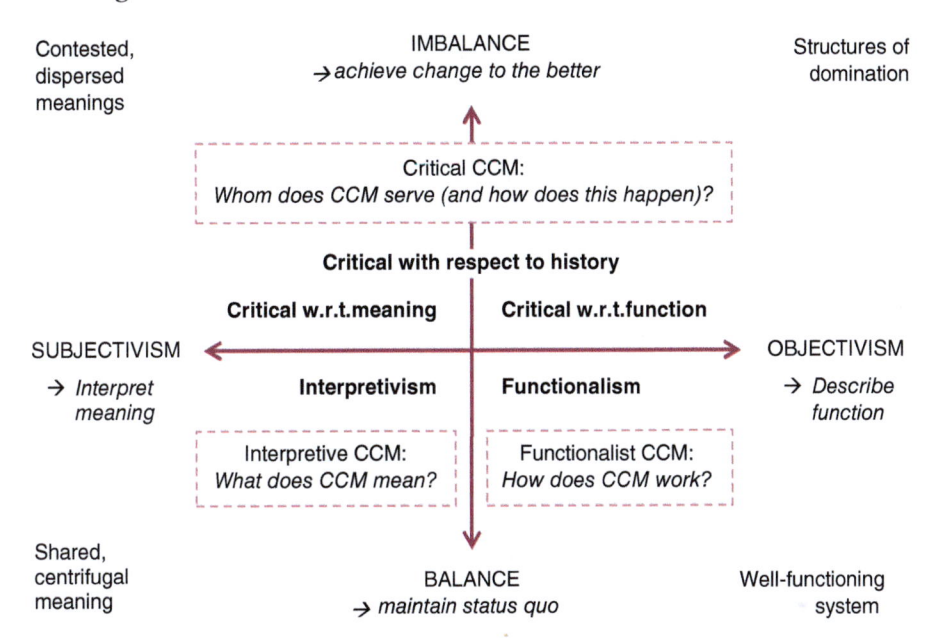

Figure 4.1 Cross-cultural management paradigms in relation to each other

Source: adapted from Burrell and Morgan (1979)

STUDENT ACTIVITY 4.1

Paradigmapping Your Study Programme and Related Disciplinary Skills

Consider the relevant subjects in your study programme and map them regarding their underlying paradigms. Consider the following aspects when doing so:

- Is the subject based on the idea of subjective or objective reality?
- Is the subject focused on meaning or function? Is power considered or not?

(Continued)

- Which subjects are **mono-paradigmatic**, which are multi-paradigmatic?
    - In case of multi-paradigmatic subjects, is one paradigm more prominent?
- Consider how paradigms underlie a certain subject as it is taught to you. Do you think that this was decided by your lecturer/those responsible for designing your study programme, or do you think that this lies in the nature of the subject?

Aggregate your insights and map your study programme, using Figure 4.1 as a template. Next, reflect upon the following:

- Are all paradigms equally represented in your study programme?
- If not, which paradigm(s) are you the most trained in? Which paradigm(s) might seem 'difficult to implement' or even 'strange' to you?
- Alternative 1: If you now realize that your study programme is rooted in a single paradigm/that not all paradigms are equally represented in your study programme:
    - What can you do to train yourself in using all paradigms equally?
    - Why *should* you train yourself in using all paradigms equally? Or, in other words, what would be the benefits of you being trained in all paradigms equally (for yourself, for your employer, for others)?
- Alternative 2: If you now realize that your study programme is rooted in all paradigms/that all paradigms are equally represented in your study programme:
    - What are the benefits of you being trained in all paradigms equally (for yourself, for your employer, for others)?
    - How can you make sure that you *really* consider all paradigms equally in your own practice?

Contrasts and Connections Between the Paradigms

Mono-paradigmatic Building theories and applying methods within a single paradigm

Paradigms are the major tools available to the cross-cultural researcher and manager. To decide upon which tool to use for which purposes, the cross-cultural researcher or manager has to understand the available paradigms in light of each other. They have to interplay CCM paradigms in practice.

Connections and contrasts between functionalist and critically functionalist CCM

Based on the understanding that social reality is objective (see Figure 4.1), both functionalist approaches to CCM wish to describe reality objectively. This requires a detached researcher (see Table 4.1).

From both functionalist perspectives, culture functions in certain, identifiable ways. Power is not considered by functionalism (culture functions *well*); therefore a single description suffices. Conversely, from a critically functionalist perspective, a single description is not enough, because of power effects in an imbalanced social world. This brings about systems of inequality which do *not* function well, and, therefore, an anti-description is required. The classic example are Marxist theories (see Nelson and Grossberg, 1988) which maintain that the workers' perspective is *always* contrary to the perspective of capital, yet excluded from the theory and practice that has become dominant. This makes it essential to critique the system via anti-theory or action, for example to counterbalance the negative effects of unconstrained capitalism, to facilitate workers' emancipation and to build a better system. The argument is not so much that workers' *perspectives* differ but rather that some parts of the objective analysis are missing in the dominant theory and practice: facts and consequences that have been neglected, and that are brought to surface by a critically functionalist analysis. The reality of Tian and the Chinese team (as subordinate to Ewoud, Koen and corporate headquarters) can be viewed in this light: What is it that the system does to *them*?

Connections and contrasts between functionalist and interpretive CCM

Functionalism and interpretivism share the idea that the social world balances itself out. It tends towards equilibrium, which means that it is not a necessity to question and challenge the status quo of 'how things work' and of 'what things mean'. Simply speaking, if Bedrijf's approach to global CRM would not work for and make sense to most of the people involved, people would have changed it.

The difference between both paradigms lies in their idea about reality. Functionalism maintains that reality is objective (Ewoud and the facts of culture are separated – he is detached), whereas interpretivism considers reality to be subjective (Ewoud himself has a cultural perspective – he is involved).

Connections and contrasts between critically functionalist and critically interpretive CCM

Critically functionalist and critically interpretive CCM oppose the idea of a social world that drifts towards a balanced status quo quasi 'automatically'. They maintain that the social world is characterized by divergent and opposing forces, and that the status quo is simply the meaning or structure that has somehow come to dominate potential alternatives. The critical cross-cultural manager/researcher should thus consider the power effects in an imbalanced social world. They should 'care' about change to the better, and not just accept the present state of 'how things work' or 'what things mean'. They should also reflect upon how they themselves are part of and produce power inequalities. This might place them in the role of an 'activist' (an 'angry' manager/researcher) who speaks for those who are presently neglected or disadvantaged. As Chapter 7 will show, this role is not without its own dangers, but at this point it suffices to state that the *critical* cross-cultural manager/researcher cannot hide behind theories and methods. Rather, they need to think about how to use their power responsibly, based on a careful analysis of 'how things *should* work' or 'what things *should* mean'.

Power is conceptualized differently across the two critical perspectives. Based on the idea of an objectively 'true' reality (see Figure 4.1) critically functionalist CCM assumes that power is large and stable, resulting in self-perpetuating systems of inequality. For example, objective corporate reality involves the differentiation between headquarters and subsidiary – an unequal power structure that is *real*.

A critically interpretive perspective looks at how it happens that certain meanings and inequalities emerge. It thus understands power as emerging from small processes. For example, Bedrijf believes that their CRM values are global, and it takes pride in its 'participative approach' to creating and maintaining a global CRM. But the ideas and practices behind Bedrijf's global CRM approach are created by people who are part of the structurally advantaged (Dutch) culture, who are located at headquarters, and who make sense of the situation mainly together with people sharing the same perspective. Therefore, does Bedrijf *really* ask for participation by all, or just for 'contributions' *within* (but not beyond) an already decided upon idea of what 'participation' is? How can the company make sure that what they understand as 'participation' really *is* the best of all alternatives, not just the one that has 'somehow' emerged as dominant?

Connections and contrasts between interpretive and critically interpretive CCM

Based on the understanding that social reality is subjective (see Figure 4.1), both interpretive CCM and critically interpretive CCM focus on meaning. However, their understanding of meaning differs.

Interpretive CCM assumes that cultural meaning is shared (culture is homogeneous). This implies that macro-cultures such as 'Dutch' and 'Chinese' can be identified as distinct and large 'meaning units'. Therefore, the main divergent perspectives which Ewoud has to consider are the inside and outside view on culture. This is the point which Koen tries to make for societal culture. There *must* be Chinese ways of providing feedback, it is just that Ewoud, as a cultural outsider, cannot identify them as such. Likewise (from a Chinese view), what Ewoud does when inviting 'feedback' is perceived differently by the Chinese team, who are an outsider to the 'Dutch' perspective. The purpose of the involved cross-cultural manager and researcher is thus to uncover and learn inside meanings.

Conversely, critically interpretive CCM[4] challenges the idea of large, shared and stable meaning units in a balanced social world. Rather, it assumes that meaning units are small, and that meanings are contested and fluid (how does meaning 'happen'?). Ewoud should therefore question the idea of stable core meanings in societal or organizational cultures and rather understand that meaning emerges from people in a situation. Maybe what Tian does is a reaction to what Ewoud did, and vice versa, and not a result of a stable 'Chinese' cultural trait. Ewoud, too, tries out several interpretations of the situation ('Is it culture? Is it communism?'), and which meaning emerges as 'true' will depend on what people do in relation to each other.

The idea of small meanings also implies that different people interpret the same situation differently (based on their own interests and fears), and that 'what things mean' cannot be pinned down to a single interpretation. Furthermore, individuals often link situations and phenomena in unexpected ways, thus creating new inequalities. For example, Ewoud interprets the behaviour of Tian and the Chinese team in relation to own negative perceptions of ethnic minorities in the Netherlands, whereas Koen does not.

From a critically interpretive perspective, power is conceptualized as many interrelated processes. These emerge from and inform how people position themselves in relation to each other. It is thus what individuals *do* in relation to each other that brings specific meanings intertwined with specific power inequalities into existence. For example, Ewoud exercises power *and* perpetuates and creates meaning when demanding 'participation' in certain ways. This also implies that Ewoud, and Tian and the Chinese team, have a choice: they can perpetuate dominant meanings and related power inequalities or they can resist and change both, simply by doing other things in a situation.

---

4 Alternatively, and more academically, postmodern CCM (see Romani et al., 2014; based on Deetz, 1996).

> ### STUDENT ACTIVITY 4.2
>
> **Paradigms and the CCM Skillset**
>
> Relate the Opening Case and what you already know about paradigms back to Table 4.1.
>
> - Which paradigm(s) do you think that Ewoud, as a customer relationship manager, is the most trained in?
> - Can Ewoud be expected to be equally versed in all paradigms?
> - If not, which paradigm(s) might seem 'difficult to implement' or even 'strange' to him?
>
> Provide reason for your arguments. If you wish, you can research what customer relationship management (CRM) involves beforehand.

CCM in Practice: Case Advice from the Different Paradigms

Paradigms are to be used in practice, and each paradigm offers distinct advice to cross-cultural managers. This section further deepens these practice implications by applying one tool from each paradigm to the Opening Case. It leads the way to the final chapter activities, and the more detailed overview on functionalist, interpretive and critical CCM perspectives and tools in Chapters 5, 6 and 7.

A functionalist tool example: Comparing leadership scores

The comparison between different countries with regard to a certain cultural feature, such as the expected leadership style in a certain country, is one way of giving advice to cross-cultural managers. The so-called GLOBE (Global Leadership and Organizational Behavior Effectiveness) study (Chhokar et al., 2007; House et al., 2004, 2014) is one of the major comparative studies. By means of large-scale, quantitative methods, six leadership styles were identified as cross-culturally relevant:

Table 4.2 GLOBE leadership styles

Leadership style	Explanation
Charismatic	The ability to inspire, to motivate and to expect high performance outcomes from others based on firmly held core values.
Team-oriented	The ability to effectively build teams and implement a common purpose or goal among team members.
Participative	The degree to which managers involve others in making and implementing decisions
Humane Oriented	The degree to which leaders are supportive and considerate but also includes compassion and generosity
Autonomous	The degree to which leaders are independent and individualistic
Self-protective	The degree to which leadership focuses on ensuring the safety and security of the individual and group through status enhancement and face saving

Source: adapted from GLOBE (2020a)

The study then investigated which leadership style is accepted as contributing to 'outstanding leadership' in which country. Table 4.3 depicts the aggregated GLOBE leadership scores of China and the Netherlands in comparison to each other.

Table 4.3 GLOBE leadership styles for China and the Netherlands

Leadership style	\multicolumn{3}{c}{Contribution to 'outstanding leadership'}			
	China			The Netherlands		
Charismatic	++	5.56	Below average	++	5.98	Above average
Team-oriented	++	5.57	Below average	++	5.75	Average
Participative	+	5.04	Below average	++	5.75	Above average
Humane Oriented	+	5.19	Above average	+	4.82	Below average
Autonomous	0	4.07	Above average	0	3.53	Below average
Self-protective	0	3.8	Above average	–	2.87	Below average

Explanation to score and visualization:
1 = greatly inhibits; visualization: (– – –)
2 = somewhat inhibits; visualization: (– –)
3 = slightly inhibits; visualization: (–)
4 = has no impact; visualization: (0)
5 = contributes slightly; visualization: (+)
6 = contributes somewhat; visualization: (++)
7 = contributes greatly; visualization: (+++)

Source: adapted from GLOBE (2020b, 2020c)

The column 'above average' and 'below average' relates a country's score to the average score across all GLOBE study countries. This puts the absolute score in relation to how valued a certain leadership style is across all countries; e.g. charismatic leadership is more valued in absolute terms on a global scale than self-protective leadership. The highest deviation from the GLOBE average is marked in bold letters. In comparison to the GLOBE average, 'outstanding leadership' in the Netherlands is thus charismatic, team-oriented and, most of all, participative. It is not very humane-oriented, not autonomous and, most of all, not self-protective. China scores the exact opposite. The data can thus explain why Ewoud assumes that Tian is a 'bad manager' because of his behaviour, and why Bedrijf's approach to Global CRM emerged in this shape in the first place.

STUDENT ACTIVITY 4.3

Comparing Cultural Data on 'Outstanding Leadership'

'Good leadership' – as an invisible managerial quality – can only be deduced from visible aspects of culture. Thus, have a look at the description and the explanation of the GLOBE leadership styles (Table 4.2), and the absolute and relative scores of China and the Netherlands in relation to each other (Table 4.3). Answer the following questions:

1. How can the GLOBE study data help you to understand the Opening Case?

Guiding example: Tian compiles reports on behalf of the team. This can be considered as an expression of 'self-protective' leadership which is defined as 'The degree to which leadership focuses on ensuring the safety and security of the individual and group through status enhancement and face saving'. According to GLOBE study scores, China scores higher than average on this leadership style (in relative terms). However, in absolute terms, self-protective leadership still is assumed to slightly inhibit outstanding leadership in China. Ewoud can therefore draw the conclusion that, either, Tian is *not* an outstanding manager, or that Tian faces a situation wherein he feels that he needs to either protect himself or the team.

2. Summarize your analysis of the Opening Case with the help of the GLOBE study leadership dimensions. What do you see now that you have not seen before?
3. Draw conclusions from there. What leadership advice do you give Ewoud?

An interpretive tool example: Locating and overcoming meaning-making gaps in CCM

The interpretive perspective assumes that members of different cultural groups learn different perspectives on social reality. This involves both visible and invisible aspects of culture. Interpretive CCM states that it is the learned, culture-specific connections between 'what is visible' and 'what things mean' which create perceived cultural differences (see Figure 4.2).

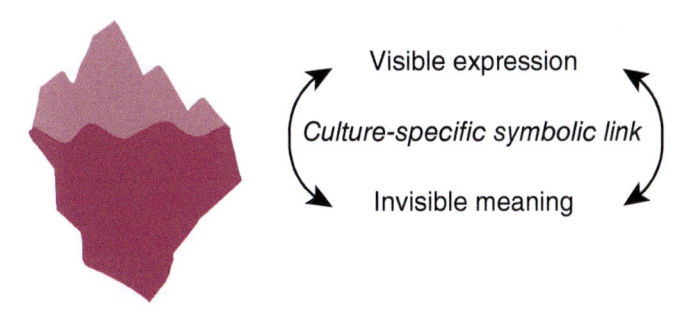

Figure 4.2 Culture as an iceberg: The symbolic meaning perspective

The link between visible and invisible culture is **symbolic**. A symbol is something that means more than can be seen. Symbols can be objects, such as a flag, which, to the cultural insider, is more than just a piece of cloth.

> **Symbol** Something that means more than can be seen

Behaviour, too, can be symbolic. For example, depending on the cultural context wherein it takes place, a smile might mean happiness, or hide sadness or discomfort. Likewise, someone who has hurt themselves might say so or make a joke about it. This means that the way in which Ewoud has learned to 'see' an invisible ideal such as 'participation' is neither universal to all groups of people nor is it the only option for expressing 'participation'. The link is selective and culture-specific.

STUDENT ACTIVITY 4.4

Mapping Symbolic Meaning Across Cultures

The previous case description suggests that Ewoud has a different idea of 'good leadership' and 'how to see it' than Tian.

(Continued)

1. To make Ewoud more aware of these differences in meaning and his own meaning-making gaps, please fill in the Table 4.4.

   Table 4.4 Meaning-mapping Ewoud's and Tian's perspective

Ewoud's perspective	Tian's perspective
What kind of behaviour does Ewoud *expect* from (a) Tian and (b) the Chinese team?	What kind of behaviour does Tian *expect* (a) from his team and (b) from Ewoud?
What does the behaviour which Ewoud expects from (a) Tian and (b) from the Chinese team *mean* to Ewoud?	What does the behaviour which Tian expects (a) from his team and (b) from Ewoud *mean* to Tian?
What kind of behaviour (a) by Tian and (b) by the Chinese team does Ewoud *experience*?	What kind of behaviour (a) by his team and (b) by Ewoud does Tian *experience*?
What does the behaviour (a) by Tian and (b) by the Chinese team *mean* to Ewoud?	What does the behaviour (a) by his team and (b) by Ewoud *mean* to Tian?

2. Next, look at the table and answer the following questions:
   - Which similarities and differences do you see between Ewoud's and Tian's perspectives?
   - Are there meaning-making gaps? For example, is one perspective completely hidden (for whom)? Is one perspective less clear or less complete than another (for whom)?
   - Do you see meanings that are completely opposite in relation to each other?
   - Do you see irreconcilable differences, or differences that can potentially complement and enrich each other?

3. Finally, draw implications for your overall analysis of the Opening Case:
   - How has your analysis improved since using the functionalist tool of comparing leadership scores? What do you see now that you have not seen before?
   - What advice do you give Ewoud now?

Critical tool examples: Investigating the power effects of ethnicity

Many contemporary societies are multi-ethnic, and immigration is one contemporary root cause for increased ethnic diversity 'at home'. At the same time, many people work together with people from other countries and within global corporate hierarchies. From a critical perspective, the danger here is that people might connect both experiences when making sense of a new or confusing cross-cultural situation. This section introduces three critical tools for approaching this topic. These tools are meaning-related, history-related and facts- or function-related.

Critical tool 1: A focus on meaning

STUDENT ACTIVITY 4.5

Questioning the Meaning(s) of Ethnicity

Ewoud compares Tian and the Chinese team to 'all these ethnic minorities in their own *wijken*, unwilling to integrate'. This way, he makes a new connection between his experiences of ethnic diversity 'at home' and his current cross-cultural experiences. From a critically interpretive perspective, Ewoud has to investigate the power implications of this connection, starting with the meaning which he gives to the term 'ethnic minority'. For becoming aware of this, Ewoud needs to first check the available definitions, for example, via consulting two major online dictionaries.

The *Cambridge Dictionary* (n.d.) defines

- ethnicity as 'a particular race of people, or the fact of being from a particular race of people'
- ethnic minority as 'a group of people of a particular race or nationality living in a country or area where most people are from a different race or nationality'

The Oxford Learner's Dictionaries (n.d.) define

- ethnicity as 'the fact of belonging to a particular nation or people that shares a cultural tradition' and give the following additional hint:

(Continued)

'Many factors are important, for example class, gender, age and ethnicity'.
- ethnic minority as 'a group of people from a particular culture or of a particular race living in a country where the main group is of a different culture or race'.

Now, please answer the following questions:

- Which contradictions do you see in the definitions above? Why are these contradictions problematic?
- Is **ethnicity** a clearly defined concept or is it 'fuzzy'?
- How does Ewoud use the term ethnicity? What does it mean to him? Is the meaning positive, negative or neutral? What kind of person does he have in mind?
- What is the power position from which Ewoud speaks of 'ethnic minorities'? Does he place himself above, below or within the group of 'ethnic minorities'? Why do you come to this conclusion?
- What does Ewoud say about Tian and the Chinese team, their way of work, and their underlying motivations, when comparing them to 'ethnic minorities who are unwilling to integrate'?

Critical tool 2: A focus on history

Small meanings and large power structures are connected in many ways, for example by history. This implies that – even though Ewoud is the one who has made the connection – the connection does not *emerge* from him. Rather, it can be traced back to real practices and real historical events involving ethnicity. Ewoud has experienced specific ways of how a country made sense of and acted towards immigrants, and this has contributed to how he made sense of the present situation. It is thus important to investigate the *real* conditions from which the idea of Tian and the Chinese team as 'ethnic minorities in their own *wijken*, unwilling to integrate' emerged.

Ethnicity An oftentimes problematic category describing and defining people by means of a combination of culture and race

Spotlight: Multiculturalism and Cultural Assimilation

After World War II, ethnic diversity in the Netherlands started to increase. At that time, Dutch policy concerning non-Western European immigrants and people relocating from former colonies was rooted in *multiculturalism*, the idea that, in a diverse society, each cultural group 'keeps' their own culture and language (Kymlicka, 2010). Ethnic minorities thus often settled in specific city districts or *wijken*. From a multiculturalist perspective, such cultural distinctness is not perceived as problematic (Entzinger and Biezeveld, 2003). In addition, there was the general understanding that the low-skilled workers who had been encouraged to settle in the Netherlands would return to their home country after a few years, yet this turned out not to be the case (Sniderman and Hagendoorn, 2007: 1).

Due to the economic crisis in the 1970s and subsequent economic restructuring towards a high-skilled economy, unemployment rose disproportionally amongst low-skilled workers, amongst them a large proportion of immigrant and descendants of immigrants (ethnic minorities). The policy of multiculturalism therefore became thought of less as a way towards inclusion, resulting in negative **segregation** (Koopmans, 2010).

Segregation covers the negative perception and/or reality that people migrating to a country fail to adopt elements of the receiving culture and *only* keep their own cultural traits (Entzinger and Biezeveld, 2003). These individuals are then perceived as one homogeneous and distant 'immigrant cultural group', as evidenced, for example, by them living in separate communities (in this case: *'wijken'*).

> **Segregation** The perception or reality of two cultural groups living apart

As this negative image – fuelled by socio-economic challenges – became prominent, Dutch immigration policy moved towards **assimilation** (Michalowski, 2005) which is based on the idea that minority groups need to adapt to a majority or 'lead' culture. The purpose of assimilation is to establish common values, cultural coherence and community, yet, viewed critically, it might lead to

> **Assimilation** The expectation or reality of a (minority or less valued) cultural group becoming part of another (majority or more valued) cultural group

(Continued)

a hierarchy of cultures, if only one culture (the 'lead' culture) is seen as positive and desirable, and if the image of the 'lead' culture is discriminatory or exclusive, e.g. because it is linked to a dominant ethnicity, race, gender, worldview or religion (Entzinger and Biezeveld, 2003).

> **Integration** The expectation or reality of two cultural groups adapting to each other in relevant ways whilst still retaining elements of uniqueness

Integration can bridge multiculturalism and assimilation. As the European Commission (2003: 17–18) states, it requires a two-way process:

on the one hand that it is the responsibility of the host society to ensure that the formal rights of immigrants are in place in such a way that the individual has the possibility of participating in economic, social cultural and civil life and on the other, the immigrants respect the fundamental norms and values of the host society and participate actively in the integration process, without having to relinquish their own identity.

Integration is thus the expectation that members of a minority group adapt towards the majority *in relevant* aspects, e.g. regarding law abidance, whilst still retaining some uniqueness, e.g. regarding cultural practices. This then also requires a relevant change in majority culture. Thus, the expectation that it is *only* the immigrant or ethnic minority group which is required to change, confuses integration with assimilation (Philipp, 2008).

STUDENT ACTIVITY 4.6

Tracing Dominant Meaning Back to Real Historic Events

To increase your knowledge of the situation, read the Spotlight on 'Multiculturalism and Cultural Assimilation'.

1. Answer the following questions:
    - Are there similarities in the power relations between ethnic majorities and ethnic minorities in countries, and the power relations between headquarters and subsidiaries in companies (a) in general and (b) in this specific case? Describe them.

- Which of the aforementioned concepts (multiculturalism, inclusion, segregation, integration or assimilation) underlie Ewoud's statements and his approach to Tian and the Chinese team? Why do you come to this conclusion?
- Which of the aforementioned concepts *should* Ewoud implement in his interactions with Tian and the Chinese team? Why?
- *How* should Ewoud implement the concept(s) which you have identified as the best way(s) of working together?
- Why is it important that Ewoud as a successful cross-cultural manager overcomes his negative perception regarding ethnic minorities in the Netherlands, even though his job is working together with people outside of the Netherlands?

Critical tool 3: A focus on facts

Finally, Ewoud also needs to consider the objective facts about ethnicity, as detached from his own experiences. These can help him understand systems of inequality – a critically structuralist perspective. At this point, however, Ewoud has no idea of Tian's ethnicity, and of ethnicity in China in general.

STUDENT ACTIVITY 4.7

Facts About Ethnicity in China

- What should Ewoud know about ethnicity in China? Are there favoured and less favoured ethnicities, and majority and minority ethnic groups in China? Do some research, if required.
- What is the Chinese policy regarding ethnicity? Can you classify it in terms of inclusion, segregation, integration or assimilation (see Spotlight)? Do some research, if required.
- What do you think is the ethnicity of Tian and the Chinese team?
- Assign three different ethnicities (based on 'ethnic groups' which are commonly identified as such in China) to Tian. How does your case analysis change?

Critical tools: Summary

As this section has shown, ethnicity is one way in which power connects with culture in contemporary CCM. Its critical effects involve both meaning and function, and both small power processes and large power structures. History is a major connector between both. Thus, the critical CCM perspective cannot be reduced to a specific method. Rather, it involves a certain power sensitive mindset regarding whatever emerges as problematic.

What is problematic in the Opening Case is the way in which Ewoud connected his perception (not the reality) of ethnic minorities in the Netherlands with his perception (not the reality) of Tian and the Chinese team. Ewoud making this connection signifies more than a mere individual interpretation because his individual interpretation is rooted in and informed by *real* historic and actual events, and power structures. This way, people, like Ewoud, are both producers and products of power – like they are of culture.

> ### STUDENT ACTIVITY 4.8
>
> **A Final Critical and Multi-Paradigmatic Analysis**
>
> Draw implications for your overall analysis of the Opening Case:
>
> - How has your analysis improved since using the functionalist tool of comparing leadership scores, and the interpretive tool of mapping meaning? What do you see now that you have not seen before?
> - What advice do you give Ewoud now?

Chapter Summary

CCM as a discipline is multi-paradigmatic, which implies that it can be approached from different angles. These angles offer different insights and lead to different role requirements. Cross-cultural managers thus need to learn how to 'juggle' the available theories and methods in practice, in order to enlarge their scope of analysis and action. Multiple ways of doing so have been proposed in theory (overview in Schultz and Hatch, 1996). This chapter has applied **interplay** as the most feasible multi-paradigmatic approach in practice (Romani et al., 2011). Interplay means to view paradigms in light of each other, focusing on connections and contrasts between them. This way, the researcher/manager can move back and forth between the paradigms, with each level of the analysis delivering further insights.

In a Nutshell: Paradigm Interplay in Practice

Paradigm interplay in practice is like zig-zagging straight ahead – with a clear eye on the distant goal, but also with never losing sight of either side of the road. The two sides of the road are the dual qualities of culture/power as discussed in this chapter, such as:

- humans are both products and producers of culture/power
- culture/power is both stable and changing
- culture is both acquiesced to and contested
- culture/power is both objective and subjective
- culture/power is both homogeneous and heterogeneous
- culture/power is both visible and invisible
- culture/power is both large and small
- cultural power-related demarcation lines are both distinct and fuzzy

If cross-cultural managers hold these opposing yet interrelated 'truths' in mind when acting across cultures, they will constantly find new aspects in a situation, and also improve upon their knowledge and skills. This increases managerial role flexibility, and their scope of analysis and action. It might also bring to light additional dualities of culture to be juggled in practice.

Key Points

- As a discipline, CCM is multi-paradigmatic.
- Different paradigms are associated with different CCM tools.
- These CCM tools are useful for different purposes.
- Cross-cultural managers need to know which tool to use for which purposes.
- Interplay is a key technique for utilizing the respective strengths of each paradigm.
- CCM involves both facts and interpretations, and objective and subjective factors.
- Power aspects of CCM are related to meaning, history and facts. They intertwine with culture.
- The three key questions to assess and manage a cross-cultural situation are: How does CCM work? What does CCM mean? Whom does CCM serve (and how does this happen)?
- Depending on the question asked, different aspects of the situation and managerial implications emerge.
- For the best analysis, action or solution, CCM researchers and managers should alternate between these three key questions and 'juggle' them in their practice.

Review Questions

1. What are paradigms, and how are they relevant to cross-cultural managers?
2. Which paradigms are commonly considered in management and organization studies?
3. What is interplay, how is it employed and why is it relevant to cross-cultural managers?
4. What are the major contrasts and connections between functionalist and interpretive CCM?
5. What are the major contrasts and connections between functionalist and critically functionalist CCM?
6. What are the major contrasts and connections between interpretive and critically interpretive CCM?
7. Please name one major tool for each paradigm and outline the main characteristics of this tool.
8. Using the example of ethnicity, why and how does each of the five paradigmatic angles contribute to understanding the impact of ethnicity on CCM?
9. Is it helpful or dangerous to classify CCM tools into paradigms? Why (not)?
10. How can cross-cultural managers make sure that they use CCM paradigms in a way that is 'useful' and to the benefit of the situation and those involved?

Opening Case Revisited

So far, the Opening Case has solely been written and analysed from Ewoud's perspective. This is a clear limitation of the case, because, this way, one perspective becomes relevant and, hence, dominant. Also, Ewoud becomes the 'fix-it-all' protagonist of the situation; he is assigned both the freedom (power) *and* the responsibility (burden) of the situation. Conversely, Tian and the Chinese team are freed from both; their case role is to be 'managed' and 'interpreted' by others. The final critical insight from this case is thus that unequal power relations create active and passive actors and organizational units. Some manage others, and others are the ones to be managed. In settings wherein both sides need to contribute their knowledge for the best possible solution (such as the best possible global CRM at Bedrijf), this condition obscures and neglects potentially valuable insights. To overcome this limitation, you should engage in the Closing Activity of this chapter.

Closing Activity: Cross-Cultural Management Beyond the Active–Passive Divide

The goal of a contemporary CCM is to utilize cultural differences in positive ways. This means to focus on:

- *Complementarities between cultures*: How perceived and actual differences imply a higher variety of potential approaches and, thus potential solutions, to a certain problem.
- *Synergies between cultures*: How the combination of the different approaches and solutions to a certain problem is more than the sum of its parts (i.e. the single approaches).

With this in mind, re-write the Opening Case from Tian's and the Chinese team's perspective. The purpose of this task is to overcome the active–passive divide which characterizes the present case description (only Ewoud and Koen are actors), and to activate Tian and 'the Chinese team' (presently, their only purpose is 'being managed' – see Opening Case Revisited above). Consider all previous paradigms, and their connections and contrasts, for example, by considering guiding questions such as:

- What is it that Tian and the Chinese team *do*?
- What do things *mean* from the perspective of Tian and the Chinese team?
- What are the power inequalities which Tian and the Chinese team experience and perceive?
- What should Tian and the Chinese team reflect about and challenge?
- How should Tian and the Chinese team proceed in order to involve Ewoud in their own ideas and ways of doing things?
- What would the cultural middle look like from the perspective of Tian and the Chinese team?

You can and should be creative to fill in those gaps in the present case description which you have identified from the various paradigmatic angles (see previous student activities).

When compiling the case, in particular when filling in present 'gaps', make sure that you don't impose your own cultural assumptions (e.g. your idea of 'how Chinese people are') onto Tian and the Chinese team. These are the recommendations for avoiding a dominant author perspective:

- Give names to each individual you write about. This makes them 'real' people and not just an unidentifiable part of a homogeneous collective ('the Chinese team', as people are presently labelled in the Opening Case, is already a symptom of a dominant outside perspective on culture, and of the dominant idea that

it is their collective 'Chineseness' which characterizes people as different). This way, you increase the likelihood that you do justice to the cultural complexity (see Chapter 2) and the unique identity (Chapter 3) of the individual person.
- Write as if Tian and the (now named) team members are the readers of your case description, and if your future career depends on whether this case seems 'true' to your readers.
- When proofreading your own writing, think about how Tian and his (now named) team members would react to your description of themselves.
- Change perspective when proofreading your own writing. Answer the question: How would you, as the reader of this case, feel if you were Tian or one of this (now named) team members?

For compiling your case, you can re-use material from the previous student activities of this chapter. If you wish, you can do additional background research. Don't forget to document additional sources, should you decide to use any. Make sure that Ewoud and Koen remain 'active enough' – the goal is higher balance, not counter-dominance.

It is very unlikely that your case description will result in a reversal of the active–passive divide (so that Ewoud and Koen are fully passive) because structural conditions are not balanced (Ewoud and Koen are more in power anyway). Therefore, the purpose of activating Tian and the (now named) team members is to make structural and interpretive conditions more inclusive. It is not to 'make the same mistake' (excluding others) from the opposite ('Chinese') perspective. Still, you should check whether Ewoud, Koen and Bedrijf's corporate culture remain an active part of the story.

Further Reading

Romani et al. (2018a) provide an academic overview on paradigms in CCM studies. Part I of *The Sage Handbook of Contemporary Cross-Cultural Management* (Szkudlarek et al., 2020) is dedicated to the multiple research paradigms in CCM studies. It includes chapters on positivist (*here*: functionalist) CCM (Sackmann, 2020), interpretive CCM (Cardel Gertsen and Zølner, 2020) and critical CCM (Romani et al., 2020a). Schultz and Hatch (1996) summarize the emergence and contours of the paradigms debate in management and organization studies and outline interplay and other avenues for a multi-paradigmatic research. Building upon this work, Romani et al. (2011) provide an example of how to perform interplay in CCM studies, and Mahadevan (2013) shows how interplay can be applied to CCM practice and corporate intercultural training.

References

Alvesson, M. and Deetz, S. (2000) *Doing Critical Management Research*. London: Sage.

Berlin, B. and Kay, P. (1969) *Basic Color Terms*. Berkeley: University of California Press.

Burrell, G. and Morgan, G. (1979) *Social Paradigms and Organizational Analysis: Elements of the Sociology of Corporate Life*. London: Heinemann Educational Books.

Cambridge Dictionary (n.d.) 'Ethnicity'. Available at: https://dictionary.cambridge.org/de/worterbuch/englisch/ethnicity [last accessed 2 September 2020].

Cambridge Dictionary (n.d.) 'Ethnic minority'. Available at: https://dictionary.cambridge.org/de/worterbuch/englisch/ethnic-minority [last accessed 2 September 2020].

Cardel Gertsen, M. and Zølner, M. (2020) 'Interpretive approaches to culture: What is interpretive cross-cultural management?', in B. Szkudlarek, L. Romani, D.V. Caprar and J.S. Osland (eds), *The Sage Handbook of Contemporary Cross-Cultural Management*. London: Sage. pp. 34–50.

Chhokar, J.S., Brodbeck, F.C. and House, R.J. (eds) (2007) *Culture and Leadership across the World: The GLOBE Book of In-Depth Studies of 25 Societies*. Mahwah: Erlbaum.

Comte, A. (1907) *A General View of Positivism*. London: Routledge.

Deetz, S. (1992) 'Critical interpretive research in organizational communication', *Western Journal of Speech Communication*, 46: 131–149.

Deetz, S. (1996) 'Describing differences in approaches to organization science: Rethinking Burrell and Morgan and their legacy', *Organization Science*, 7(2): 191–207.

Entzinger, H. and Biezeveld, R. (2003) *Benchmarking in Immigrant Integration*. Available at: https://ec.europa.eu/home-affairs/sites/homeaffairs/files/e-library/documents/policies/legal-migration/pdf/general/benchmarking_final_en.pdf [last accessed 14 September 2020].

European Commission (2003) *On Immigration, Integration and Employment*. Available at: https://eur-lex.europa.eu/LexUriServ/LexUriServ.do?uri=COM:2003:0336:FIN:EN:PDF [last accessed 14 September 2020].

GLOBE (2020a) Available at: https://globeproject.com/study_2004_2007?page_id=data#data) [last accessed 3 August 2021].

GLOBE (2020b) Available at: https://globeproject.com/results/countries/CHN?menu=list#list [last accessed 3 August 2021].

GLOBE (2020c) Available at: https://globeproject.com/results/countries/NLD?menu=list#list [last accessed 3 August 2021].

Hatch, M.J., with Cunliffe, A. (2006) *Organization Theory – Modern, Symbolic and Postmodern Perspectives*. Oxford: Oxford University Press. 1st edn, 1996.

House, R., Hanges, P., Javidan, M. and Gupta, V. (2004) *Culture, Leadership, and Organizations: The GLOBE Study of 62 Societies*. Thousand Oaks: Sage.

House, R.J., Dorfman, P.W., Javidan, M., Hanges, P.J. and Sully de Luque, M.F. (eds) (2014) *Strategic Leadership Across Countries: The GLOBE Study of CEO Leadership Behaviour and Effectiveness in 24 Countries*. Thousand Oaks: Sage.

Jack, G. and Westwood, R. (2009) *International and Cross-Cultural Management Studies – A Postcolonial Reading*. Basingstoke: Palgrave Macmillan.

Kay, P., Berlin, B., Maffi, L., Merrifield, W.R. and Cook, R. (2009) *The World Color Survey*. Stanford: CSLI Publications.

Koopmans, R. (2010) 'Trade-offs between equality and difference: Immigrant integration, multiculturalism and the welfare state in cross-national perspective', *Journal of Ethnic and Migration Studies*, 36(1): 1–26.

Kymlicka, W. (2010) 'The rise and fall of multiculturalism? New debates on inclusion and accommodation in diverse societies', *International Social Science Journal*, 61(199): 97–112.

Lowe, S., Moore, F. and Carr, A.N. (2007) 'Paradigmapping studies of culture and organization', *International Journal of Cross Cultural Management*, 7(2): 237–251.

Mahadevan, J. (2013) 'Performing interplay through intercultural simulations: Insights on tacit culture in Taiwanese-German management team', *International Journal of Cross-Cultural Management*, 13(3): 243–263.

Mahadevan, J. and Schmitz, A. (2020) 'HRM as an ongoing struggle for legitimacy: A critical discourse analysis of HR managers as "employee-experience designers"', *Baltic Journal of Management*, 15(4): 515–532.

Michalowski, I. (2005) 'What is the Dutch Integration Model, and has it failed?', *Focus MIGRATION*, Policy Brief No. 1. Available at: www.bpb.de/system/files/pdf/VXMT6N.pdf [last accessed 14 September 2020].

Moore, F. and Mahadevan, J. (2020) 'Ethnography and cross-cultural management', in B. Szkudlarek, L. Romani, D.V. Caprar and J.S. Osland (eds), *The Sage Handbook of Contemporary Cross-Cultural Management*. London: Sage. pp. 127–140.

Nelson, C. and Grossberg, L. (eds) (1988) *Marxism and the Interpretation of Culture*. Urbana: University of Illinois Press.

Oxford Learner's Dictionaries (n.d.) 'Ethnicity'. Available at: www.oxfordlearnersdictionaries.com/definition/english/ethnicity [last accessed 2 September 2020].

Oxford Learner's Dictionaries (n.d.) 'Ethnic minority'. Available at: www.oxfordlearnersdictionaries.com/definition/english/ethnic-minority [last accessed 2 September 2020].

Philipp, P. (2008) *Opinion: Integration Doesn't Mean Assimilation*. Available at: https://p.dw.com/p/D7Kt) [last accessed 14 September 2020].

Primecz, H. (2020) 'Positivist, constructivist and critical approaches to international human resource management and some future directions', *German Journal of Human Resource Management*, 34(2): 124–147.

Primecz, H., Romani, L., and Sackmann, S.A. (2009) 'Cross-Cultural Management Research: contributions from various paradigms', *International Journal of Cross-Cultural Management*, 9(3): 267–274.

Romani, L., Primecz, H. and Topçu, K. (2011) 'Paradigm interplay for theory development: A methodological example with the Kulturstandard method', *Organizational Research Methods*, 14(3): 432–455.

Romani, L., Primecz, H. and Bell, R. (2014) 'There is nothing so practical as four good theories', in B. Gehrke and M.-T. Claes (eds), *Global Leadership Practices – A Cross-Cultural Management Perspective*. London: Palgrave Macmillan. pp. 13–50.

Romani, L., Barmeyer, C., Primecz, H. and Pilhofer, K. (2018a) 'Cross-Cultural Management studies: State of the field in the four research paradigms', *International Studies of Management & Organization*, 48(3): 1–17.

Romani, L., Mahadevan, J. and Primecz, H. (2018b) 'Critical Cross-Cultural Management: Outline and emergent contributions', *International Studies of Management & Organization*, 48(4): 403–418.

Romani, L., Boussebaa, M. and Jackson, T. (2020a) 'Critical perspectives on cross-cultural management', in B. Szkudlarek, L. Romani, D.V. Caprar and J.S. Osland (eds), *The Sage Handbook of Contemporary Cross-Cultural Management*. London: Sage. pp. 51–65.

Romani, L. Mahadevan, J. and Primecz, H. (2020b) 'Methods of critical Cross-Cultural Management', in B. Szkudlarek, L. Romani, D.V. Caprar and J.S. Osland (eds), *The Sage Handbook of Contemporary Cross-Cultural Management*. London: Sage. pp. 141–155.

Sackmann, S. (2020) 'Culture in cross-cultural management: Its seminal contributions from a positivist perspective', in B. Szkudlarek, L. Romani, D.V. Caprar and J.S. Osland (eds), *The Sage Handbook of Contemporary Cross-Cultural Management*. London: Sage. pp. 17–33.

Schultz, M. and Hatch, M.J. (1996) 'Living with multiple paradigms: The case of paradigm interplay in organization culture studies', *Academy of Management Review*, 21(2): 529–557.

Schwartz-Shea, P. and Yanow, D. (2012) *Interpretive Research Design – Concepts and Processes*. London: Routledge.

Sniderman, P.M. and Hagendoorn, L. (2007) *Multiculturalism and its Discontents in the Netherlands: When Ways of Life Collide*. Princeton: Princeton University Press.

Spencer-Oatley, H. and Franklin, P. (2009) *Intercultural Interaction – A Multidisciplinary Approach to Intercultural Communication*. Basingstoke: Palgrave Macmillan.

Swingewood, A. (1991) 'Critique of positivism: I Durkheim', in A. Swingewood, *A Short History of Sociological Thought*. London: Palgrave. pp. 97–127.

Szkudlarek, B., Romani, L., Caprar, D.V. and Osland, J.S. (eds) (2020) *The Sage Handbook of Contemporary Cross-Cultural Management*. London: Sage.

Functionalist Cross-Cultural Management

5

How does CCM work?

Learning Objectives

After reading this chapter, you should:

- understand the main premises of a functionalist and comparative CCM and its major tools, cultural dimensions or cultural value orientations
- know the cultural dimensions of Kluckhohn and Strodtbeck, Hall, Hofstede, Trompenaars and Hampden-Turner and project GLOBE, and be able to apply them
- be able to use cultural dimensions as hypotheses to be tested upon a situation
- be able to compare societal cultures with the help of cultural dimensions
- be able to apply cultural dimensions to alternative cultural levels.

Reading Requirement

- You should have read Chapter 4 of this book

Introduction

The previous chapter has introduced the paradigms underlying contemporary CCM. This chapter deepens your understanding of functionalist CCM (see box) by introducing tools for comparing societal **macro-cultures** with each other. A functionalist CCM wishes to find out how different cultures have found specific solutions to culturally universal questions. For example, task differentiation is relevant to any social organization (this is a selected universal aspect of culture), but what does 'good task differentiation' involve? (Here, cultures differ in their answers.) A major goal of a functionalist CCM is thus to establish causalities between selected universal aspects of culture, and culture-specific ways of management and organization.

> **Macro-culture** Large units of culture, such as nations or societies

This chapter highlights the major assumptions underlying the functionalist perspective, such as **cultural universalism**, and the focus on selected aspects of culture, such as values and culture as communication. It introduces cultural dimensions and cultural value orientations as major tools of a functionalist perspective, in particular a macro-comparative CCM, and provides advice on how (not) to use them.

> **Cultural universalism** The assumption that certain elements exist in all cultures, albeit in different configurations

In a Nutshell: Functionalist CCM

Functionalist CCM involves studies and practices that seek to uncover the *objective* ways in which CCM works, in particular regarding how large units of culture (macro-cultures), such as societies or nations, differ from each other. The underlying idea is that there *is* one best way to manage across cultures, and that this way is best identified by means of quantitative data. Functionalist CCM maintains that cross-cultural reality does not depend on perspective (cross-cultural researchers and managers can be *objective* regarding culture). Therefore, the cultural identity of the cross-cultural manager and researcher is not relevant to how they study culture. They are detached from their object of interest (cultures and cross-cultural differences). A major goal of functionalist CCM is to establish causalities between selected universal aspects of macro-cultures, and management and organization. A major tool for uncovering relative differences between macro-cultures are the so-called cultural dimensions or value orientations.

Opening Case

'Tech-guys'

A French multinational pharmaceutical company with a production subsidiary in Switzerland has offshored part of its IT infrastructure to the Vietnamese town of Thành Phố. Three men in their mid-thirties are the ones in charge of managing global IT for all corporate locations worldwide. These are: Pierre, from corporate headquarters in Ville; Ralf from Altstadt in the German-speaking part of Switzerland; and Minh Đúc from Thành Phố. All three hold a postgraduate degree in computer engineering, and all of them have worked in Silicon Valley at a certain point in time. There, they have experienced the same tech culture, with a focus on flat hierarchies, on solving problems as they occur, and on self-motivation based on a personal interest in developing excellent technological solutions. All three consider themselves experts in their fields, and, if they'd have to weigh customer-friendliness over digging deeply into technology, all three of them would choose the latter. Also, none of them is fond of the multiple regulations and safety checks that characterize working in the pharmaceutical industry, and, regarding their work, they value freedom and creativity above all. They have been called 'nerds' by colleagues from other, non-technological departments, but in a friendly and fond way. In summary, to outsiders, all three of them are alike in their 'being tech-guys'.

Pierre, Ralf and Minh Đúc have been asked to improve internal helpdesk operations and, together, they have come up with a new approach. This involves changes to customer service, and to the software and hardware components of the internal helpdesk interface. Pierre, Ralf and Minh Đúc have also thought about how they can convince the company of their ideas. As part of this process, they have identified key helpdesk users at the three corporate sites (Ville, Altstadt and Thành Phố), all of them corporate line managers and project managers, with a degree in pharmaceuticals or medicine. Pierre, Ralf and Minh Đúc need to convince these key persons of the new helpdesk, so that they [the key users] will support and promote the helpdesk change within the organization.

As a first step, Pierre, Ralf and Minh Đúc need to prepare a virtual meeting with the key helpdesk users from all three sites. They wonder what will convince the key users of the new helpdesk. Which arguments should they bring forward, and how should they communicate? How should they prepare, structure and run the meeting itself?

Functionalist CCM   137

All three of them share common ideas of how French, Vietnamese and Swiss employees normally tick. But, still, the insights which they share sound more like stories and not sound facts. They also realize that they themselves seem to have different expectations and ideas of what is important and what is not, and they even start to get emotional over the right approach.

'This is no good', says Ralf. 'We developed the new helpdesk together: We agreed on it, and we had good reasons. Why all this fighting now? – We are acting like managers in a Dilbert cartoon.' 'Well, the random acts of management...,' Pierre says with a smile. 'Is there *really* no way of getting reliable data on the cultural preferences of our internal customers from different countries?' he asks. Minh Đức remembers that he had once attended a soft skills course on 'how to work internationally' as part of his graduate degree. 'There are some studies on cross-cultural differences, I believe. We should look them up.' And this they do.

Minh Đức has remembered studies of cross-cultural differences, also known as **Comparative CCM**. These compare large units of culture, such as countries or societies (macro-culture). They use quantitative methods that enable the researcher to handle large amounts of data. The focus is on selected aspects of macro-culture, also known as cultural value orientation or **cultural dimensions**. These are assumed to be universal (to exist in all cultures), and Pierre, Ralf and Minh Đức could use them for further advice on how to proceed.

Comparative CCM (Quantitative) analyses of relative differences across (macro-)cultures

Cultural dimensions Selected universal aspects for (macro-)cultural comparison

The Formation of Comparative CCM

Early cultural dimensions: Kluckhohn and Strodtbeck, and Hall

The earliest concepts of cultural dimensions were developed across the disciplines of anthropology, psychology and linguistics. These early studies are not yet based on the 'reliable' quantitative data which Pierre, Ralf and Minh Đức of the Opening

Case wish for; however, they already depict key elements of what later became Comparative CCM. This section highlights two interdisciplinary early studies.

> **Cultural value orientations** Invisible, socially learned motivations and expectations underlying people's behaviour that are assumed to differ across cultural groups

Anthropologist Clyde Kluckhohn and psychologist Fred Strodtbeck (1961) were amongst the first to propose **value orientations** as universal and comparable aspects of culture. Bridging anthropology and linguistics, Edward T. Hall (e.g. 1966, 1976, 1983) applied the idea of studying and comparing selected universal aspects of culture to the level of societal and national culture. Borrowing from applied linguistics, he proposed that only those parts of culture need to be considered which are *communicated* by means of language or other ways (*culture as communication*).

Both studies were driven, in different ways, by the need to provide useful advice to people working across cultures, and this required them to only focus on selected universal aspects of culture. This enabled immediate learning via simplified models of culture which helped learners understand how cultures are different in relation to each other (a focus on *relative difference*). This means they do not depict culture in absolute terms (how a certain culture *is*) but in relative terms (how two cultures *are when compared to each other*).

Both studies mark the beginning of cultural theory being applied to other activities, such as management. They introduced the main principles of what later became Comparative CCM, namely:

1. A focus only on selected aspects of culture (values or communication).
2. The assumption that some aspects of cultures are universal, which makes them objectively identifiable and comparable.
3. The goal to draw implications for larger units of culture, ideally country culture.
4. The idea of training managers and other occupational groups in objective patterns of relative differences across cultures (cross-cultural differences).

For Pierre, Ralf and Minh Đức of the Opening Case, these early studies imply that they don't have to study and understand the whole of culture by means of longitudinal exposure. Rather, it will be enough if they focus on those aspects of culture which are universal and, thus, comparable across cultures, in order to prepare for a cross-cultural situation, such as the virtual meeting which they plan. The two major options available to them are a focus on cultural value orientations, and a focus on culture as communicated between individuals.

However, in order to apply this theory correctly, Minh Đức, Ralf and Pierre have to keep in mind the limitations of this approach. Cultural value orientations don't apply to the whole of culture as an experienced and shared sense of 'how we normally do things around here', but only to those cultural elements which are universal. Thus, cultural value orientations don't predict what people *really* do but only point out which value orientations or communicative patterns *might* underlie people's behaviour. Therefore, the validity test to cultural value orientation is how the individual *uses* them in practice. Pierre, Minh Đức and Ralf need to test them as hypotheses for what *might* cause a certain behavioural pattern, motivation, interpretation or expectation, and then to figure out whether and to what extent they might or might not inform people's actual doings.

For this, it is helpful to consider a prominent definition of values, namely as criteria or blueprints by which people judge a situation (Schwartz, 1992: 1). The properties of values, understood in this way, are:

1. Values are concepts or beliefs
2. [they] pertain to desirable end states or behaviours
3. [they] transcend specific situations
4. [they] guide selection or evaluation of behaviour and events
5. [they] are ordered by relative importance (Schwartz, 1992: 4).

Therefore, if one understands these underlying concepts or beliefs *in general*, one can draw conclusions for how people act in a *specific* situation.

STUDENT ACTIVITY 5.1

How Do Values Influence People?

Consider the aforementioned definition of values. Imagine that you are part of the team which needs to plan the online meeting (see Opening Case).

1. Reflect upon your own value orientations. What do you think are criteria against which your team's approach should be measured? Should your approach be, for example, 'well-planned', 'well-communicated', 'collaborative', 'structured', etc.? Write down what would be important to you in this task in terms of values.
2. Next, exchange what you have found with three to four other students. Have you found similar or different value items? Why (not)? What

(Continued)

> influencing factor has caused these similarities/differences in value orientation? In your discussion, do not only focus on how you have labelled a certain value orientation but also describe to each other how you would expect to 'see' this value orientation in your own and other people's behaviour in the situation. For example, 'well-planned' and 'structured' might refer to similar or the same type of behaviour, as might 'collaborative' and 'well-communicated'. On the other hand, people might label a value orientation the same way, yet have different images in mind of how, for example, 'collaborative' looks like when translated into actual behaviour.

The 'culture as value orientations' approach: Dimensions by Kluckhohn and Strodtbeck

Anthropologists Clyde Kluckhohn and Fred Strodtbeck (1961) based their work on participant observation and qualitative interviews which they conducted among five cultural groups in the Southwest of the USA, amongst them Navajo Indians and members of The Church of Jesus Christ of Latter-day Saints. They defined six universal *value dimensions*, each of them involving three orientations and proposed that cultures can be compared by means of these orientations (see Table 5.1).

Table 5.1 The cultural dimensions of Kluckhohn and Strodtbeck

Dimension	Explanation	Orientations
Relationship to nature/ environment	The degree to which members of a group believe in a need or duty to control nature (mastery), to maintain harmony between people and nature, or to submit to nature (subjugation). *Example: Corporate sustainability strategies as an example for moving beyond mastery of the environment and towards harmony between company and environment.*[1]	Mastery Harmony Subjugation
Human relations	The degree to which members of a group emphasize independence of individuals or of immediate teams within a larger group (individualistic), emphasize consensus within an extended group of equals (collateral), or emphasize hierarchical principles and deference to higher authorities within the group (hierarchical). *Example: The allocation of managerial incentives in a company: on individual basis (individualistic), team-based (collateral) or depending on hierarchical position (hierarchy)*	Individualistic Collateral Hierarchical

---

1 Subjugation is difficult to apply to the corporate level. One could argue for subjugation in case of companies who are highly dependent on the environment, e.g., offshore wind-parks, but on the other hand the same phenomenon might also signify mastery. Potentially, one can find subjugation in the informal economy, e.g., individual fishers with non-industrialized equipment depending on the tides for fishing.

Functionalist CCM

Dimension	Explanation	Orientations
Beliefs about human nature	The degree to which members of a group believe that people are inherently good, mixed or evil. *Example: degree to which high-skilled employees' working hours are controlled by the company (higher control signifies a less positive image of employees' work-attitude).*	Good Mixed Evil
Time orientation	The degree to which members of a group believe that people should make decisions with respect to events in the past, in the present, or in the future. *Example: The assumptions regarding time-orientation which underlie corporate strategy and decision-making.*	Past Present Future
M Human activity	The degree to which members of a group believe that people should live for the moment (being), should aim for personal growth as defined by personal beliefs (being-in-becoming), or should focus on achieving goals which are defined externally (doing/achieving). *Example: the assumptions underlying a company's human resource development (HRD) strategy: becoming better at doing one's job as a means of personal growth (being-in-becoming) or objectives for employees which are set externally (doing/achieving) versus providing no HRD opportunities at all (being).*	Being Being-in-becoming Doing/Achieving
Conception of space	The degree to which members of a cultural group believe that space should belong to individuals (private), to all (public), or that the distribution of space should be a combination thereof (mixed). *Example: Individual offices (private space) versus open offices/cubicles (public space), or the combination thereof (mixed) as organizing principles for corporate space*	Private Mixed Public

Source: adapted from Kluckhohn and Strodtbeck (1961)

As Table 5.1 suggests, cultural dimensions cannot be observed directly, they can only be deduced from what is visible or known about a situation. For example, if managers in a company devise detailed mechanisms of control, then one can deduce an underlying belief in hierarchical relationships between people (employees will not work if uncontrolled by a higher authority). Conversely, if a company allows employees to use discretion at work, this implies a belief in collateral relationships (employees work because they share a common goal towards which they orientate themselves).

To complicate the picture, managers are also influenced by other cultural levels, for example, industry culture, when devising corporate relationship structures. For example, in the Opening Case, the 'tech-culture' which Minh Đùc, Ralf and Pierre share is much more oriented towards collateral relationships (open innovation) than the industry culture of the pharmaceutical industry, wherein patient safety (and thus control, e.g. of the production process of pharmaceuticals) is much more important, resulting in hierarchical relationships between employees involved in production but not so much between those in IT.

STUDENT ACTIVITY 5.2

Value Orientations in the Opening Case

Cultural dimensions are hypotheses to be tested by the cross-cultural manager and researcher. When doing so, you need to consider each case as unique and see how far the application of cultural dimensions brings you to understanding more of the situation.

Consider the cultural dimensions by Kluckhohn and Strodtbeck (Table 5.1).

1. Which cultural dimensions by Kluckhohn and Strodtbeck do you see in the Opening Case? Describe how you see them. You don't have to be sure that something *really* signifies a certain cultural dimension – this would actually be the wrong approach, because it presses culture into a 'rule book', which does not do the concept justice. Rather, try to formulate a plausible hypothesis, as done via the examples in Table 5.1.
2. What would you need to know about the situation in order to learn more about the impact of those cultural dimensions which you cannot see in the case at present?
3. In general, what can you learn by applying cultural dimensions to a situation or phenomenon, also in your own life?

The 'culture as communication' approach: Dimensions by Hall

Edward T. Hall, originally trained as an anthropologist, had joined a team of academics at the US-American Foreign Service Institute (FSI) after World War II. There, they were tasked with preparing diplomats, military personal and development aid workers for cultural differences abroad (Pusch, 2004). Culture was thus understood on national level.

Because the participants in the workshops and courses offered by the FSI demanded immediately applicable concepts (Leeds-Hurwitz, 2010), not in-depth theory, a new approach to 'teaching culture' was developed (Hall and Trager, 1953). It drew from descriptive linguistics and focused on those aspects of culture which are 'communicated' via language, behaviour and perceptions. The purpose was to help individuals to 'decipher' the cultural patterns and cross-cultural differences underlying an interaction. For this, Hall and Trager (1953) provided the models that described cross-cultural differences, and they also developed role plays and case examples to train participants in using these concepts in practice. Out of this, the practice of **intercultural training** as a standard tool for people's skills development was born (Leeds-Hurwitz, 1990). Chapter 11 of this book, focusing on the cross-cultural manager's skills development, will apply such techniques of intercultural training.

> **Intercultural training** Group activity for training people in how to work together across cultures; a standard human resource development tool

After he had left the FSI, Hall then went on to publish these ideas on his own (1959, 1966, 1976, 1983) and with his wife, Mildred R. Hall (Hall and Hall, 1990). He coined the expression: 'Culture is communication, and communication is culture' (Hall, 1959: 186). Communication, to him, is thus a very large concept which is not limited to verbal and non-verbal aspects, but also involves *time, space, context* and the *speed of information*. He thus moved beyond a narrow definition of communication.

Communication in the narrow sense

In the narrow sense, communication can be differentiated into *verbal*, *non-verbal* and *para-verbal* communication. Verbal communication involves spoken words and utterances. Non-verbal communication adds mimics and gestures, as well as posture and body language. Para-verbal communication introduces, for example, the degree of overlap between speech acts to the previous two. According to Hall (1959) and colleagues, all three modes of communication are culture-specific.

> **Link to Practice: A Finnish-Spanish Conversation**
>
> Because communicative norms vary across culture, different expectations can get into the way of a successful interaction. For example, as a norm, Spanish conversations involve much overlap between speakers whereas there is a distinct 'pause' between Finish speakers. As a consequence of this relative difference in cultural patterns, the average Finnish person is likely to feel interrupted by the average Spanish person (who interacts with the best intentions), whereas the average Spanish person is likely to perceive the average Finnish person as disinterested (because they are too slow to react) (also see Mahadevan, 2017: 40).

Proxemics

Proxemics, that is the organization of space as linked to social relations, are another cultural factor impacting upon communication. The concept refers to the literal and figurative distance which people maintain between each other. Or, in other words, people communicate space. As Hall (1966) shows, people learn a certain organization of space, e.g. when growing up, and this becomes part of their 'mental maps'. For example, there is a certain norm regarding how to greet each other in every cultural situation, and this norm also involves space in the sense of how much distance is kept and whether the greeting brings people 'physically closer' or not.

> **Proxemics** How space is perceived and communicated socially

Hall (1966) differentiates between the 'space bubbles' that surround a person, and he also allocates 'distance measures' to these bubbles (see Figure 5.1).

1. Intimate space (0–2 feet)
2. Personal space (2–4 feet)
3. Social space (4–12 feet)
4. Public space (more than 12 feet)

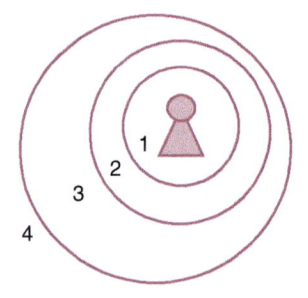

Figure 5.1 Space bubbles (proxemics) according to Hall

Hall argues that people start feeling uncomfortable when others enter the wrong space bubble, without being able to locate the root cause of their feelings in a violation of culturally learned allocations of space. He also states that different cultures have different ideas of how large these space bubbles should be, how they should interrelate, and to what extent they should overlap (if at all). For example, if related to Figure 5.1, certain greetings, e.g. the handshake, enter the personal space – even if exchanged in the social sphere – whereas others, e.g. the bow, do not. The understanding of proxemics can therefore help a cross-cultural manager and researcher to view the situation more objectively than before and not to interpret a handshake (if the bow is expected) as overly intrusive and a bow (if the handshake is expected) as a lack of 'openness'.

On an even larger scale, Hall classifies whole business cultures with regard to whether it is expected that personal and social sphere are mixed up (*diffuse relations*) or whether both are kept strictly separate (*specific relations*). For example, Hall argues that US-American business culture is characterized by diffuse relations, which means that personal topics are touched upon in business. However, this does not imply that people have become 'close friends' because entering the personal sphere is just a normal part of business interactions. Conversely, specific relationship patterns (Hall gives the example of Germany) imply that the personal sphere is reserved for close friends and should also not be touched upon in business.

Specific relations also imply that people at work are not judged based on the whole of their personal qualities. What is relevant is how they function on the job. Conversely, diffuse relations imply that a person on the job is judged based on their personality and how they relate to people on a personal basis, e.g. the manager as a person who 'cares' about their employees and who is present with their 'whole self'. According to Hall, this implies that one needs to build relationships first before focusing on business. It might also mean that managers will bring in personal details, e.g. tell a story about their lives, in order to make a point about business, which – if looked at from the standpoint of specific relations – is just bad management, because what is then perceived as 'personal anecdotes' are assumed to 'have nothing to do' with objective job descriptions and tasks at work.

Link to Practice: The Psychology of Space

Space influences the outcome of a business interaction (Waida, 2022). For example, if people are seated at one rectangular table, then the most important person (VIP) should sit at the table, and their advisors should flank them. However, this then automatically places the person opposite to the – thus created or identified – VIP in opposition and makes them more likely to disagree. Those seated in the middle are likely to find themselves in the 'listener role'. Therefore, the rectangular table is also often used strategically in two-party negotiations in order to establish position. Conversely, a round table used for the same purposes might soften disagreements.

Time-orientation (chronemics)

Hall (1983) furthermore suggests and differentiates between culture-specific concepts of time (also called **chronemics**). He states that people from different cultures are 'on different times', namely M-time and P-time.

Monochronic time orientation (M-time) signifies a preference for doing 'one thing at a time', and for a clear sequence or steps, events, etc. Time is apportioned, e.g. into 'work-time', 'lunch-time', 'leisure-time', which means that one can run out of one portion

Chronemics How time is perceived and communicated socially

of time (time can stress you out). The main goal is thus to 'keep time', which implies a focus on schedules, procedures, tasks and goals, as well as on planning activities. Hall states that M-time fits a communicative style that is 'to-the-point' and thus low on context-orientation (see next).

Polychronic time orientation (P-time) is associated with 'juggling time'. From this perspective, time is just there, and the individual uses the existing time in the best possible way. This often means synchronous, holistic actions (more than one thing at a time, with a wide focus on the action itself). It can also take the shape of responding to a number of demands or people simultaneously or to establish connections between previously unlinked demands or people. According to Hall, P-time is a perfect fit to a communicative style which considers the multiple influencing factors of a situation and pays attention to the relations between people (high-context orientation, see next).

> ### Link to Practice: Time for Small Talk
>
> How much time is spent on small talk, and how this small talk is orchestrated in a business meeting shapes the nature and the quality of the relationships of those involved. For example, refreshments automatically signal a more diffuse relationship than a facts-oriented beginning. Thus, small-talk, when experienced, should be carefully participated in and reflected upon. It serves a purpose, and it is the cross-cultural manager's task to identify this purpose and to devise their own interaction strategies accordingly.

Context and communication

Communication, from Hall's (1976) perspective, can be further differentiated by the ways in which it is linked (or not so linked) to its boundary conditions. He identifies two opposing patterns. First, a communicative style which puts emphasis on the content of a message and not on the boundary conditions (context) wherein the message is offered. This is called a low-context orientated style or simply *low-context communication*. Conversely, a communicative style which values context over content is called *high-context communication* (because it is highly context-oriented). High-context orientation means that people adapt the content of their messages based on relevant context factors such as: Who is speaking? Who is listening? Where does the interaction take place? How well do people know each other? Is there hierarchy involved? What is the purpose of the interaction? Which interests and obligations underpin the interaction?

Communication is thus linked to wider social aspects, such as relations between people. For example, high-context communication implies the differentiation between in-group and out-group. Those who are similar to or affiliated with the sender of the message in a certain way are members of the in-group and hence possess contextual knowledge for deciphering it. Other members of society or of an organization (out-groups) who are different from the immediate in-group or not affiliated in a certain way, lack the contextual knowledge for deciphering the high-context message. Additionally, out-group relations are influenced by a fine and complex web of status-related interdependencies.

High-context includes a variety of styles, from direct, explicit and verbal to indirect, implicit and non-verbal. Conversely, low-context communication tends to focus solely on direct, explicit and verbal messages, with only minor variations across contexts. High-context is thus not the opposite of low-context, but rather encompasses this style, too, should context demand for it (e.g. in-group communication amongst equals).

Low-context orientation is focused on speed. However, there is also a maximum speed to it because everything has to be said in order to be understood. Which means that, for example, longer specifications or agreements are needed *regardless of the context* (planning documentation can actually become 'boring' for experienced employees, but, still, this information needs to be exchanged explicitly). Conversely, high-context communication can go into both directions. It can be very slow, e.g. communicating negative messages across out-groups or when there is not yet an established relationship, but on the other hand it can be very fast within an in-group, or if all context factors are known to all participants, then a simple 'handshake' might be enough to finalize, for example, a contract (because everyone already 'knows' from the context, what this handshake implies). Viewed long-term, high-context orientation thus starts slowly, but might become very fast whereas the speed of communication does not vary that much in low-context. This also implies that 'building relationships' or other investments into strengthening the context can pay off with speed and reliable communication in only a few words.

Context orientation, like other cultural dimensions, cannot be observed directly, but has to be deduced from the situation. Table 5.2 provides an overview of potential questions to be asked in order to identify a situation as high- or low-context. Please note that Table 5.2 depicts 'ideal' characteristics which do not exist in such clarity in real life. In reality, situations 'lean' to a certain style, and it is the task of the cross-cultural manager to find, interpret and reflect upon the respective clues. In Table 5.2, communication is compared to 'driving a car'.

Table 5.2 Overview of high- and low-context orientation

Question	Low-context	High-context
What do we listen to?	Listen to what I say (and only to what I say). This also means that details have to be said and written down in order to be understood and to 'count' (e.g., car insurance policy).	Read between the lines and also listen to what I don't say. Not every detail has to be said and written down, because people fill in the gaps with their knowledge of the context.
Which communicative road are we on?	We are on a speed-'Autobahn': The direct and fastest way to the destination. When we arrive, we might be stressed out.	We are driving on a winding country-road: A nice drive, but not the fastest one. When we reach our destination, we should not be stressed out.
What do we concentrate on while driving?	We want to reach our destination; we don't look left or right.	We take in the landscape; driving is an enjoyable experience.
What, if we don't like the drive?	We show it, because, this way, driving can be improved.	We hint at it, so that the nice atmosphere is not destroyed. If we know a person well, we might voice our opinion more strongly.
What unites and separates groups of people?	People are pooled into cars as required, based on where they need to go at this point in time. Individual messages are preferred.	Some people have formed long-term affiliations; they like to go for a drive together (in-group). Others, are part of other groups (out-group). Groups don't change that easily, and individual messages should consider groups.
What schedule are we on?	Time is highly organized (monochronic): Reaching the destination is more important than how to get there.	Time is open and flexible (polychronic): The drive itself is more important than reaching the destination.

Source: adapted from Hall (1976)

Table 5.3 Summary of Hall's cultural dimensions

Dimension	Definition/source
Diffuse vs specific relationship	Personal and public sphere overlap versus a private sphere which is reserved for close friends (Hall, 1966).
Monochronic vs polychronic	Singular and sequential time versus time as many parallel flows (Hall, 1983). Linked to relationships, communication and organizing at work.
Low context vs high context	Degree to which communication is direct, explicit and verbal versus indirect, implicit and non-verbal. (Hall, 1976). Also linked to relationship patterns, such as in-group and out-group differentiation in highly context-oriented cultural groups. Furthermore, high-context implies polychronic time-orientation, and low-context implies monochronic time-orientation. High-context orientation is also characterized by a higher variance, e.g. regarding communicative style, and the speed of the information flow.

Source: adapted from Hall (1966, 1976, 1983)

Functionalist CCM

Link to Practice: Meeting Culture as Communication

How a meeting runs is largely determined by how relations and topics are communicated by those leading and participating in these meetings. For example, if one uses a more high-context oriented approach to tell a person that they are off topic, this is more conductive to the meeting than calling them out directly. Schwarz (2016) summarizes eight such communicative 'ground rules for great meetings'.

STUDENT ACTIVITY 5.3

Culture as Communication

Note the summary of Hall's 'culture as communication' dimensions in Table 5.3. Then, assume the relative differences in cultural orientations shown in Figure 5.2.[2]

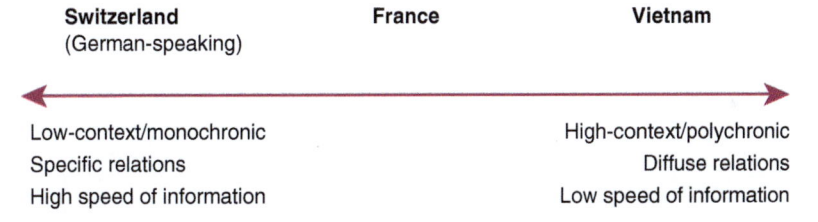

Switzerland (German-speaking)	France	Vietnam
Low-context/monochronic		High-context/polychronic
Specific relations		Diffuse relations
High speed of information		Low speed of information

Figure 5.2 Switzerland, France and Vietnam, and Hall's cultural dimensions

With this insight in mind, re-read the Opening Case. Next, answer the following questions:

1. When planning the virtual meeting, how should Ralf, Minh Đùc and Pierre consider the impact of this relative cultural difference? Differentiate your answer into:

(Continued)

---

[2] Hall (1959) did not develop his cultural dimensions by means of large-scale quantitative data. Therefore, this Figure 5.2 is not an exact 'measurement' of cultural orientations. Rather, it is Hall's ideas of what differentiates these three countries which have later been applied by other researchers and practitioners, also by means of quantitative studies. Nonetheless, cultural dimensions are never 'exact' data; they are hypotheses to be tested, with the goal to 'see' more in a situation.

- *Participants*: Who should be invited to this meeting? Can every topic be discussed with every group of people (think about in-group/out-group differentiations)? Do you need one meeting with all key users or should you think about multiple meetings (and for which groups of people)? Keep in mind that the purpose of the meeting is to turn organizational key users into promoters of the new helpdesk.
- *How to start the meeting*: What would be a good way of starting the meeting in order to convince participants to support the new help-desk? Are there different best ways in the different cultures, and, if so, how can these different ways be integrated? Keep in mind that integration is different than compromise; it means to fully consider each perspective, not to reach a 'half–half solution'.
- *Schedule*: What should the schedule look like? For answering this question, consider the wider aspects of communication. For example, what comes first – presentation of the topic or an acknowledgement of the people involved, the easy or the more difficult changes?
- *Utilizing the benefits of diversity*: Pierre, Ralf and Minh Đừc should assume that they are also more familiar with some cultural styles than with others. What will each of them be good at in this meeting? What might be difficult for each of them? Based on their thus identified cultural strengths, which roles would you assign to Pierre, Ralf and Minh Đừc? (Consider preparation of the workshop, the workshop itself and what needs to be done afterwards in order to ensure future success.)

2. Have a look at your answers to question 1). Would you say that the idea of cultural dimensions is helpful, or did it just result in more stereotyping? How (not) so?
3. How should Pierre, Ralf and Minh Đừc apply the idea of cultural dimensions to the situation, so that the benefits outweigh the potentially negative effects?
4. How can *you* use cultural dimensions in a good way in your own life?

Large-Scale Comparative Studies

The cultural dimensions so far were generalizations derived from small-scale research. From small investigations of culture in context, large implications for nations and countries were deduced. Geert Hofstede's (1980) work changes the methodology. It marks the beginnings of large-scale Comparative CCM research (also known as Quantitative Societal Cultures Research (QSCR) – Peterson and

Søndergaard, 2011). QSCR uses quantitative methods (surveys, questionnaires, also standardized interviews) on a large scale (many respondents) and aggregates findings to draw implications for large units of culture. Essentially, this means to, for example, translate a cultural dimension into a survey item, and to offer participants' standardized ways of how to respond. For example, to test high versus low context communication, you can give a manager a conflict scenario and then two options of how to solve it: by means of confrontational and direct communication (low context) or by means of integrative action (high context). Hofstede's studies and selected follower studies are presented in the following pages.

The beginnings of large-scale comparative research: The Hofstede studies

Hofstede developed his six cultural dimensions over the course of many years.

In 1980, Hofstede proposed four dimensions, namely *power distance, individualism versus collectivism, masculinity versus femininity* and *uncertainty avoidance*. These dimensions are based on data from employee surveys in a multinational company (1967–1972) which Hofstede analysed with regard to culture. However, those countries which were not accessible to Hofstede at that time, and for which these cultural dimensions exist as well, were added at a later stage and with the help of different methods.

In 1988, Hofstede introduced a fifth dimension, namely *long-term orientation versus short-term orientation*, also known as Confucian work dynamism (Hofstede and Bond, 1988). This dimension is based on a survey which was conducted in 23 countries and tried to take presumably 'Confucian' values into account.

In 2010, Hofstede added a sixth dimension, namely *indulgence versus restraint*.

All six cultural dimensions are summarized in Table 5.4. For each, an example is provided.

Table 5.4 The cultural dimensions by Hofstede

Dimension	Definition
Power distance	The degree to which members of a society expect and accept an unequal distribution of power. High power-distance means that a higher degree of inequality is accepted and expected.
	Open offices (low) versus separate offices for higher management (high power distance)
Individualism vs collectivism	The degree to which members of a society put forward their own interests against the group and hold self-reliance to be valuable (individualism) versus the degree to which members of a society align their interests with those of the group and consider this valuable (collectivism).
	Individual versus team-based (collective) incentives at work

(Continued)

Table 5.4 (Continued)

Dimension	Definition
Masculinity vs femininity	This dimension has two implications: First, a masculine business style implies the dominance of values that are considered 'masculine' such as assertiveness and competitiveness. In contrast, a 'feminine' business style implies the dominance of values that are considered 'feminine' such as care, cooperation and modesty. As a consequence, Hofstede assumes societies with masculine business styles to be dominated by men, and the business spheres of societies with a feminine business style to have more gender equality in business. *Small-talk as an opportunity to show one's qualities in direct competition with others (masculinity) versus small-talk as the opportunity to establish a 'we'-feeling (femininity).*
Uncertainty avoidance	The degree to which members of a society feel uncomfortable when facing uncertainty and ambiguity. High uncertainty avoidance means that there is a high tendency to avoid uncertainty, e.g. via planning the task or via establishing relations. Low uncertainty avoidance is associated with accepting uncertainty as part of life. *Feeling a high versus low need to be insured against potential negative events in one's life (high versus low uncertainty avoidance).*
Long-term vs short-term orientation	This dimension combines multiple aspects. Long-term orientation implies that members of a society pay attention to status differences and value seniority, have a strong work ethic and perseverance, and respect tradition. Short-term orientation implies that members of a society do not place high priority on status, try to postpone old age, are concerned with short-term results and aim for quick satisfaction of needs. *Doing business together over the course of many generations, e.g. because one's parents already did business together (long-term orientation), versus doing business with those how are the most profitable partners today (short-term orientation).*
Indulgence vs restraint	The degree to which members of a society receive gratification of basic human desires versus the degree to which members of a society are controlled in this gratification. *A tendency to accumulate savings (restraint) versus spending money to fulfil one's immediate wishes (indulgence).*

Source: adapted from Hofstede (1980, 2001, 2010; Hofstede and Bond, 1988)

Link to Practice: How (Not) to Use Cultural Dimensions

Hofstede's cultural dimensions are widely published on the internet. You will find, for example, rankings of countries based on Hofstede's cultural dimensions, as well as details of the cultural dimensions themselves, e.g. concerning how they impact on people's behaviour at work. However, you cannot be sure that every piece of information is equally reliable or 'objective'. For example, the perspective on culture, let's say, in Brazil will differ depending on whether culture in Brazil is described, let's say, from a US-American or from a Portuguese perspective (relative difference manifests itself only *between* two or more cultures). Also, you need to ask yourself what the purpose behind a website is. For example, if it is an intercultural training agency, offering preparation to US-American managers working in Brazil, then they will present cultural dimensions differently than, for example, an academic institute in Portugal focusing on the history of the Lusophone (Portuguese-speaking) world.

Based on these insights, it is part of the cross-cultural manager's and researcher's task to judge the available Comparative CCM tools with regard to their qualities and purposes. If applied without such considerations, cultural dimensions might actually do more harm than good, for example, by promoting stereotypes about cultures.

STUDENT ACTIVITY 5.4

Seeking Cross-Cultural Advice on the Internet

Please read the box above on 'How (Not) to Use Cultural Dimensions'. Next search the internet to find out how France, Switzerland and Vietnam score regarding the Hofstede dimensions, while at the same time evaluating the quality of the sources.

1. Identify an internet source which you consider an academic source of good quality regarding Hofstede's cultural dimensions.
   i. Document the source and write down your arguments why this is a good quality academic source.
   ii. Next, consider the implications of this information for Pierre, Ralf and Minh Đức of the Opening Case. Which differences in national culture do they need to consider when preparing the workshop?

If you cannot identify a source, then please document the sources which you found, together with your considerations *why* they are not good quality academic sources.

(Continued)

2. Identify an internet source which you consider a 'good quality' source for managers regarding Hofstede's cultural dimensions.

   i. Document the source and write down your arguments why this is a good-quality managerial source.
   ii. Next, consider the implications of this information for Pierre, Ralf and Minh Đức of the Opening Case. Which differences in national culture do they need to consider when preparing the workshop?

If you cannot identify any good source at all, document two 'bad-quality' sources for managers (question 3) instead.

3. Identify an internet source which you consider a 'bad-quality' source for managers regarding Hofstede's cultural dimensions.

   i. Document the source and write down your arguments why this is a bad-quality managerial source.
   ii. Next, consider the implications of this information for Pierre, Ralf and Minh Đức of the Opening Case: Why should they not follow this information when preparing their workshop? What harm will this information do?

Cultural dimensions by Trompenaars

Fons Trompenaars (1993) conducted another large-scale study of culture which identified seven cultural value orientations. It is based on a questionnaire which was distributed to managers from 28 countries over a period of ten years and which was later applied to a much larger number of countries (Trompenaars and Hampden-Turner, 1997). These dimensions (see Table 5.5) relate back to previous studies and have refined and integrated existing concepts.

Table 5.5 The cultural dimensions by Trompenaars and Hampden-Turner

Dimension	Definition	Link to previous studies
Universalism vs particularism	The degree to which members of a society treat everyone equally and favour one rule or norm for all situations (universalism) or to which members of a society treat groups of people differently, e.g. based on relations, and favour many context-specific norms (particularism).	Partly similar to Hall's concept of low-context vs high-context communication

Functionalist CCM

Dimension	Definition	Link to previous studies
Individualism vs communitarianism	The degree to which members of a society put forward their own interests against the group and hold self-reliance as a value (individualism) versus the degree to which members of a society align their interests with those of the group and consider this to be valuable (communitarianism).	Linked to Hofstede (1980): individualism vs collectivism. Addition to concept: communitarianism as specific to 'communist countries'
Affectiveness vs neutrality	The degree to which emotions are hidden or shown.	
Specificity vs diffuseness	The degree to which members of a society engage others in specific areas of life and single levels of personality, or diffusely in multiple areas of their lives and at several levels of personality at the same time.	Partly similar to Hall: specific vs diffuse relations
Achieved vs ascribed status	The degree to which status is either ascribed based on family background or titles, or achieved by proven competence at work.	Linked to Kluckhohn and Strodtbeck: hierarchical vs collateral relations
Sequential vs synchronic time	The degree to which time is understood and planned as a sequence of portioned and separated events versus the degree to which time is filled with many activities in parallel and not separated into several portions of time.	Linked to Hall: monochronic vs polychronic time
Internal vs external control/inner direction vs outer direction	The degree to which members of a collective believe in a need or duty to control nature (internal control/direction) versus the degree to which members of a collective believe that human life is a product of nature and environment and therefore aim at achieving balance and harmony (external control/direction).	Linked to Kluckhohn and Strodtbeck: relationship to the environment (mastery, harmony, subjugation)

Source: adapted from Trompenaars (1993); Trompenaars and Hampden-Turner (1997)

Link to Practice: How to See and Prove Managerial Competence

Major conflicts may occur if there are divergent understandings of what proves managerial status at work. For example, will a manager's competence be accepted because they come from the 'right kind of family' (ascribed status)

(Continued)

or because they have acquired the 'right kind of diploma' (achieved status)? Furthermore, the expected ways of how to *prove* achievement might differ, even if an achievement orientation is generally accepted. For example, in the USA, it is common for industrial managers to prove their competencies via a Master of Business Administration (MBA). Conversely, in Germany, industrial managers are expected to have some technical expertise, proven, for example, via a degree in engineering or industrial engineering. In the USA, the management qualification is the one to be proven via achievement, in Germany it is the opposite. For both countries, the respective other qualification (USA: engineering; Germany: management) is more ascribed than proven; it follows from the proven one (USA: management; Germany: engineering). But which managers are the better ones, and could *fully* ascribed status be a global managerial option as well?

STUDENT ACTIVITY 5.5

'Tech' and 'Pharma' Culture in Light of Each Other

Originally intended for establishing relative difference between countries, cultural dimensions, such as the ones by Trompenaars and Hampden-Turner, can nonetheless be applied to other levels of culture, such as professional or industrial cultures. If this is done, then the purpose of these dimensions changes from 'preparing for objective cultural differences' to 'learning more about a situation'. This activity applies this learning.

1. Go back to the Opening Case. Can you identify hints for a relative difference in cultural orientations (dimensions by Trompenaars and Hampden-Turner) between the 'tech-culture' of Pierre, Ralf and Minh Đức and the culture of the pharmaceutical industry wherein they work? This is not about factual 'proof' but more about you working as a 'cultural detective'. Which cultural dimensions *could* be in there? You will not find all cultural dimensions in the case.
2. Now, consider that the three 'tech-guys' need to hold their workshop for line and project managers in the pharmaceutical industry, with a background in pharmaceutics and/or medicine. What cultural differences (dimensions by Trompenaars and Hampden-Turner) between 'tech culture' and 'pharma culture' should Pierre, Ralf and Minh Đức prepare for and how? Note, you can search the internet for descriptions of both cultures.

> You will find something. Don't take it at face value but interpret what is behind it (people who speak about 'tech' and 'pharma' culture are also part of certain cultures and therefore not objective in their viewpoints).

Project GLOBE

The GLOBE (Global Leadership and Organizational Behavior Effectiveness) study is the most recent large-scale research project on culture (House et al., 2004). GLOBE data was collected by 170 scholars from various cultures through more than 17,000 interviews with middle managers from 62 countries in three industries (House et al., 2004).

During research, House et al. (2004) intended to capture culture on two levels, namely *practices* and *values*. Interviewees were asked, for example, to evaluate their actual cultural practices – 'as is' – and the level of cultural values – 'should be'. The intention was to uncover differences between cultural reality and the cultural ideal. For example, in a culture, there might be the ideal to be gender equal ('should be'), but at the same time, there might be gender unequal practices ('as is'). GLOBE proposes nine cultural dimensions which are presented in Table 5.6.

Table 5.6 Cross-cultural dimensions according to GLOBE

Dimension	Definition
Performance Orientation	The degree to which a collective encourages and rewards (and should encourage and reward) members for performance improvement and excellence.
Assertiveness	The degree to which individuals are (and should be) assertive, confrontational, and aggressive in their relationship with others.
Future Orientation	The extent to which individuals engage (and should engage) in future-oriented behaviours such as planning, investing in the future, and delaying gratification.
Humane Orientation	The degree to which a collective encourages and rewards (and should encourage and reward).
Institutional Collectivism	The degree to which organizational and societal institutional practices encourage and reward (and should encourage and reward) collective distribution of resources and collective action.
In-group Collectivism	The degree to which individuals express (and should express) pride, loyalty, and cohesiveness in their organizations or families.
Gender Egalitarianism	The degree to which a collective minimizes (and should minimize) gender inequality.
Power Distance	The extent to which a collective accepts and endorses (and should accept and endorse) authority, power differences, and status privileges.
Uncertainty Avoidance	The extent to which a collective relies (and should rely) on social norms, rules, and procedures to alleviate unpredictability of future events. The greater the desire to avoid uncertainty, the more people seek orderliness, consistency, structure, formal procedures, and laws to cover daily situations.

Source: GLOBE (2020a)

These cultural dimensions involve a few innovations. First, according to Hofstede (1980), collectivism is the degree to which individuals are expected to give priority to group interests before their own individual interests. House et al. (2004) critiqued this dimension for being a mixture of (1) external collective encouragement (institutional collectivism) and (2) the inner personal valuation of groups (in-group collectivism) and considered each aspect as a separate dimension. Secondly, Hofstede's (1980) concept of masculinity was split up into assertiveness (the expected business style) and the degree to which both genders are considered equally (gender egalitarianism). Third, GLOBE renamed Hofstede's (2001) construct of 'long-term orientation' into future orientation, questioning its quality as a specifically 'Chinese' cultural concept (Ashkanasy et al., 2004). The GLOBE dimension of humane orientation, which is a new addition, refers to the institutionalized aspects of caring for each other in a society, and it can be related back – amongst others – to Kluckhohn and Strodtbeck's understanding of relations between people and the nature of people.

According to the data, in-group collectivism is the dimension in which the GLOBE societies differ the most (Javidan et al., 2004: 31–32), and assertiveness the one with the least spread (ibid.: 32). High power distance and 'being somewhat male orientated' is what most GLOBE societies have in common (ibid.: 30–31).

Furthermore, GLOBE (House et al., 2004) identified two relations which are not directly related to culture but nonetheless are crucial considerations for the contemporary cross-cultural manager.

Firstly, the data suggests that culture is an explanatory variable only if a country is sufficiently developed. For example, if child labour is prevalent in a country, this might have less to do with cultural value orientations and more with the sheer necessity to survive. Likewise, high performance orientation might be impossible to achieve and pursue if a country lacks the required infrastructure and the stable economy and political system for enabling companies and individuals to perform.

Secondly, there is a gender bias in the study itself. Of the middle managers from whom the data stems, approximately one third were women and two thirds were men. Across all societal cultures studied, women managers judged gender egalitarianism in their own societal culture to be lower than male managers. Furthermore, the mean score of the dimension Gender Egalitarianism is the lowest among all practice orientations, 'indicating that GLOBE societies are reported to be male oriented' (Javidan et al., 2004: 31). The implications of this finding are firstly that all societal cultures are characterized by an imbalance of the proportion of men and women in management, and secondly that men – across all societal cultures – underestimate gender inequality compared to women (Emrich et al., 2004).

Link to Practice: Gender Gaps in Entrepreneurship

There is a gender gap – that is, an underrepresentation of women – in many sectors, entrepreneurship not being an exception. Yet, according to the Global

Entrepreneurship Monitor (GEM) for 2020/2021, the number of founding women has risen and has even surpassed those of founding men in Kazakhstan, Angola, Indonesia and Togo (GEM, 2021: 53–54), whereas the gender gap in entrepreneurship is the highest in Italy, India and Egypt (ibid.: 54). The absolute levels of female entrepreneurship in the Middle East, Latin America and the Caribbean, and Sub-Saharan Africa are generally higher than those in Europe and North America (GEM, 2021: 53–54). What might explain these gender gap differences, and why is there less female entrepreneurship in many European and North American countries compared to many other parts of the world?

STUDENT ACTIVITY 5.6

Cultural Values and Cultural Practices in Light of Each Other

Please look up the visualizations of the results of the 2004 GLOBE study for France, Switzerland and Vietnam (GLOBE, 2020b; see QR code).

If you click on the map, you are directed to the results for each country. Please only consider the cultural dimensions (*not* the leadership scores of Chapter 4).

1. Which gaps in cultural practice can you identify between the three societal cultures?
2. Which gaps in cultural value can you identify between the three societal cultures?
3. Are there gaps between cultural value and practice *within* one societal culture? If so, what do you think does this mean?
4. Have a look at the GLOBE average for each cultural dimension. Which scores (a. value; b. practice) of which of the three societal cultures are far away from this average score? What do you think could be the implications of this for Pierre, Ralf and Minh Đùc, respectively, when holding a workshop?
5. What can you learn from applying the GLOBE study dimensions?

Chapter Summary

This chapter focused on functionalist CCM; that is, an approach that wishes to provide objective advice to managers regarding the differences between cultures. Its purpose is to help managers identify a best way of 'how to manage across cultures'.

A main tool for doing so are cultural dimensions. Cultural dimensions are presumably universal, selected aspects of culture which enable direct comparison between cultures with regard to these selected aspects of culture. Thus, relative difference between cultures can be established, which provides a more reliable ground for managerial strategy and actions.

The three main characteristics of Comparative CCM are:

1. A focus on selected aspects of culture (e.g. values or communication).
2. The assumption that some aspects of cultures are universal, which makes them objectively identifiable and comparable.
3. The idea of training managers and others in objective patterns of relative differences across cultures (cross-cultural differences).

Early comparative studies, such as the ones by Kluckhohn and Strodtbeck, and by Hall, put forward these main characteristics, but were not yet engaged in providing large-scale quantitative data on societal and national cultures. This happened for the first time with Hofstede (1980). Since then, other large-scale studies have built upon and have refined Hofstede's cultural dimensions; however, only a few cultural dimensions have been added to the CCM toolkit (e.g. humane orientation, assertiveness and gender egalitarianism). This might signify that there is only a limited number of universal cultural aspects and a finite list of cultural dimensions to be identified. Nonetheless, it is relevant to constantly try to improve upon this tool because, in the process, certain cultural dimensions can be refined, e.g. the differentiation of collectivism (Hofstede, 1980) into in-group and institutional collectivism (House et al., 2004).

Investigating national or societal patterns are one potential way of becoming aware of the imprint which culture has upon individuals. It can provide relevant advice to managers, e.g. when making international market entry decisions or when developing international business strategies (see Chapter 8). However, any model trying to shed light onto the 'essence' of national cultures must necessarily involve simplification. If one takes inner-societal diversity and cultural complexity into account, it would be impossible to establish useful managerial advice, and this is the limitation of this approach. Cultural dimensions should thus be used as hypotheses to be tested upon a situation, not as an answer to how this situation 'really' is.

Key Points

- Cultural dimensions are a key tool of functionalist CCM, in particular Comparative CCM.
- Cultural dimensions focus only on selected universal aspects of culture – such as values or communication – to make cultures comparable.
- By means of cultural dimensions, managers and other occupational groups can be trained in objective patterns of relative differences across societal cultures.

- If applied to a situation as hypotheses to be tested, cultural dimensions provide a first entry point for learning new cultures on multiple levels.
- The actual benefits – or potential dangers – of using cultural dimensions thus depend on how well the cross-cultural manager handles them in practice.

Review Questions

1. What are cultural dimensions, how are they constructed and what do they wish to depict?
2. What are the main premises of a functionalist CCM and how are these reflected in the construct of cultural dimensions?
3. Please name and explain the cultural dimensions by Kluckhohn and Strodtbeck and provide an example for each of them. How are these cultural dimensions different from other and later cultural dimensions?
4. Please name and explain the cultural dimensions by Hall and provide an example for each of them. What are the key ideas underlying Hall's approach?
5. What is meant by Quantitative Societal Cultures Research (QSCR), and which QSCR studies do you know?
6. Please name and explain the cultural dimensions by Hofstede and provide an example for each of them.
7. Please name and explain the cultural dimensions by Trompenaars and Hampden-Turner and provide an example for each of them.
8. Please name and explain the cultural dimensions by project GLOBE and provide an example for each of them.
9. Which cultural dimensions build upon or are similar to each other?
10. How should cross-cultural managers use cultural dimensions to utilize their benefits? Which usage of cultural dimensions might be detrimental or even dangerous, and should therefore be avoided?

Opening Case Revisited

The Opening Case of this chapter depicts a very common scenario in today's work environment; that is, three people who are culturally different in some aspects and culturally related in other aspects need to engage in a common task which involves other people who are also culturally different in some aspects and culturally related in other aspects. Cultural dimensions are a useful tool to be applied in practice. They can provide people who need to achieve a certain goal across cultures with first hypotheses as to which cultural differences might occur and how these might manifest themselves. Still, they never provide you with the 'complete' picture of culture in all its depth.

When conducting the workshop, Pierre, Ralf and Minh Đùc should therefore pay particular attention to those incidents when what is happening does not meet the expected cross-cultural differences for which they have prepared. This way, they will prevent cultural dimensions from becoming a 'self-fulfilling' concept which they project upon people but which does not do justice to the cultural complexity of the situation and the multiple cultural identities of those involved (see Chapters 2 and 3).

Pierre, Ralf and Minh Đùc should also observe themselves and others while conducting the workshop. They should reflect upon what is going on (alone and together), in particular concerning situations wherein opinions diverge or conflict emerges, and then check whether cultural dimensions provide additional insights. This way, they will make the unit of analysis even smaller, they will learn from experience and they will further develop their cross-cultural skills.

Closing Activity

In this chapter, you have engaged with the concept of cultural dimensions in depth. With this experience in mind, answer the following questions:

1. How has the 'picture' which you hold in mind about France, Switzerland and Vietnam changed?
2. In what aspects (if any) do you now have a more objective picture of each country?
3. How has your understanding of your own cultural patterns (values/behaviour) changed? What difference will it make when you interact across cultures?
4. What is still unclear? What could be your next steps for closing these gaps?

Further Reading

Peterson and Søndergaard (2011) provide an overview of how Comparative CCM studies have developed, and Sackmann (2020) outlines the contours of functionalist CCM in Chapter 1 of *The Sage Handbook of Contemporary Cross-Cultural Management*. A special issue on values in the *Journal of Cross-Cultural Psychology* (Vol. 42, Issue 2, March 2011) highlights the merits of the comparative study of selected universal aspects of culture. However, this approach is also critiqued for its simplicity – Ailon (2008) offers a much-cited example. On the other hand, Osland and Bird (2000) provide advice on how to use cultural dimensions as more than mere 'sophisticated stereotyping'. Mahadevan (2017, Chapter 2) argues that the usefulness of cultural dimensions is not determined by this tool itself, but rather by those using it for appropriate purposes and from an appropriate mindset.

References

Ailon, G. (2008) 'Mirror, mirror on the wall: Culture's consequences in a value test of its own design', *Academy of Management Review*, 33(4): 885–904.

Ashkanasy, N., Gupta, V., Mayfield, M. and Trevor-Roberts, E. (2004) 'Future orientation', in R. House, P. Hanges, M. Javidan and V. Gupta (eds), *Culture, Leadership, and Organizations – The GLOBE Study of 62 Societies*. Thousand Oaks: Sage. pp. 282–342.

Emrich, C.G., Denmark, F.L. and Den Hartog, D.N. (2004) 'Cross-cultural differences in gender egalitarianism: Implications for societies, organizations and leaders', in R. House, P. Hanges, M. Javidan and V. Gupta (eds), *Culture, Leadership, and Organizations – The GLOBE Study of 62 Societies*. Thousand Oaks: Sage. pp. 343–394.

Global Entrepreneurship Monitor (GEM) (2021) *2020/2021 Global Report*. Available at: www.gemconsortium.org/file/open?fileId=50691 [last accessed 31 July 2022].

GLOBE (2020a) *Data from the 2004 Study*. Available at: https://globeproject.com/study_2004_2007?page_id=data#data [last accessed on 30 September 2020].

GLOBE (2020b) *Visualizations of the 2004 Study*. Available at: https://globeproject.com/results?page_id=country#country [last accessed on 30 September 2020].

Hall, E.T. (1959) *The Silent Language*. Garden City: Doubleday.

Hall, E.T. (1966) *The Hidden Dimension*. Garden City: Doubleday.

Hall, E.T. (1976) *Beyond Culture*. Garden City: Doubleday.

Hall, E.T. (1983) *The Dance of Life: The Other Dimension of Time*. Garden City: Doubleday.

Hall, E.T. and Hall, M.R. (1990) *Understanding Cultural Differences*. Yarmouth, ME: Intercultural Press.

Hall, E.T. and Trager, G.L. (1953) *The Analysis of Culture*. Washington: American Council of Learned Societies.

Hofstede, G. (1980) *Culture's Consequences: International Differences in Work Related Values*. Beverly Hills: Sage.

Hofstede, G. (2001) *Culture's Consequences: Comparing Values, Behaviors, Institutions and Organizations across Nations*. London: Sage.

Hofstede, G. (2010) *Cultures and Organizations: Software for the Mind*. New York: McGraw-Hill.

Hofstede, G. and Bond, M. (1988) 'The Confucius connection: From cultural roots to economic growth', *Organizational Dynamics*, 16(4): 4–21.

House, R., Hanges, P., Javidan, M. and Gupta, V. (2004) *Culture, Leadership, and Organizations: the GLOBE Study of 62 Societies*. Thousand Oaks: Sage.

Javidan, M., House, R. and Dorfman, W. (2004) 'A nontechnical summary of GLOBE findings', in R. House, P. Hanges, M. Javidan and V. Gupta (eds), *Culture, Leadership, and Organizations – The GLOBE Study of 62 Societies*. Thousand Oaks: Sage. pp. 29–48.

Kluckhohn, C. and Strodtbeck, K. (1961) *Variations of Value Orientations*. Westport: Greenwood.

Leeds-Hurwitz, W. (1990) 'Notes in the history of intercultural communication: The foreign service institute and the mandate for intercultural training', *Quarterly Journal of Speech*, 76(3): 262–281.

Leeds-Hurwitz, W. (2010) 'Writing the intellectual history of intercultural communication', in T.K. Nakayama and R.T. Halualani (eds), *The Handbook of Intercultural Communication*. Chichester: Wiley-Blackwell. pp. 17–33.

Mahadevan, J. (2017) *A Very Short, Fairly Interesting and Reasonably Cheap Book about Cross-Cultural Management*. London: SAGE.

Osland, J. and Bird, A. (2000) 'Beyond sophisticated stereotyping – understanding cultural sensemaking in context', *Academy of Management Executive*, 14(1): 65–79.

Peterson, M.F. and Søndergaard, M. (2011) 'Traditions and transitions in quantitative societal culture research in Organization Studies', *Organization Studies*, 32(11): 1539–1558.

Pusch, M.D. (2004) 'Intercultural training in historical perspective', in D. Landis, J.M. Bennett and M.J. Bennett (eds), *Handbook of Intercultural Training*. Thousand Oaks: Sage. pp. 13–36.

Sackmann, S. (2020) 'Culture in cross-cultural management: Its seminal contributions from a positivist perspective', in B. Szkudlarek, L. Romani, D.V. Caprar and J.S. Osland (eds), *The Sage Handbook of Contemporary Cross-Cultural Management*. London: Sage. pp. 17–33.

Schwartz, S.H. (1992) 'Universals in the content and structure of values: Theoretical advances and empirical tests in 20 countries', *Advances in Experimental Social Psychology*, 25: 1–65.

Schwarz, R. (2016) 'Eight ground rules for great meetings', *Harvard Business Review*, 15 June. Available at: https://hbr.org/2016/06/8-ground-rules-for-great-meetings [last accessed 1 August 2016].

Trompenaars, F. (1993) *Riding the Waves of Culture*. Burr Ridge: Irwin.

Trompenaars, F. and Hampden-Turner, C. (1997) *Riding the Waves of Culture: Understanding Cultural Diversity in Global Business*. London: Nicholas Brealey.

Waida, M. (2022) '8 must-know types of seating arrangements for events', Socialtables. Available at: www.socialtables.com/blog/meeting-event-design/types-of-seating-arrangements/ [last accessed 31 July 2022].

Interpretive Cross-Cultural Management

6

What does CCM mean?

Learning Objectives

After reading this chapter, you should:

- understand the main premises of an interpretive CCM, and be aware of how culture emerges from an interpretive perspective
- know the concept of emic and etic and be aware of the positionality of CCM
- understand the concept of symbolic meaning
- know the ways in which meaning is transmitted (language, being-in-the-world and technology)
- be able to interpret culture in context
- be able to interpret symbolic meaning in interaction
- understand the main principles of engaging in intercultural interactions
- know how to refine and contextualize your categories of difference.

Reading Requirement

- You should have read Chapter 4 of this book

Introduction

The previous chapter has introduced functionalist CCM with its focus on identifying the best, objective ways of how CCM *works*. This chapter deepens another, complementary approach, namely interpretive CCM with its goal of uncovering what CCM *means*, and to whom.

Interpretive CCM is informed by linguistics, anthropology and sociology (overview in Cardel Gertsen and Zølner, 2020). It is based on the premises of *perspectivity* and *positionality*. In simple terms, this means to approach a question such as: 'What is an elephant?' from the insight that a person standing in front of the trunk will experience a different animal than a person standing behind the elephant's tail. Out of this difference in perspective then follow different conclusions about what the elephant might be useful for, whether and how it is dangerous, how it should be taken care of, and so forth. Likewise, cultural reality as interpreted and experienced differently by different groups of people, leads to a variety of conclusions of what constitutes 'good' management.

What is an elephant, and from which position does one 'manage' or 'study' it?

Figure 6.1 **The perspectivity of reality and the positionality of CCM**

Culture (that is, how people have come to view the elephant) provides managers with the 'glasses' through which to look at the situation. Consequently, the elephant comes to mean certain, and not other, things to them. Or, in other words, people approach situations equipped with a certain – and not another – cultural backpack in which previous experiences and tools for how to interpret and handle situations are stored. This way, culture interprets experience and generates behaviour.

Emic and etic as two complementary perspectives

The starting point is the insight that there is no objectively 'true' view on reality, and that every cultural viewpoint is limited. People only 'know' and experience the trunk or the tail of the elephant, respectively. This means that they are insiders to their own, and outsiders to the worldviews of others. In academic terms, this differentiation has become known as **emic** (inside) and **etic** (outside) perspective (Pike, 1967).

Emic Inside (perspective)

Etic Outside (perspective)

Application: Emic and Etic

Revisit Figure 6.1.

- An **emic view** is the perspective and position of a cultural insider. For example, only if you are positioned in front of the trunk, will you experience the elephant from this perspective: You have access to the whole of this **emic meaning.** The same is true for the person positioned in front of the tail – two distinct cultural realities of what an elephant *means* and how it should be handled emerge.
- An **etic view** is the perspective of a cultural outsider who experiences social reality from another position. For example, you are still positioned in front of the trunk, but you are now asked to view the elephant from the perspective of someone standing behind its tail. You are now a cultural outsider to this perspective (etic view), and your access to what the elephant *means* from this angle (emic meanings) is limited.

Because every cultural viewpoint is selective, and, thus, limited, interpretive CCM rejects the idea that there is a single best way of how to manage (no one sees the 'real' or complete elephant, and no one can handle it perfectly). Out of this follows the need to change perspective, and to try to look at the elephant from alternative angles, in order to enrich one's understanding of the situation, and to enlarge one's repertoire for handling it. Developing the abilities for doing so is what the tools in this chapter are for.

To achieve its goals, this chapter first highlights social constructivism, as the main premise underlying interpretive CCM. It then elaborates the different ways in which interpretive CCM focuses on meaning in context. This leads to insights on how and why people construct and maintain cross-cultural differences when interacting. Out of this follow recommendations for managing intercultural interactions. The starting point are the divergent stories told about a multinational project in the Opening Case.

Figure 6.2 Interpretive cross-cultural management of emic meanings

Opening Case

Making Sense of Project Alpha

This is the story of project Alpha, as told by several members of a multinational company (company Beta). The purpose of this case, with its different narratives, is to highlight the tools required for interpreting cross-cultural situations, on both subjective and inter-subjective level.

The Wider Context

Beta's headquarters are located in the USA, production takes place in the USA and India. Beta produces medical equipment which is essential to pharmaceutical companies for manufacturing patented products. After a certain period of time, these patents will run out. Therefore, Beta's customers want to produce and sell as much and as quickly as possible before patent protection comes to an end. Afterwards, other companies will be able to access research and development data freely and, without the original investment, will produce cheaper versions, so called generics, of the same pharmaceutical product. If Beta does not produce and deliver in time and exactly to specification, penalties will need to be paid. This makes every project at Beta highly time critical.

The technical equipment produced by Beta is also customized specifically for each client. This implies that every project is unique. Moreover, the pharmaceutical products manufactured by means of Beta's equipment concern the health of human beings, which means that each project also needs to meet high safety standards. Markets for pharmaceutical products differ across countries in their requirements, but all of them tend to be regulated, with high-quality demands. Since 2005, Beta has shifted most of its production from the USA to India, currently one of the biggest producers of generics and other pharmaceutics.

Prior to project Alpha, the production site in India had to be built by the company from scratch. As the US-American head of global production recalls (quote 1):

> we literally had to build it into the jungle outside of the city and pave our own roads, there was nothing there.

Project Alpha

Project Alpha was carried out during the last two years by the US-American and the Indian production site. First, project management (PM) control was exerted by the US-American site. After a year, the Indian site was given full responsibility for project Alpha. At this time, it was the biggest project ever executed directly by the Indian site. The goal was to manufacture and deliver customized technical equipment for an Indian customer. Direct customer interaction was to be handled by the Indian site as well.

After control had been given over to the Indian site, Project Alpha was to be led by an engineer from the Indian site who had been with the company for several years. He had executed smaller projects for Indian customers previously. Immediately after this decision was announced, the global head of production at the US-American site expressed his concerns that the Indian site would not be able to handle a project of this size.

The US-American head of global production, formerly in charge of project Alpha, said that (quote 2):

> During the previous project, which was much smaller and only partially handled by the Indian site, we had lots of PM issues and ended up with additional costs of 60,000 USD. And, the board asks me: 'XY, are

(Continued)

you crazy?' And I go: 'What shall I do?' It's these crazy Indian people, and their lack of cost-consciousness! And now, with project Alpha, the same thing is happening again, and my boss is breathing down my neck. I mean, of course, you cannot say for sure who has caused the overhead because of our global matrix design, but this Indian 'do it today, do it tomorrow' thing definitely plays a role. And the leadership qualities are definitely lacking at the Indian site.

Yet, the Indian project manager now in charge of project Alpha tells the following story about the previous project (quote 3):

During the last time when we handled a project in cooperation with the American site here in India, we experienced some issues. The main issue was that costs were allocated to the Indian site but actually were caused by delays in global engineering which is comprised of both sites. But when I tried to raise this point towards our colleagues in the US, the production manager in particular, I was told that this was due to insufficient project controlling in India.

The US-American head of production's direct boss represents the board's perspective when she says (quote 4):

When the two sites started working together on this project, it started out just fine. But then, the managing directors at the US-American and the Indian site stopped talking to each other. And this is why we are facing these cost issues. Of course, the level of development in India is also much lower than in the US.

As a result of the board's concern which are aggravated by the US-American head of production's narrative (quote 2) and a generally expressed feeling at headquarters that the project will not work out because the Indian site has implemented insufficient project monitoring tools, an external project manager, originally from France, but working globally since decades, is hired to get the Indian site 'up to speed'. This does not go well.
A Brazilian member of the board noted that (quote 5):

The cooperation with the new external project manager is going very badly. You cannot let him see an Indian customer. We had one incident during which he practically insulted the Indian customer.

> The customer walked out of the meeting and threatened to end the cooperation, and the Indian colleagues were completely annoyed. You know, in India, you need to find a diplomatic way and involve people: bluntness will boomerang. Also, he seems to operate from a standpoint of superiority: to him, India is simply an underdeveloped country, and people are less qualified, and this is why he treats people like they are not equal, much like my American colleagues treat people from Brazil. There is a lot of arrogance involved.

The US-American head of production, formerly in charge of project Alpha says (quote 6):

> The behavior of the external project manager is not good, and the Indian colleagues like to see his butt the most. You simply cannot talk as straightforwardly with an Indian customer as with an American customer. At one point, the customer threatened to cancel out contracts, and I even had to step in and to do it the Indian way, I mean, communicate politely, and beat around the bush, and so on. This is why I have now taken care that any interaction with the customer is solely handled by the Indian site.
>
> He [the external project manager] has learned PM from scratch. He is very experienced. The only reason why I keep him on the project is that I do not want the project to fail. The external project manager tells me: 'the Indians are capable of nothing. They are at the very beginning. Their project management skills equal zero.' The Indian project manager has phoned me twice. He and his people want to de-install the external project manager. But I don't believe that they can do it on their own. I have to increase the pressure on India now. If I let it run along just like that, I would not do the Indians a favour, they are not ready yet. The external project manager is necessary. He will teach the Indian colleagues how to manage projects this size. He is costing me a hell of a lot of money, though. But what else can I do?

The Indian global project manager meanwhile states that (quote 7):

> We are no children ... We work for the same company and are trained the same way. Pharmaceutics is a global business, and we have proven ourselves in it. An overbearing parent to take care of it is what

(Continued)

> we need the least. What we *really* need is to be taken seriously. For example, after the last project we suggested improvements to global accounting procedures, but they just dismissed it as a 'stupid Indian idea'. And that is the general attitude.
>
> Such are the perspectives on project Alpha as of today. What do these narratives *mean*, where does the project *really* stand and what are the managerial implications?

From an interpretive perspective, the question is not 'how to make project Alpha function in the best possible way' but, rather, what does project Alpha *mean* (and for whom and for what reasons)? People involved in intercultural interactions also try to figure this out, and, when they look back onto a situation with the aim of grasping its meaning, this is called *sensemaking*.

STUDENT ACTIVITY 6.1

What is the Status of Project Alpha?

Read the Opening Case above and answer the following questions:

- What is the status of project Alpha?
- What are the main problems to be addressed?
- What would you, as a cross-cultural manager, recommend to improve the situation?

The Social Construction of Reality

Interpretive CCM is underpinned by the idea that reality is constructed socially (Berger and Luckmann, 1966). This means that culture emerges 'between' people; it is *inter*-subjective. This happens via a two-way process between individuals and the world. On the one hand, culture (the meanings 'between' people) provides people with 'blueprints' of what a situation – in this case, Project Alpha – means. In such ways, culture is the invisible intermediate layer between people and the world. At the same time, people constantly try to figure out what events, such as project Alpha, mean – they *interpret* reality. When doing so, they are no mere passive by-standers of culture unfolding. Rather, they also shape what the project *means* via their individual (*subjective*) interpretations and consecutive actions. This way, they *create* inter-subjective reality. In these mutually constitutive ways, humans are products and producers of culture (see Figure 6.3).

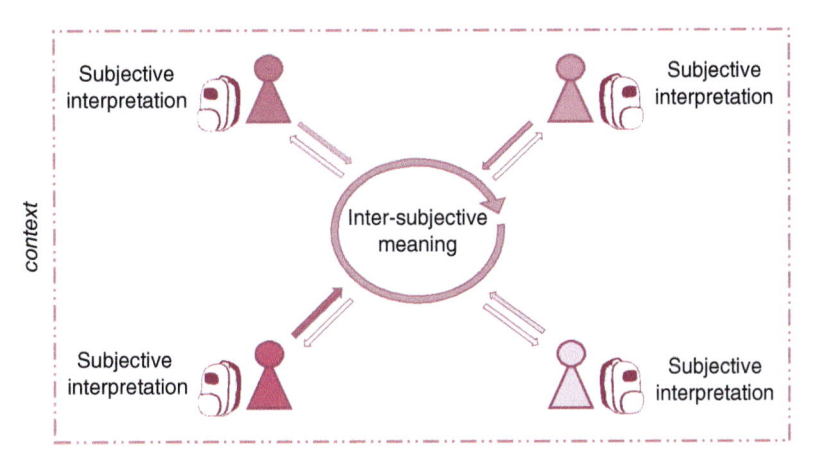

Figure 6.3 How culture emerges from an interpretive perspective

> ### Link to Practice: 'What Modern Arranged Marriages *Really* Look Like' (Emery, 2022)
>
> Across cultures and individuals, there are many divergent ways of how to get married and what this means, and emic and etic perspectives on the matter tend to differ. This article in *Brides* online (Emery, 2022) focuses on the matter and it exemplifies the construction of multiple (inter-)subjective realities in practice. See: www.brides.com/story/modern-arranged-marriages

A Focus on Meaning and Experience in Context

Meaning and experience are central to interpretive CCM. This section sheds further insight into how culture interprets experience and generates behaviour.

Symbolic meaning

If the world is socially constructed, as interpretive CCM maintains, then cultural clues can never contain a single 'true' content. Rather, they are signs or 'indicators' as they refer to ('signify') something else (the signified), which others need to interpret. What they stand for, and thus 'signify', are cultural ideas or concepts; something largely invisible, yet meaningful, if one knows the code. Visible aspects of culture (behaviour, language, but also objects and technology) thus transport deeper cultural meaning – they act as symbols. This way, they stand for more than one can see – but only if one has learned how to correctly 'decipher' the cultural code transmitted.[1] Figure 6.4 visualizes this process.

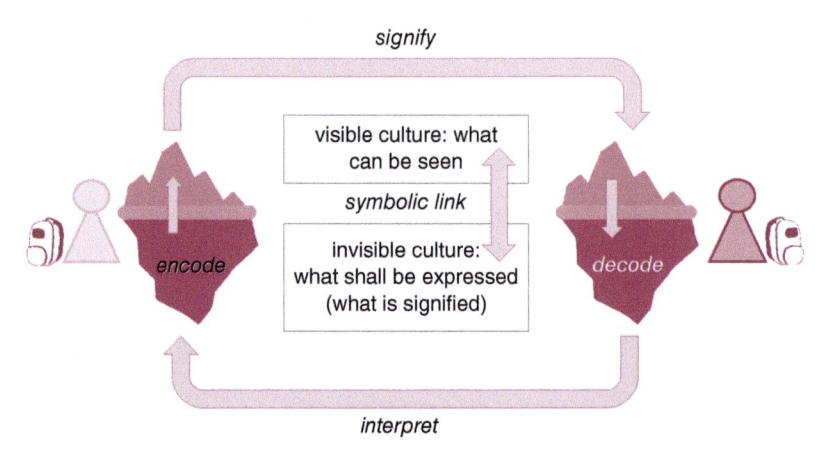

Figure 6.4 Culture as an iceberg: The symbolic meaning perspective

Spotlight: Symbolic Interactionism

Symbolic interactionism is a prominent lens for interpretive CCM. Meaning, as defined by social psychologist H. Mead (1934: 67), can be understood as 'action on a common basis'. Meaning according to Mead arises, for example, when a person asks another person to bring a chair for a visitor and that person reacts to the request and brings the chair. Both share the same understanding of what it means to 'bring a chair'. At the same time, the person making the request could go and fetch the chair by themselves in case the other

---

1 The aforementioned considerations are a combination of semiotics: the study of how language produces meaning through signs in situated contexts (de Saussure, 1977), and interpretive anthropology which assumes that 'culture' is a text to be interpreted symbolically (Geertz, 1973). The manager's and researcher's task is thus to uncover and learn the 'grammar' behind the cultural language, as symbolically expressed. Or, in other words, cross-cultural interactions will go wrong if people do not share the same symbolic cultural language and fail to learn the respective other cultural language.

person moves too slowly. By triggering the same response/action also within one's own person, the meaning becomes significant or symbolic.

Herbert Blumer proposed three premises upon which symbolic interactionism rests:

1. Individuals act based on the meaning that things have for them.
2. Meaning results from the social interaction between individuals.
3. Individuals modify meanings through interpretative processes when they encounter new situations and things (Blumer, 1986: 2).

Central to symbolic interactionism is thus not only meaning but also how people 'enact' meaning by taking up certain 'roles'. Roles, such as 'manager' or 'employee', inform how people interact because they create certain expectations and templates of how people 'should' behave in certain situations (Goffman, 1959). Symbolic interactionism can therefore shed light onto how individuals communicate with each other, act upon things, interpret the actions of the others, and develop new ways of acting and behaving in various situations.

> **Symbolic meaning** Invisible meaning attached to visible expressions of culture which only a cultural insider can decode

How meaning is transmitted: Language, being-in-the world and technology

As Figure 6.4 suggests, meanings are dynamic and emerge in context. One person codes culture symbolically, in order to signify something deeper, the other person – ideally – decodes the sign accordingly, thus interpreting what is signified as it was originally intended. Yet, what are the options for coding and transmitting meaning?

One way of producing meanings is language – how people talk about reality, also shapes how they experience this reality. Major focus points of interpretive CCM are therefore textual analyses, discourse (speech events, but also the conditions framing a speech event), narrative (verbal communication) and stories.

Another way is how people experience the world via the senses (being-in-the-world, also referred to as phenomenology), how they present themselves to each other (gestures, body posture, distance, dress) and how they interpret these features in others.

A third way by which meaning is symbolically interacted is the material world. People interpret the objects which they have created, and technology with which they interact. At the same time, meaning also emerges from objects and technology and influences people.[2]

> ## Link to Practice/Student Activity 6.2: Communication and Meaning in Context
>
> Relevant ways of signifying meaning are also **proxemics**, the culturally learned ideas and practices of which distance to keep in which context (Hall, 1966), and **chronemics**, the culturally learned ideas and practices of how to deal with time (Hall, 1976). Both have been introduced in Chapter 5 as a functionalist CCM tool. However, if applied from a different angle, they also contribute to an interpretive CCM.
>
> Revisit 'the culture as communication approach' of Chapter 5. This section summarizes Edward T. Hall's idea that invisible symbolic meaning is expressed and interpreted by means of communication. Or, to put it another way, culture can only be deduced from the acts communicating it. With this interpretive understanding, re-read this section and re-consider all four of Hall's communicative dimensions: time, space, context and the speed of information. Next, answer the following questions:
>
> - How might a person used to M-time *perceive* a person used to P-time, and vice versa? Which misinterpretations are likely because time *means* different things to each of the individuals involved? Which strengths of the other person might remain hidden to the other person?
> - Answer the same questions also for space, context and the speed of information.

Meaning beyond understanding

Out of the previous sections emerges the question of whether interpretation and experience are reflexive or pre-reflexive. In other words, to what degree can people become aware of how they interpret and experience the world? Do they know which cultural meanings they transmit and receive, and are they aware of how they code and de-code meaning, and of what shall be signified by what they do?

Two philosophical traditions come to different conclusions here: *Hermeneutics* (Gadamer, 2013; Schleiermacher, 1998) proposes that people seek to and are able

---

2 Traditionally, interpretive CCM focuses mainly on language and meaning, based on the philosophical tradition of hermeneutics, i.e. the search for understanding meaning – see Cardel Gertsen and Zølner, 2020. Being-in-the-world (phenomenology), as well as objects/technology, are additions of the author, based on the understanding that contemporary CCM conditions require the acknowledgement of both.

to understand meaning; conversely, *phenomenology* (Heidegger, 2005; Husserl, 1970; Merleau-Ponty, 1965) proposes that people *experience* the world via their senses, and that it is via this pre-reflexive being-in-the-world (and not via a conscious search for understanding meaning) that people 'know' what the world 'means'. For example, hermeneutics might focus on how people reflect and talk about a stone and its potential purposes and thus give 'meaning' to it, whereas phenomenology proposes that people can only 'know' what a stone 'means' when they stumble upon it.

For the cross-cultural manager, this implies that they might need to look for interpretive trigger points outside of what people say, reflect upon or are aware of in order to assess and manage the situation. For example, there are powerful sensory experiences associated with other cultures, such as how a country 'smells', how the temperature 'feels'. The US-American global head of production recalls these experiences (quote 1), and one can assume that they have contributed to shaping his picture of 'how the Indian site can manage Alpha', regardless of whether he is aware of this effect or not.

Link to Practice/Student Activity 6.3: Sensory Experiences in CCM

Reflect upon your own being-in-the-world. Has it ever happened to you that you experienced a powerful sense of 'feeling at home' and/or 'experiencing difference' in a situation based on sensory experiences? If so, write them down. Keep them for a follow-up activity.

Culture in context

Symbolic cultural expressions, regardless of whether people are aware of them or not, emerge in a certain situation and under certain boundary conditions. Acknowledging **context** is thus central to an interpretive CCM.

Context The factors influencing a situation and how it is interpreted

Context can be differentiated into immediate, wider, virtual and communicative factors.

- Relevant immediate context factors are, for example, time, place and people involved. A management meeting is different if held in different locations or if conducted by different people. Even if both of the previous are the same, then the point in time of the meeting will matter.
- Relevant wider context factors are, for example, the organizational unit, corporate structures and hierarchies, the professional background of those involved, the status of the organization (stability, change, crisis), and the wider societal, political, economic and legal structures wherein the organization or company operates.

- Additionally, virtual interactions have become increasingly relevant to management. Therefore, also features of the virtual environment, the technology used (and its potential failures), and dispersion factors such as time-zone differences need to be taken into account.
- Finally, the communicative context is shaped by the language(s) spoken, the decisions made regarding language (e.g. which language should be the language of choice for international interactions), and the communicative media used (e.g. e-mail, spoken language, written reports). In case of virtual interactions, also the richness of communication needs to be considered (meeting virtually is 'richer' than sending e-mails because a virtual meeting also involves non-verbal communication and enables the synchronous exchange of messages).

Culture in context (see Figure 6.5) thus implies that a group of people share a certain way of experiencing reality at least to a certain extent (their cultural backpacks are similar). Thus, they interpret and act upon what is happening in context in similar ways.

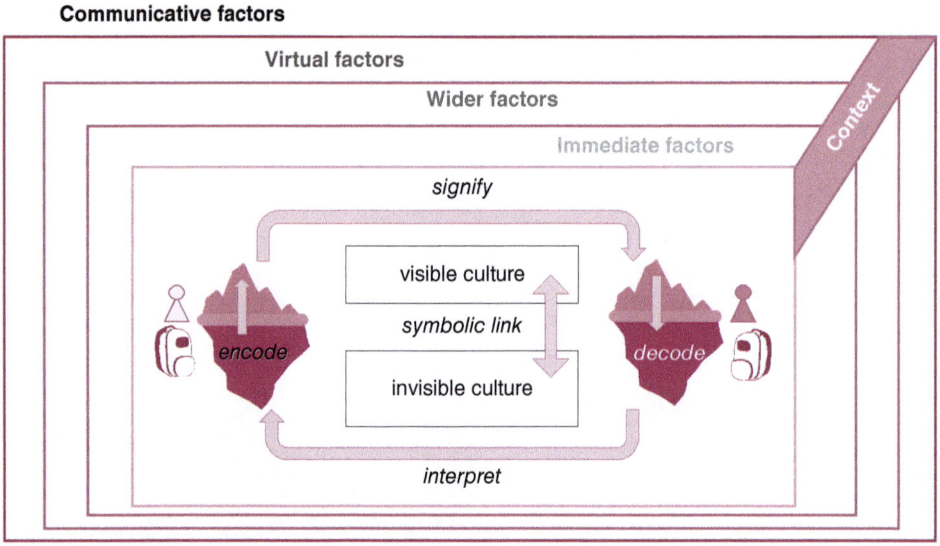

Figure 6.5 Meaning-making in context

> **Framing** The (selective) process by which people assign meaning in context, based on what they culturally know

Framing refers to the processes by which experience is put into context. For example, the global head of production has learned certain ways of 'how to see a good project leader'. These are his

frames of reference for making sense of the situation, and he relates current experiences back to this frame.

Recontextualization (Brannen, 2004) is the ongoing process through which meaning is altered when ideas, expectations or practices travel across cultural contexts, such as teams, corporate sites, companies, industries or countries. As a result, the same visible aspects of culture, e.g. a certain verbal expression or a certain way of doing things, might be interpreted in new, unforeseen ways, based on other, culturally learned meanings, which were already present in the new context. If this happens, **meaning negotiation** is required: via interacting, people have to figure out which meanings to ascribe to the situation. Figure 6.5 is thus also a way of understanding processes of meaning negotiation by which new 'frames' are created (meaning-making).

> **Frames of reference** The socially learned categories into which people categorize their experiences
>
> **Recontextualization** The ways in which meaning changes to fit another context
>
> **Meaning negotiation** The cross-cultural interactions across divergent frames by which new meaning is made

In the case of project Alpha, the US-American global head of production's sensemaking is informed by what he *knows* about how to lead a project this size, and what he *thinks* he knows is cultural: it comes from experience in context. Being faced with a specific question – can the Indian site manage the project? – he re-applies previous frames of reference to the situation; yet, they do not fit anymore, because what 'good project management' means and how it is signified and deciphered has been re-contextualized.

STUDENT ACTIVITY 6.4

Project Alpha in Context

Task 1

This task trains your ability to identify culture in context. For doing so, go back to the Opening Case and your notes from the previous activities. Next, try to identify which context factors might influence the sensemaking of the people involved.

(Continued)

The task is not to *prove* that a certain context factor *determines* individual and collective sensemaking (humans are no victims of culture), but rather to come to plausible assumptions by means of which interpretive CCM links individuals, immediate and wider context, and objects and technology.

Task 2

This activity enables you to become aware of how you yourself frame and contextualize meaning. There is no perspective 'free of culture', nonetheless people tend to view others as 'more limited by culture' than themselves. This activity helps you to overcome this danger of seeing culture only in others, and not in yourself.

a. Think about your own ideas of *what Project Alpha means*. What do you believe in?
   - Why did the previous project develop a cost overhead of 60,000 USD?
   - What should be done to make sure that project Alpha is carried out excellently by the Indian site?

b. Figure out what makes you interpret the situation in these ways, by means of questions such as:
   - Which interpretations about project Alpha seem 'true' to you the most? Why?
   - Which interpretations about project Alpha seem the least 'true' to you? Why?
   - Which previous experiences and presumed 'knowledges' might have contributed to why you interpret the status of project Alpha in such a way?

Engaging in Intercultural Interactions

People's sensemaking abilities are informed and, thus, limited by their cultural glasses. When interacting across cultures, it is difficult for them to grasp what could be beneficial, advantageous or potentially even better about an alternative idea or way of how to do things. Yet, if they engage with and relate to the other, initial cross-cultural differences might give way to new *inter*cultural meanings. Figure 6.6 visualizes this process.

Interpretive CCM

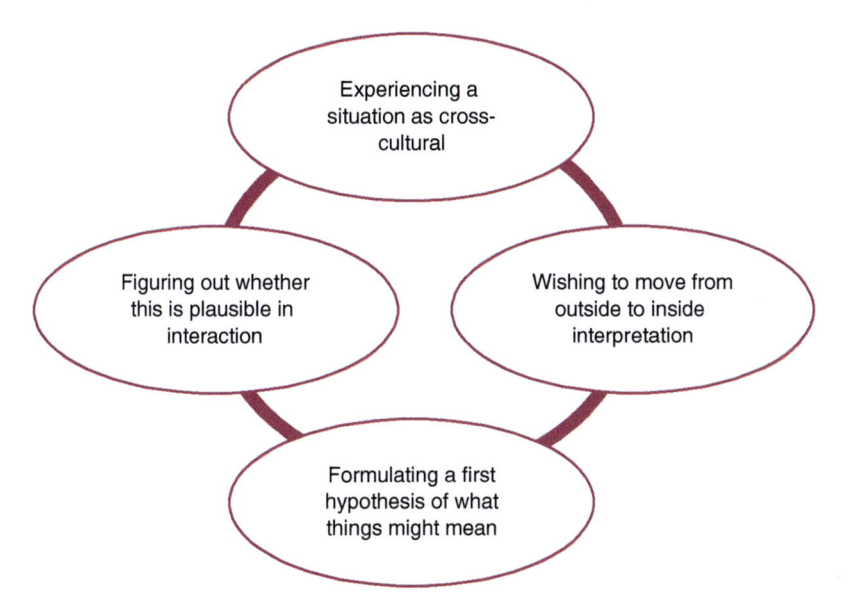

```
        ┌─────────────────┐
        │ Experiencing a  │
        │ situation as    │
        │ cross-cultural  │
        └─────────────────┘
       /                   \
┌──────────────┐      ┌──────────────┐
│ Figuring out │      │ Wishing to   │
│ whether this │      │ move from    │
│ is plausible │      │ outside to   │
│ in interaction│     │ inside       │
│              │      │ interpretation│
└──────────────┘      └──────────────┘
        \                   /
        ┌─────────────────┐
        │ Formulating a   │
        │ first hypothesis│
        │ of what things  │
        │ might mean      │
        └─────────────────┘
```

Figure 6.6 **The circle of intercultural interactions**

The description of a situation and how it is interpreted is usually experienced as one. For example, meeting a person might give you a somewhat 'strange' feeling, yet, you might not know what action on the part of the other person (or yourself) creates this feeling. The cycle of intercultural interaction helps you differentiate between the situation and how it is interpreted from emic and etic perspective. It is a model that improves your CCM skills in action. These are the steps involved:

- A situation is experienced as cross-cultural: describe what happens accurately.
- The first interpretation arises from how the other behaviour is not what it should be: become aware of it.
- Acknowledge that the immediate outside (etic) interpretation is insufficient because it fails to acknowledge the emic meanings behind the other person's action.
- Recognize that you need to try to step into the other person's shoes and view the situation from their perspective: what could be reasons for this to 'make sense' to the other?
- For achieving this crucial step, build first hypotheses of what motivates the other person.
- Put these hypotheses into practice via own behaviour and further interaction, and, this way, test them.

The required mindset behind this process is the insight that, 'what other people do must make sense to them', even though I (as an outsider) cannot see this 'sense' behind their actions, and even though people themselves might not be fully aware of it.

The starting point: Cross-cultural differences as experienced in the situation

From an interpretive perspective, cross-cultural situations are a constant process of experiencing and making sense of difference in context. The starting point can be any interaction between people. Two scenarios are possible:

- If the situation evolves as expected, culture is likely to remain unnoticed – 'this is just the way we normally do things around here'; the situation is just 'cultural'. For example, the global head of production might be so preoccupied with his own way of doing things that he does not even notice potential alternatives. In companies, this often happens if those with superior authority ('the bosses') do not give others room for bringing alternative solutions to a situation.
- If the situation is perceived as 'this is *not* how we normally do things around here' by some of those involved, it is experienced as *cross*-cultural. This is then the starting point for the next step – interpretation and sensemaking – as immanent in the quotes regarding project Alpha.

Project Alpha is unique and new to all involved, and established ways of 'how to normally do things' fail to make sense out of the situation. Therefore, the situation is experienced as 'cross-cultural' by those involved. The task is now to clearly describe what happens, without mixing this description up with interpretations.

Interpretation, part 1: Etic shortcomings

Interpretation tends to begin with an outside (etic) view on what other people do. People are interpreted based on one's own backpack, not based on what they carry to the situation. Therefore, difference, when experienced, is not just an objective and rational category. It might challenge oneself, and it might be experienced as scary or even threatening. Interpretive CCM takes this into account.

For example, the US-American head of global production clearly sees that there is a certain 'Indian' way of how to interact with customers, Yet, he cannot imagine that this way of doing things might be a good or even superior way of doing things, because if he were to entertain this possibility, he would also have to question his own way of doing things. Thus, he proceeds with the 'safer' alternative, namely judging the Indian team from his own perspective. Such an approach which imposes one's own culture as the measuring rod on other cultures is called ethnocentrist.

Ethnocentrism

Ethnocentrism refers to 'a view of things that one's own group is the centre for everything, and all others are scaled and rated with reference to it' (Sumner, 1906: 13). It lets people undervalue alternative cultural orientations and to view their own approach as superior. For example, if the trunk of the elephant is 'normal', and if this idea is not questioned, then anyone arguing for the need to view it from its tail would be 'strange'. For example, headquarters' representatives might be so sure of their own superiority that they lose sight of local employees' needs (see also Perlmutter and Heenan, 1974).

> **Ethnocentrism** Measuring others against the scale and in terms of one's own culture

Essentially, ethnocentrism means looking down on other cultures. It overshadows a more objective description of the situation, and it also prevents people from seeing what could be good about another viewpoint or behavioural style ('what is good about the Indian way of doing things?') and how this could enrich oneself ('what could the American global head of production learn?').

Othering and saming

Othering and **saming** (see Spotlight below) describe the self-related purposes of ethnocentrist tendencies, and they often go hand in hand. Basically, they involve the construction of a single cultural demarcation line, by which two presumably homogeneousand irreconcilably 'different' groups of 'they' and 'we' are created. Both processes are somewhat artificial because those who are now perceived as 'others' are never merely different, and they are also not a homogeneous mass of people. Likewise, those who are now the 'we' are never merely similar, and they, too, are not a homogeneous mass of people. Processes of othering and saming thus make other people more alien than they actually are (they are only perceived as an artificially coherent mass of 'them'), and they also affirm an artificially coherent group of 'us' as superior.

> **Othering** Making others more alien then they actually are, often in order to maintain one's own position or identity

> **Saming** Making oneself and others more similar than they actually are, often in order to maintain one's own position or identity

For example, when employing an external project leader, the US-American head of production proceeds from the assumption that the Indian team-members are less capable of handling project Alpha on their own – he makes them the 'other'. When doing so, he places himself into a presumably superior group of 'we' and distances himself from the thus constructed 'others'. He thus simplifies both categories, stressing the difference across them and neglecting the variance within them. By **saming** the members of each group, he erects 'cultural containers' in a situation wherein culture in context is much more complicated (see quote 6). This enables him to upload the image of himself being more experienced and his superiority being justified.

Because of these self-related purposes, it might thus even happen that difference is exaggerated and ascribed to the wrong root causes. Therefore, is 'the Indian team' *really* different because of 'Indian culture' (and is macro-culture even the right level of culture to be considered?), or is this just the explanation promoted by the US-American head of production, for reasons related to his own interpretive needs?

Spotlight: Social Identity Theory

Social identity theory is a way of explaining the behaviour across small groups (inter-group behaviour). It was developed by social psychologists Henri Tajfel and John Turner (1986) who showed by means of social experiments that students who were put into different groups – without any information as to what makes these groups different – started to behave *as if these groups were different*. Tajfel and Turner observed both a tendency to exaggerate the differences between one's own and other groups (other groups are made more 'different' than they actually are; people are 'othered'), and a tendency to exaggerate the similarities among the members of one's own group (the own group is made more similar than it actually is; people are 'samed'). From a cross-cultural perspective, this implies that people are likely to exaggerate the differences across cultures, and to neglect the variance within them once they have 'identified' themselves as part of a certain culture.

Tajfel and Turner identify three underlying processes, namely

- *social categorization* – the process of deciding which group one belongs to
- *social identification* – the tendency to identify with this group as soon as one is part of it, and to take over characteristics, attitudes and behavioural aspects of this group
- *social comparison* – the process by which one's own concept of self is increased via belonging to this group (creation of Us) and via identifying others as negatively different (creation of Them).

Social comparison creates the distinctiveness of the in-group; one can only identify as 'someone' if one identifies others as 'different'.

Tajfel and Turner also found out that, when being offered gratification (e.g. money), a group was more likely to choose a gratification that maximized the difference compared to another group, then to choose the highest gratification in absolute terms. For example, instead of choosing 30 USD for their in-group and 20 USD for their respective out-group, students would rather choose 20 USD for themselves and 5 USD for the other group.

In psychology, this has been understood as **similarity-attraction phenomenon**. Those who perceive each other as similar are attracted to each other in the sense that they favour their own group, are also more willing to work together, and that they trust each other more.

> **Similarity-attraction phenomenon** Human tendency to be attracted to others who are similar to themselves in relevant aspects

People then try to affirm the sameness of this in-group and tend to ascribe difference towards other out-groups to certain, sometimes arbitrary markers. For example, in the Tajfel and Turner experiment, students were simply 'told' to be in one group or the other. However, in the process, these distinctions then became 'reality' via how students interpreted them and interacted with each other.

Naïve realism

When viewing the world through their cultural glasses, people are often unaware of the perspectivity and positionality of the reality which they experience. Rather, they assume that this is an objectively and universally 'true' reality, a limitation referred to as naïve realism. **Naïve realism** is the 'taken-for-granted belief that the way in which we perceive the world is how the world actually is' (McCurdy et al., 2005: 9). For project Alpha, this implies that those involved are not aware of the fact; none of them sees the whole of project reality, because of their own, cultural, perspective.

> **Naïve realism** Unquestioned belief that reality really *is* as it is perceived

Native categories

Naïve realism might result in **native categories**, that is, taken-for-granted cultural assumptions (Moore, 2015; based on Buckley and Chapman, 1997) which are not questioned anymore by a group of people and which thus constitute 'cultural blind-spots'.

> **Native categories** Taken-for-granted cultural assumptions of a person or group

For example, the US-American head of global production *really* believes that the Indian team is less capable of managing project Alpha, and the ways in which he interprets the objective facts of project Alpha support him in this viewpoint. However, this is not the only fathomable interpretation. The Brazilian member of the board, for example, identifies the global head of production's statement as othering, and the Indian global project manager points out the negative job-related consequences of it.

> ### STUDENT ACTIVITY 6.5
>
> ### The Shortcomings of Etic Interpretations
>
> Re-investigate the Opening Case and figure out:
>
> - Which native categories remain unquestioned (and by whom)?
> - Which naively realistic practices/ideas about project reality can you identify?
> - Which incidents of othering can you identify?
> - What is the danger to the project should some perspectives become dominant?
> - Which practices/ideas about project reality should you support or at least further investigate in order to balance project reality, as socially constructed?

Interpretation, part 2: Approximating emic meanings

Ethnorelativism Judging other cultural standpoints in their own (emic) terms

The general goal of an interpretive CCM is achieving **ethnorelativism**, which is in many aspects the opposite of ethnocentrism. Ethnorelativism refers to the ability and practice of judging alternative cultural orientations in their own terms. Basically, it means to not interpret another person based on one's own standpoint, but to step into and walk in the other person's shoes, thus, to train oneself in looking at the world from their perspective, and to also translate the insights gained into action.

The starting point is the formulation of first hypotheses of why and how alternative ideas about 'what things mean' and practices of 'how things should be done' might make sense from the perspective of those promoting them. At this stage, it is of no importance that this interpretation is 'right' (from an interpretive perspective, there is no single right or wrong cultural reality) – it is the motivation and process of engaging in the task that counts. The idea is that such a process is enriching because it will enable people to pack new items into their cultural backpack and, thus, to enrich their managerial repertoire.

STUDENT ACTIVITY 6.6

Emic and Etic

Re-visit the Opening Case. In which quotes do you identify a person changing from etic to emic perspective, that is an incident of 'walking in the other person's shoes' and looking at the world from their perspective?

In practice, even a partial approximation of an alternative perspective is a good starting point for developing one's intercultural competencies. A person's guess does not have to be 'perfect' but it should be offered from an attitude that values the other position and perspective or that tries to give positive meaning to a difference that is experienced as difficult.

Building new hypotheses

From an interpretive perspective, cross-cultural differences in a situation are simply those differentiating lines which a certain number of people in a situation have highlighted above others, thus creating a simplified picture of 'us' (who are 'the same') versus 'them' (who are 'different'). The purpose of this simplification is to be able to deal with an otherwise too complex and too uncertain cultural reality. The explanations used for differentiating 'us' versus 'them' are on the one hand 'given' to those involved (people are products of existing ideas and about cross-cultural difference) and on the other hand 'created' by them (people are producers of emerging ideas about cross-cultural differences).

In any case, what managers believe about cross-cultural differences will influence their further interpretations and actions. For example, the Indian project leader's approach is viewed as different by the global head of production, and this might well be true – but it might just as well not be so. However, as soon as it is sufficiently believed that there is 'an Indian way of doing things', the differentiating lines of 'American' versus 'Indian' culture then influence how people behave in and judge the situation – they become the project's reality. Likewise, ideas such as 'the Indians are too inexperienced to handle the project', or 'Indians are less capable of managing the project efficiently and effectively' shape further actions. Managers might then decide to make project members aware of the cultural dimension scores of their respective countries, train the Indian team in the project management methods which they presumably lack or – as is done in this case – install an external project leader. Again, ideas become reality.

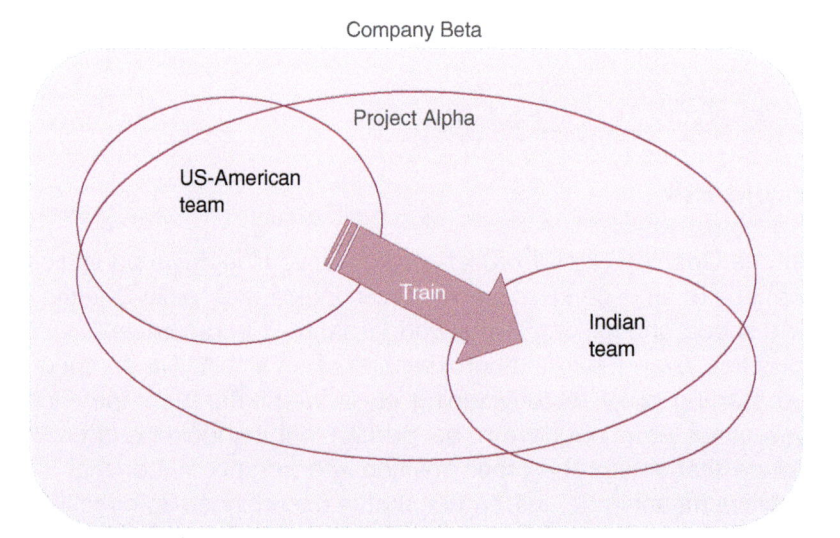

Figure 6.7 Assumptions about cross-cultural reality and their consequences

STUDENT ACTIVITY 6.7

Comparing the Societal Cultures of Project Alpha

Cultural dimensions are a major tool of comparative CCM; that is, an approach which investigates the relative differences in selected universal orientations across societal (macro-)cultures. If you are not certain about how cultural dimensions function and what they describe, revisit Chapter 5 (Functionalist CCM).

Consider the cultural dimension scores for India, Brazil, France and the USA. Use either the cultural dimensions by project GLOBE or the scores by Hofstede (you will find the relevant databases on the internet).

1. Which relative differences do these cultural dimensions describe? Build hypotheses of how the cultural dimension scores of their respective societal cultures might influence the actions and interpretations of those involved (e.g. French project leader, US-American team and head of production, Indian global project leader).

2. Next, come to managerial conclusions. Assuming that it is, indeed, relative difference in macro-cultural dimensions which impacts on project Alpha – what should be done about the project?

Also consider the GLOBE study leadership dimensions. Which leadership style is considered to be outstanding in France, India, Brazil and the USA? Answer questions 1) and 2) for relative differences in accepted leadership behaviour and leadership ideals in the respective countries as well.

Cultural dimensions or cultural value orientations are thus one hypothesis to be tested by the cross-cultural manager. They can provide one with first clues as to what things might mean from another person's perspective, even though there were not intended to be used in such a way.

However, as interpretivism suggests, there are always other potential realities. Part of the cross-cultural manager's task is thus also to consider how it is *not* macro-cultural differences which impact the project negatively but, for example, insufficient financial accounting procedures (the Indian project team leader mentions this aspect). Out of this exercise might then emerge a more complex picture of the same reality, for example, as depicted in Figure 6.8 below.

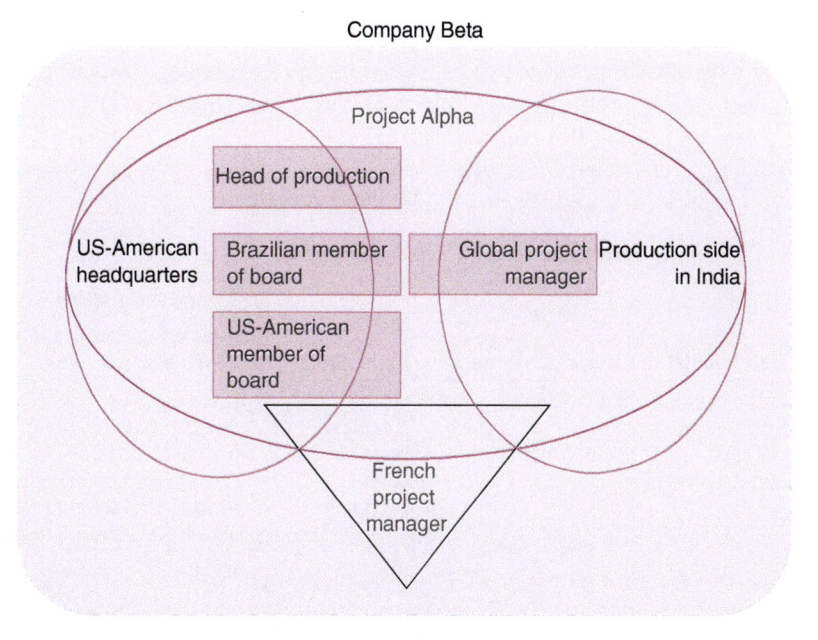

Figure 6.8 Another cross-cultural map of project Alpha

STUDENT ACTIVITY 6.8

What Happens, and What Does it Mean, and Why and for Whom?

This activity trains your ability to assess how people interpret reality. This interpretive skill is the basis for any further managerial action taken.

Re-read the Opening Case with the understanding that it contains both facts about project reality (what is happening?) and subjective interpretations of project realities (what does it mean, and for whom?).

1. Write down those aspects of the case which are objective, i.e. the indisputable facts about project Alpha. Reflect upon what you found. Is it more or less than you expected? How difficult was it to make the distinction between objective facts and subjective interpretations?
2. Consider the quotes regarding project Alpha in the Opening Case. Identify and write down or mark those parts of the quotes wherein you see that the speaker tries to 'make sense' out of the situation, i.e. wherein they give 'meaning' to it.
3. Try to link objective facts and subjective interpretations from the perspective of those involved. This means, write down the facts about the situation, and then try to figure out what the situation means, for whom and – most importantly – *why* it makes sense to the person to interpret reality in such a way. The question 'for whom' lets you identify the perspectivity of culture; different people see different things in the same situation. The question 'why' lets you grasp the positionality of culture – a person (subject) arrives at a certain perspective because of a certain logic which they construct.

Table 6.1 Mapping objective and subjective culture

What is happening?	What does it mean?	For whom?	Why does this make sense? (plausible logic from the subject's perspective)
Previous project was smaller than Alpha, yet 60,000 USD above budget.	'the Indian site is not capable of handling project Alpha'	US-American head of global production	• I was held responsible ('boss breathing down my neck') • I had to give up my power • Indian manager is too young (less experienced than I am) • …

Refining and contextualizing your categories of difference

Testing hypotheses about the situation in interaction enables managers to move from simplified, large categories of culture and cross-cultural differences to more complex, contextualized ones, or in other words, from simple, selective causalities (cultural dimensions) to an in-depth and more holistic understanding of culture. It prevents them from overstressing the importance of presumed cross-cultural demarcation lines and helps to deduce finer cross-cultural differences from the context itself. For example, at the beginning, the US-American head of global production or the Indian project leader of Alpha might work with large cultural categories such as 'Indian' versus 'US-American'. Then, they might come to realize that organizational hierarchies play a role. Out of this follow the categorizations 'headquarters' versus 'subsidiary'. Next, they might see how people are not only the same because of a shared nationality or organizational location; they might also differ because of age, experience, profession, hierarchical position and so on – a step towards even smaller and more refined categories.

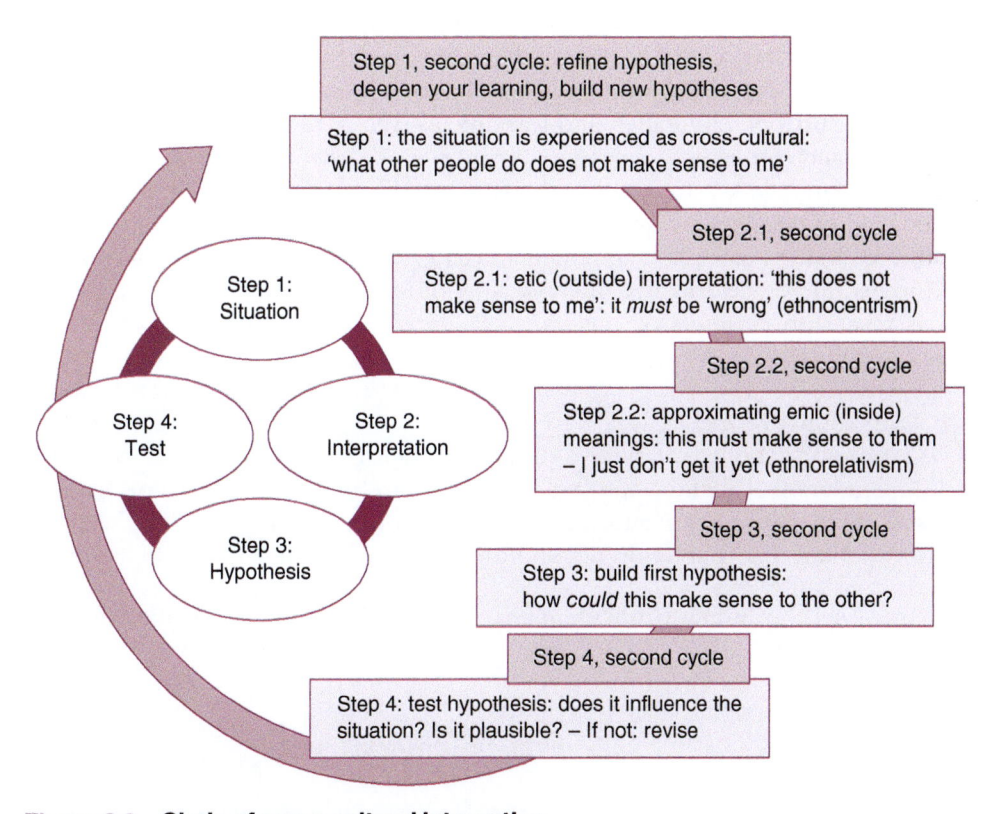

Figure 6.9 Circle of cross-cultural interaction

> **STUDENT ACTIVITY 6.9**
>
> ### Is the Indian Style of Leading the Project *Really* Different?
>
> You have by now put a lot of effort into your analysis of project Alpha. With this expertise in mind, is the Indian style of leading the project *really* different because of culture, or are there alternative explanations of what is going on? Secondly, is the Indian way of executing the project *really* inferior, or is it just that some people need to believe that this is the case? Provide examples from the quotes to make your point.

Cross-cultural management as the negotiation of meaning

From an interpretive perspective, cross-cultural managers are asked to negotiate meaning across perceived differences and beyond culture-specific frames and prevalent ideas of difference, and to also design the organizational context in such a way that this can be achieved. On the micro-level, this requires a managerial mindset and ensuing practices of exploration and learning, as well as the willingness to act as an interpreter and mediator of meaning (Primecz et al., 2009). On the meso-level, this requires organizational structures and communication channels which allow for the negotiation of meaning, an appropriate choice of the language(s) of communication (Barmeyer and Davoine, 2019; Brannen and Salk, 2000), and appropriate technology.

Another, more performance-oriented, way of looking at how to negotiate meaning is related to its intended outcomes. These can be differentiated broadly into four categories:

1. Adaptation: one group adapts to the other.
2. Compromise: both groups give up part of their position.
3. Separation: the work of both groups is split up into distinct work packages so that there is no need for further negotiation of meaning.
4. Innovation: a new solution beyond the initial approaches is developed.

Together, these techniques provide managers with the tools for negotiating meaning across cultures.

Chapter Summary

This chapter has introduced the main premises, as well as the main focus points, of interpretive CCM. It has shown how the interpretive researcher and cross-cultural manager are interested in how reality is *perceived* (and by whom it is perceived similarly and differently), and for what reasons (due to which cultural 'glasses'), and under which boundary conditions. Out of the idea that culture and cross-cultural differences are constructed socially follows the need to acknowledge the positionality and perspectivity of culture, to entertain multiple possibilities of difference, and to deduce cultural demarcation lines from the context itself. Out of this follow three recommendations for cross-cultural managers, namely to manage interpretive processes in interaction, to relate to the other and approximate emic meanings, to pay attention to the recontextualization and framing of meaning, and to refine and contextualize their categories of difference. Models, such as the circle of intercultural interaction, the cultural backpack and the cultural iceberg can serve as an entry point for doing so.

On a meta-level, the stories and activities of project Alpha also exemplified storytelling as both a key interpretive practice in which managers engage to make sense out of their cross-cultural reality, and also a key means for gaining insights into how people perceive and construct cross-cultural differences. The activities related to the multiple stories about project Alpha exemplified the required process of interpretive learning.

What managers can gain from interpretive CCM tools is the ability to experience more and more complex things in context, to relate to more and more diverse people, and to manage more contexts in more and more appropriate and effective ways – a constant process of personal growth.

Key Points

- Culture and cross-cultural differences are constructed socially.
- Culture emerges between people; it is inter-subjective.
- Meaning and experience in context are central to interpretive CCM.
- It is unclear whether and to what extent people are aware of how they construct, interpret and experience cultural meaning and ensuing similarities/differences.
- Much of cultural meaning is tacit; it cannot be put into words.
- Invisible and often tacit culture is signified by symbolic elements of visible culture.
- Only an insider to a cultural context can decode symbolic meaning.
- Outside (etic) perspectives are insufficient and often negative.
- The task is thus to change from outside (etic) to inside (emic) perspective.
- Context plays a key role in how meaning and experiences emerge. It needs to be differentiated into virtual/technological context, and micro-, meso- and macro-levels.
- Meaning is framed in context and is prone to recontextualization.
- Managers need to contextualize and refine the categories of difference from which they operate.
- Storytelling, as exemplified by project Alpha, is a key tool of interpretive CCM.

Review Questions

1. What are the main premises of an interpretive CCM?
2. How does culture emerge and manifest from an interpretive perspective?
3. What is meant by emic and etic, and how are these concepts central to an interpretive CCM?
4. What is meant by culture in context, and how is this focus central to an interpretive CCM?
5. What is meant by symbolic meaning, and how is symbolic meaning transmitted?
6. Why do cross-cultural managers need to be able to differentiate between emic and etic perspectives?
7. What can cross-cultural managers learn from engaging in intercultural interactions?
8. How shall cross-cultural managers engage in intercultural interactions?
9. How can cross-cultural managers refine and contextualize their categories of difference?
10. How do the functionalist and the interpretive perspective complement each other, or, in other words, what can *only* be uncovered by employing interpretive tools, and what is missed by using them?

Opening Case Revisited

Project Alpha represents a common scenario in the contemporary business world: a cross-cultural, cross-site, cross-functional, knowledge-intensive cooperation in a multinational company, with a common goal to be achieved. These scenarios cannot be assessed by means of simple categories of difference. Rather, events unfold, and people contribute to them and make sense of them. The benefit of interpretive CCM tools is that they uncover the inevitable blind-spots from which managers and organizations operate in such scenarios. Rather than providing definitive answers, the interpretive perspective makes it more certain that the right kind of assumptions are questioned, that the right kind of questions are being asked, and that all required perspectives are included. It also acknowledges how people make sense of reality by means of stories. Project Alpha highlights how managers are essentially storytellers.

For Project Alpha, there is no definitive answer as to what constitutes project reality. Is the external project manager more beneficial than harmful to the project? Is the global head of production's attitude towards the 'Indian team' mere arrogance, or does his experience, indeed, enable him to know how to perform better? Is the Indian way of managing the project different because of societal culture, and, if so, is this way of doing things better, worse or simply different? These are the interpretive processes which need to be managed in the situation, and the more hypotheses those involved can entertain, the more they will see in the situation. Sustaining an interpretive mindset and 'puzzling with culture in context', rather than 'solving the problem' once and for all is thus the major implication of this case.

Closing Activity

Consider the aforementioned four potential outcomes of meaning negotiation for project Alpha. Based on your previous case analysis:

- Which outcome will be the best for whom, and why?
- Which outcome will be the best for project Alpha in general, and why?

Now, consider the stated micro- and meso-level requirements:

- What will it take to achieve the afore defined best possible outcome for project Alpha?
- Which skills do cross-cultural managers need to work towards this best outcome?
- What contextual requirements must be met so that this outcome can be achieved?
- Which technologies, e.g. for communication and collaboration, might be used?

Come up with a business case analysis and strategic suggestions for further development.

It is helpful to conduct this activity in two steps: first, individually, second, in groups. When starting to work on a group solution, also take note and reflect upon how subjective and inter-subjective interpretations of the task differ and interrelate.

Further Reading

Brannen, in her seminal study (2004), describes how meaning changes when travelling across cultures and contexts. In this case, it is what Disneyland stands for in different countries. Mahadevan (2011) considers engineering identities in a multifunctional and multi-sited engineering project – another example of how 'we' and 'others' are made in interaction. Moore (2015) reflects upon native categories prevalent in a multinational corporation, in particular the idea that 'production work is nothing for women', and draws implications for a gender-aware and inclusive human resource management from there. An overview on the theoretical foundations of interpretive CCM can be found in Cardel Gertsen and Zølner (2020). The edited collection by Primecz et al. (2011) applies an interpretive lens to practical cases, and the editors also offer advice on how to negotiate meaning across cultures in practice (Chapters 1 and 12).

References

Barmeyer, C. and Davoine, E. (2019) 'Facilitating intercultural negotiated practices in joint ventures: The case of a French-German railway organization', *International Business Review*, 28(1): 1–11.

Berger, P. and Luckmann, T. (1966) *The Social Construction of Reality*. New York: Doubleday.

Blumer, H. (1986) *Symbolic Interactionism. Perspective and Method*. Berkeley: University of California Press. (1st edn, 1969)

Brannen, M.Y. (2004) 'When "Mickey" loses face: Recontextualization, semantic fit and the semiotics of foreignness', *Academy of Management Review*, 29(4): 593–616.

Brannen, M.Y. and Salk, J. (2000) 'Partnering across borders: Negotiating organizational culture in a German-Japanese joint-venture', *Human Relations*, 53(4): 451–487.

Buckley, P.J. and Chapman, M. (1997) 'The use of native categories in management research', *British Journal of Management*, 8(4): 283–300.

Cardel Gertsen, M. and Zølner, M. (2020) 'Interpretive approaches to culture: What is interpretive cross-cultural management?', in B. Szkudlarek, L. Romani, D.V. Caprar and J.S. Osland (eds), *The Sage Handbook of Contemporary Cross-Cultural Management*. London: Sage. pp. 34–50.

De Saussure, F. (1977) *Course in General Linguistics*. New York: Collins.

Emery, L.R. (2022) 'What modern arranged marriages really look like', *Brides*, 23 February. Available at: www.brides.com/story/modern-arranged-marriages [last accessed 31 July 2022].

Gadamer, H.G. (2013) *Truth and Method*. London: Bloomsbury Academic.

Geertz, C. (1973) *The Interpretation of Cultures, Selected Essays*. New York: Basic Books.

Goffman, E. (1959) *The Presentation of Self in Everyday Life*. New York: Doubleday.

Hall, E.T. (1966) *The Hidden Dimension*. Garden City: Doubleday.

Hall, E.T. (1976) *Beyond Culture*. Garden City: Doubleday.

Heidegger, M. (2005) *Die Grundprobleme der Phänomenologie*. Frankfurt am Main: Klostermann. (1st edn, 1927)

Husserl, E. (1970) *The Crisis of the European Sciences and Transcendental Phenomenology*. Evanston: Northwestern University Press. Originally published in German (1936) *Die Krise der Europäischen Wissenschaften und die Transzendentale Phänomenologie*. Belgrade.

Mahadevan, J. (2011), 'Engineering culture(s) across sites – implications for cross-cultural management of emic meanings', in H. Primecz, L. Romani, and S. Sackmann (eds), *Cross-Cultural Management in Practice: Culture and Negotiated Meaning*. London: Edward Elgar. pp. 156-174.

McCurdy, D.W., Spradley, J.P. and Shandy, D.J. (2005) *The Cultural Experience – Ethnography in Complex Society*. Long Grove: Waveland Press.

Mead, G.H. (1934) *Mind, Self and Society from the Standpoint of a Social Behaviorist*. Chicago: University of Chicago Press.

Merleau-Ponty, M. (1965) *Phenomenology of Perception*. London: Routledge & Kegan Paul.

Moore, F. (2015) 'Towards a complex view of culture: Cross-cultural management, "native categories", and their impact on concepts of management and organisation', in N. Holden, S. Michailova and S. Tietze (eds), *The Routledge Companion to Cross-Cultural Management*. London: Routledge. pp. 19–27.

Perlmutter, H.V. and Heenan, D.A. (1974) 'How multinational should your top managers be?', *Harvard Business Review*, 52(6): 121–132.

Pike, K.L. (1967) *Language in Relation to a Unified Theory of the Structures of Human Behavior*. The Hague: Mouton & Co. (1st edn, 1954)

Primecz, H., Romani, L. and Sackmann, S.A. (2009) 'Cross-cultural management research: contributions from various paradigms', *International Journal of Cross-Cultural Management*, 9(3): 267–274.

Primecz, H., Romani, L. and Sackmann, S.A. (eds) (2011) *Cross-Cultural Management in Practice: Culture and Negotiated Meanings*. Cheltenham: Edward Elgar.

Schleiermacher, F. (1998) *Hermeneutics and Criticism and Other Writings*. Cambridge: Cambridge University Press.

Sumner, W.G. (1906) *Folkways*. New York: Ginn.

Tajfel, H. and Turner, J.C. (1986) 'The social identity theory of intergroup behavior', in S. Worchel and W.G. Austin (eds), *Psychology of Intergroup Relations*. Chicago: Nelson-Hall. pp. 7–24.

Critical Cross-Cultural Management

7

Whom does CCM serve, and how does this happen?

Learning Objectives

After reading this chapter, you should:

- be aware of the multiple facets of power in CCM
- be able to identify power and its effects on CCM
- have encountered first tools to work towards a more balanced and inclusive CCM.

Reading Requirement

- You should have read Chapter 4 of this book.

Introduction

From a critical perspective, management is not just about functional factors such as performance, efficiency and effectivity (how management and business *is*). Rather, it involves the responsibility to question the status quo and to figure out how management and business *should* be in the best interest of all. Power, and the goal to improve the situation for those who are presently disadvantaged, is thus a key focus point of a critical management theory and practice. Key theories that have inspired critical CCM are postcolonial studies, critical theory, Marxism and postmodern thought (overview in Romani et al., 2018, 2020). The diverse approaches are united by the understanding that power inequalities – however conceptualized – and CCM are inseparable. This has implications for the role of the cross-cultural manager and researcher, understood as the involved person responsible for working towards a more equal and inclusive CCM.

Relevant critical considerations to be dealt with in this chapter are thus: What is power? What does a power-sensitive cross-cultural management involve, and what does this mean for the role of the cross-cultural manager? Critical CCM is thus like putting the bits and pieces of a power puzzle together, and the pieces of the Opening Case facilitate the development of this skill.

Engaging in critical CCM inevitably requires challenging one's own implicit assumptions, biases and stereotypes; it is a very personal, sometimes deep engagement with how one has learned to categorize the world, and oneself and others in it. In the process of challenging previously held assumptions, negative feelings might occur. The challenge of a critical CCM thus lies in facing what seems uncomfortable or even offensive. The goal is to move beyond these feelings by a differentiated understanding of how power and culture intersect in people's lives, on a level that is not only individual, but also systemic (part of the system). Out of this follow insights of how one may contribute to a change to the better and whose responsibility it is to do so.

Opening Case

CCM as a Power Puzzle

The critical search for the interrelations between power and CCM is like putting together bits and pieces of a power puzzle. The Opening Case will introduce relevant pieces, and your task is to put them together. By acquiring knowledge and engaging in activities throughout, you will train your ability to identify and manage power in CCM.

Piece 1

An African-American manager is sent to Paris by her company for three years. In the beginning, she speaks French with an American accent, and

(Continued)

is immediately identified as American. Over time, her foreign accent fades, and she notices an increase in negative interactions.[1]

Piece 2

An ethnic German professor teaches a Business Negotiation course in the French language in a highly subscribed trilingual Master's programme in International Management at a German university. 'We have several students from Cameroon,' he says, 'and they come with very poor skills. They don't speak any German, and their English and French is very bad. Our German students can hardly understand them, and it is the same for me.'

Piece 3

A female Tunisian engineer is employed as a doctoral researcher in a cross-national research project in the area of sustainable product development. The project is conducted in Tunisia and funded by the European Union. She says,

Whenever I meet someone from the European team, they ask me about Islam: 'Do you pray, why do you not cover your head, how come you are not shy, what does the Quran say about this and that?' And I have no idea of Islam, I am just me, I am a woman, I am from the city, I am an engineer. And now, I have to search the internet to come up with answers to all these religious questions I know nothing about, and this is taking me far too much time. And this is what I told one of the important European science ministers asking about how the project is going: 'See, you are saying that you are funding us because you want to support global sustainability. But actually, what you want is that *your people* learn about Islam and don't stereotype Muslims, and this is what you think we are there for. But we are not.'[2]

Piece 4

The annual corporate Christmas party takes place in a Hungarian multinational company. Employees are expected to attend and enjoy themselves. The party is not viewed as something 'religious' but simply as a way to build corporate team spirit.[3]

---

[1] This piece has been inspired by Kassis-Henderson and Cohen (2020): 12–21.
[2] Quote from unpublished interview with the Tunisian research engineer, interviewer J. Mahadevan (2014).
[3] This piece has been inspired by Hidegh and Primecz (2020).

Piece 5

LGBT+-friendly mosques have been founded in numerous cities around the globe.

Piece 6

A student from North Wales who describes himself as being 'working class' and who has never been far away from home receives a scholarship for a prestigious International Business programme at a cosmopolitan English university. During orientation week, he figures out that he is the only person in his year with no first-hand experience of any other country. He strongly feels that he is at a disadvantage, and the financially well-off, bicultural and/or well-travelled student crowd and staff from all over the globe who surround him seem to think so as well.

Piece 7

The Brazilian census conducted in regular intervals by the Brazilian Institute of Geography and Statistics (IBGE) knows five racial categories. These are branco (white), preto (black), pardo (brown), amarelo (yellow) and indígena (indigenous). People are asked to self-identify within these categories (Petrucelli, 2015).

Piece 8

In 1921, *The Story of the Irish Race: A Popular History of Ireland* (MacManus, 1921) was published.

STUDENT ACTIVITY 7.1

Grasping Power

Have a look at the pieces of the Opening Case. All of them are about power somehow. Your task is to figure out how exactly. At this point, however, it might still be unclear how power is part of these pieces. To identify power, you thus need to come up with first ideas of what the underlying 'problems' are which each piece refers to. Is there a certain inequality, an imbalance, an uneasiness, a majority–minority relation to be considered? Are there

(Continued)

unequal structures, divergent ideas about the situation, or different ways of how to handle the situation? Is the outcome of the situation already clear, or are its effects still in the making?

- What is each piece about? Write one sentence.
- What, if anything, is problematic about the situation described in the piece? Write one sentence.
- What, if anything, would you do about the piece? Write one sentence.
- How are these pieces connected? Visualize by means of a mind-map.

Keep your notes for the next activities.

What is Power? A Multi-Dimensional Approach

There are several, interrelated ways in which power has been approached in the social and managerial sciences. This section provides a very brief overview of them and thus lays the foundation for a critical CCM practice. When reading this chapter, keep your insights from Student Activity 7.1 in mind and try to identify to which dimension or facet of power a certain piece of the Opening Case refers.

Four properties of power

To understand how power is part of 'how we normally do things around here', it is helpful to differentiate the concept into *power, power over, power to* and *domination*.

The starting point is the insight that every person acts in certain so-called '**fields**' (Bourdieu, 1989), in which they make choices, interact and are judged by others. For example, a manager is acting in the field of management. The manager is judged against certain expectations and rules of practice, and will also orientate herself towards it. Fields are furthermore influenced by certain structures and other boundary conditions. For example, the labour law regulations in a country partly shape the work of the manager. Still, individuals have the freedom to act. They choose between different actions (scope of action), and, because others also act, the same actions can result in different outcomes. Person, sphere of action of others, field and boundary conditions are interdependent and mutually constitutive. In this way, fields are both an existing reality and something constantly 'in-the-making'.

Field A system of social positions that is structured by internal power relationships

The four properties of power are not an either/or, but interrelated. Together, they cover the whole bandwidth between power as an everyday interpersonal process and a fully discriminatory system. Out of this follows that power is not always negative. Rather, it is the specific field analysis which determines what, if anything, should be done about power.

Consider the example of two fictional managers, A and B, attending a meeting.

Power: Both managers state opinions in the meeting. A's actions affect B's scope of action, and vice versa. This is the 'normal' power of everyday life. Everyone possesses it and can act upon it. There is no clear or unified direction or intent of this power.

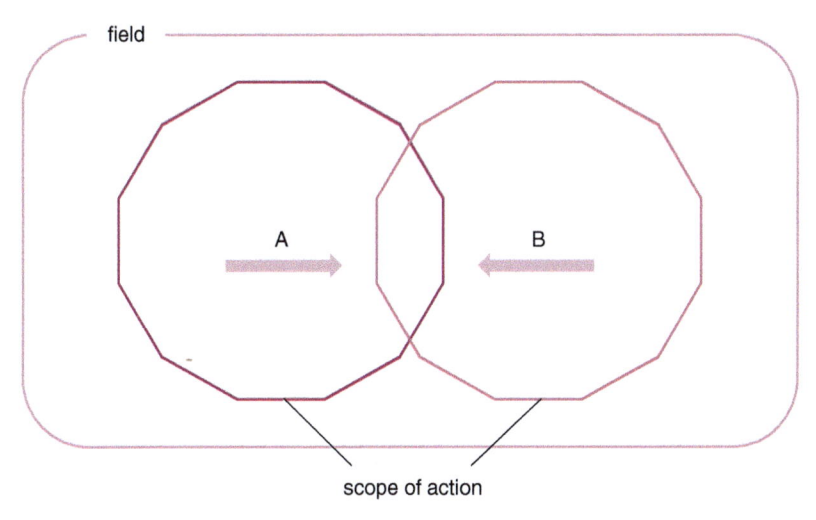

Figure 7.1 The everyday power of A and B

Power over: A wishes to convince B of a certain business strategy. A's actions then modify B's scope of action. Suddenly, B cannot 'just say something' anymore as whatever B says on the matter will be placed in relation to A's prior suggestion. The outcome of this suggestion could either be good or bad or none at all; the whole process is ongoing. Many actors have a say in it, and A might also change her power strategy. Still, 'power over' has a direction (it flows from A to B), and is thus more unequal or forceful as 'normal' power.

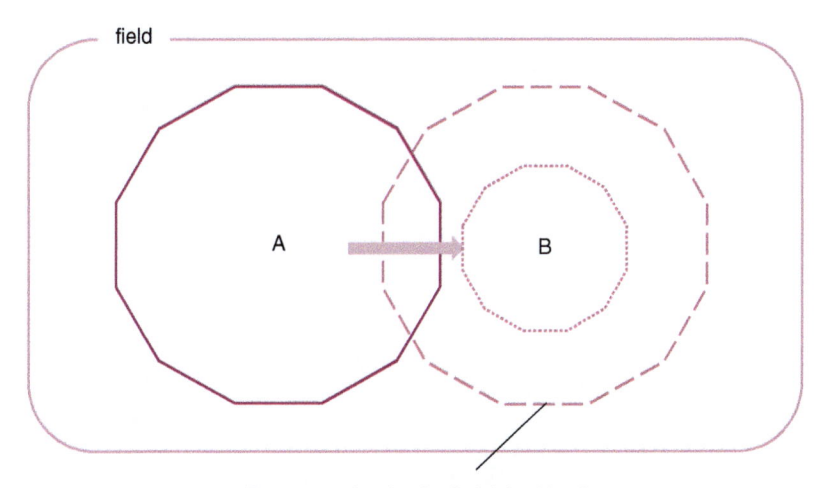

Figure 7.2 A exercises power over B

Power to: B speaks out against A's suggestion. This way, B might change A's power strategy or introduce new power strategies. This ability to resist, and subvert and change a system is called agency (Foucault, 1980).

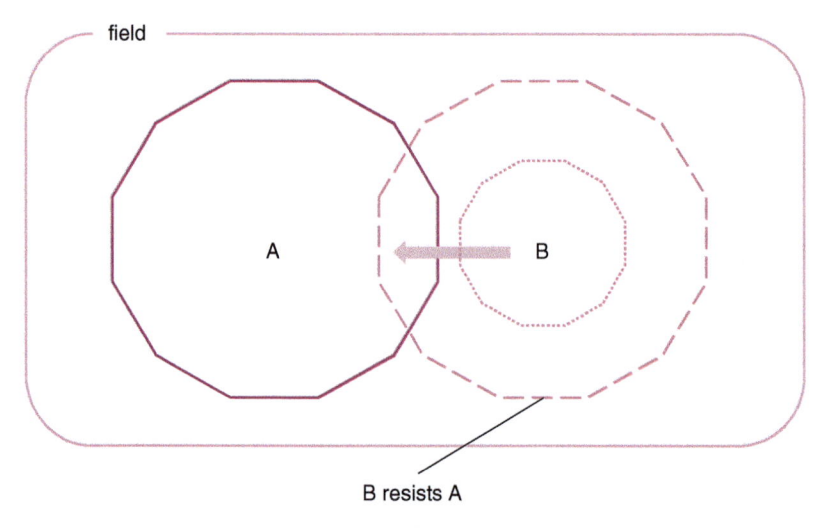

Figure 7.3 B's power to resist A's power over

Domination: B does not or cannot resist A's proposal, for example because everyone else agrees upon it, and because new business regulations are implemented to put the proposal into practice, even though it is harmful to B. This means that A modifies B's sphere of action with permanent consequences. Their power relations, and thus also the direction and effect of power, are fixed, and power becomes an unequal system which is to the advantage of A and to the disadvantage of B.

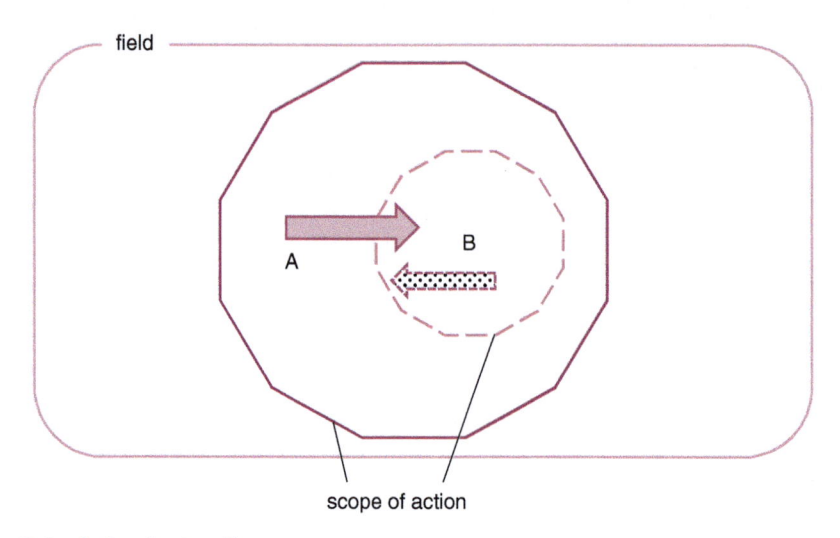

Figure 7.4 A dominates B

STUDENT ACTIVITY 7.2

A Multi-Dimensional Approach to Power

The previous paragraph introduced the four properties of power: *power, power over, power to* and *domination*. Revisit the pieces of the Opening Case and, for each of them, establish:

- What is the relevant field of this piece?
- Who are its actors? Which actors are missing?
- What are its boundary conditions?
- Which elements of *power, power over, power to* and *domination* can you identify?
- Where do these power elements originate from? Whom/what are they directed towards?
- Is the outcome of the power elements in each piece already fixed or are power relations and their effects still 'in-the-making'?

Visualize your analysis for each piece. Now, look back onto your outcome of the previous activities and answer the following question: How and in what aspects has your analysis changed or been improved? Which understanding of power did you add to your tool-box? What is still unclear?

Link to Practice: Whistleblowing

If an employee makes corporate wrongdoings public, this is known as whistleblowing. From a power perspective, whistleblowing is a reaction by which a person uses their personal ability (power to) to expose a certain corporate malpractice, thus challenging power over or even domination which would otherwise have gone unnoticed. In order to protect the whistleblower against negative corporate actions, many countries and regions, such as the United Kingdom (UK) or the European Union, have issued laws specifying a whistleblower's rights and also when and how whistleblowing is legal. You can look up the UK laws at: www.gov.uk/whistleblowing (UK Government, 2022).

Towards a Multifaceted Kaleidoscopic Practice

As the four properties of power suggest, identifying power effects in CCM is much like looking through a kaleidoscope as depending on how you turn it, the pieces of it are re-shuffled, and a different reality emerges. The effects of the kaleidoscope are largely unforeseen and you, as the person holding it, are not in full control of how the pieces are brought into place. The pieces are given, yet their position is not fixed; you shuffle them with a certain intention in mind, but this intention might not be put into effect.

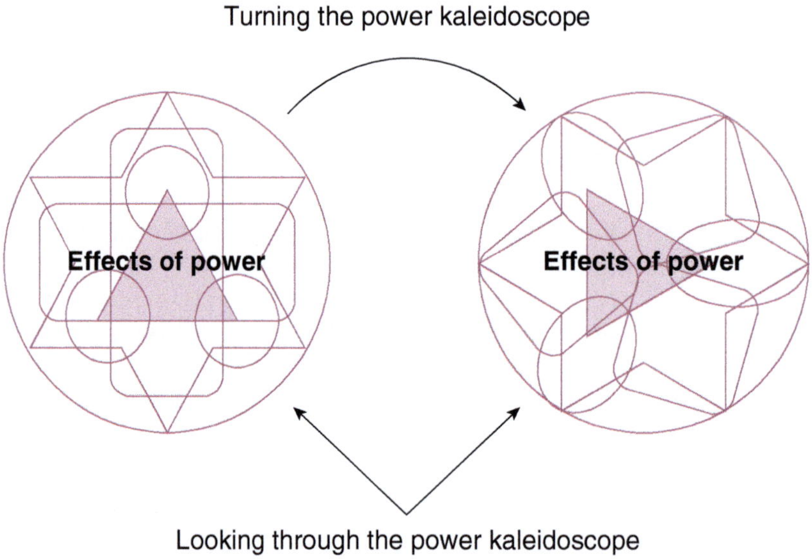

Figure 7.5 A power kaleidoscope

This section focuses on key pieces which should be part of your future kaleidoscopic managerial practice, and on general patterns of how the pieces might fall into place and what you should consider when shuffling them. Building on these insights, the section thereafter will then suggest how you view all pieces in light of each other.

Fact and discourse

Power, like culture, is both objective and subject to interpretation, with mutual interdependencies. For example, people might have certain ideas in mind about other groups of people, and these ideas influence how they act. If these effects then become 'real', power is an objective reality. This reality is then further experienced by people, who further act upon it.

Critical CCM

A term for how to grasp these inter-relations is **discourse**. From a narrow linguistic perspective, discourse only refers to language. From a wider cultural or social viewpoint, discourse involves a system of thought which informs peo-

> **Discourse** A system of thought which informs practice and vice versa

ple's socio-cultural practices, e.g. their habits, rituals, practices, routines, judgements, norms and many more, and which is, in return, informed by these practices.

Discourse is also a power mechanism, because once a certain 'way of doing things' has become normalized as part of the system of thoughts, it then might pre-structure further action and interpretation.

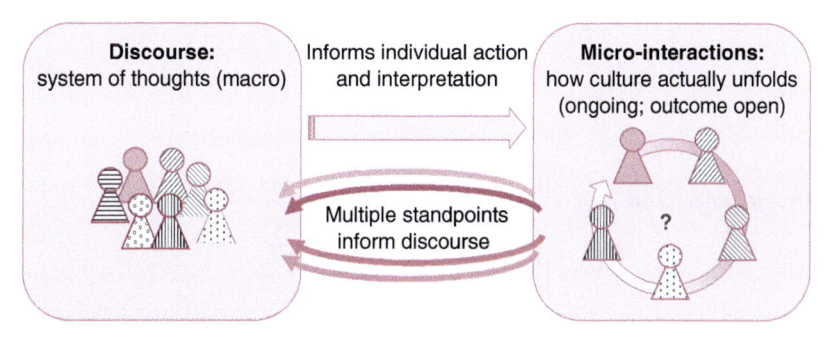

Figure 7.6 Discourse

What a critical cross-cultural manager thus needs to find out is: to what extent discourse is hegemonic. **Hegemonic discourse** implies that a general system of thought (macro) is more powerful than how culture unfolds in a situation (micro). The danger of hegemonic discourse is that it fixes micro-level interactions and prescribes their outcome. Dominant power relations emerge which further affirm hegemonic discourse, and alternative standpoints are not even considered anymore; they are assigned a position 'at the margins', or, in other words, they are marginalized, or even excluded.

> **Hegemonic discourse** A system of thought which has become dominant

For example, it is part of general discourse that successful international managers should be able to converse fluently in English. In today's world, fluency in English language comes in different shapes and varieties. For example, one might speak Australian, South African, Singaporean or Jamaican English, also those who learn English at school in most countries around the globe and speak it with the accent of their respective first languages. This discourse of 'English language fluency' is hegemonic, if it is also underpinned by a certain idea of how to speak English,

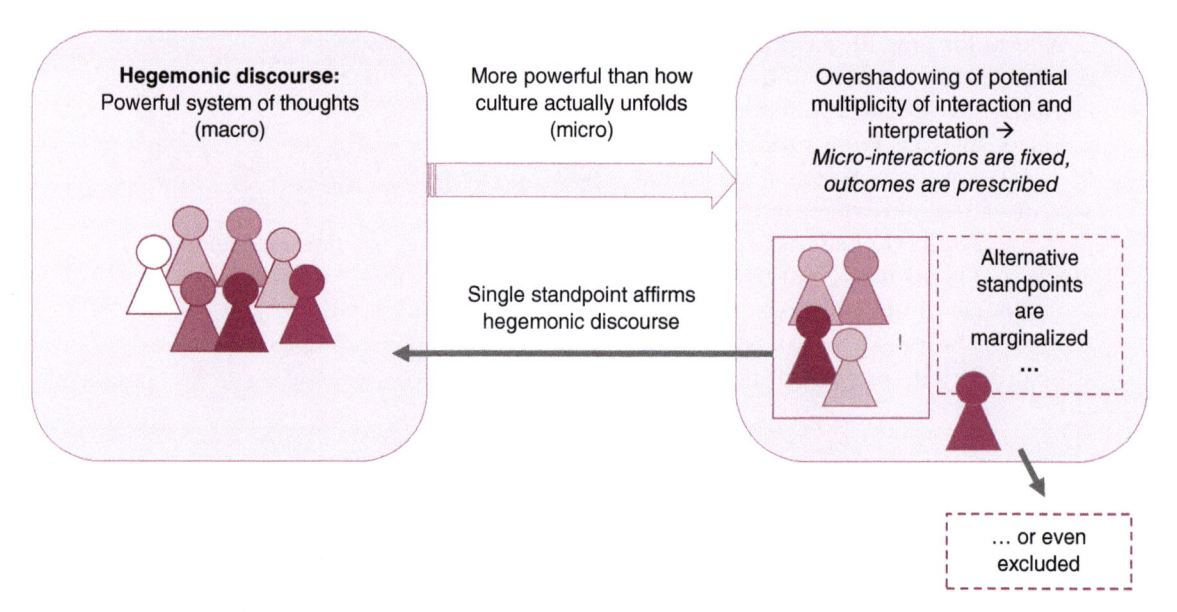

Figure 7.7 Hegemonic discourse

for example, as a first language, preferably with what is commonly perceived as 'upper-class' English or 'well-educated' US-American English. If this is the case, then a certain type of people would be excluded (those speaking English with alternative accents, dialects and sociolects, or as a second language) because they don't fit the dominant idea of how to identify 'English language fluency'. Regardless of how well they perform in the job interview or the skills which they have, it would already be clear from the first sentences spoken that this individual fits into the category of 'not being fluent enough'.

Therefore, the difference between 'normal' discourse and hegemonic discourse is that the first leaves the outcome of micro-interactions open and all people have the opportunity to contribute to the system of thought via their actions. This way, there is a multiplicity of standpoints, and the possibility to interpret discourse in more than one way and to contribute to a further development and change of discourse. Conversely, hegemonic discourse does not open up the discussion – it closes it. *Critical discourse analysis* (CDA, see Fairclough and Wodak, 1997) is a technique that traces such power effects of discourse. The next activity is based on it.

STUDENT ACTIVITY 7.3

The Power of Discourse

Revisit the pieces of the Opening Case. Consider whether and how each of them is characterized by 'normal' or hegemonic discourse. Clearly identify what is hegemonic about certain discourses, and also who is affirmed, marginalized and potentially excluded by them.

Habitus and the power of fields

A relevant insight from the previous study is that the perception of competencies is not objective but depends somehow on how a certain 'type of person' is perceived. For understanding this effect, Pierre Bourdieu proposed the concept of **habitus.**

> **Habitus** The fine distinctions by means of which social differentiation manifests

Habitus, or the fine distinctions

Habitus describes how fine social distinctions are inscribed into people. For example, the ways in which people dress, furnish their living room, speak, interact and so on is also indicative of social class, ethnicity, age, gender and so on. This is a relevant closure effect when it comes to work. A **closure effect** is a mechanism by means of which only some, but not all people are allowed to enter a field.

> **Closure effect** A social inequality mechanism which allows some, but not all people to enter a field

Simply speaking, a person with a presumably 'lower-class' sociolect (as based on dominant perceptions) or who made a presumably 'wrong' choice of dress (again, as based on dominant perceptions) will be perceived as less competent than a person who fits expectations. Now, habitus explains that people have learned or not learned to speak and dress the right way based on their social upbringing and previous experiences. The 'right' way to speak and dress as a manager may come naturally to a manager's child, but not necessarily to a worker's child.

CCM Perspectives

The latter has to learn the rules of the game; the former is 'born into' them and has automatically internalized them. These 'rules of the game' are not objective as they are just what managers perpetuate unconsciously to distinguish themselves from other groups, let's say workers. And in order to maintain this 'fine distinction', they are thus less willing (on an unconscious level) to let a worker's child in (closure effect).

Symbolic capital, or the power of perception

When an individual enters a field (see above), for example, the job market, they bring with themselves so called capital. Capital are the resources which the person possesses and which will be judged by those already in a field. Capital can be differentiated into the following types:

- *Economic capital* – capital which a person can directly convert into money, such as money, ability to work or material possessions. It is the fundamental basis for the accumulation of the other types of capital, but it is not the most important one.
- *Social capital* – the resources and networks which a person has access to because they belong to a certain social group; they are known and recognized by others, and, because they themselves are part of networks, they can instil trust in others.
- *Cultural capital* – a person's education and 'how to' knowledge. This 'how to' knowledge involves a variety of aspects. The first aspect is *incorporated cultural capital*. Cultural capital is part of a person's body and outward appearances, such as how to dress for a job interview, or the accent or sociolect with which a person speaks. It is the capital that the field 'deduces' from the person. The second one is *objectified cultural capital*: material objects which make cultural capital visible, such as wearing the right kind of clothes, the right kind of accessories, how to furnish one's living room, etc.; it is the capital that is 'shown' to the field. The final one is *institutionalized cultural capital*, e.g. academic credentials or professional qualifications as formally recognized by institutions in this field (e.g. a company); it is the capital that is formally 'proven'. There is an overlap between the types of cultural capital; for example, a university certificate is both objectified and institutionalized cultural capital – depending on how it is used and by whom.

Symbolic capital   A person's skills and competencies as manifesting in a field

Upon entering a field, such as management, these three forms of capital have the potential to be translated into **symbolic capital**. If this happens, others believe in a person's competencies. High symbolic capital signifies that the person entering the field fits the norms, expectations and rules of this field. Low symbolic capital signifies a lack of 'fit' in the eyes of those who are already in the field and who thus determine access to it. This is not an

Doxa Unquestioned rules of the field by means of which capital is assessed

objective process, but dependent on the 'rules of the game' which are seen as normal and natural by those acting in a certain field and which are not questioned, the so called **doxa**. Based on the doxa already in place, people will be judged unequally and have unequal opportunities (manager's child versus worker's child). Symbolic capital is thus a form of power. It is unequal, because not every person has the same access to it. Basically, this model says that factors such as social class, ethnicity, gender, age and so on matter for how people are perceived, often regardless of objective qualifications.

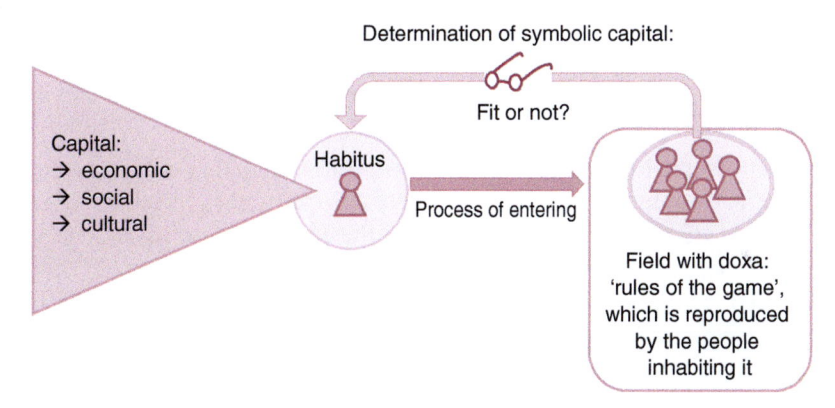

Figure 7.8   Capital and field – an overview

STUDENT ACTIVITY 7.4

Habitus and Symbolic Capital in CCM Fields

Revisit the pieces of the Opening Case. Which ones can be explained with the help of concepts such as field, habitus, symbolic capital and doxa? Give reasons for your solution.

> **Link to Practice: The Price of Wine**
>
> Have you ever wondered how the price of wine is determined? In fact, most people cannot differentiate between 'low priced' and 'costly' wines by means of objective sensory characteristics (Beckert et al., 2017: 206). If this is so, what justifies the price? It originates from the degree of symbolic capital which it ascribes to its buyer. Symbolic capital is relational. It must be recognized by others in order to exist, and one can only be sure of it if recognition is achieved. Thus, by choosing or producing the 'right' kind of wine, wineries and consumers affirm 'class hierarchy' in their own eyes and the eyes of others (ibid.: 206), and distinguishing oneself from a thus constructed 'lesser group' of buyers or producers is what justifies the price.

Structure versus agency

The previous insight into discourse, habitus and field theory might give you the impression that people are victims of structural power effects, such as *domination* and *power over*. However, this is only half of the picture as on an individual level, there is always *power to*.

In the social sciences, this has come to be understood as the dilemma between *structure* and *agency*. Both concepts will be explained in the following and then applied via activity.

Structure refers to the ways in which power is inscribed into the system. For example, racial segregation as a formal system is a structural power effect. Structural power effects might create domination by cancelling out an individual's *power to* (*agency*).

From an agency-oriented perspective, power is never a one-way process. One can only be ruled if one lets oneself be ruled. This means that both the rulers and those ruled need to contribute to structural inequality in order to maintain it. Which, in return, implies that every unequal system bears in itself the possibility to be overthrown because, in order for domination to manifest, those dominated need to be complicit in it.

Still, agency does not always play out. For example, a low-cost unskilled production worker might not have the *power to* work against their own domination. Yet, a white-collar employee just might. On a second level, agency depends on whether individuals *believe* that they have agency or not, and then act upon their respective beliefs.

> **STUDENT ACTIVITY 7.5**
>
> **Structure Versus Agency**
>
> Research these three individuals: Mohandas Karamchand (Mahatma) Gandhi, Martin Luther King and Rosa Louise Parks.
>
> - All of them faced unequal systems, and all of them resisted by means of agency. Find out how exactly by researching their lives and actions.
> - Discuss what weighs more in people's lives – structure or agency?
> - Can each of us be like Mahatma Gandhi, Martin Luther King or Rosa Parks, if we desire so? Why (not)?

Rules of practice

The idea of *rules of practice* is one way of bringing the paradox of structure versus agency together (see Clegg, 1989). Rules of practice refer to the normalities of 'how things are done and should be done' in a field (they are less fixed and more related to the actual doings of people than doxa). These informal rules are not written down and often differ from formal rules or structures. For example, a company might have a formal rule against gender discrimination; that is, discrimination because of people being categorized as 'male', 'female' or 'non-binary'. However, the rules of practice might be different; for example, it might be that the most important meetings are conducted in the evenings when it is more difficult for people with social obligations (e.g. children) to participate. Because of socially learned gender roles in society, namely the idea that childcare is a 'woman's job', this might then advantage some men over some women, but also those without childcare obligations over those with. As an indirect effect, both younger and older age groups might be advantaged as well.

Rules of practice thus create *power over*, sometimes even *domination*, which might be more difficult to pinpoint and less obvious than structural inequalities. The measuring rod is the degree to which *power to* (agency) is cancelled out. To what degree do the ways in which discourse and structure are put into practice (via rules of practice) still allow for individual room to manoeuvre and to devise counter-strategies (agency), which in return can then change the rules of practice in existence and, potentially, existing structures of domination?

STUDENT ACTIVITY 7.6

Corporate Christmas as a Means of Corporate Team-Building

Piece 4 of the Opening Case states that the annual corporate Christmas party takes place in a Hungarian multinational company. The idea that this event takes place and that employees attend is thus part of corporate rules of practice. The Christmas party shall contribute to a strong corporate team spirit.

Have you ever attended a religious ceremony at work which was not considered to be religious but simply a corporate team-building event? If yes, use this experience for working on the following task. If not, ask people who are employed in a company and, if experienced by them, let them describe the event. Use these descriptions for answering the following questions:

- How can it happen that it is considered 'normal' practice that people do something religious at work, yet what they do is not considered to be religious?
- Would this 'normality' apply to all religious practices at work, or only to some? Why?
- Why is it important for the power relations at work that employees receive gifts by their managers during the occasion? Or, in other words, how is the building of 'team spirit' also linked to maintaining power relations?

Link to Practice: Seasonal Greetings

'Seasonal greetings' is what is most commonly sent out by companies worldwide when the end of the year is approaching. By this choice of wording, a reference to a specific religious tradition is avoided. Nonetheless, the underlying reason for sending out greetings at this time of the year remains a specific, not a universal one.

Managing the Circuits of Power

In 1989, Stuart Clegg introduced the idea of *frameworks of power* in order to integrate structure, agency and rules of practice (see previous section). He proposed that all three facets of power can be understood as *circuits of power*, through which power flows into a certain, but not the alternative, direction. He also suggests that there are *obligatory passage points*, also called *nodes of power*, which are the 'switches' that determine the direction of the power flow. All action needs to pass these nodes of power. In simple terms, whoever owns or takes possession of the switches, controls the circuit.

- One direction of power is from macro to micro, or in other words, from structure to agency – control. In this case, *systems of domination* shape and fixate *rules of practice* which then empower some over others. Rules of practice are the doxa of 'what things mean' and 'who is a member' in a relevant, contested field.
- The alternative direction is from micro to macro, or, in other words, from agency to structure – resistance and, ultimately, structural change. The ongoing process of people playing out their agency against each other is called *episodic power relations*. These describe the process by which people position themselves.
- Based on the outcomes of such processes, people acquire the means and resources to control the *nodes of power* and, thus, to change the direction into which power flows.

In simple terms, one can understand the two possible directions as control or resistance:

- Control implies that structural, stable power establishes successful systems of domination. Power as a system-wide factor has factual effects on people: some are empowered, others are disempowered, and existing rules of practice reproduce systems of domination. Those resisting do not succeed in gaining control over the nodes of power, and what people do in episodic power relations continues to fixate the rules of practice and their meanings. Thus, the system of domination is further affirmed and remains stable, and power continues to flow from macro to micro.
- Resistance implies that those resisting dominant power have acquired resources and means for taking control of the obligatory passage points. Episodic power relations have thus resulted in counter-interpretations and counter-actions which are strong enough to facilitate system change. This way, the rules of practice and associated meanings are being transformed, and a new power system is 'in-the-making'. Power flows from micro to macro, and a system change is facilitated.

CCM Perspectives

A factor to be considered are external contingencies; for example, technological innovation might facilitate systems of control, or a certain change in the law system might empower some actors more than previously, both of which can result in a change of the rules of practice and of what is required to become an accepted member in a certain field.

These interrelations are depicted in Figure 7.9.

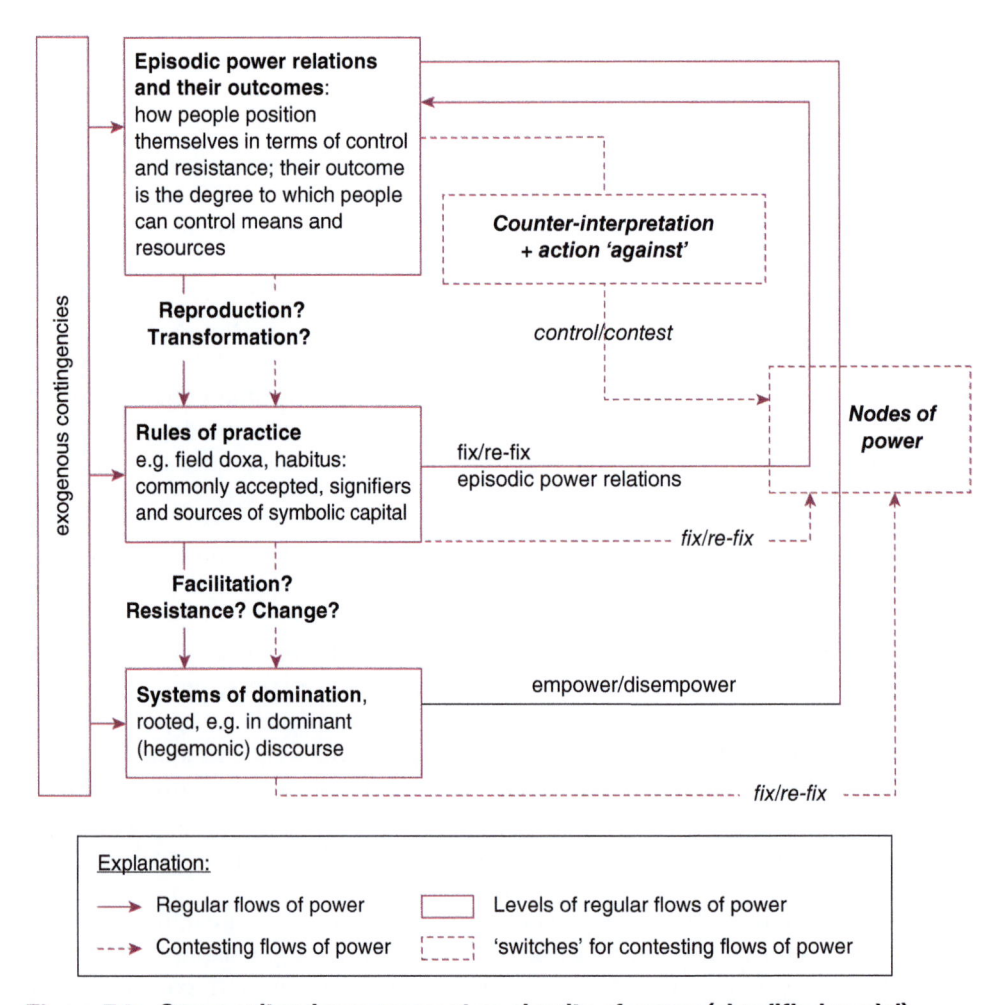

Figure 7.9 Cross-cultural management as circuits of power (simplified model)

Source: adapted from Clegg (1989: 214); Mahadevan (2012)

The following application delivers further insights into these interrelations.

Application to practice: Student activity 7.5 revisited

The example of Mahatma Gandhi shows how individuals (micro) can change a system (macro): they have managed to take control of the switch and thus change the flow of power. It thus serves as a practice example for Clegg's (1989) circuits of power (Figure 7.9)

- The British Empire perpetuates an unequal colonial society.
- Gandhi has a counter-interest to change this.
- He is well-positioned enough in the system (London-educated lawyer in South Africa) for his agency not to be cancelled out by domination (in South Africa, Indians are 'second' to the British, they are not at the bottom of the colonial hierarchy).
- Gandhi interests others in his counter-interest and mobilizes them towards peaceful resistance.
- The counter-movement becomes powerful enough to turn the switch: power flows bottom-up and changes dominant structures.
- The British Empire cannot sustain its previous rules of domination because a large enough number of those ruled by them are not complicit to domination anymore.
- However, this then aggravates and affirms another inequality: Black South Africans are even worse off because Indian South Africans don't ally with them but only seek to advance their own position to 'White South African' status.

STUDENT ACTIVITY 7.5

Part II: The Many Faces of Mahatma Gandhi

Based on the previous considerations (Student Activity 7.5 revisited), research how Gandhi has spoken about women and 'Black South Africans' (whom he often named 'Kaffa'). Note the sources and how you feel about them.

Then, come to an opinion about whether Gandhi's actions were to the worse or the better (and for whom)? Or did Gandhi simply not 'know better',

(Continued)

given the context of his time, and any potential 'racism' and 'misogynism' (showing hate against women or expressing that men are better than women) from his side was inevitable and still led to change to the better?

Discuss your opinion and how you arrived at it with fellow students. Reflect together on why and how it is difficult to revise one's understanding of matters such as racism and misogynism. How is the topic difficult and what is required to facilitate discussion? Why is it essential to constantly challenge and revise one's understanding with the help of others? Write down your major learnings from the activity.

Pause and Reflect: When the 'Empty Signifier' Shifts

Ernesto Laclau and Chantal Mouffe (1985) propose another, related way in which one can understand how the macro and micro of power relate, and how a certain idea suddenly becomes dominant. What they focus upon is the paradox of large meta-level discourses such as 'democracy', 'religion' or 'human rights': Everyone has an 'idea' of what they mean and how they should be promoted, yet much of these ideas differ. Thus, Laclau and Mouffe identify these large ideas as 'empty signifiers': what they signify is so large and all-encompassing that they *can* mean anything to anyone. Therefore, 'democracy' or 'religion' only *do* mean something when contextualized in episodic power relations. Laclau and Mouffe then propose to observe shifts ('nodal points') in how a large meta-level discourse is interpreted or filled with meaning in order to identify critical power effects. For example, 9/11 can be viewed as a nodal point for the empty signifier 'Islam' (Rahman, 2017). The idea of what 'Islam' is became different from what it used to be before, and this then affected individuals who are identified or self-identify as 'Muslim'. As a still ongoing struggle over the nodal point of 'individual freedom', the worldwide COVID-19 pandemic can be interpreted as attempts at shifting the empty signifier of 'human rights' which was challenged by the pandemic. The underlying debate centres around the extent to which it is justified that individual freedom is restricted for a higher goal. In virtually every country, this resulted in an ongoing struggle to mobilize the resources and means for controlling the otherwise empty signifier 'human rights'. Only in retrospect, it will become visible when and how exactly the shift took place, which nodal points were involved, and who mobilized which resources and means successfully to take control.

Critical CCM   219

In summary, the idea of frameworks of power allows for precisely mapping domination, power over, and power to, and their root causes, and to also identify the switches by which one of the power circuits is switched on and off in both cases. The next activity lets you apply this learning.

> **STUDENT ACTIVITY 7.7**
>
> ### Frameworks of Power
>
> Select one piece of the Opening Case.
>
> - Identify all three circuits of power and describe them.
> - Identify into which direction power flows and why this is the case.
> - Identify the 'switch' that might reverse the direction into which power flows.
>   - Direction 1 is from macro → micro; it signifies power over and, if fixed, domination
>   - Direction 2 is from micro → macro; it signifies resistance and, if successful, system change.
>
> Throughout, be precise when defining and locating power.

> **Link to Practice: The World Day against Child Labour**
>
> 12 June is the World Day against Child Labour, and in 2022 the motto was 'Universal social protection to end child labour' (ILO, 2022). As the International Labour Organization (ILO) states, 'social protection is both a human right and a potent policy tool to prevent families from resorting to child labour in times of crisis' (ILO, 2022). With this statement, the ILO acknowledges the interrelations between structures (whether people are socially protected or not), practices (to what degree child labour takes place) and individual agency (whether families and children are enabled to choose otherwise).

The Power of History

Power does not emerge in a vacuum; there is a history to it, and out of this history a certain, but not another present emerges. For example, Columbus can only have 'discovered' the Americas if history is written from a White European perspective.

Likewise, Mahatma Gandhi can only stand for peaceful resistance and a fight for equality and human rights if his actions are interpreted in light of how he sought advanced male Indians to the status of White Englishmen.

> ### Pause and Reflect: The World as We Know it
>
> A thought experiment on world history is the historical footnote that a Chinese fleet, with navigational and weapons technology far beyond anything Europe had to offer, sailed the oceans under general Zheng He between 1405 and 1433. The fleet reached, for example, Aden and Jedda in the Gulf of Persia, and Mogadishu in East Africa. Shortly afterwards, all such expeditions were abandoned. About the same time, in 1434, captain Gil Eanes, who had been sent out by the Portuguese King known as Henry the Navigator, reached Kap Bojador on the West coast of Africa. This is considered the first stepping stone towards the circumnavigation of the African continent. It culminated in Vasco da Gama reaching Calicut in India in 1498, and also led to Christopher Columbus, another explorer in search of the passage to India, accidentally 'discovering' the Americas in 1492. One can imagine how the power map of the world would look differently if the Chinese fleet had just sailed on West from Mogadishu for a little while and had reached Portugal just prior to the 'Golden Age of Discovery' that spurred the ascent of Western European nations as global super-powers during the age of imperialism.

Thus, the way in which people categorize the world is not independent of history and their standpoint in it; moreover, even if they try to be critical and reflect upon what is taken for granted, they might only be able to do so within the wider socio-cultural, historical, economic and political context in which they are situated.[4]

Postcolonial approaches to power

Postcolonialism, which is the focus of this section, pays particular attention to how exactly contemporary systems, rules of practices and ideas are still implicated by colonial histories. This means to acknowledge that there is a historical imbalance to categories such as race – it is not that 'white' and 'non-white' are different categories (Piece 7), but also that 'white' carries a more positive connotation and is, from a historical and systemic perspective, advantaged over other categories. The root are actual historical events, such as slavery and colonialism. If companies and people

---

[4] This argument is put forward mainly by Critical Theory, but also by Postcolonial Studies (see next section). Marxism would be an alternative way of unmasking power in CCM studies on structural levels.

Critical CCM

perpetuate the same patterns – consciously or unconsciously – this is then called *neo-colonial* (newly colonial), a situation which needs to be checked for its power implications.

Colonialism in the narrow sense

In the narrow sense, **colonialism** is a historical period, predominantly in Europe, which is linked to mainly 19th-century philosophy and practices of **imperialism**. The underlying rationale was to acquire colonies in order to gain economic wealth and to also expand political territory. Colonialism is strongly linked to ideas of supremacy, for example, in terms of race, religion, civilization or culture. For example, Rudyard Kipling (1899) beseeched the USA to 'take up the white man's burden' of colonization (and to not lose their colonies, the Philippines), lest they fall behind European states. Kipling paints a picture of the 'civilized', Christian, cultured 'white man', as opposed to the 'sullen, uncivilized, barbaric, non-White heathen', out of which follows the moral obligation of every 'white man' to take up the stated 'burden'. These ideas depart from a notion of inequality, namely between the thus constructed 'white' and 'non-white' peoples.

> **Colonialism** An historical period, mainly associated with 19th century Europe

> **Imperialism** The political ideology of gaining wealth by acquiring and, afterwards, governing overseas colonies, mainly associated with 19th century Europe

Colonialism: The wider implications

Neo-colonialism implies that not only actual colonialism, but the whole history of the world has shaped the present in unequal ways; the past still informs the present. Such power patterns not only apply to individuals but also to organizations and larger geopolitical systems of power. For example, organizations from high-labour cost countries offshore and outsource to low labour-cost countries, and thus create and sometimes reproduce unequal systems of collaboration. Yet, historically, the economically more developed countries on the globe, also referred to as **Global North**, have often developed at the cost

> **Global North** Denomination for the richer and more industrialized countries, which are mainly located in the northern hemisphere. From a critical perspective, also a questionable term as the current status quo is assumed to be rooted in historic inequalities such as colonialism and imperialism (which made certain regions 'richer')

> **Global South** Denomination for the poorer and less industrialized countries, which are mainly located in the southern hemisphere. From a critical perspective, also a questionable term as the current status quo is assumed to be rooted in historic inequalities such as colonialism and imperialism (which made certain regions 'poorer').

of today's less developed countries, also referred to as **Global South**, for example, due to policies of imperialism and colonialism. Thus, there is a historic root to the inequality perpetuated by today's companies. In simple terms, the riches of the Argentinian silver mines went to the Spanish crown for a long time, and not to the local population. Could this have contributed to the economic status and relations of the two countries today? You could apply the same argument to rare earths in Inner Mongolia, copper and tin in Afghanistan, and oil in the Niger Delta. These resources are exploited by multinational companies in collaboration with national governments, and with the help of local workforces. Isn't this an arrangement that is similar to the arrangements during colonial times? From a postcolonial perspective, what one can find are new actors (you could ask, for example, whether countries like China are now a neo-colonial global power), but what has remained the same are the archetypical roles of the play.

The goal of postcoloniality

Postcoloniality describes the goal of a present which wishes to move beyond the neo-colonial remnants of the past. It requires that one checks for the power implications of the present. Are the patterns *really* neutral, or do they have a connotation which advantages some over others, because of a certain unequal history? What counts are the patterns behind the actual power mechanism; the mechanism itself does not need to be exactly the same. For example, there is no longer a system of thought wherein 'the Irish' are a 'race' (Piece 8), yet ideas of 'race' and associated hierarchies linger on, for example, the Brazilian census still differentiates people into 'race' (Piece 7). Like culture, the specifics of power in relation to race vary across time and context, but at the same time power patterns continue to exist across time and context.

The goal is thus to identify patterns and relations across presumed differences in context and experience. For example, Piece 1 and Piece 2 seem different on a factual level as one is about perfect French, the other about inadequate French. Still, the patterns underlying it are the same. In Piece 1, the 'perfect French' of the African-American manager turns out to be to her disadvantage as when speaking French with an American accent, she had been identified as 'American', an identity associated with a 'Western' country of the Global North which was to her advantage. Yet, when that accent faded, she became a certain version of 'French' when talking to others, namely a person 'from the former colonies', which put her in a socially more unfavourable position of an 'immigrant to the native country'.

The German professor teaching a French business negotiation course refers to the language skills of his Cameroonian students as inadequate, but what he actually experiences is another way of speaking French beyond what is promoted as desirable by the Académie Française. German students learn the same version of speaking French at school as has the business professor himself, and this then becomes the 'normal' and seemingly only good way of speaking French. Thus, what needs to be reflected upon is *why* one version of the same language is more desirable than another one, even if varieties of the latter one are spoken by more people worldwide.

> ### STUDENT ACTIVITY 7.8
>
> **Neo-Colonial Remnants of the Past in Contemporary CCM**
>
> Revisit those pieces of the Opening Case not yet discussed. Which ones could be examples of a certain unequal history 'lingering on'? If you are unfamiliar with the contexts which they describe, find a person who could know more and do some research.

The creative potential of power: Cultural flows, mimicry and hybridity

Postcolonialism also acknowledges that power is as much restricting as it is enabling. For example, previously colonized countries such as India would not exist in the way they do today without both the positive and negative influences of colonization. For good or bad, colonization has shaped their history and their future. If Gandhi had not profited from the educational opportunities of the British Empire, he could not have contributed to its demise (and to the perpetuation of racism against Black people). Colonialization has also played a historic part in people all over the globe receiving their education in transferable languages such as French, Spanish or English, which then enables them to pursue a global career. As the example of Gandhi suggests, it is crucial with whom this otherwise diverse group of people allies and against whom they distance themselves. It is a decisive factor as to which neo-colonial inequalities are affirmed and which ones are resisted.

The Cameroonian students of Piece 2 exemplify these new opportunities which might work towards changing the established power relations in today's world. Piece 6 provides the counter-perspective: a local student with an interest in international business who gets the strong feeling that he is not 'bicultural', 'multi-ethnic', 'upper-class' or 'well-travelled' enough to enter this field. In both cases, depending on perspective, a certain identity expectation (see Chapter 3) dominates. Who can say where negative perceptions of 'migration' end and positive connotations of 'biculturalism' and 'multilingualism' begin?

Therefore, postcolonialism is also a thought experiment. To which extent is a certain historical or present power effect to the advantage or disadvantage of whom? Who was or is empowered over others? Who complies and who resists, and out of which interests and for what purposes? Who can re-invent what it takes to succeed, and in which ways?

To uncover the unforeseen potential of power, critical cross-cultural managers need to pay attention to processes of transference and translation, so-called **cultural flows**. For example, cricket, an English gentlemen's sport, became a mass event in India; an external influence was 'made new sense of' in another location. Likewise, Indian movies, fashioned after a certain idea of 'Hollywood', but also introducing novel ideas, scripts and symbolics, have by now travelled back to North America and Western Europe, in return informing a picture of India. This example shows the change potential of power. Every knowledge, if transferred, will be interpreted in a new light, and might be used against the system from which it emerged. The example of Gandhi, who used his London-based English-language university education to mobilize peaceful resistance against the British Empire, can be viewed in this light.

> **Mimicry** The process of copying a cultural element

> **Hybridity** A cultural element which has emerged from an exchange process across pairs such as 'old' and 'new', 'foreign' or 'familiar', or 'global' and 'local'

Also, every practice might be copied, and then further developed – again, with unforeseen effects (like Indian cricket). Homi K. Bhabha (1990, 1994) has called this **mimicry**, resulting in **hybridity**. First, new knowledge is introduced to a context by those in power. Next, people copy it, and, by doing so, acquire the capital to enter the field in a position of power; they are empowered by colonial knowledge. Next, those now empowered combine 'old' and 'new', and 'local' and 'global' in new creative ways and for a unique outcome. Michel Foucault (1980) has coined this insight as *power/ knowledge*. He argues that every unequal system of power, by its mere existence, provides those ruled with the knowledge to subvert and, ultimately, change the system. In other words, experiencing inequality is a resource for one's own empowerment, if agency is activated successfully. The result is system change, but also the empowerment of new groups over even other ones. The example of Gandhi, if viewed in a different light than before, speaks of this effect.

Appropriation/'mimicry'

'Original' knowledge → Reinterpretation/Knowledge creation

Used against/'hybridity'

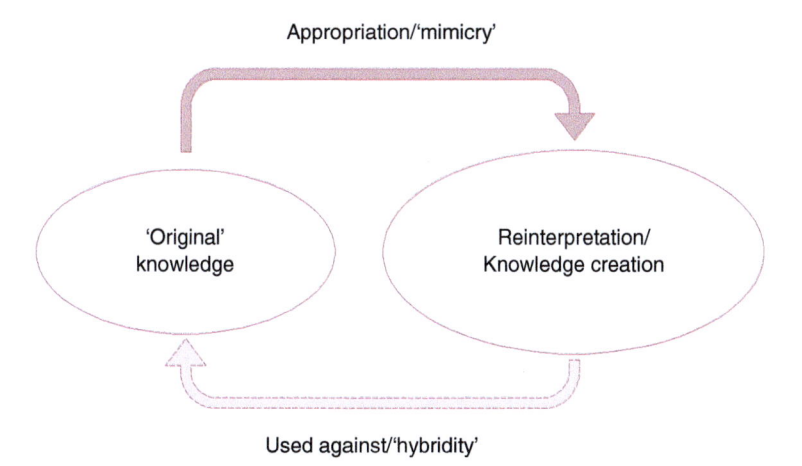

Figure 7.10 **The creative potential of power**

STUDENT ACTIVITY 7.9

A Postcolonial Reality

This activity asks you to reconsider Pieces 3 and 4 of the Opening Case.

1. Piece 3 of the Opening Case largely is a postcolonial story. How so? In order to answer this question, tell the story, its logic, its history and its present boundary conditions from the perspective of the Tunisian engineer.
2. Assume that Piece 4, which exemplifies the practice of corporate Christmas in multinational corporations across the globe, is a story of neo-colonialism and neo-imperialism.
    - For example, how did it happen that it was 'Christmas' that is now celebrated in former socialist Hungary which, in even earlier days, was a part of the (Catholic) Austro-Hungarian empire?
    - Why was it that this practice was re-appropriated in Hungary?
3. Consider Pieces 3 and 4 in light of each other:
    - How are the perceptions and practices of (non-)religiousness in Pieces 3 and 4 similar to and different from each other?
    - How can postcolonialism explain the idea that corporate Christmas is perceived to be a 'normal' practice in a multinational corporation (whereas alternative religious beliefs might not be equally endorsed on corporate level)?

Identifying subalternity whilst avoiding the dangers of help

Not every unequal or neo-colonial system results in empowerment. Another potential effect would be, for example, *self-colonization*. This means that people are exposed to opportunities within a system of domination, e.g. Indian clerks in the British colonial administration, and then also accept the system of domination as superior; they become their own colonizers. In the present world, such effects also work backwards. Piece 6, for example, highlights reverse effects of the increased need to internationalize one's own identity in management, and the Welsh student needs to decide whether he wishes to categorize himself in dominant terms or not. Viewed from this perspective, he faces the same challenge as the Tunisian research engineer (Piece 3), but in other ways.

Additionally, not everyone has access to empowerment, and this inequality is another power effect. A bottom line of this analysis are the so-called *subalterns*. These are individuals who can be assumed to be disadvantaged throughout, e.g. across time and many contexts. For example, low-skilled production workers in a low-cost country who are part of the global value chain of a multinational cooperation might not have the means and resources to resist successfully; their agency has been cancelled out by a system of domination.

The task of the critical cross-cultural manager is then to identify those who are fully disempowered and to work towards their emancipation, based on the understanding that they cannot do it themselves because they are robbed of their agency. The problem with power is that its effects are multi-layered and difficult to identify. For example, as historian Harald Fischer-Tiné (2009) suggests, well-educated colonial subjects, such as M.K. Gandhi, might have had much more system power in the British Empire than working-class, uneducated English subjects for whom Fischer-Tiné then proposes the term 'White Subalterns'.

The cross-cultural manager should also not be too eager to act for others. The first reason is that what you have not experienced, you cannot necessarily 'know', and you might get it wrong. Secondly, even an act of help might have negative consequences because it constructs inequality: one person becomes the 'active helper', the other person becomes the 'passive recipient' of this help. The helper makes the choices, and those helped can only be 'grateful' for what is offered (Mahadevan, 2012); yet another way in which unequal relations are fixed. From a postcolonial perspective, this is exactly the critique against global developmental aid as by trying to 'help' those in need, a system is put into place which makes some dependent on the very aid that aims at overcoming inequality – the perpetuation of unequal relations between Global North and South (Foroughi, 2020).

STUDENT ACTIVITY 7.10

Discourses of Help

Revisit Piece 3 of the Opening Case. Based on your previous analysis (Activity 7.9), discuss the following questions:

- Is the Tunisian engineer 'a modern woman'?
- If so, what are the reasons for it?

Orientalism and imaginative geographies

Power is also the knowledge that has become dominant, for example, when it comes to which history of the world is 'normal' and remains unquestioned. Critical CCM requires challenging these normalities. Two concepts for doing so have been proposed by Edward Said, namely Orientalism (1979) and imaginative geographies (1993). You can think of his theories as a projection of ideas of 'Us' versus 'Them' onto a map of the world.

For example, consider the categories 'West' and 'non-West'. This is more than a factual geographical classification because a country like Italy is considered 'Western' despite being located on an 'Eastern' meridian, whereas Tunisia, on a Western meridian and West of Italy, is not.

From a postcolonial perspective, the very point from which East and West is measured is already neo-colonial – there is an actual history to why the Zero meridian runs through Greenwich. Secondly, there is an identity aspect to it. When 'the West' defined itself, it largely defined itself against a 'non-Western other'.

As Edward Said (1979) maintains, this non-Western other was 'Islam': a constant political threat to 'Western' Europe, and, in order to deal with this threat, 'the West' had to identify itself as 'western'. Out of this, the interrelated categories of Occident and Orient emerged. Said calls this mechanism **Orientalism** – it means the discourses, structures, rules of practices and acts of positioning which emerge because the West needed to identify the Orient as 'other' in order to define itself as 'West'. Following Said, the West invents itself by looking into the mirror

> **Orientalism** The representation of the 'Arab world' or 'Asia' as opposite and less modern than the thus constructed 'West' in order to self-identify as 'positively Western'

of the 'Orient'. A major identifying category is religion: Christianity ('Western') versus Islam ('Oriental'). The main idea here is that 'the West' is purported to be more advanced, more modern, more rational and more secular than the presumably traditional 'Orient', due to religion. This idea then becomes a reality, and interactions between the thus constructed opposing categories are overshadowed by Orientalist thought. Present challenges faced regarding Muslim minorities in the West can be interpreted in this light, as can the idea of a 'corporate Christmas' as a presumably 'secular' team-building practice in a contemporary multinational corporation (Piece 4).

However, in English colonial language, the term 'Oriental' was also used for a diffuse group of people, covering Turkey, Arab countries, China, India, and the Far East. Said (1993) calls this imagined or **imaginative geography**: a geography that makes sense of the identity of those applying it but which does not describe the actual world. These are thus 'perceived' not 'real' geographies that serve those who apply them. However, the effect applies to both sides, because 'West' and 'non-West' are affirmed at mutually exclusive and distinct categories. What then becomes more difficult, is the hybridity, and the cultural transferences and flows envisaged by postcolonial studies.

> **Imaginative geographies** Perceived geographies that serve those applying them

STUDENT ACTIVITY 7.11

Orientalism and Imaginative Geographies

Revisit Piece 3 of the Opening Case. Based on your previous analysis (Activity 7.9), reflect on whether you find orientalist positions in your analysis. Discuss with your lecturer.

Link to Practice: Who is Not a Migrant?

The United Nations (UN) International Organization for Migration (IOM) defines a migrant as:

> any person who is moving or has moved across an international border or within a State away from his/her habitual place of residence, regardless of (1) the person's legal status; (2) whether the movement is

> voluntary or involuntary; (3) what the causes for the movement are; or (4) what the length of the stay is. (UN, 2022)
>
> Thus, factually, the term migrant covers all types of cross-border mobility, such as student exchange or refugee movements. One could therefore ask: Who is *not* a migrant in today's world?

Moving Beyond What has Become Accepted as Normal

Critical perspectives highlight how some viewpoints on the world have become normalized whereas others have not. **Normalization** means that a certain reality, which is not the only possible reality, is not challenged anymore. It is similar to native categories or naïve realism (Chapter 6) but with much larger implications concerning discourses and systems of domination.

> **Normalization** The process by which a certain reality is selected over alternative realities to attain the status of an 'unquestioned truth'

Denaturalization

The CCM technique for overcoming normalization is **denaturalization**. This means to understand that a certain reality is not 'natural' in the sense that it is the only reality that could have emerged. For example, there is the idea that 'the West' is secular and that, for example, 'the Arab world' is not (Piece 3). Yet, often, there are corporate Christmas parties in Western companies (Piece 4), which is a remnant of a certain religious tradition. The only difference, as Anna Hidegh and Henriett Primecz (2020) argue, is that some religious traditions have become more normalized in those countries which, because of history, now dominate world business. Therefore, one religion is simply 'seen' more than another which just 'vanishes', and to some people (such as Tunisian female engineers) religiousness is ascribed more to some than to others.

> **Denaturalization** The process by which a normalized reality and practice (see before) is challenged and identified as a selective adoption

Again, this points to the need to think in more complex, overlapping and indistinct categories of difference. For example, there is also the idea that 'the Orient' is homophobic whereas the West is not. Yet, there is also a strong tradition of homosexuality in Islam (Rahman and Chehaitly, 2020), and alternative combinations, such as lesbian, gay, bisexual, transgender and queer friendly mosques can be found in many countries across the globe (Piece 5). One could argue, of course, that these mosques are mainly found in 'Western' countries, therefore, the argument is not to maintain that 'Islam' is 'doing better' than 'the West' but rather to point out that there are more combinations of local and global, and of old and new, than seems imaginable at first sight. At the same time, however, anti-Western tendencies and homophobia *do* exist across the globe – the main message is that one should not simply presume that 'Western' equals 'more advanced and better'. Furthermore, there is the need to consider the hybridity of culture and identities. Just like 'attending Corporate Christmas' (Piece 7) is not merely religious, 'going to the mosque' is also a social not only a religious practice, and the underlying reasons for engaging in these practices vary across cultural contexts and individuals.

Problematization and deconstruction

Two techniques are helpful for achieving moving beyond what has become accepted as normal: problematization and deconstruction. Both facilitate alternative reconstructions.

- *Problematization* means to ask what is problematic about what is taken-for-granted as the only possibility (normalized reality).
- *Deconstruction* is the activity of 'taking things apart' (e.g. normalized reality). It is based on the understanding that everything that is written, said and done hides alternative possibilities which need to be 'excavated'.
- *Reconstruction*, as facilitated by problematization and deconstruction, is a new way of bringing the bits and pieces of reality into place, e.g. beyond systems of domination or hegemonic discourses.

For example, if not problematized, the actions and historical role of M.K. Gandhi emerge as only positive. However, if deconstructed by means of an alternative angle, for example, as to whether his actions were also to the advantage of women and black South Africans, history and its effects may be reconstructed. Out of it, a more realistic and nuanced understanding of Gandhi's role and actions emerges.

The next student activity lets you apply these deconstructive techniques.

STUDENT ACTIVITY 7.12

Who is Barack Obama? A Deconstruction

Barack Obama is often labelled the 'first African-American president of the USA'.

- Do some research and deconstruct this label. Who else is Barack Obama?
- Why was the label 'first African-American president of the USA' chosen, by whom and for what purposes?
- Finally, transfer your insights: What does this case tell you about power and CCM in general?

Chapter Summary

Critical CCM entails different approaches and methods. What is central to it, across all heterogeneity, is the awareness that power is part of everything; there can be no social interaction, no decision and action, and no social system without it. This might not necessarily be bad, but managers have to check for whether, how and when the situation becomes 'bad' and for whom, and then to identify and devise appropriate strategies and actions to change it to the better (however identified). Key techniques of a critical CCM are problematization, deconstruction and reconstruction, and denaturalization. The goal is to work towards the emancipation of those who are presently disadvantaged (*micro-emancipation*) while at the same time acknowledging that there are dangers associated with trying to 'free' others from inequality. Critical CCM is thus like putting the bits and pieces of a power puzzle together, whilst also deconstructing and reconstructing the puzzle in the process. The pieces of the Opening Case have walked you through the critically reflexive process required for a critical CCM.

The overarching technique is to view power from different angles and to oscillate between those multiple viewpoints, in order to make power small and, thus, manageable. For example, a first analysis of a situation could focus on discourse, the next on mimicry, yet another on agency, and all can then be viewed in light of each other. Out of this kaleidoscopic process, a more complete picture of how power implicates CCM emerges.

Long-term, the task of the cross-cultural manager is thus to constantly re-shuffle the pieces of the kaleidoscope of power in CCM, in order to figure out which configurations need to be overcome and which ones should be promoted and how. This is an ongoing process because the social realities of power – like culture – change.

Shuffling the bits and pieces of power, such as the pieces of the Opening Case, requires asking responsible questions such as: 'Where are we going? Is this development desirable?' (Flyvbjerg, 2001: 60), and to act accordingly, however challenging this might be. This chapter has highlighted how to implement this concerned, power-sensitive and kaleidoscopic managerial practice.

Key Points

- Power, culture and cross-cultural management are inseparable.
- Power in CCM is multifaceted, and needs to be managed kaleidoscopically.
- Main facets of power are: habitus, discourse, symbolic capital, fields, structure, agency, practice and history.
- Power leads to the normalization of certain categories and worldviews. These need to be denaturalized, problematized, and deconstructed and reconstructed from alternative and multiple angles.
- Power is not only negative, but also a creative force for system change, as indicated by cultural flows, mimicry and hybridity.
- Cross-cultural managers need to consider the effects which their actions have on those who are systematically and historically disadvantaged (subalterns) without perpetuating dominant discourses of help.
- Every action and every perspective can have unforeseen power effects: there is no neutral, innocent or fully positive CCM theory and practice.
- Nonetheless, cross-cultural managers need to act in a power-sensitive manner and to reflect upon their doings and their outcome, in order to shape CCM to the better.

Review Questions

1. What are the main premises of a critical CCM?
2. In what ways is power central to a critical CCM?
3. What is discourse, and when and how is discourse problematic?
4. What does field theory say about power, which are the central concepts, and how are these concepts helpful for cross-cultural management in practice?
5. What are 'circuits of power', which facets of power are integrated by this idea (and how), and how is it helpful for cross-cultural management in practice?
6. What is meant by postcolonial approaches to power, which problems shall be addressed by them, and how is a postcolonial approach helpful for cross-cultural management in practice?
7. What is meant by a 'multifaceted kaleidoscopic' cross-cultural management practice, what shall be achieved by such practice, and who needs to implement it?
8. Why is it relevant to denaturalize CCM, and how shall cross-cultural managers achieve this?
9. Why and how might engaging with the Critical CCM perspective be personally challenging, and how shall one move beyond such feelings?

10. What is the responsibility of the cross-cultural manager from a critical CCM perspective, and how can cross-cultural managers (you and I) make sure to have done this responsibility justice?

Opening Case Revisited

By now, you have encountered many ways in which the pieces of the Opening Case are different and related in terms of power; via the Closing Activity, you will integrate this learning.

Closing Activity

Revisit the pieces of the Opening Case with the full knowledge of this chapter.

Task 1

Briefly describe what the power aspects of each case are, and which cases are connected. The following connections are possible: cases are related, cases complement each other, or cases contradict each other. Also note whenever you struggle to find any power aspect at all in one of the pieces and state what you could do to relate yourself more to this piece. If you come up with more than one possible solution, either for the case itself or for case connections, write down all of them and state which ones are more or less likely.

Task 2

Visualize your insights from Task 1 in a mind-map. Try to acknowledge all facets and dimensions, and their root causes and effects, which were described in this chapter.

Task 3

Discuss and compare with fellow students.

1. Write down what you have learned via this comparison (consider two aspects: what you/the other student(s) found out, and how the task was approached).
2. Next, reflect collectively. What made you/the other student(s) approach the overall task and specific cases as you did? If approaches were different, why did you not 'see' what other student(s) saw? What did you 'see' and investigate which others missed, and why was that so? Write down your answers to this question as well.

Task 4

Visualize the joint outcome of the group in a second mind-map.

Further Reading

An overview on principles and methods of a critical CCM can be found in *The Sage Handbook of Contemporary Cross-Cultural Management* (Szkudlarek et al., 2020), Chapters 3 (Romani et al., 2020a) and 9 (Romani et al., 2020b), respectively, as well as in the open access paper by Romani et al. (2018). Providing specific examples and applying critical CCM concepts and tools, the book *Cases in Critical Cross-Cultural Management: An Intersectional Approach to Culture* (Mahadevan et al., 2020) is a helpful source for the critical CCM student and manager. Several pieces of the Opening Case stem from this book. Weichselbaumer (2016) provides an insightful example on 'Discrimination against female migrants wearing headscarves'. Based on a representative study in Germany, she shows how certain effects, such as discrepancies between objective skills and the subjective decision to (not) invite a job-seeker for an interview are rooted in stereotypical images of Muslim women and the headscarf. Sambajee (2016) highlights the power dynamics of language and ethnicity in the culturally complex context of Mauritius, revealing the intersecting status- and class-effects of both. Deconstructing CCM, Jackson (2017) discusses whether CCM scholars should study race (and concludes that they need to do so).

References

Beckert, J., Rössel, J. and Schenk, P. (2017) 'Wine as a cultural product: Symbolic capital and price formation in the wine field', *Sociological Perspectives*, 60(1): 207–222.

Bhabha, H.K. (ed.) (1990) *Nation and Narration*. London: Routledge.

Bhabha, H.K. (1994) *The Location of Culture*. London: Routledge.

Bourdieu, P. (1989) 'Social space and symbolic power', *Sociological Theory*, 7(1): 14–25.

Clegg, S. (1989) *Frameworks of Power*. London: Sage.

Fairclough, N. and Wodak, R. (1997) 'Critical discourse analysis', in T.A. van Dijk (ed.), *Discourse as Social Interaction: Volume I*. London: Sage. pp. 543–564.

Fischer-Tiné, H. (2009) *Low and Licentious Europeans. Race, Class and 'White Subalternity' in Colonial India*. Delhi: Orient Blackswan.

Flyvbjerg, B. (2001) *Making Social Science Matter: Why Social Inquiry Fails and How it Can Succeed Again*. Cambridge: Cambridge University Press.

Foroughi, H. (2020) 'Global North and Global South: Frameworks of power in an international development project', in J. Mahadevan, H. Primecz and L. Romani (eds), *Cases in Critical Cross-Cultural Management – an Intersectional Approach to Culture*. Abingdon: Taylor & Francis (Routledge). pp. 174–185.

Foucault, M. (1980) 'Two lectures', in C. Gordon (ed.), *Power/Knowledge: Selected Interviews and Other Writings 1972–1977 by Michel Foucault*. New York: Pantheon Books. pp. 78–108.

Hidegh, A.L. and Primecz, H. (2020) 'Corporate Christmas – sacred or profane?', in J. Mahadevan, H. Primecz and L. Romani (eds), *Cases in Critical Cross-Cultural Management – an Intersectional Approach to Culture*. Abingdon: Taylor & Francis (Routledge). pp. 46–58.

ILO (2022) 'World day against child labour', International Labour Organization. Available at: www.ilo.org/global/topics/child-labour/campaignandadvocacy/wdacl/lang--en/index.htm [last accessed 15 July 2022].

Jackson, T. (2017) 'Should cross-cultural management scholars study race?', *International Journal of Cross Cultural Management*, 17(3): 277–280.

Kassis-Henderson, J. and Cohen, L. (2020) 'The paradoxical consequences of "the perfect accent" – a critical approach to cross-cultural interactions', in J. Mahadevan, H. Primecz and L. Romani (eds), *Cases in Critical Cross-Cultural Management – an Intersectional Approach to Culture*. Abingdon: Taylor & Francis (Routledge). pp. 12–21.

Kipling, R. (1899) 'The white man's burden', *McClure's Magazine*.

Laclau, E. and Mouffe, C. (1985) *Hegemony and Socialist Strategy*. Verso: London.

MacManus, S. (1921) *The Story of the Irish Race: A Popular History of Ireland*. Ireland: The Irish Publishing Co.

Mahadevan, J. (2012) 'Translating nodes of power through reflexive ethnographic writing', *Journal of Organizational Ethnography*, 1(1): 119–131.

Mahadevan, J., Primecz, H. and Romani, L. (2020) (eds) *Cases in Critical Cross-Cultural Management – an Intersectional Approach to Culture*. Abingdon: Taylor & Francis (Routledge).

Rahman, M. (2017) 'Islamophobia, the impossible Muslim, and the reflexive potential of intersectionality', in J. Mahadevan and C.-H. Mayer (eds), *Muslim Minorities, Workplace Diversity and Reflexive HRM*. London: Taylor and Francis. pp. 35–45.

Rahman, M. and Chehaitly, S. (2020) 'From impossibility to visibility: An intersectional approach to LGBT Muslims and its benefits for CCM', in J. Mahadevan, H. Primecz and L. Romani (eds), *Cases in Critical Cross-Cultural Management – an Intersectional Approach to Culture*. Abingdon: Taylor & Francis (Routledge). pp. 33–45.

Romani, L., Mahadevan, J. and Primecz, H. (2018) 'Critical Cross-Cultural Management: Outline and emergent contributions', *International Studies of Management & Organization*, 48(4): 403–418.

Romani L., Boussebaa M. and Jackson, T. (2020a) 'Critical perspectives on Cross-Cultural Management', in B. Szkudlarek, L. Romani, D.V. Caprar and J.S. Osland (eds), *The Sage Handbook of Contemporary Cross-Cultural Management*. London: Sage. pp. 51–65.

Romani, L., Mahadevan, J. and Primecz, H. (2020b) 'Methods of critical Cross-Cultural Management', in B. Szkudlarek, L. Romani, D.V. Caprar and J.S. Osland (eds), *The Sage Handbook of Contemporary Cross-Cultural Management*. London: Sage. pp. 141–155.

Said, E. (1979) *Orientalism*. New York: Vintage Books.

Said, E. (1993) *Culture and Imperialism*. New York: Vintage Books.

Sambajee, P. (2016) 'The dynamics of language and ethnicity in Mauritius', *International Journal of Cross-Cultural Management*, 16(2): 215–229.

Szkudlarek, B., Romani, L., Caprar, D.V. and Osland, J.S. (eds) (2020) *The Sage Handbook of Contemporary Cross-Cultural Management*. London: Sage.

UK Government (2022) Whistleblowing. Available at: www.gov.uk/whistleblowing [last accessed 15 July 2022].

UN (2022) Migration. Available at: www.un.org/en/global-issues/migration [last accessed 15 July 2022].

Weichselbaumer, D. (2016) 'Discrimination against female migrants wearing headscarves', IZA Discussion Paper No. 10217. Available at: http://ftp.iza.org/dp10217.pdf [last accessed 12 December 2016].

PART III
CCM APPLICATIONS

In Part II, you have familiarized yourself with contemporary CCM perspectives. This section highlights key applications of CCM today. The purpose of Part III is to provide you with the knowledge and tools required for developing and refining your cross-cultural management skills for specific application areas. Based on the characteristics of contemporary management, organization and business, these application areas are international business (Chapter 8), organization (Chapter 9), and technology and social Media (Chapter 10). These application areas span and cross meso- and macro-levels of culture and interrelate with the individuals and teams engaged in CCM (micro-level). Figure III.0 visualizes these interrelations.

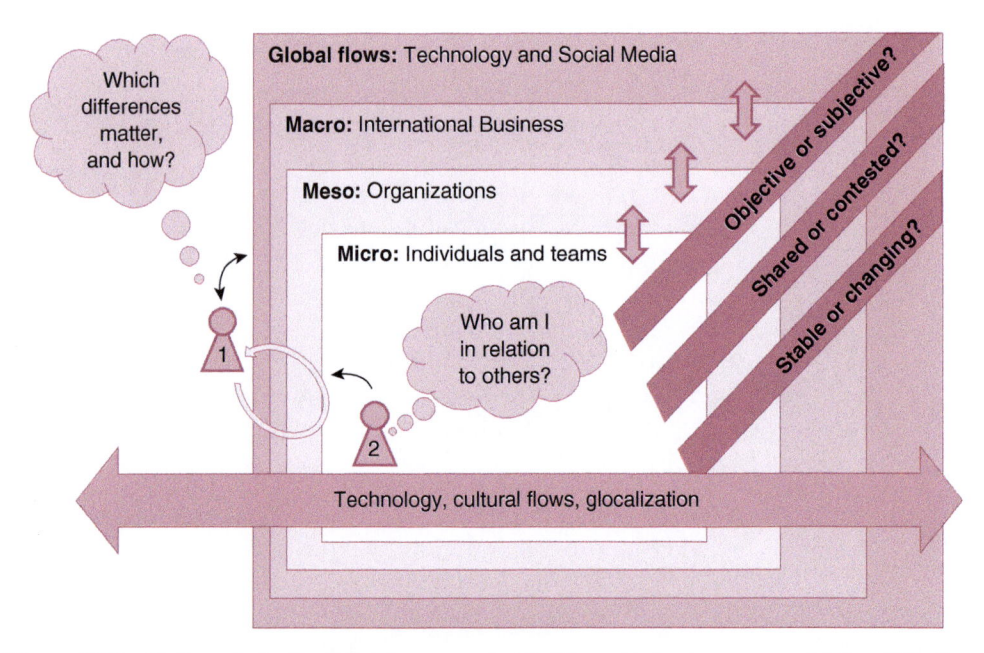

Figure III.0   Culture in today's business, organizations and management (simplified)

All chapters consider culture – as interrelated with individuals, organizations, business, and technology and social media – as both objective and subjective, as simultaneously stable and changing, and as shared and contested. The chapters also acknowledge that individuals play a double role in how contemporary CCM realities emerge. On the one hand, they are reflecting upon culture at large, asking the question: Which cultural differences matter, and how? (Figure III.0, Position 1). On the other hand, individuals also apply these realities to themselves, constantly asking the question: Who am I in relation to others? (Figure III.0, Position 2).

For making the most of Part III, you should have a good understanding of the configurations of culture (Chapter 2) and identities (Chapter 3) in contemporary CCM.

CCM and International Business 8

Learning Objectives

After reading this chapter, you should:

- understand how the international business environment is shaped and which ideas underpin it, and how these conditions interrelate with cross-cultural management
- understand trade-offs, interrelations and potential combinations related to being global and being local on individual and corporate levels
- know main philosophies and principles underlying corporate internationalization
- know and be able to apply specific modes of market entry and cultivation
- understand the specifics of contemporary corporate and managerial international exposure
- be able to address questions of corporate social responsibilities and ethics.

Reading Requirements

- You should have read Part I of this book.
- You should have read Chapter 4 on CCM paradigms and have a good understanding of what characterizes functionalist, interpretive and critical CCM.

- You should also be familiar with comparative CCM and its major tool, cultural dimensions (Chapter 5).
- You should know how power is part of the international business environment and be familiar with postcolonial and critical perspectives (Chapter 7).

Introduction

International Business The study of international trade and investment, and of corporate internationalization processes

International business (IB) refers to the trade of goods, services, technology, capital and/or knowledge across national borders. It also involves the question as to when, how and why companies – in particular multinational enterprises (MNEs) – internationalize or are active on a global scale (Hill, 2009). Cross-cultural management knowledge and skills are essential for the success of these activities, as well as for the strategic decisions underlying them. To this end, this chapter highlights selected aspects of IB, as relevant to the cross-cultural manager. Topics which will be addressed in this chapter are:

- the IB environment and its stakeholders
- companies in their local and global environment
- questions of ethics and sustainability in IB
- CCM requirements stemming from corporate internationalization and the IB environment

Opening Case

Piece 1

A US-American manufacturer of smart watches offshores part of its research and development (R&D) to China. The competitive strength of the company is the quality of its products, yet its main weaknesses are the high production costs and the fact that its corporate presence on East Asian markets is weak. Therefore, the strategic decision has been made to lower R&D costs by taking advantage of lower labour costs in China. Also, time-to-market for new products in East Asia will be reduced. The hope is that this move will enable the company to build up know-how on East Asian markets and to target the local customer base in better ways. However, people in the R&D department at headquarters are not happy about this move; there is the rumour that jobs might be lost. Soon after this decision has been implemented, headquarters' R&D engineers start to complain about the capabilities of the Chinese engineers: 'They simply follow orders and don't care about quality. Whatever we give them, they copy, and they are not motivated to contribute and think on their own.'

Piece 2

A Chinese company wins the governmental bid for operating a copper mine in a remote hinterland of Pakistan (Kakar and Mahadevan, 2020). For the first time in history, the contract has not gone to a company from Australia, the traditional country of origin of the mining consortia operating in Pakistan and one of the global key players in global mining. There is the hope amongst Pakistani government officials that this move will enable the country to free itself from the legacies of the British Empire and to decrease existing dependencies on economically more developed members of the Commonwealth such as Australia. For the Chinese company this is a highly prestigious project, and managers and engineers are proud of the achievement which it signifies. They believe that China has come a long way in the last decades, that it has overcome poverty and embraced development, and that it is their obligation to also help other countries of the non-West world, such as Pakistan, to achieve the same. Chinese managers and mining engineers promoting this spirit are sent to Pakistan to operate the mine with the help of local Pakistani workers and technicians. Soon afterwards, it becomes apparent that both sides mistrust each other's capabilities and motivations. These are the main themes in how both sides talk about each other.

Table 8.1 Chinese and Pakistani perspectives on IB cooperation

Chinese managers on Pakistani workers	Pakistani workers on Chinese managers
'They have lower standards of work and want spoon-feeding.'	'Pakistani are neither invited nor told about the daily or monthly production.'
'We need to monitor them constantly.'	'You must play dumb and say "yes" to everything, so that you don't lose your job.'
'They don't care about goals and drink tea* all the time.'	'They don't speak English well, and they don't even drink their tea like we do.' **
'We need to make them realize that this is about the future of Pakistan.'	'Our government sells out the country, and the local population suffers.'

* The Pakistani drink black tea with milk and sugar (English style), poured from the stove, through a tea strainer, and served in cups. Tea is consumed after lunch or during breaks, at specific times, in groups.

** The Chinese drink green tea, often from a personal thermos, whilst working. This is an individual activity throughout the day, and the thermos may be refilled with hot water anytime.

Source: based on insights from Kakar and Mahadevan (2020)

Underpinnings of International Business

Whether IB is a recent or age-old phenomenon depends on perspective. If one understands IB broadly, as any transfer of goods or services across distance and boundaries, then it has been in place for ages. Examples are prehistoric travel routes, the Silk Road, or – less well-known, but one of the prominent academic examples – the exchange of cowrie shells (as a commodity or as 'shell money') in many parts of the world. It is only if one understands IB in the narrow sense, namely as the transfer of goods, services and capital *across national borders*, that it becomes a more recent phenomenon.

STUDENT ACTIVITY 8.1

Your Own IB Exposure

Which activities in your everyday life make you part of today's international business, that is economic activities which cross national borders? Find examples for those key roles which you might occupy in International Business:

- Consumer
- Producer
- Supplier
- (Past, present or future) employee
- Investor
- Other

Which drivers of the respective activities and roles can you identify, in particular, where or what does the global or cross-national influence originate from?

The idea of trade as a positive-sum game

IB takes place in the global market sphere. Markets are 'places' where offer and demand meet. Historically, these places were physical locations; nowadays, markets can also be a shared idea of the place held in mind by all those who interact on this market (e.g. the internet).

Due to certain factors, it has become much easier for companies to target markets across national borders. Reasons are, for example, the relevance of immaterial technology and services, and the reduced transport costs of physical goods and technology, as well as the supra-national and cross-border integration of markets.

The *'invisible hand of the market'* (Smith, 1776) refers to the idea that, in an ideal market, the price and quantity of goods will float towards the perfect equilibrium; in the perfect market, consumers will be able to buy exactly as much as they want at the optimum price. This then implies that those making offers on a market (e.g. companies) should specialize on those offers which they can produce and sell the most effectively and efficiently.

- *Effectiveness* means that the desired output (the market offer) can be reached.
- *Efficiency* means that the desired output (the market offer) can be achieved with the least input (e.g. labour, raw material).

Out of this follows that IB actors such as countries, companies, organizations, etc. will specialize in those marketable offers which they can produce the best. The idea is that, via specialization and trade that is facilitated on a global scale, more products will be available at lower prices to more people. For example, New Zealand should not invest in producing rice, but rather concentrate on sheep, whereas India should do the opposite, and both should trade these commodities with each other. One could therefore also mark the beginnings of IB with a crucial step of how the theories underlying it developed, namely with the idea that *International Business is a positive-sum game* which is beneficial to those involved (Ricardo, 1817; overview in Hill, 2009). The idea is that, via specialization and trade that is facilitated on a global scale, more products will be available at lower prices to more people.

Cross-cultural application: Functionalist approaches to culture in IB

IB is related to the macro-environment of CCM ('large-scale culture'), which means that functionalist and causal approaches to culture are highly relevant to it. Functionalist CCM is concerned with how CCM works (Chapter 5); it tries to establish the impact which selected universal aspects of culture (cultural dimensions or cultural value orientations) have, for example, on the international activities of companies or consumer behaviour. For example, Hofstede (2001) differentiates between 'indulgence' and 'restraint' – these are two cultural dimensions indicating whether people are likely to indulge (satisfy needs immediately) or restrain (postpone gratification). Countries score differently regarding these dimensions. For making strategic decisions such as 'should we internationalize our product to country A or B?', these scores are relevant because they suggest a certain causality for actual consumer buying behaviour and the degree of the general willingness to spend money. Functionalist approaches to CCM are thus highly suited for making strategic decisions regarding when, how and why companies should go international.

The need for IB integration and regulation

In an ideal market, there are no distortions; that is, no barriers to the intended outcome. Consequently, the costs for all will be reduced, and more and/or better products at lower prices will be made available to more people. However, in real life, markets are not perfect, more so on international or global level. Common distortions are, for example,

- an unequal distribution of information
- lack of or more difficult access to the market
- perishable goods and not fully transferable services.

In the IB environment, such distortions multiply. Also, new distortions occur, such as:

- language barriers
- difference in political, economic and legal systems
- gaps in living standards, health and income
- and last, but not least, cross-cultural differences.

Therefore, many IB theories suggest that these distortions need to be minimized for IB to be beneficial not only in theory, but also in practice ('New Zealand and India are both better off because of specialization and trade').

The general idea of IB as a positive-sum game thus only works if all IB actors adhere to shared principles. For example, if one country decides to protect its market and to demand tariffs for any imports, then others might do the same to retaliate. Certain institutions and principles therefore try to ensure fair rules of the game to all.

Institutions are elements of IB which strengthen the trust in a certain exchange – in this case international trade and investment – and the international mobility of knowledge, ideas and people. Institutions can be formal (structural) or informal (language-based, social or cultural). For example, the World Bank is a formal institution facilitating trust in international money exchange. Shared behavioural patterns ('the culture') of those who do business with each other are informal institutions. Conclusively, an *institutional view on IB* (Peng and Meyer, 2011) proposes that it is institutional knowledge and skills which are the most crucial to managers and organizations for achieving international success.

> **Institutions** Elements of IB that intend to strengthen the trust in and the reliability of the exchange

Principles are those 'rules of the game' which aim at ensuring the potential benefits of IB for all. For example, the 'most favoured nation' clause to which all countries that are members of the World Trade Organization (WTO) need to adhere. The clause specifies that a WTO member country which grants a special favour to another WTO member (such as lower tariffs for importing goods) has to do the same for all other WTO members. As of 2021, the WTO (2021) counts 164 of the world's 195 countries as its members. This implies that (in theory) most countries on the globe need to adhere to the principle of 'treat every nation as you treat the most preferred one', thus reducing market distortions.

Regional economic integration is another, related process. For example, the European Union (EU), originally intended as an economic union, has brought about further political integration. Regional economic integration lowers internal barriers, e.g. as related to individual mobility, and to trade and investment, but raises access barriers to companies and people outside of the integrated sphere. It is one aspect of how the ideal of the perfect international market is distorted in reality.

Principles IB rules that shall ensure that IB is the most beneficial to all (or most)

The Local and Global Exposure of People and Companies

When going or being international, companies need to manage global, local and cross-cutting (glocal) forces. This section highlights these challenges and their CCM implications.

Globalization, localization and glocalization

Globalization is both a driver and a consequence of IB. Certain production factors, such as materials or people, are increasingly mobile, also because of lower transportation costs. Additionally, because of information and communications (ICT) technology, location matters less in IB today, and corporate and any business activities are now pursued across distance. Due to the exposure to global media and global products, as well as to ICT, some lifestyles and consumer behaviours are streamlined. National economies are increasingly integrated, and markets have grown together to a higher degree. Together, these factors create interlinkages between people, companies, societies and countries.

Globalization Global integrative forces and streamlining of consumer behaviour and other spheres of life and work

> **STUDENT ACTIVITY 8.2**
>
> **International Business Then and Now**
>
> - Re-consider your own roles in IB which you have previously identified. Consider the lives of a previous generation. How are your roles in IB and your exposure to IB different compared to members of a previous generation?
> - Revisit the pieces of the Opening Case. Which aspects of them would have been unthinkable and/or undoable 30 years ago?

Globalization does not imply that everyone's lives are 'the same'. It only states that there is a global dimension to life and work today, which accompanies local experiences. **Glocalization** (Robertson, 1994) is the term that covers the specific processes by which the global and the local come together for a certain group, context or activity. Companies glocalize when adapting their global offers to local preferences. Fast food chains, for example, serve different types of burgers in different national contexts, e.g. lamb burgers in the Middle East, vegetarian burgers in India and beef burgers in North America. Glocalization has thus also been referred to as the 'McDonaldization' of IB.

Customer needs, too, are characterized by a combination of global and local factors. What is required is thus a careful analysis of how culture impacts markets. Whitening creams, for example, are a sought-after product only in countries wherein the cultural ideal of 'light skin colour' prevails, and self-tanning sprays are a desirable product only in locations wherein a sun tan constitutes the ideal – a culture-specific difference in what customers deem beautiful. In this case, companies thus need to pursue a localized strategy. At the same time, all these consumers might buy the same equipment for working online. If they have equal buying power and if the product is equally available to them, then global is better, and companies should standardize their offers.

> **Glocalization** A (cultural) force that is characterized by simultaneous global and local influences

STUDENT ACTIVITY 8.3

Glocalization

Consider your own life. Which elements of it are glocalized?

Remember that glocalization means that global and local influences come together in people's lives. For example, spices from all over the globe can now be bought in cities worldwide, yet only a specific number of people in a certain locality mixes a certain global influence (certain spices) into their own lives.

Your task is to find at least five aspects of your own life which are glocalized, and to identify the relevant cultural group or community which you share this pattern with.

Link to Practice: Disneyland in Paris

Why was Disneyland more successful in Tokyo than in Paris? Key elements here were wrong assumptions from the side of the US-American managers planning the Euro location of the theme park (overview in Euro Disney, 2022). For example, when the location had to be chosen, Disney selected Paris (in France) over a location in Spain, due to the city being in the very heart of Europe. The assumption was that the park would be within reach of more visitors this way, despite the climate being less favourable to winter visitors compared to Tokyo. However, what Disney had not considered was that cultural distance outweighs factual distance: to travel from Berlin or Prague to Paris is experienced as a vaster distance than travelling the same factual distance within the USA. Furthermore, difference in language and customs were neglected, and, as Brannen (2004) showed, 'Mickey' as a cultural image also does not integrate well with the cultural image of France. As a result of this poor choice in location, visitor numbers have remained well below expectations since the opening of Euro Disney and much below Disney in Tokyo.

Trade-offs between standardization and adaptation

IB brings about strategic trade-offs between **efficiency** and effectivity. On the one hand, standardization bears opportunities in terms of efficiency. Producing more quantities of the same product, for example, results in less fixed costs per

> **Efficiency** Here, economic advantage put into effect via utilizing operating on, beyond and across localities (economies of scale)

> **Effectivity** Here, economic advantage put into effect via being closer to the market or a local environment

items (economies of scale) and also enables companies to acquire more and faster learning about the process (learning curves) – global is better, and this pushes the company to the global sphere. However, standardization also means to be less close to the local customer, for example, in terms of culture-specific preferences or market conditions – a loss in **effectivity**. From this perspective, *local is better*, and this pulls the company towards local markets. For example, it is common in India for truck drivers to transport passengers in order to increase their income, and it is therefore preferable to have as many seats as possible in the front of the truck – a specific local demand to be considered. On the other hand, standardizing truck production will enable a company to integrate their global operations, and to exploit learning curves and economies of scale.

STUDENT ACTIVITY 8.4

Economies of Standardization and Adaptation

Consider the pieces of the Opening Case.

- Piece 1 describes a consumer product (smart watches). To what extent is this a global, and to what extent is this a local product? Differentiate the features of the product into its standardized and localized elements.
- Piece 2 describes how a key raw material for production is made accessible. Research the internet. For what is copper used nowadays? Who requires it? Where can copper be sourced, where is it processed, who buys it and for what purposes? Trace the supply chain of copper in IB and identify those who have an interest in global copper mining.

The appropriate management of local responsiveness versus global integration (differentiation versus standardization) is a key success factor for MNEs. Bartlett and Ghoshal (1989) have developed a typology to classify the strategies pursued (see Figure 8.1).

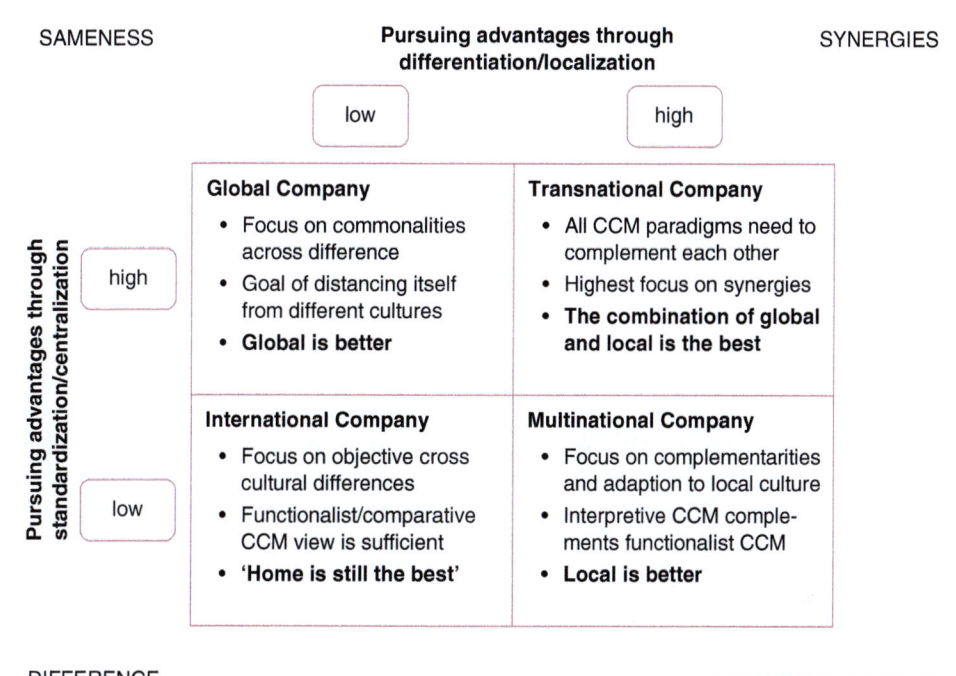

	Pursuing advantages through differentiation/localization	
	low	**high**
high	**Global Company** • Focus on commonalities across difference • Goal of distancing itself from different cultures • **Global is better**	**Transnational Company** • All CCM paradigms need to complement each other • Highest focus on synergies • **The combination of global and local is the best**
low	**International Company** • Focus on objective cross cultural differences • Functionalist/comparative CCM view is sufficient • **'Home is still the best'**	**Multinational Company** • Focus on complementarities and adaption to local culture • Interpretive CCM complements functionalist CCM • **Local is better**

SAMENESS (top-left) — SYNERGIES (top-right)
DIFFERENCE (bottom-left) — COMPLEMENTARITIES (bottom-right)
Left axis: Pursuing advantages through standardization/centralization

Figure 8.1 Typology of multinational companies and its CCM implications

Source: adapted from Bartlett and Ghoshal (1989)

An **international company** is exposed to the global business environment the least. Cross-cultural differences, if experienced at all, are thus mainly experienced in terms of objective cross-national differences, e.g. in political, economic or language-related aspects. A functionalist, comparative CCM perspective might suffice, because 'home is still the best', and the approach to cross-cultural differences never exceeds the notion of 'difference' and otherness.

A **global company** is exposed to the international business environment to a higher degree, yet makes it a point to distance itself from cross-cultural differences (*global is better*). The purpose is thus to identify commonalities in comparative CCM perspectives; the CCM focus lies on 'sameness'.

A **multinational company** wishes to adapt to different IB environments (*local is better*) and to identify complementarities. It thus needs to understand culture in context to a higher degree and beyond mere comparative perspectives. An interpretive approach needs to complement the functionalist one in order to identify complementarities across cultures.

A **transnational company** aims at utilizing both potential dimensions of competitive advantage by assessing each part of its functions separately for their standardization and differentiation potential. For example, a company might standardize its human resource management operations but run independent advertising campaigns all around the globe (differentiation). It might also centralize the IT-support function at headquarters but employ sales representatives locally (a localization decision). This implies that cross-cultural considerations are crucial to the success of the company on all levels and in all aspects. The integration of functionalist, interpretive and critical perspectives is required to achieve the best possible overall combination of global and local (*the best combination between global and local is the best*) and to identify synergies across cultures.

> **International, global, multinational, transnational company** Typology classifying four ways in which companies may utilize local and global IB advantages

STUDENT ACTIVITY 8.5

The Strategic Orientation of Companies in IB

Consider the pieces of the Opening Case.

- Do the companies pursue advantages from adaptation or standardization, or of a combination thereof?
- Which trade-offs can you identify between the conflicting needs for global integration and local responsiveness?
- Would you classify the companies described as international, multinational, transnational or global?

Provide reasons for your answers, and also highlight which further information beyond the case descriptions you require to come to a grounded conclusion.

CCM and International Business

The IB strategies pursued by companies have CCM implications (see Table 8.2). In an international company, there is not much engagement with CCM, and superficial knowledge, e.g. regarding which cultural dimensions, might suffice. Multinational and global companies pursue specific advantages in IB. Thus, managers need to possess both knowledge (theory) and skills (knowledge-in-action) to put strategy into practice. The highest demand on managerial capabilities follows from a transnational orientation. Here the cross-cultural manager is the one actively shaping how global and local come together. This requires not only knowledge and skills, but a mindset and organizational framework that motivates individuals and organizational units to engage with the task and to navigate it.

Table 8.2 Types of companies and cross-cultural management requirements

Type of company	Source of competitive advantage	Cultural focus	Approach to cultural differences	Required CCM capabilities
International	–	On home culture	Distancing oneself from culture	Low: knowledge
Multinational	Localization / differentiation	Be near to local cultures; many cultural orientations	Maintaining and exploiting differences	Medium: knowledge and skills
Global	Standardization / centralization	Be detached from local cultures, focus on global culture	Streamlining differences	Medium: knowledge and skills
Transnational	Combine and mix as proves best	Combine and mix as proves best	Utilizing differences as proves best and moving beyond	High: knowledge, skills and mindset

Link to Practice: Transnational by Evolution?

With employing more than 148,000 people across the world, with 400 brand names in 190 countries, and with its complex organizational design, Unilever (Unilever, 2022) fits the characteristics of a transnational company as proposed by IB studies. However, as Maljers (1992) argued 30 years ago, this is 'not the outcome of a conscious effort'. Rather, 'the company has evolved mainly through a Darwinian system or retaining what was useful and rejecting what no longer worked'. This suggests that it is actual corporate practice, evidenced by the degree to which a company responds to market needs (and how well it does so), that helps a company integrate the conflicting demands of being global and local in the long run.

Philosophies and aims underlying corporate internationalization

What do companies expect from the IB environment? The underlying corporate philosophies can be classified into ethnocentric, polycentric, regiocentric and geocentric (Perlmutter, 1969). This typology describes how the advantages pursued by a company (from standardization or differentiation) are linked to the company's approach to culture, and to how the company utilizes the cultural capabilities of its managerial staff. The implementation of these corporate philosophies furthermore requires a certain managerial 'mindset', to be differentiated into the categories defence, exploration, control and integration (Kedia and Mukherji, 1999).

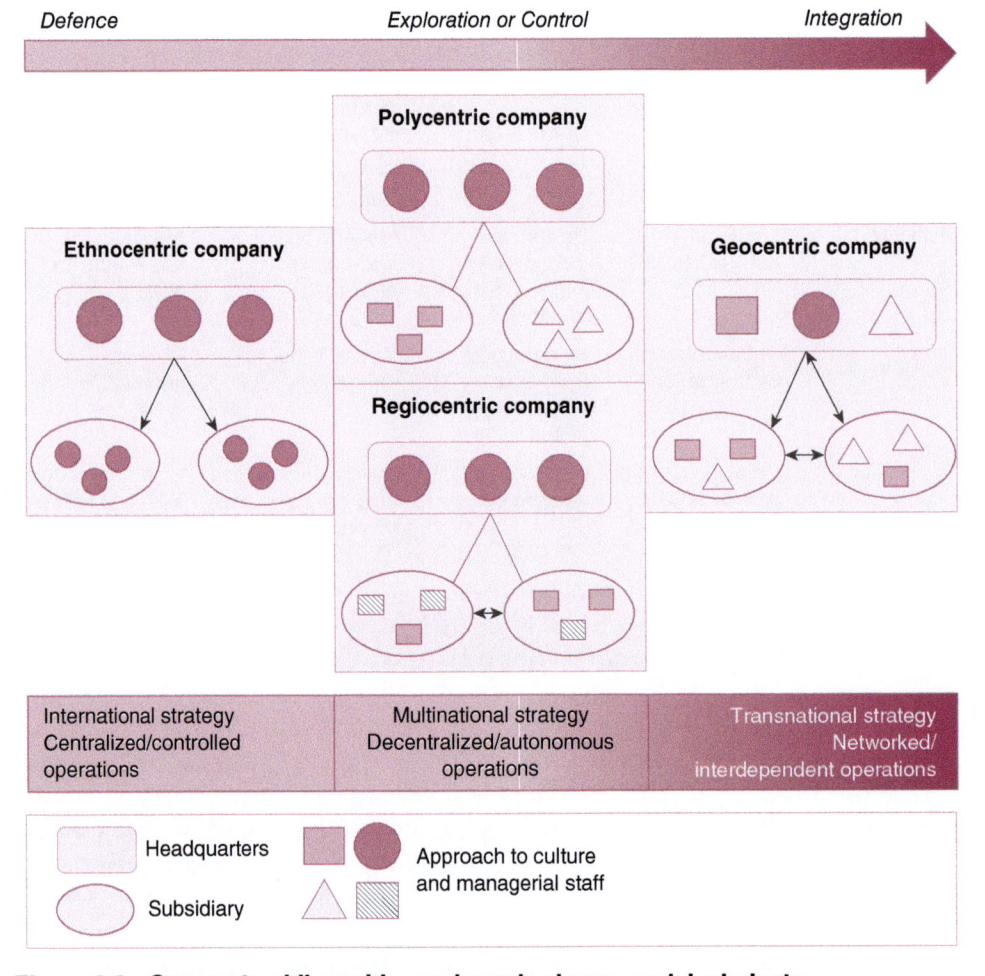

Figure 8.2 **Corporate philosophies and required managerial mindsets**

Source: adapted from Perlmutter (1969); Kedia and Mukherji (1999)

In an **ethnocentric company**, headquarters' corporate culture, as well as managerial staff from headquarters, are transplanted to all subsidiaries worldwide. Therefore, there is a sort of cultural imperialism associated with this type. The idea is 'how we do it at home, is how we should do it everywhere'. Thus, the focus is on cultural control, and the main advantage comes from centralization. In terms of the underlying cross-cultural mindset, the opportunities and willingness for cross-cultural learning are limited, and, therefore, the ethnocentric company signifies a low level of IB exposure. In terms of the Bartlett/Ghoshal typology (see above), corporate strategy is international, and the advantages from both differentiation and standardization are low.

The **polycentric company** is the opposite of the ethnocentric company in that local management and culture dominates at all sites. This type might be chosen if local demands are highly culture-specific or differ from each other, and local responsiveness is thus a key requirement. This type achieves strong local cohesion, yet brings about higher coordination costs and a lack of global integration.

A **regiocentric company** mixes polycentrism with integration on a regional level. For example, there will be exchange within larger regions, such as Asia, Europe or North or Latin America, yet not beyond these regions. Headquarters' culture and managerial staff remain remote.

Both polycentric and regiocentric companies are characterized by cultural relativism: 'how they do it over there (and we over here), is how they should do it over there (and we over here)'. Their focus is on decentralized and autonomous decision-making within the separate units. In terms of the Bartlett/Ghoshal typology (see above), corporate strategy is multinational, and it is mainly the advantages from differentiation which are pursued. In terms of the underlying cross-cultural mindset, there is the willingness to exploit cross-cultural differences if they bring about market success abroad, yet, there is no exploration of how these differences might inform other locations; there is no integration or the creation of synergies from difference.

A **geocentric company** signifies the highest levels of combined global integration and local responsiveness. Management techniques, styles and concepts ('culture'), as well as managerial staff are mixed and combined in the best possible ways, and there is no pre-classification of people and cultures. In terms of the underlying mindset, there is the willingness to explore both local and global dimensions of culture, and both standardization and differentiation advantages are pursued, as seems best. The outlook is on interdependent and networked strategies and practices. Managers proceed from a global perspective, and, in terms of the Bartlett/Ghoshal typology (see above), corporate strategy is transnational.

Ethnocentric, polycentric, regiocentric, geocentric company Typology to classify the aims and philosophies underlying corporate activities in IB (Perlmutter model)

> ### STUDENT ACTIVITY 8.6
>
> **Philosophies Underlying Corporate Internationalization**
>
> Consider the pieces of the Opening Case.
>
> - Classify the corporate approach to cross-cultural differences and staffing policies in terms of the aforementioned typology as ethnocentric, polycentric, regiocentric or global.
> - Next, consider what kind of approach to cross-cultural differences the companies pursue. Is the focus on knowledge, skills or mindset?
> - Do you find this approach sufficient? Why (not)?

Why and How do Companies Internationalize?

The corporate strategic decision to internationalize largely stems from the aim of utilizing the advantages of the IB environment (its 'markets'). Examples for advantages to be pursued are, for example, low labour costs, higher efficiency and effectiveness in operations, reduction of the costs of logistics, closeness to suppliers and/or customers, and access to certain raw materials, new markets, technology and know-how. Ideally, companies should internationalize with a purpose, and not by chance, and they should do so when it seems likely that internationalization will bring about *competitive advantage*.

Traditionally, corporate internationalization has been differentiated into two phases:

- **Going international** involves management challenges such as which foreign markets to select and how to act on them (*target marketing*, such as niche marketing), how to enter and cultivate these markets (*market entry and cultivation*), and when and in which order and intensity to do so (*timing*).
- The main focus of **being international** is on *allocation* (such as the international, global, multinational and transnational allocation of resources and activities), and related *coordination challenges*, which include the configuration of structure, human resources, technology and corporate culture. The typologies presented in the previous section exemplify this task.

In the contemporary IB environment, internationalization is no longer a defined, step-by-step process from 'low' to 'high' internationalization, but involves waves and cycles. For example, companies might choose to de-internationalize at a certain

CCM and International Business

point and then re-enter international markets again. Furthermore, there are external and internal disruptions to the corporate internationalization process, such as the ones caused by the 2020 COVID-19 pandemic. Figure 8.3 depicts these contemporary IB conditions. It also shows how it is still helpful to split up the contemporary IB challenge into its five main focus points in order to make it small and, thus, manageable.

> **Going international** A company entering the international market

> **Being international** A company sustaining its presence on the international market

Exogenous shocks — Market entry and cultivation — Disruptions

Target marketing — Coordination

Timing — Allocation

Explanation:
- Going international focus
- Being international focus
- Internationalization: Waves and circles

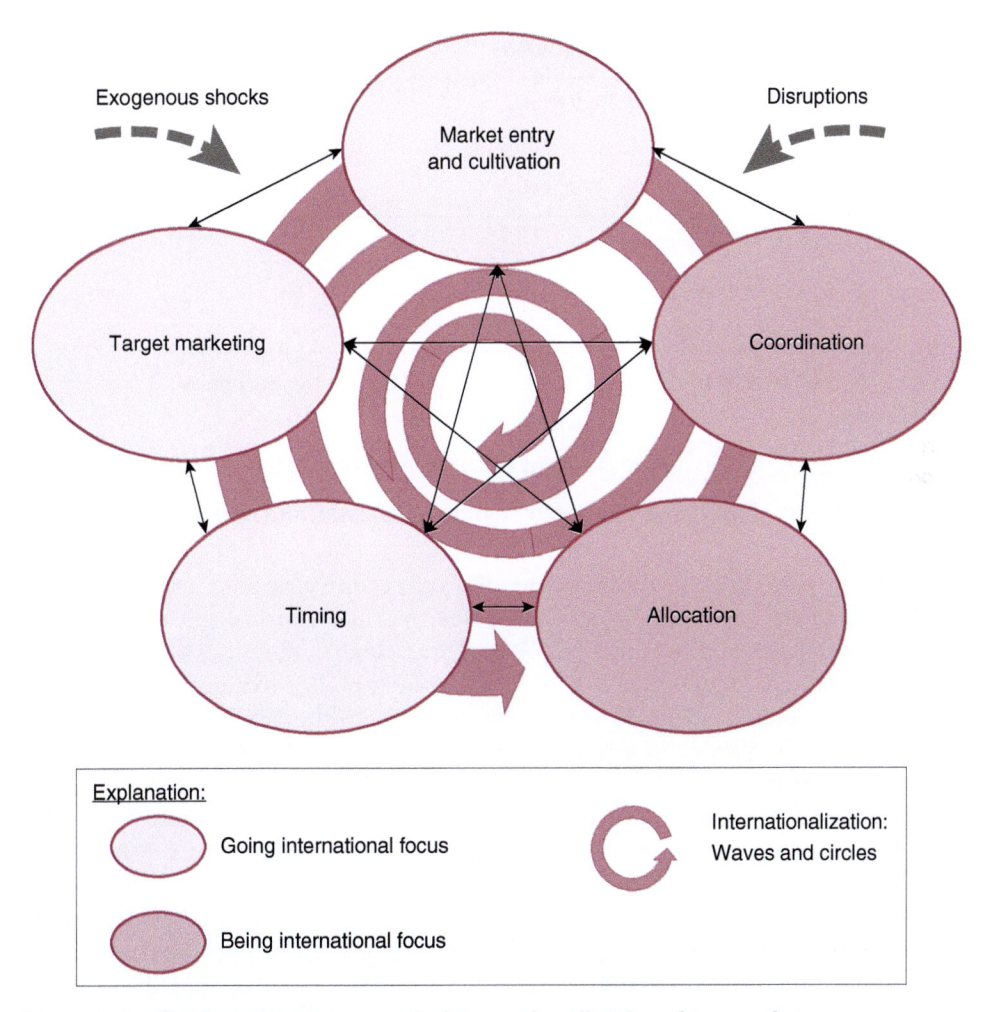

Figure 8.3 Contemporary corporate internationalization: An overview

Source: adapted from Schmid (2007: 14)

How to enter and cultivate international markets

The modes of market entry which are available to companies can be classified with regard to their risk, required investment, and degree of control (see Figure 8.4). Generally speaking, low-risk and low-control modes of going international, such as export, do not involve investment across borders, but merely the transportation of goods across borders.

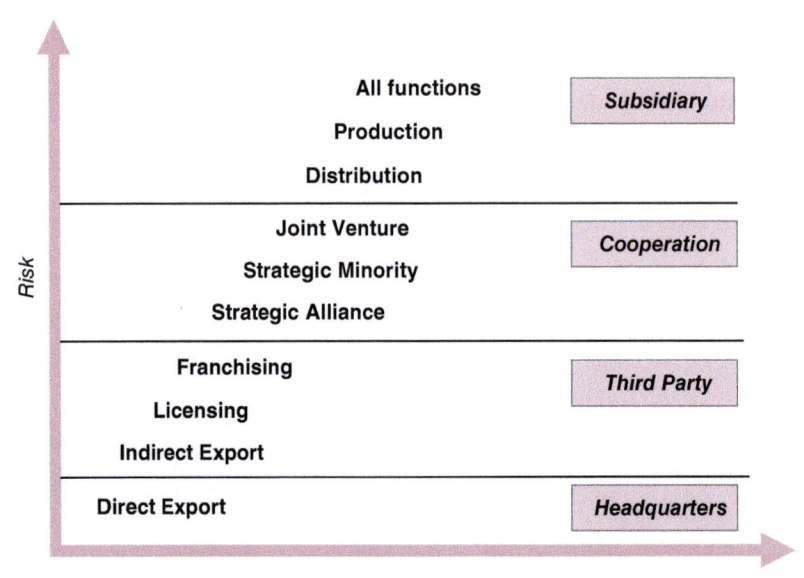

Figure 8.4 Modes of market entry and cultivation, and risks and opportunities

Risk (vertical axis) / *Resources required for/ability to control activities at new location* (horizontal axis)

- All functions / Production / Distribution — **Subsidiary**
- Joint Venture / Strategic Minority / Strategic Alliance — **Cooperation**
- Franchising / Licensing / Indirect Export — **Third Party**
- Direct Export — **Headquarters**

Underlying the choice of the mode of market entry should be considerations of corporate strengths and weaknesses, market opportunities and risks, and associated costs and potential returns of investment. Potential cross-cultural differences and similarities contribute to these factors. For example, a company that wishes to enter a culturally distant market might choose indirect export as first mode of market entry to minimize first entry risks and to learn culture from local export partners.

The cross-cultural implication of market entry and cultivation arises from the insight that a company which knows its home market (in CCM terms, how to do things around *here*) does not necessarily know a foreign market (in CCM terms, how to do things around *there*) in terms of customer needs and wishes. It is thus part of the international challenge to be aware that one does not know a certain market environment (which is then perceived as 'foreign'), to account for and manage the risks involved, and to gain the required cultural knowledge.

Simply speaking, it is the company's problem to make themselves familiar to the foreign market and to account for the associated costs. This is referred to as **liability of foreignness**; that is, the costs faced by companies operating outside their home market above those experienced by companies that are 'native' to this market. Part of this liability is expressed as **psychic distance** (Johanson and Vahlne, 1977); that is, the perceived differences that make the company 'alien' to the foreign market and its potential customers, suppliers or business partners. It is assumed that a company that internationalizes needs to develop specific assets to counter the liability of foreignness as, for example, brought about by psychic distance. Cross-cultural competencies are such a potential asset.

> **Liability of foreignness** Need to account for corporate alienness on a foreign market

> **Psychic distance** (Perceived) differences that make a company 'alien' to a market

The factors contributing to 'psychic distance' are both objective (quantifiable and measurable) and subjective (rooted in divergent interpretations). They can be grouped into four categories, namely:

- linguistic differences and translation issues
- cultural factors, such as differences in societal norms, values and customs
- difference in economic factors
- effects of the political and legal system.

Cross-cultural differences when dealing with 'foreign' markets are thus both perceived (e.g. psychic distance) and actual (e.g. language, economic system, political regulations), and that both factors result in actual difference to be factored in by the company.

How to time international market entry and cultivation

Regarding the timing of their internationalization, companies might enter several markets simultaneously (**sprinkler strategy**) or one after the other (**waterfall strategy**), or use a combination thereof. Managers thus need to configure the speed and intensity of corporate internationalization. Generally speaking, a sprinkler strategy seems suitable if a product seems sufficiently attractive on a global level and is not specific to a certain national cultural environment, whereas a waterfall strategy might allow the company to internationalize step-by-step and adapt their offers and cultural competencies to each new market. Cultural dimensions and insights on cultural distance can provide advice on this matter.

Cultural distance is a concept developed from Hofstede's cultural dimensions by Kogut and Singh (1988). One finding of their study on foreign direct investment (FDI) in the USA was that cultural distance influences the market entry mode. However, there are also processes that close this distance, such as globalization, geographical proximity, foreign experience, acculturation, or the cultural attractiveness of countries (Shenkar, 2001). Cultures and countries are thus in a constant process of 'friction' at their respective interfaces.

> **Sprinkler strategy** Entering foreign markets simultaneously, a specific timing strategy

> **Waterfall strategy** Entering foreign markets sequentially, a specific timing strategy

To minimize a company's liability of 'foreignness' (see previous), the so-called **Uppsala model** (Johanson and Vahlne, 1977), a specific type of waterfall model, suggested that companies internationalize from culturally similar to culturally alien markets – or, in other words, from lower to successively higher psychic distance – in order to maximize the changes of success and to transfer learning from one market to the other. This way, the model proposed, companies will successively build up the required cross-cultural knowledge that reduces their own foreignness to other national markets. IKEA is said to have followed this internationalization path (Schmid, 2007).

> **Uppsala model** Model suggesting corporate internationalization from culturally similar to culturally alien markets in order to minimize costs and maximize success

Since the first publication of this model, relevant changes to it have been proposed by the authors themselves (Johanson and Vahlne, 2009).

- Firstly, 'markets' have now become so integrated that the cultural differences experienced by companies and people cannot be clearly differentiated along national lines anymore.
- Secondly, organizational borders, such as between customers and suppliers, have become blurred and even integrated into complex organizational networks of which companies are 'insiders' or 'outsiders'.
- Thirdly, the organizational uncertainties brought about by network 'outsidership' are more fundamental than the (perceived and actual) differences emerging from foreignness to markets. Rather than focusing on 'entering markets', contemporary organizations and managers thus have to build multiple relations for achieving 'insidership' in relation to as many cultural contexts and groups of people as possible.

In summary, one can thus understand the initial Uppsala model (Johanson and Vahlne, 1977) as an example of how corporate success might be achieved when going international in the classic, sequential sense (Figure 8.4). The revised Uppsala model (Johanson and Vahlne, 2009) informs managers about what has changed under contemporary conditions (Figure 8.3). As an additional level to be addressed by cross-cultural managers, the revised Uppsala model also highlights the relevance of the organizational context for corporate internationalization and intercultural interactions. The organizational dimension of CCM will be highlighted in Chapter 9.

How to target international markets

The basic premise of target marketing is that the market needs to be profitable enough; it must comprise a sufficiently large customer base. Here, IB provides opportunities that might not exist on a single national market. For example, long-distance runners in one location would be too few to be considered a profitable 'market' for washing liquid for functional running wear. Yet, grouping those of the same interest globally makes this need economically relevant. From a marketing perspective, this means to target a **niche**, that is a very specific customer segment, across national borders, thus creating a so-called **transnational market segment**.

This advantage has also been exploited by highly specialized small- and medium-sized enterprises (SMEs). For example, there are companies offering in-situ engine repairs to large container ships. This niche service might not be profitable enough in just one country, yet, is highly sought after globally. Thus, these SMEs have been called '**born globals**' (Rennie, 1993), that is, companies with a very specialized purpose that need to be 'global' from the beginning onwards or shortly after their inception in order to gain the return of investment they need for profitable operations.

> **Niche** A specialized segment of the whole of a potential market

> **Transnational market segment** Customer needs which are homogeneous across national markets and which are targeted as a single market with multiple locations. Often, a transnational market segment unites many national niche markets

> **Born global** A company that targets global market segments from the beginning onwards and does not follow the phase model of going and being international

Spotlight: Born Global

In their original Uppsala model, Johanson and Vahlne (1977) describe a stepwise internationalization process, which requires experiential market knowledge and the management of psychic distance. Yet, some companies leapfrog these internationalization stages (Rennie, 1993).

Ferguson et al. (2021: 263) define born global firms 'as start-ups with at least 25% of their sales in exports within three years of founding'. Advances in technology (from physical infrastructure such as railroads and highways up to the internet), reduced barriers for trade between countries, free movement of people and capital are seen as parameters facilitating the appearance of born global firms (Rennie, 1993).

Holtbrügge and Wessely (2007) identify the following company- and market-related success factors in the rapid internationalization of born global companies. These are: international experience, certain characteristics of the managers (age, knowledge of international markets, networks, etc.), company's vision, innovative products, etc., as well as growth opportunities in foreign markets, the degree of market regulation, industry type, etc. Logitech (founded in 1981) and eBay (founded in 1995) are regarded as companies that underwent within a few years a rapid internationalization process (Holtbrügge and Wessely, 2007), yet more recent companies such as Comodule, Khar & Partners, Frog Bikes (founded between 2013 and 2014) started their international activities immediately or within a mere few months (Eurofound, 2018). The internationalization challenges faced by born globals are similar to non-born global companies (different legislation, different product requirements, different technical standards, etc.), and access to capital proves to be an important barrier in the internationalization process (Eurofound, 2018). Yet, operating in niche markets, having a powerful innovation culture and being led by founders who often share the same educational background and a common vision of the future, born global companies are able to compete on the international market even though their resources and experience are rather scarce in comparison (Cavusgil and Knight, 2015).

Link to Practice: IKEA's Path to Internationalization

IKEA is a Swedish-founded, Europe-based multinational company that is frequently used as an example to illustrate the original Uppsala model (Schmid, 2007). IKEA's practices exemplify the corporate strategy to internationalize step-by-step from culturally familiar to culturally alien markets, and to also use hybrid markets as 'fountain heads' for accessing new cultural regions. In terms of timing, this signifies a 'waterfall strategy' with some 'fountain head' elements in the case of culturally hybrid markets. For example, from Sweden, the company internationalized to Norway and, next, Denmark – two Scandinavian countries. To build up knowledge on other cultural regions, the company then turned to Switzerland – due to its cultural hybridity, a small test market for Germany, France and also Italy. As products proved to be the most successful in German-speaking Switzerland, the company then moved on to Germany. Australia functioned as a smaller test market for the English-speaking world and afterwards, utilizing the combined French- and English-speaking corporate experience from Switzerland and Australia, Canada was approached. Applying the Uppsala model obviously is only one of many informed readings of corporate reality. However, the general skill of applying theory to reality is something the cross-cultural manager needs to train themselves in, thus have a look at the full internationalization path of IKEA (Figure 8.5) to draw further conclusions.

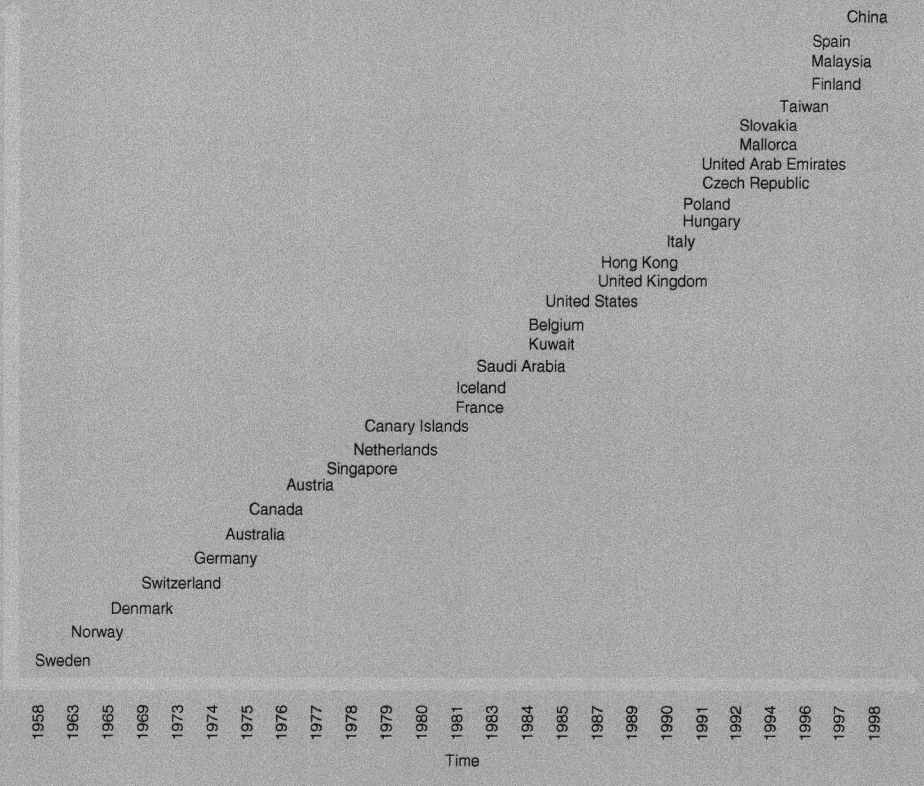

Figure 8.5   IKEA's internationalization path
Source: Schmid (2007); Internet Archive (1999)

Towards a Responsible Stakeholder Management in IB

Beyond pure market considerations, the interests of those whose needs are not marketable in the purely economic sense need to be integrated in IB. For this, a stakeholder approach to IB has been proposed. **Stakeholders** (Freeman, 1984) are all who have an interest in a certain business activity; **shareholders** are those who have invested money in it. Key IB stakeholders are, for example, workers, consumers, companies, employers, governments, ecology and societies. Some of these stakeholders are internal to the organization, some of them are external, and some of them are closer to or further removed from the situation or task at hand. However, they are all part of the CCM context, and part of the managerial task is to find out which stakeholders are relevant, and how exactly.

> **Stakeholders** Those who have an interest ('stake') in a company and its activities

> **Shareholders** Those who have invested in and thus 'own' (a part of) a company

STUDENT ACTIVITY 8.7

Stakeholders in IB

Consider the pieces of the Opening Case.

- Which stakeholders can you identify for each of them? Which ones are internal, which ones are external? Which ones are closer to, which ones are further removed from the situation?
- Based on your analysis, which conflicts of interest can you identify between which stakeholders?

As a strategic management tool, a stakeholder analysis provides managers with a much wider lens on the task at hand, and it also enlarges the view on what constitutes corporate 'costs' or 'return on investment'. For example, whereas a shareholder view on IB would only consider the interests of those who have invested money in business, a stakeholder view also considers the non-monetary and intangible costs to the environment, the society or underprivileged workers. A stakeholder view can thus enable companies and managers to become aware of wider requirements and strategic options, such as the global customer's need for sustainable products or environmental costs as caused by corporate waste; it can highlight relevant market distortions in IB or aspects not yet regulated but relevant to certain stakeholders.

A stakeholder view on IB is focused not only on how IB works the best, but on how it *should* work in the best interest of all; it is an example of a critical IB approach (see In a Nutshell).

In a Nutshell: Critical Perspectives on IB

Critical IB is an approach to IB that requires that managers consider where the knowledge of their theory and practice comes from, also in light of IB history (Cairns and Śliwa, 2008). For example, prevalent management theories and practices underpinned by Western, in particular US-American, culture are still deemed to be universally applicable to all countries and cultures (Boyacigiller and Adler, 1991). IB theory and practice has therefore been critiqued as 'Westocentric'. **Westocentric**' means that a subject or task is approached from a 'Western' point of view, with the term 'West' encompassing Western European nations and some of their former settler colonies, such as Canada, the USA, Australia and New Zealand. Conversely, so called 'indigenous management knowledge', a vague and often contradicting concept (Li et al., 2016), is thought of as solely being applicable to the presumably 'local' context from where it emerged (Jackson, 2013). Exceptions are mainly found for countries, such as the BRIC states (Brazil, Russia, India, China) that challenge existing power relations in IB (Holtbrügge, 2013), with whole continents, such as Africa, remaining seriously underrepresented as the source of an equally valuable global knowledge (Kan et al., 2015).

Westocentric Approaching something/someone from a 'Western' point of view

Questions of corporate social responsibility, ethics and sustainability

The stakeholder approach to IB is partly rooted in the 1960s (US-American) social movements for civil rights, women's rights, consumer rights and environmentalism (Carroll, 2015: 91) which posed new legal requirements on companies, beyond

> **3Ps (people, profit, planet)** The three main trajectories and impact directions of a sustainable (international) business

> **Circular economy** A regenerative model of production and consumption wherein existing materials and products are used as long as possible. This involves sharing, leasing, repairing, recycling and upcycling them.

purely economic considerations (see Figure 8.5). From there, corporate requirements shifted from corporate social responsibility to corporate social *responsiveness*, and, next, to corporate social *performance*. The starting point was a certain ideal image of companies as being socially responsible, which was not yet measurable. Consumer pressures, for example, the need to prove that one's product was 'child-labour free', then demanded for concrete actions to prove that this ideal has been put into practice (corporate social *responsiveness*). The last and current concept, corporate social *performance*, is thus something that is measurable via action. Its scope has been constantly enlarged since the 1980s; it now involves not only business ethics and stakeholder management, but also corporate citizenship and sustainability. *Corporate citizenship* implies that companies are aware of their responsibility as 'global citizens'. Sustainability is usually defined in terms of the **3Ps**: **people** (social sustainability), **profit** (economic

Philanthropic responsibilities → Since 1990s: sustainability, corporate citizenship, business ethics, stakeholder management

Ethical responsibilities → Since 1980s: business ethics, stakeholder management

1970s–80s: corporate social **performance**: *measurable via action*
1970s: corporate social **responsiveness**: *reacting to market/customer requirements*
1960s: corporate social **responsibility**: *an ideal which is not measurable*

Legal responsibilities → 1960s: civil and women's rights, consumerism, environmentalism

Economic responsibilities → Basis of doing business since before 1960s

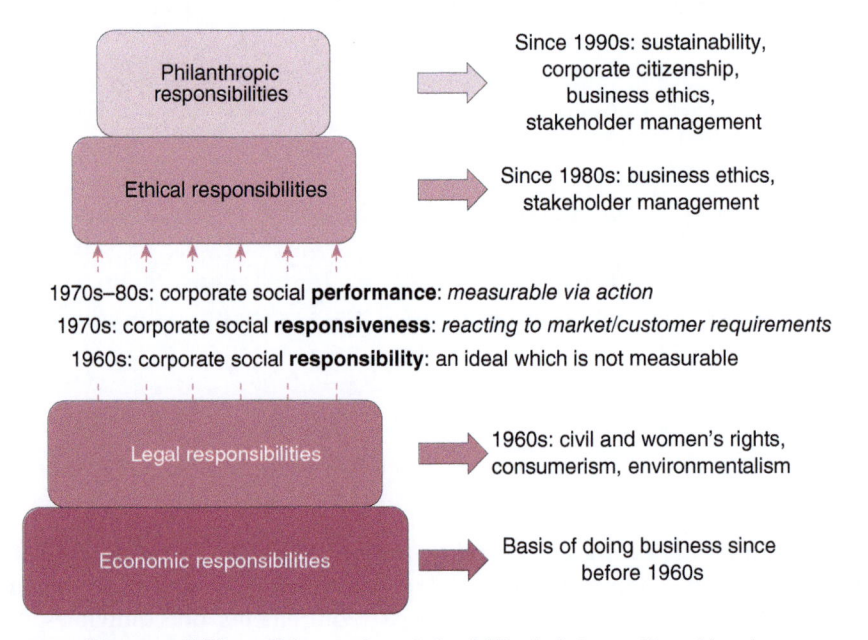

Figure 8.6 Responsibility, ethics and sustainability in international business

Source: adapted from Carroll (2015, 2016)

sustainability) and **planet** (ecological sustainability), all three of which shall not be exploited by the present generation at the cost of future generations (Verbeke et al., 2014). All concepts can also be a source of competitive advantage in contemporary IB. The goal of a sustainable business is the **circular economy**.

Such an action-based approach to ethics, sustainability and corporate social performance (the enlarged understanding of CRS) moves beyond the traditional approach to ethics in IB which discusses ethics in terms of large typologies, such as ethical imperialism versus ethical relativism (Peng and Meyer, 2011).

- **Ethical universalism** refers to the assumptions that ethics are independent of culture and local conditions. An example is the understanding that human rights are universal.
- **Ethical relativism** is the idea that ethics depend on culture and location; there is no universal standard of ethics. In practice, however, neither approach provides managers with feasible advice of how to make decisions in action.
- **Ethical imperialism** means that headquarters impose home-country standards of ethics upon local stakeholders and subsidiaries. It is thus a specific, often inadequate solution to the question of how to deal with divergent ethics in IB, namely in such a way that everyone should do as they do at home and/or by making one's own ethical standards the measuring rod for all.

> **Ethical universalism** The idea and practices that there should be one standard of ethics across the globe

> **Ethical relativism** The idea and practices that ethics differ across markets and localities

> **Ethical imperialism** A philosophy that applies one's own ethical standards worldwide

Furthermore, there is the question upon which principles to base one's actions (Hill, 2009):

- Is an action good because it is based on a non-negotiable standard of ethical principles which can govern all action? This idea of an absolute standard is referred to as a **categorical imperative**, first proposed by philosopher Immanuel Kant. In the case of child-labour, a common occurrence in the global value chain, this would

> **Categorical imperative** An approach to ethics by Immanuel Kant that holds an action to be 'good' if it may serve as the principle for all actions. An absolute, abstract standard of ethics

> **Utilitarianism** An approach to ethics that holds an action to be 'good' if the outcome of this action is positive. A situational, practice-oriented standard of ethics

imply that child-labour is never okay, even though a whole family might starve without it.
- Or, is an action good if it creates good outcome? If this principle, **utilitarianism**, is applied, then any risky technology or potentially life-threatening activity would be good as long as it does not cause negative effects. Or is an action good if the position of the least advantaged stakeholder is improved upon by it? This would mean that a pay rise for top management is good, if the situation of the lowest paid global worker is also improved upon.

Seeking answers to these questions is part of the cross-cultural challenge in IB today.

STUDENT ACIVITY 8.8

CSR and Ethics in IB

Consider the pieces of the Opening Case.

- What is the corporate social responsibility in each case, and how can the respective corporate social performance be measured?
- Which measuring rod for 'ethics' (ethical relativism or ethical imperialism, utilitarianism or categorical imperative) would you propose for each case, and why?
- How can each company be sustainable (what does sustainability mean in each case?), and what are the corporate citizenship requirements in each of the cases?
- Finally, which similarities and differences do you find across the cases when it comes to stakeholder management, corporate social performance, sustainability, ethics and corporate citizenship?

Link to Practice: Avoiding Harm or Doing Good?

Which ethical guidelines shall companies follow when facing different environments, and what shall they learn from these differences? Corporate dilemmas – and ensuing learning opportunities – may be exemplified by example of IKEA, a multinational furniture company originating from Sweden and selling 'Scandinavian lifestyle' by means of its products. In 2012, IKEA was critiqued by media worldwide for 'erasing women' from its Saudi Arabia catalogue (e.g. *Al Jazeera*, 2012; *The Guardian*, 2012). Essentially, the 2012 catalogue was the same as the Swedish one except that pictures of women had been airbrushed from it. According to *Al Jazeera* (2012), 'Saudi Arabia applies strict rules of gender segregation, banning women from driving and requiring them to have permission from a male guardian before travelling or receiving medical care'. IKEA's decision not to show women in their Saudi Arabian catalogue was later on felt to clash with corporate values (*The Guardian*, 2012) as well as with the 'values of the Swedish population' who, according to *Al Jazeera* (2012), 'pride themselves on egalitarian policies and a narrow gender gap'. What should IKEA have done? To navigate such dilemmas, companies may consider which of the actions they take to 'avoid harm' and which ones 'do good' in terms of their corporate global citizenship (overview in Miska and Pleskova, 2016). On a larger level, the case points to the question as to whether ethics are independent of culture (ethical universalism) or culture-specific (cultural relativism). For approximating which approach IKEA has chosen to pursue, it is informative to have a look at the company's current catalogue for Saudi Arabia in relation to the catalogues distributed in other countries, such as Sweden, and to reflect upon the current corporate choice of how to represent people. Does IKEA 'do good' now, or does it merely avoid harm? All current catalogues are accessible online.

Phronēsis as a practical approach to navigating ethics in IB

To implement critical perspectives in IB, George Cairns and Martyna Śliwa (2008) propose drawing from Aristotle's (2004 [350 BC]) concept of phronēsis. Phronēsis can be broadly understood as 'prudence' or 'practical wisdom'. The idea behind it is that humans are capable of identifying what is in the best interest of humanity at present, and in the future. The requirement is that they consider what is 'good action' in a situation and to act upon this assessment. Phronēsis is thus a practical approach to present and future IB challenges such as corporate social responsibility (CSR), ethics and sustainability.

From a phronēsis perspective, ethics are not a large, theoretical concept but rather the willingness to engage with ethical issues when and as they occur. The underlying view on human beings is thus a positive one – managers are capable of ethical behaviour, yet because they are 'only human' they might not make their lives difficult enough to pause and reflect, and to actually deal with ethics.

Flyvbjerg (2001: 60) has formulated guiding questions which help managers to make ethical considerations a part of their daily business, and to navigate ethics as part of their decision-making processes. He suggests that managers facing a problem, situation or decision ask the following:

- Where are we going?
- Is this development desirable?
- What, if anything, should we do about it?
- Who gains, and who loses, and by which mechanisms of power?

These questions are the guiding questions of a responsible action in practice. Basically, this responsible practice is determined by the willingness to pause and to ask the question how IB *should* be configured to the best interest of the weakest or least advantaged stakeholder.

Phronēsis Prudence or practical wisdom (Aristotle)

STUDENT ACTIVITY 8.9

The Application of Phronēsis

Imagine that you are part of the top management of the two companies of the Opening Case. Your task is to analyse the current situation and its strategic implications. For each company, fill in Table 8.3:

Table 8.3 A strategic stakeholder analysis (application of phronēsis)

Where are we going?	Is this development what we want?	What, if anything, should we do about it?	Who gains, and who loses...?	... and by which mechanisms of power?
[Hint: consider the previous content of this chapter for identifying key aspects, such as: competitive advantage, effectiveness, efficiency, ethics, culture, strategy...]	Yes, because...		Winners: Stakeholder 1 Stakeholder 2 Stakeholder 2 ...	Because Mechanism A Mechanism B ...
	No, because...		Losers: Stakeholder 4 Stakeholder 5 ...	Because ...

Chapter Summary

IB refers to the activities by which trade and investments cross borders. It is supported and framed by processes of integration which shall ensure that IB remains to the benefit of all. However, for this to be the case, the interests of those IB stakeholders whose needs are not marketable in the purely economic sense, need to be considered as well. Born globals, transnational niche markets, networks of insidership and outsidership and the constant experience of cultural friction exemplify the contemporary CCM condition wherein national borders do not equal cultural borders anymore. These conditions also show how countries, people and companies today are both similar (in certain aspects) and different (in other aspects), and that one needs to think in terms of multiple 'cross-cultural niches' instead of making one concluding assessment of cultural differences across nations. Out of these considerations, a complex web of relations emerges, to be managed and sustained under uncertain and potentially changing boundary conditions. Cross-cultural managers in a glocalized world who face culturally complex situations and need to manage multiple cultures thus have to be aware of their own 'liability of outsidership', and to try to assess and reduce it via constant cross-cultural adjustment. What managers believe in – the cultural 'mindset' from which they approach how IB should be configured – will influence the degree to which a company manages its stakeholders responsibly. For example, if managers stop at criteria such as effectiveness and efficiency, their approach to IB will remain purely functionalist. However, if they stop and pause to reflect upon how IB *should* be configured to the best interest of the least advantaged stakeholder, then they will make questions of sustainability, ethics and corporate social responsibility part of their daily business.

Key Points

- International business refers to trade, investment and other economic connections across borders.
- If freed from market distortions, IB is supposed to be to the advantage of all, offering more goods at lower prices to more people.
- However, the market approach to IB neglects the role and requirements of non-economic stakeholders, such as society and environment.
- Companies internationalize to take advantage of IB opportunities, and the degree and qualities of their international, global and transnational exposure can be assessed by means of various models which the cross-cultural manager should be familiar with.
- Companies need to manage trade-offs between being global and being local, and between standardization and adaptation.

- The philosophies and aims underlying corporate internationalization vary and influence corporate strategies and actions. Companies may therefore be classified, for example, into geocentric, polycentric, regiocentric and ethnocentric.
- Corporate internationalization can be differentiated into several aspects, such as target marketing, market entry and cultivation, timing, coordination and allocation. All of these need to be considered – sequentially or simultaneously, and under the conditions of stability or change – by the cross-cultural manager.
- Traditionally, companies internationalized sequentially. Increasingly so, contemporary companies are 'born global'.
- To acknowledge the needs of all stakeholders and to factor in external costs neglected by a purely market-oriented approach, companies need to answer questions of corporate social responsibility, ethics and sustainability and to consider the demands of their global citizenship and the desired circular economy.

Review Questions

1. How and why has international business developed and what is supposed to be achieved by it?
2. What are the problems in practice that hinder IB realizing its benefits?
3. What is the difference between the shareholder and the stakeholder approach to IB?
4. How does IB have to be configured (and who needs to do it) in order to utilize its theoretical benefits in practice? What are the limits of reaching IB goals?
5. How do global and local interrelate in IB on the level of nations, companies and individuals, and what are corporate options for managing the interrelations between global and local?
6. By means of which typology may corporate international exposure be classified? Describe the different corporate orientations and their CCM implications.
7. By means of which typology may the philosophies and aims underlying corporate international exposure be classified? Describe the different corporate orientations and their CCM implications.
8. What are the different elements of going and being international, and how does corporate internationalization today differ from internationalization in the past?
9. Why and how are questions of sustainability and ethics relevant to companies today?

10. How shall managers act in order to contribute to the goal of an ethical, responsible and sustainable circular IB economy? Which conditions do they require in order to succeed? Which problems of the global future are larger than individuals, companies and countries, and how shall these be addressed (and by whom)?

Opening Case Revisited

IB today mainly takes place in English language, and the two pieces of the Opening Case exemplify this condition. It is therefore relevant to ask what the effects of language are, and which history and developments brought these effects about (see Spotlight).

Spotlight: English as a Lingua Franca

As of 2021, English is the world's most widespread language with 1,348,000,000 speakers, yet, only some 370,000,000 of these are native ones (Eberhard et al., 2021). The second most widespread language is Mandarin Chinese, with the largest number of native speakers (921,000,000), but only some 199,000,000 non-native speakers (Eberhard et al., 2021). English is thus the main language of communication for people who speak different mother tongues, and this is how a lingua franca is defined.

The level of proficiency of the non-native speakers who use English as a lingua franca (ELF) can vary greatly; what matters most is to convey a message and make oneself understood. Some approaches to ELF include native speakers, others do not. For example, Seidlhofer (2011: 7) defines ELF as 'any use of English among speakers of different first languages for whom English is the communicative medium of choice, and often the only option'. Firth (1996: 240) defines ELF as the 'chosen *foreign* [emphasis in original] language of communication'. Sometimes, the demarcation line between the two definitions is unclear, because in some countries, such as Liberia, India, Pakistan, Singapore or Nigeria, English functions as the internal lingua franca, either officially or unofficially (Corradi, 2017).

Three main factors have been identified for the spread of ELF, namely the rise of the British Empire with its numerous overseas colonies

(Continued)

> (Michelman, 1995: 218), trade and the British industrial revolution with its technical innovations, and the emergence of the USA as a superpower after World War II. Later events such as demographic mobility, international markets, international political associations, advancements in communication technologies and internationalization of tertiary education then further reified ELF (Seidlhofer, 2011).

With the previous knowledge of the two Opening Cases in mind, revisit Chapter 6 (Critical CCM) and read the section 'The Power of History'. Now, re-consider the pieces of the Opening Case and reflect critically upon how those involved perceive each other. For example, is how the Chinese engineers are described in Piece 1 an objective representation of their capabilities or not (why)? Which roles does colonial history play, e.g. the fact that Pakistan was part of the British Empire and that now, for the first time, it is a non-Commonwealth, non-English-speaking, non-Western nation that is represented by the mine's management? What about language, in particular ELF, and the history of the countries involved in relation to ELF?

Consider these questions in light of the critical postcolonial tools suggested in Chapter 6, such as imagined geographies, discourses (of help), neo-colonialism and neo-imperialism and Orientalism. The key question to be answered is: How come the ways in which the Chinese managers talk about the Pakistani workers in Piece 2 has so much in common with how the Chinese are perceived by the Americans in Piece 1? In both cases, these perceptions are explained with culture – but: Are they about culture or are they about something else, such as power and history in IB?

Closing Activity: Oil in the Niger Delta

The Niger Delta is one of the key oil-producing regions on the African continent. Oil is, of course, a highly sought-after product in the global economy.

Task 1

Do some research and answer the following questions: Which phenomena distort the market? Which stakeholders are neglected and by whom? What should be done to consider the perspective of these stakeholders, and why might this be relevant to corporate activities in the contemporary world?

- Weak governmental standards…
- Economic power of MNCs…

- Poverty of local population…
- Lack of interest by supra-national institutions…
- Lack of interest by global media and global interest groups…

Task 2

Consider trade as a positive-sum game. What would it take to make sure that trade and investment is also a positive-sum game (and for whom?) when it comes to oil in the Niger Delta? To what extent is the situation in agreement with or a violation of existing regulations? Which formal and informal institutions and principles would be required to improve upon the status quo? Which problems remain unsolved?

Further Reading

Hill (2009) provides a mainstream overview of international business. A discussion of the Bartlett and Ghoshal typology can be found in Harzing (2000), and Perlmutter's typology of multinational managers is applied to practice by Perlmutter and Heenan (1974). Ladkin (2015) highlights the ethical dimension of management and organization. A critical approach to IB is provided by Cairns and Śliwa's (2008) introduction, and, with a focus on organizations, management and culture, by Boyacigiller and Adler (1991).

References

Al Jazeera (2012) 'Swedish firm erases women in Saudi catalogue', *Al Jazeera*, 1 October. Available at: www.aljazeera.com/news/2012/10/1/swedish-firm-erases-women-in-saudi-catalogue [last accessed 15 July 2022].

Aristotle (350 BC) [2004] *The Ethics of Aristotle: The Nicomachean Ethics* (J.A.K. Thomson (1955) (ed.)). *Penguin Classics*. [Re-issued 1976, revised by Hugh Tredennick.]

Bartlett, C.A. and Ghoshal, S (1989) *Managing Across Borders. The Transnational Solution*. Boston: Harvard Business School Press.

Boyacigiller, N.A. and Adler, N.J. (1991) 'The parochial dinosaur: Organizational science in a global context', *Academy of Management Review*, 16(2): 262–290.

Brannen, M.Y. (2004) 'When "Mickey" loses face: Recontextualization, semantic fit and the semiotics of foreignness', *Academy of Management Review*, 29(4): 593–616.

Cairns, G. and Śliwa, M. (2008) *A Very Short, Reasonably Cheap and Fairly Interesting Book about International Business*. London: Sage.

Carroll, A.B. (2015) 'Corporate Social Responsibility: The centerpiece of competing and complementary frameworks', *Organizational Dynamics*, 44: 87–96.

Carroll, A.B. (2016) 'Carroll's pyramid of CSR: Taking another look', *International Journal of Corporate Social Responsibility*, 1(3): 1–8.

Cavusgil, T.S. and Knight, G. (2015) 'The born global firm: An entrepreneurial and capabilities perspective on early and rapid internationalization', *Journal of International Business Studies*, 46(1): 3–16.

Corradi, A. (2017) *The Linguistic Colonialism of English*. Available at: https://brownpoliticalreview.org/2017/04/linguistic-colonialism-english/ [last accessed 15 March 2021].

Eberhard, D.M., Gary, F.S. and Charles, D.F. (eds) (2021) *Ethnologue: Languages of the World*, 24th edn. Available at: www.ethnologue.com/guides/most-spoken-languages [last accessed 15 March 2021].

Euro Disney (2022) *The Marketing Failure of Euro Disney: A Prime Example of Not Knowing Your Audience*. Available at: https://eurodisney.weebly.com/ [last accessed 15 July 2022].

Eurofound (2018) *Born Globals and Their Value Chains*. Luxembourg: Publications Office of the European Union. Available at: www.eurofound.europa.eu/sites/default/files/ef_publication/field_ef_document/fomeef18005en.pdf [last accessed 14 May 2021].

Ferguson, S., Henrekson, M. and Johannesson, L. (2021) 'Getting the facts right on born globals', *Small Business Economics*, 56: 259–276.

Firth, A. (1996) 'The discursive accomplishments of normality: On 'lingua franca' English and conversation analysis', *Journal of Pragmatics*, 26(2): 237–259.

Flyvbjerg, B. (2001) *Making Social Science Matter: Why Social Inquiry Fails and How it Can Succeed Again*. Cambridge: Cambridge University Press.

Freeman, R.E. (1984) *Strategic Management: A Stakeholder Approach*. Boston: Pitman.

Harzing, A.W. (2000) 'An empirical analysis and extension of the Bartlett and Ghoshal typology of multinational companies', *Journal of international Business Studies*, 31(1): 101–120. Available at: https://link.springer.com/content/pdf/10.1057/palgrave.jibs.8490891.pdf [last accessed 15 July 2022].

Hill, C.W. (2009) *International Business – Competing in the Global Marketplace*. Boston: McGraw-Hill Irvin.

Hofstede, G. (2001) *Culture's Consequences: Comparing Values, Behaviors, Institutions and Organizations across Nations*. London: Sage.

Holtbrügge, D. (2013) 'Indigenous management research', *Management International Review*, 53(1): 1–11.

Holtbrügge, D. and Wessely, B. (2007) 'Initialkräfte und Erfolgsfaktoren von Born Global Firms [Initial Forces and Success Factors of Born Global Firms]', in M.-J. Oesterle (ed.), *Internationales Management im Umbruch. Globalisierungsbedingte Einwirkungen auf Theorie und Praxis internationaler Unternehmensführung*. Wiesbaden: Deutscher-Universitäts-Verlag. pp. 169–205.

Internet Archive (1999) *International Directory of Company Histories, Vol. 26*. Available at: https://archive.org/details/internationaldir0026unse/page/211/mode/2up [last accessed 15 July 2022].

Jackson, T. (2013) 'Reconstructing the indigenous in African management research: Implications for international management studies in a globalized world', *Management International Review*, 53(1): 13–38.

Johanson, J. and Vahlne, J.-E. (1977) 'The internationalization process of the firm: A model of knowledge development and increasing foreign market commitments', *Journal of International Business Studies*, 81(1): 23–32.

Johanson, J. and Vahlne, J.-E. (2009) 'The Uppsala internationalization process model revisited: From liability of foreignness to liability of outsidership', *Journal of International Business Studies*, 40(9): 1411–1431.

Kakar, Q. and Mahadevan, J. (2020) 'Configurations of power and cultural explanations – the case of a Chinese–Pakistani mining project', in J. Mahadevan, H. Primecz and L. Romani (eds), *Cases in Critical Cross-Cultural Management – an Intersectional Approach to Culture*. Abingdon: Taylor & Francis (Routledge). pp. 86–99.

Kan, K.A.S., Apitsa, S.M. and Adegbite, E. (2015) '"African Management": Concept, content and usability', *Society and Business Review*, 10(3): 258–279.

Kedia, B.L. and Mukherji, A. (1999) 'Global managers: Developing a mindset for global competitiveness', *Journal of World Business*, 24(3): 230–251.

Kogut, B. and Singh, H. (1988) 'The effect of national culture on the choice of entry mode', *Journal of International Business Studies*, 19(3): 411–432.

Li, P.P., Sekiguchi, T. and Zhou, K. (2016) 'The emerging research on indigenous management in Asia', *Asia Pacific Journal of Management*, 33(3): 583–594.

Maljers, F.A. (1992) 'Evolving transnational company', *Harvard Business Review*, September–October. Available at: https://hbr.org/1992/09/inside-unilever-the-evolving-transnational-company [last accessed 15 July 2022].

Michelman, F. (1995) 'French and British colonial language policy: A comparative view of their impact on African literature', *Research in African Literatures*, 26(4): 216–225.

Miska, C. and Pleskova, M. (2016) 'IKEA's ethical controversies in Saudi Arabia', in C. Barmeyer and P. Franklin (eds), *Intercultural Management: A Case-Based Approach to Achieving Complementarity and Synergy*. London: Palgrave Macmillan. pp. 120–134.

Peng, M. and Meyer, K. (2011) *International Business*. London: Cengage Learning.

Perlmutter, H.V. (1969) 'The tortuous evolution of multinational enterprises', *Columbia Journal of World Business*, 4(1): 9–18.

Perlmutter, H.V. and Heenan, D.A. (1974) 'How multinational should your top managers be?', *Harvard Business Review*, 52(6): 121–132.

Rennie, M.W. (1993) 'Global competitiveness: Born global', *McKinsey Quarterly*, 4: 45–52.

Ricardo, D. (1817) *On the Principles of Political Economy and Taxation*. London: John Murray.

Robertson, R. (1994) 'Globalisation or glocalisation?,' *Journal of International Communication*, 1(1): 33–52.

Schmid, S. (2007) *Strategien der Internationalisierung [Strategies of Internationalization]*, 2nd edn. Munich: Oldenbourg Wissenschaftsverlag GmbH.

Seidlhofer, B. (2011) *Understanding English as a Lingua Franca*. Oxford: Oxford University Press.

Shenkar, O. (2001) 'Cultural distance revisited: Towards a more rigorous conceptualization and measurement of cultural differences', *Journal of International Business Studies*, 32(3): 519–535.

Smith, A. (1776) *The Wealth of Nations*. London: W. Strahan and T. Cadell.

The Guardian (2012) 'Ikea apologises over removal of women from Saudi Arabia catalogue', *The Guardian*, 2 October. Available at: www.theguardian.com/world/2012/oct/02/ikea-apologises-removing-women-saudi-arabia-catalogue [last accessed 15 July 2022].

Unilever (2022) 'We are Unilever'. Available at: https://www.unilever.com/ [last accessed 01 November 2022]

Verbeke, A., van Tulder, R. and Strange, R. (eds) (2014) *International Business and Sustainable Development*. Bingley: Emerald.

World Trade Organization (2021) Members and Observers. Available at: www.wto.org/english/thewto_e/whatis_e/tif_e/org6_e.htm [last accessed 1 August 2021].

CCM and Organization

9

Learning Objectives

After reading this chapter, you should:

- be aware of what organizing, organization and organizational design involves, and how organization interrelates with culture and CCM
- have a good understanding of the basic building blocks of organization
- be able to manage organizational change, learning and transformation, also from a cross-cultural perspective
- know and be able to apply key metaphors of organization
- have a first understanding of tacit knowledge management in organizations
- be able to make responsible, sustainable, effective and efficient organizational design choices, as related to the organizational environment and as involving various organizational stakeholders, also from a cross-cultural perspective.

Reading Requirements

- You should have read Chapter 8 on CCM and international business, as well as Part I of this book. You should have familiarized yourself with functionalist CCM (Chapter 5) and interpretive CCM (Chapter 6).

Introduction

For the cross-cultural manager, the organizational level is a relevant intermediate layer (**meso-culture**) between the interaction of **micro-culture** in context and the **macro-cultural** environment. This chapter details the role of organizing and organization in contemporary CCM, in particular as related to organizational design, culture, stakeholder networks, learning and change. This chapter does not present an overview on the whole of organization studies, but rather concentrates on those aspects which are of particular relevance to the cross-cultural manager.

> **Meso-culture** Intermediate layers of culture, such as organizational culture, regional cultures

> **Micro-culture** Small-scale cultural contexts, such as teams or interpersonal interactions

> **Macro-culture** Large-scale culture, such as societal, national or greater regional cultures

---

Opening Case

The COVID-19 Pandemic as an Organizational Challenge

The COVID-19 pandemic (WHO, 2020) hit countries all over the globe in 2019 and 2020 (see Chapter 2). To contain the spread of the newly discovered coronavirus and its subsequent mutations, social distancing became a major strategy in many countries, at least until vaccines had been developed and vaccination campaigns had taken effect. Thus, remote work and education, wherever possible, became the global premise of the time (Wiles, 2020). Schools and childcare facilities were fully or partially closed, and activities and jobs were re-organized as telework or remote work.

New pandemic-induced environmental requirements created major organizational challenges. How to organize work and transfer knowledge? How to encourage commitment and measure performance? How to acknowledge employees' diverse and changing needs, such as caring commitments and family work? How to establish organizational belonging and care for employees' wellbeing?

(Continued)

Organizational change The actions by which a company, business or non-profit organization alter major or relevant components of how they operate; often a reaction of changing environmental conditions

Organizational learning The processes by which organizations change

Organizational transformation A learning and change process that has altered the organization in major, relevant ways that are beneficial to the organization. Often required to survive changes in the organizational environment.

What might have looked as a 'phase' to be over soon, soon manifested in a need for **organizational learning, change** and **transformation**, as second, third, fourth and fifth waves of the pandemic hit countries all over the globe in 2021 and thereafter. It became clear that learning, work and organization would not be the same in the future as it had been before.

But what if one's blue-collar job could not be done remotely? What if necessity demanded leaving home for one's own or one's family's survival? What if one's home country lacked the infrastructure for successful digitization, was politically instable or economically disadvantaged? What if social distancing was never a feasible technological, political, economic or social option? What if there was no opportunity to be vaccinated against the coronavirus, even two or three years into the pandemic?

STUDENT ACTIVITY 9.1

Experiences of Organization During the COVID-19 Pandemic

Look back to your experiences during the first wave of the COVID-19 pandemic. If you attended school or university, choose this context. If you were employed during this time, choose this context. Imagine that, ten years into the future, a friend asks you, 'Interesting, so you attended school/went to work when the COVID-19 pandemic hit ...'

- How was school/work organized differently compared to how it had been organized before?
- How did the first wave of the pandemic change how school/work was organized afterwards?
- And what did you personally learn from this experience of 're-organization'?

What would you answer? Write this down as if you would tell it to a friend.

Alternative: you can research how a country reacted to the first wave of the COVID-19 pandemic and re-organized school/work on the internet, or you can talk to another person who has experienced the onset of the COVID-19 pandemic.

Principles of Organizing and Organization

In order to emerge, organization requires a coordinated effort (organizing). Hatch (2011: 1–2) provides the following example (see Figure 9.1): a person wishes to move a large piece of rock uphill (A) and engages others in this goal – a process of organizing. However, their efforts are not yet coordinated, and they thus fail to achieve the desired outcome (B). Once organization is established via improved processes of organizing, the piece of rock can be moved (C). Out of this, a formal organization, such as a 'rock moving' company might emerge.

The initial processes of organizing can be classified by means of the following characteristics:

- Organization can happen spontaneously or planned.
- Organization might be directed towards the everyday or towards the exceptional.
- Organization might involve simple or complex activities.

The aforementioned differentiation is not so much based on the task but rather on what this task means and what shall be accomplished by it. For example, 'pushing a rock uphill' can be a one-time, spontaneous and simple act of organizing if the road is blocked by it due to bad weather, or it can be part of a complex and planned organization, if this boulder is part of the next Egyptian pyramid to be built.

Therefore, organization is always linked to the environment: the input which the organization receives from the environment (the quantity and quality of 'pushers') and the output which the environment demands from the organization (a pyramid or an accessible road). This explains why changes in the organizational environment, such as the onset of the COVID-19 pandemic, always affect organization. An *organization transforms inputs into outputs* – if the inputs change, outputs are at stake, and established transformation needs to be reconsidered (and changed accordingly).

Figure 9.1 How organization happens and becomes permanent

Source: adapted from Hatch (2011: 2)

Culture is part of how organization and its environment interrelate. For example, depending on their cultural orientations, people might like to work in certain ways more than in others, and, depending on the prevalent value orientations in society, certain outcomes of organization might be preferred over others. Or, to refer back to the Opening Case, COVID-19 induced new ways of 'how to do things', also how to organize work.

Make the link: Organization and cultural dimensions

Cultural dimensions or cultural value orientations (Chapter 5) are selected, universal aspects of societal or national macro-cultures which allow for cross-cultural comparison. Key studies are the ones by Hofstede (1980, 2001) and project GLOBE (House et al.,

2004). Cultural dimensions are a suitable tool for reflecting upon which approach to organization might be preferred by whom. For example, there is the cultural dimension 'uncertainty avoidance' which, according to GLOBE (2020) describes:

> the extent to which an organization relies (and should rely) on social norms, rules, and procedures to alleviate unpredictability of future events. The greater the desire to avoid uncertainty, the more organizations seek orderliness, consistency, structure, formal procedures, and laws to cover daily situations.

This then implies that a higher degree of uncertainty avoidance in practice, such as indicated for Germany, might support planned processes of organizing and hinder spontaneous ones, and that a lower degree of uncertainty avoidance, such as indicated for Brazil, might have the exact opposite effects.

Functionalist and causal CCM tools (originally intended for macro-cultural comparison) can thus also be used on organizational meso-level. They are hypotheses to be tested, but not determinants of organizational behaviour. For example, if there are a lot of rules and procedures in a company, this suggests – but does not prove – high uncertainty avoidance. Conversely, a small business with a 'start-up' culture points to – but does not prove – low uncertainty avoidance.

Link to Practice: Why There Is No 'Cultural Inclination Towards Child Labour'

When being applied to organization, culture must be considered in light of the economic, political, social and ecological development and stability of a country. As the GLOBE study (House et al., 2004) states, culture is an explanatory variable only if a country is sufficiently developed. For example, child labour as prevalent in a country is not indicative of cultural values being attached to this practice but rather a consequence of economic hardship and the need to survive. In such a situation, people simply cannot afford 'culture'. Therefore, when considering culture as an explanatory variable for organizations, managers must also consider whether culture has any explanatory power *at all* for the situation which they analyse. For child labour, it most likely does not.

Building blocks of organization

As a minimum, organizing requires **collaboration and coordination, and differentiation and integration**. For example, a single person cannot push the rock (lack of collaboration, Figure 9.1A). However, a group is not helpful if they work in an uncoordinated manner and without a differentiation into organizational roles such as pusher and instructor (Figure 9.1B). At the same time, these differentiated roles have to be sufficiently integrated in order to work in sync.

Organization, as a more permanent manifestation, emerges when the relationships between the people who organize are formalized as in Figure 9.1C. From there, organizations – as entities – are built. For example, the longer the four people push the rock uphill in a permanently coordinated manner and according to differentiated roles, the more their activities become routines and can be formalized, e.g. by means of an organizational chart.

> **Collaboration and coordination; differentiation and integration** The four main principles of organization to be balanced out

> **Role** What a person stands and is responsible for in the organization

A **role** can be broadly understood as how a 'task and responsibility per person' is understood and sometimes formally defined. For example, student and teacher are organizational roles at school. The re-organization required due to the COVID-19 pandemic might have resulted in new ideas of how these roles should be 'filled' with tasks and responsibilities.

Four elements, to be grouped in pairs, are essential to the emergence of more formal and permanent organization.

First of all, there is the **differentiation** into roles and tasks. Differentiation enables people to focus on the task, yet it might make it more difficult to communicate critical information across distinct functions and roles. Vertical differentiation refers to levels of hierarchy (formal authority), horizontal differentiation to the division of labour. Both types of differentiation thus need to be counterbalanced by **integration**.

In order to achieve organizational goals, there secondly needs to be **cooperation**, coupled with **competition**. Both exist internally (the best pusher is being promoted to instructor) and externally (organizations compete with each other), and none of them can exist without being balanced by the other. For example, if all pushers only compete with each other, they won't achieve the required collaboration. If all pushers only collaborate, they are not motivated to excel.

There are trade-offs and interlinkages between differentiation and integration, and cooperation and competition. For example, division of labour increases individual efficiency and effectiveness, yet also weakens the ties between the individual and the overall organizational goal (because the individual is now more alienated from it). Vertical differentiation results in clear chains of command, yet it becomes more difficult to pass critical information up several levels. From a CCM perspective, all four elements are permeated by culture. For example, higher individualism suggests a tendency towards competition at work whereas higher collectivism is conducive of collaboration.

> ### STUDENT ACTIVITY 9.2
>
> #### Organizational Citizenship, Responsibility and Sustainability
>
> Re-read the section on corporate social responsibility, ethics and sustainability in Chapter 8. Now, apply these insights to the onset of the COVID-19 pandemic (Student Activity 9.1):
>
> - Which new demands did the COVID-19 pandemic put on organizations?
> - What are the new requirements regarding sustainability and responsibility?
> - How should organizations react to these new demands?
>
> When answering these questions, use examples and describe your suggestions, and classify them in terms of collaboration and cooperation, and integration and differentiation. Consider how the organizing involved is spontaneous or planned, directed towards the everyday or the exceptional, and involving simple or complex activities. Make sure to differentiate your descriptions into initial processes of organizing and the subsequent emergence of more formalized organization, which involve, for example, new task descriptions and new organizational roles.

Acts and goals of organizing are underlined by certain motivations and assumptions. For example, it can be argued that, if all human wishes were fulfilled effortlessly, there would be no need to organize. Organization thus stems from the desire to improve upon present conditions, and it happens when a single person cannot reach the desired end state or goal on their own. For organization to happen, there first must be certain desires and motivations to fulfil them, which are then coupled with assumptions as to how this should be done. Cultural dimensions can thus shed light onto how people organize differently when wishing to improve upon the present status of things.

STUDENT ACTIVITY 9.3

Making the Link – Organization and Cultural Dimensions

Revisit the concept of cultural dimensions (Chapter 5, Tables 5.4 to 5.6) and make sure that you are familiar with the concept. If required, re-read the whole of Chapter 5.

- Which of the aforementioned organizational configurations seem to be a fit or misfit to a certain cultural dimension score?

Visualize your findings by means of a table (see examples below in Table 9.1).

Table 9.1 Organization and cultural dimensions

Organizational characteristic	Fit	Misfit
High cooperation	Collectivism (Hofstede, 1980)	Individualism (Hofstede, 1980)
High vertical differentiation	High power distance (Hofstede, 1980)	Low power distance (Hofstede, 1980)

Explanation: A high degree of organizational cooperation seems to fit collectivism, but not individualism (Hofstede, 1980).

Afterwards, discuss your findings with fellow students.

Organizational Design and Roles

If the coordinated efforts of organizing are repeated long enough, interactional patterns and approaches develop into structures; organizations emerge and continue to exist independent of their members. For example, job descriptions (pusher, instructor, see Figure 9.1C) might be developed so that vacancies can be filled with people who fit the profile. Job descriptions are part of **organizational social structures**; that is, processes of organizing made permanent.

> **Organizational social structures** Roles, responsibilities, job descriptions, workflow documents and other means by which processes of organizing are made permanent

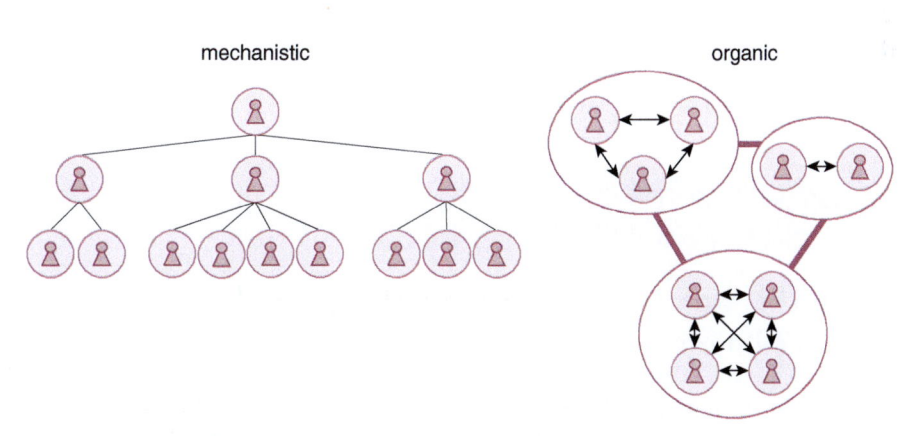

Mechanistic and organic organizational designs

As the previous considerations suggest, organization is not static, but rather an ongoing process to achieve the best possible combination of certain elements. The process by which managers intentionally create and change organizational structures and processes to enhance **organizational performance**, and the theories which they use for doing so, are referred to as **organizational design**. Organizational design is effective if it focuses employees' attention on the differentiated activities they are responsible for *and* if it achieves integration across differentiated parts (Hatch, with Cunliffe, 2006). For achieving these conflicting goals, managers can choose between more mechanistic and more organic organizational designs.

> **Organizational performance** The degree to which an organization is effective and efficient (also, responsible and sustainable) when transforming inputs into outputs

> **Organizational design** The process by which managers intentionally create and change organizational structures and processes to enhance organizational performance, and the theories they apply for doing so

Figure 9.2　**Mechanistic and organic organizational designs**

The strength of **mechanistic designs** are clear, efficient and effective reporting relationships. However, this comes at the expense of flexibility, adaptability to the environment and the capability of rapid change, all three of which are strengths of more **organic designs**. Managers therefore need to carefully balance the more structural and stable aspects of organization with the more process-oriented and flexible ones. Table 9.2 provides an overview on the key questions underlying this choice.

Table 9.2 Key decisions of organization

Mechanistic ←	Key design question →	Organic
Centralized control by only a few	To what degree shall decision-making and control be centralized?	Decentralized control by many
Formalized rules, procedures and channels	To what degree shall rules, procedures and communication channels be formalized?	Individual discretion (freedom of choice and action) at work
Highly formalized standards	To what degree shall tasks be standardized?	Low standardization, scope for discretion
High degree of specialization, narrow width of tasks	To what degree shall individual and collective tasks and responsibilities be specialized?	Low degree of specialization, broad width of tasks
(Only) managers meet and exchange information formally	How shall integration be achieved?	Managers and employees exchange information, as needed (often informally)
Grouping based on function (task, responsibility)	By which criteria shall people be grouped into departments?	Grouping based on shared identifiers, outcomes and goals (products, regions)

STUDENT ACTIVITY 9.4

Making the Link – Organizational Design and Cultural Dimensions

Revisit the concept of cultural dimensions (Chapter 5, Tables 5.4 to 5.6). Which of the aforementioned organizational design variants, such as high versus low standardization, seem to be a fit or misfit to a certain cultural dimension score? Write down your findings. Afterwards, discuss with fellow students.

Organizational design, bureaucracy and CCM

Organizational designs are models to achieve a certain desired way of organization, not a strict 'how to do'. For example, mechanistic designs instil a stronger sense of cultural belonging within each function, yet not across. Therefore, if cross-functional projects need to be managed across national cultures and distance, they are not the ideal solution. However, if one ensures cultural diversity within each function, this might facilitate cross-cultural learning and higher innovativeness in each function.

In practice, most larger companies are thus characterized by **hybrid designs**. Their goal is to achieve the best combination of the building blocks of organization in relation to external and internal influences and demands, the required inputs and outputs, the required stability and change, and the desired organizational transformation.

> **Mechanistic, organic, hybrid** Three main organizational design orientations

Every organizational design is limited in the sense that it weighs organizational stability over flexible processes of organizing. By visualizing a 'structure', a more permanent idea of organization comes into existence. Therefore, organizations almost inevitably develop a certain amount of bureaucracy as they grow.

Bureaucracy (based on Weber, 1947) is the prime example of a purely mechanistic organization. Bureaucracy develops if organizations are large, and rely upon recognized technical or functional expertise, or continue over a long period of time (e.g. governments). It can be partially avoided by more organic designs, but is still prone to emerge due to sheer organizational size, which then encourages mechanistic approaches.

The idea of bureaucracy is to establish rules which are fair to all because they are independent of the person, to promote people for merit-based grounds and to ensure reliable decision-making based on offices (not individuals). For example, job descriptions, if developed based on objective criteria, can be filled with the best possible applicant, regardless of the personality or personal traits of the individual. Every manager can make this hiring selection according to impersonal criteria, again, regardless of the personality or personal traits of the individual. This way, bureaucracy turns average people into competent administrators and ensures fair rules of the game for all.

However, by removing the individual from the organization, bureaucracy also tends to develop a life of its own and to hinder innovation, change and creativity. If the individual cannot bring their own innovative ideas and personal strengths to the job anymore and if they cannot use discretion at

> **Bureaucracy** An inevitable consequence of organization, especially in large companies; employed to ensure fairness via objectivity and impersonal rules and procedures

work (decide on their own), bureaucracy becomes an 'iron cage' to those involved in it. Bureaucracy should thus be particularly avoided by small organizations and by those employing knowledge workers and relying on creativity. At the same time, bureaucracy keeps individual aims at personal power in check and also ensures a minimum standard for all. Avoiding it completely might thus have severe consequences in the sense that some can abuse their power in the organization. Nonetheless, bureaucracy 'fixes' the role, tasks and responsibilities of an individual in the organization. Therefore, it might not encourage diverse managerial styles or non-conformity with a resulting potential loss of innovativeness and of the benefits of diversity.

STUDENT ACTIVITY 9.5

Making the Link – Bureaucracy and Cross-Cultural Management

Re-consider the contemporary CCM goal of utilizing cross-cultural differences for achieving synergies and complementarities. Discuss with fellow students:

- Revisit the concept of cultural dimensions (Chapter 5, Tables 5.4 to 5.6). Which cultural orientations seem more conducive of bureaucracy to you than others? What does this tell you about cross-cultural organization?
- Is bureaucracy good or bad – for organizations in general, and from a CCM viewpoint, in particular?
- What are the risks and opportunities of cross-cultural organization without any bureaucracy, and of cross-cultural organization with too much of it?
- How shall managers identify and maintain the perfect ratio between cross-cultural learning and bureaucracy, and how can they design the organization accordingly?

The enactment of organizational roles

As Figure 9.1 suggests, differentiation – e.g. into roles and functions – is an essential part of organization. An organizational **role** is what a person 'stands for' in the organization; it is the smallest unit of organizational culture. An organizational function usually involves more than one person. It represents one of the portions of work into which the overall goal is broken down in order to achieve it. In C, there are, for example, three pushers (an organizational function) and the instructor (another organizational function). People are thus allocated two distinct roles: pusher and instructor. Organization also involves hierarchy in relation to roles (instructors coordinate the pushers) and interdependency between otherwise distinct functions (pushers need instructors and vice versa; nonetheless, their tasks are also clearly differentiated). For organizational performance, critical information needs to be communicated across functions and organizational units.

> **Organizational role** What a person stands for in the organization.

For managing roles, Erving Goffman's (1956) notion of *social play* is helpful. His approach highlights how *sensemaking* (how people interpret the organization) is not only in people's minds – it is in people's actions (*enactment theory*). People 'play out' ideas of 'good organization' and 'good management', and how these should be achieved (Weick, 1995). The three main stages on which this play is performed are onstage, differentiated into **frontstage** (a person plays a role on centre stage) and **backstage** (a person plays a role but not on centre stage), and **offstage** (the role is not enacted). The next section provides you with further details on this approach.

(Cross-cultural) management as social play

In order to illustrate how roles are enacted, Goffman (1956) uses the idea of 'theatrical performance'. 'Performance' refers to actions directed at influencing others involved in an interaction; 'theatrical' refers to the fact that individuals take up social roles when interacting, just as actors play different roles on stage. Goffman suggests three stages for role enactment: **frontstage**, **backstage**, or in a region outside of the two, the **offstage**. Roles are enacted according to these stages because all involved in a social interaction have an interest in impression management, meaning that the performers and the audience alike are concerned with conveying a certain image of the self and with maintaining certain appearances ('saving the show', Goffman, 1956: 153).

Frontstage, an individual displays a formal conduct in a formalized setting (a boardroom, a church, a meeting room, etc.) in front of an audience, making use of the 'personal front': 'insignia of office or rank; clothing; sex; age; and racial characteristics; size and looks; posture; speech patterns; facial expressions; bodily gestures; and the like' (Goffman, 1956: 14–15). Frontstage is thus also a 'power stage'.

Backstage, an individual (or a team) can prepare for a frontstage performance, but can also 'drop [their] front, forgo speaking [their] lines, and step out of the character' (Goffman, 1956: 70). This means that, backstage, the enactment rules are less strict, yet still exist. Offstage, however, the roles do not pre-structure the interaction anymore, and other roles might become relevant (imagine a manager who meets a worker on the playground, with both their children playing there – here, the roles of manager versus worker gives way to the shared role of parents).

The borders between frontstage and backstage are not clear cut, and performers can choose to combine them (imagine a meeting with coffee breaks). Sometimes, there is even a mix up of all three stages. Goffman (1956) gives the example of a person entering a meeting unannounced. Such a situation can lead to various impression management problems: the person holding the meeting might be confused due to the unexpected outsider, the audience is unsure what attitudes to adopt, and the outsider might be confused about what is happening in that meeting. Goffman's (1956) recommendation is to handle such situations with great care. If possible, a performer should keep the audience of one of their roles separated from the audience of another of his/her roles. A priest, for example, might want to avoid going swimming with his parishioners, as this would infringe on the distance and the conduct that the role of a priest imposes.

Culture accompanies any act of performance, irrespective of the stage on which it takes place (frontstage, backstage or outside of the two). For example, think of a project presentation at the corporate headquarters of a multinational company. The team presenting is all dressed up for this occasion, gets on the stage (the meeting room), employs and shows familiarity with the technology in the room, speaks the corporate language, etc. The audience, too, behaves in accordance with the corporate culture of the organization as it shows politeness, commitment to the objectives of the meeting, etc. In Goffman's (1956) words: 'A tacit agreement is maintained between performers and audience to act as if a given degree of opposition and of accord existed between them' (p. 152). During the break and when among themselves, the team members might display a slightly different behaviour as they might speak their native language, group hierarchy might become apparent, they might speak louder and all at the same time, etc.

Frontstage, backstage, offstage The three main stages on which roles are played

When playing a role in an interaction, one also enacts culture. This then implies that cross-cultural managers can switch between performances, for example, via consciously using a backstage scenario (coffee break) to mediate a conflict, e.g. of cultures, as apparent in the frontstage meeting. This way, they might integrate divergent expectations because (potentially culture-specific) role performances and expectations are pre-structuring the interaction more on frontstage than on backstage.

STUDENT ACTIVITY 9.6

Making the Link – Organizational Roles, CCM and IB

Like interpretive CCM (Chapter 6), interpretive approaches to organization investigate how culture is constructed socially. Discuss the following questions in student groups:

1. Which interpretive CCM tools have you encountered in Chapter 5 which also fit the meso- (organizational) level?
2. Consider how social distancing was interpreted and enacted in your home country during the COVID-19 pandemic. Which role expectations and cultural dimensions (see Chapter 5) were prevalent? Provide examples and descriptions.
3. Link the concepts of role enactment and social play to your insights on international business (Chapter 8). How and for what purposes should cross-cultural managers use ideas of social play, impression management (frontstage – backstage – offstage) and enactment theory in IB? Consider, for example, the need to manage multiple networks of insidership and outsidership (revised Uppsala model), and the management of cultural friction (revised concept of cultural distance).

Link to Practice: Leadership Roles Across Cultures

As Erin Meyer writes in the *Harvard Business Review*, 'cultural differences in leadership styles often create unexpected misunderstandings' (Meyer, 2017). 'Being the boss' in Brussels, Boston and Beijing thus poses different requirements on the individual. While this might seem self-evident, the article also provides specific advice: namely not to conflate attitudes towards authority and attitudes towards decision-making. To understand how culture influences leadership roles in organization, one needs to assess authority and decision-making separately. For example, in Japanese–American interactions, 'Japanese find Americans confusing to deal with' (Meyer, 2017: 70). On the one hand, 'American bosses are outwardly egalitarian – encouraging subordinates to use first names and to speak up in meetings', yet, they also 'seem to the

(Continued)

> Japanese to be extremely autocratic in the way they make decisions' (ibid.). This presumed paradox can be found in many cultures; for example, German leadership roles are said to be characterized by high members' involvement in decision-making processes such as team workshops or discussion rounds – yet, in the end, it is the formal leader who makes and communicates the decision, 'using' team input for doing so but speaking with a single authoritative voice (Brodbeck et al., 2002). When organizing across cultures, authority and decision-making thus need to be assessed and managed separately.

Organizational Networks and Stakeholders

Organizational networks and virtual organization

Organizational networks are formed by non-hierarchical relationships via human points of contact (so called *nodes*). They are a reaction to rapid technological change, shortened product life cycles, and fragmented, specialized markets. Their flexibility and adaptability stem from lateral partnerships and horizontal communication between more or less equal organizational units. The focus is more on collaboration, less on hierarchy. Figure 9.3 visualizes a network, its nodes, and inter-nodal processes of transference and exchange.

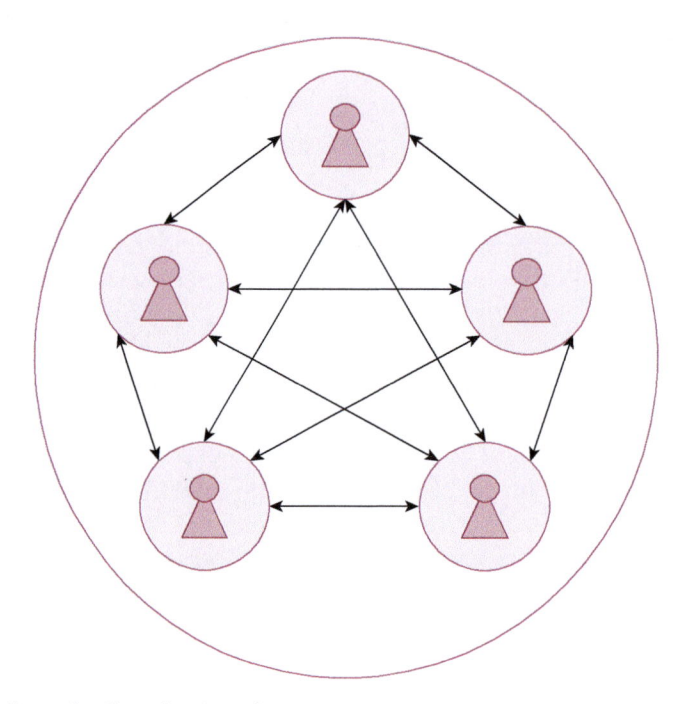

Figure 9.3 Organizational networks

Virtual organizations are specific organizational networks whose connections are mediated largely by information and communications technology. Usually, a distance factor is involved, but does not need to be, as the example of COVID-induced virtual organizing suggests. Virtual or network organization challenges certain, more 'traditional' aspects of organization, such as bureaucracy or centralized control. It also favours processes of organizing across nodes and virtual technology (the flexible component of organization) over organizational structure (its fixed component).

> **STUDENT ACTIVITY 9.7**
>
> **(Virtual) Networks**
>
> Which virtual networks are you a part of? Choose one network.
>
> - Visualize this network, name the different nodes of the network, and highlight what is exchanged in the network and between whom.
> - Which strengths of virtual networks can you identify for organizing across cultures, what might be the weaknesses? Which opportunities might be utilized by virtual networks across cultures, which threats do they need to overcome?
>
> Write down your findings and discuss with fellow students.

Organizations, stakeholder networks and the organizational environment

As Figure 9.1 suggested, organizations and processes of organizing are linked to their environments in multiple ways. At their core, organizations engage in a *transformation process* which requires a certain input (such as human resources, in the case of Figure 9.1, pushers and instructors) in order to create a certain output (in the case of Figure 9.1, removal of a piece of rock).

Organizations are not in sole control of their internal transformation processes because they draw their input from the environment, they deliver their output to the environment, and they are also contingent upon wider boundary conditions (see Figure 9.4). For example, in the case of organizing 'how to push a rock uphill' (Figure 9.1), how many people are available for the task of pushing the piece of rock? Who will require the piece of rock? How difficult is the terrain, and what are the weather conditions?

Relevant sectors of the environment are, for example, the legal, economic and political system of a country, society, the physical and technological environment, and ecology. All these sectors manifest on multiple levels, for example, there are global and local social demands, as well as national and international ones. The relevant environmental conditions that shape organizations and organizing are both objective and subjective. For example, technology creates objective differences in different national environments, e.g. when it comes to the availability of high-speed internet. On the other hand, technology is also made sense of by members of the organization, e.g. when it comes to how desired or relied upon internet connectivity is.

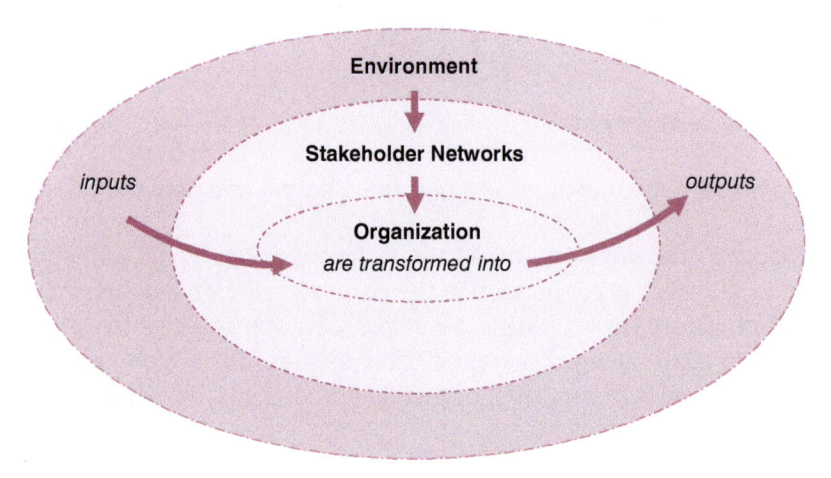

Figure 9.4 **Organizations, stakeholder networks and the environment**

Sustainability The organizational goal and practice to use resources in such ways that the present does not impact negatively upon future generations

3 Ps (people, profit, planet) The three main resource categories, trajectories and impact directions to be considered by a sustainable business and organization. Also known as society, economy and ecology.

The organization is influenced by various stakeholder groups and networks to be managed (Figure 9.4). These stakeholders provide an intermediate, permeable layer between the organization and its environment. For example, there are global supply chains in many organizations, and the border between the core organization and suppliers (network) is often subject to change, as companies make their 'make or buy decisions'. Relevant external stakeholders are, for example, investors, competitors, customers, suppliers, partners, interest groups, unions and regulatory agencies. Relevant internal stakeholders are, for example, workers and management

(Hatch, with Cunliffe, 2006: 67). Wider aspects of the organizational environment refer to 'mega-trends' such as the goal of a sustainable organization for a **circular economy**. For meeting these environmental demands, **sustainable organization** is required; that is, using and transforming resources in such ways that **people, profits and the planet** (society, economy and ecology) are not exploited at the expense of future generations.

> **Circular economy** A regenerative model of production and consumption wherein existing materials and products are used as long as possible. This involves sharing, leasing, repairing, recycling and upcycling them.

From the perspective of Resource Dependency Theory (Pfeffer and Salancik, 2003), stakeholders are relevant external forces which control the organization. For example, capital investors provide capital inputs, suppliers provide raw material inputs, competitors influence the organization's strategy, and customers buy the organizations' outputs.

STUDENT ACTIVITY 9.8

Stakeholders of Organization

Imagine that you work in a company which announces that it is going to offshore part of its core activities to a lower-cost country.

- How do input and output factors change?
- Which stakeholders can you identify, what are their interests, and how will they try to influence future organizational transformation?
- Which resources is the organization dependent upon?

A crucial socially constructed input which the organization needs from the environment is *social legitimacy*: organizations require the acceptance of stakeholders in order to continue to exist and be trusted. The environment provides the organization with a cultural blueprint of 'how it should look like' and 'how it should behave'.

> **Institutionalization** Processes by which certain ways of 'doing things' are repeated and given meaning. An organizational way of achieving legitimacy and trust

Together, the environment, the organization and its stakeholders are engaged in a process of **institutionalization**, the process by which certain ways of 'doing things' are repeated (e.g. by the organization) and are then given similar meaning by those involved (which then results in a fit between the organization and its external stakeholders) From the perspective of *institutional theory* (Selznick, 1957), it is these processes of institutionalization which create organization.

Application: Organizational Politics of National Culture

It has been debated whether organizational stakeholders and organizations might also consciously *use* culture in their own interests, thus choose (not) to collaborate across cultures. This question is rooted in the insight that organizations, particularly multinational companies (MNCs), are zones of competition and power plays. For example, it might be that a MNC ponders whether to change their corporate language from language A to language B. This is not just a language change but a change in the power relations between people and organizational units. For example, (near-)native speakers of language B will be empowered over the previously (near-)native speakers of language A. Language is a visible aspect of organizational culture, and speakers of language B might therefore choose to strategically 'sell' the work ethics of macro-culture B within the company so that language B is chosen. At the same time, speakers of language A now have an interest in promoting the work ethics of macro-culture A in order to prevent this corporate language change from happening.

Likewise, when in danger of their jobs being offshored to a low-cost country, headquarter employees might choose to consciously devalue the work ethics of the offshore site in order to 'prove' their own national culture as superior to secure their jobs. Again, a power play between divergent interests and the need to achieve organizational legitimacy in the eyes of relevant stakeholders.

Betina Szkudlarek (2009) has therefore asked the question to what ends people *use* the cross-cultural knowledge and skills which they acquire, and will these skills improve or worsen the situation. She argues that it is only an elite of Western managers who are trained in CCM, and that this elite might use their knowledge and skills to dominate employees and organizational stakeholders from non-Western and less developed countries even more.

STUDENT ACTIVITY 9.9

Institutionalization and Achieving Social Legitimacy

Go back to the previous example of a company wishing to offshore part of its core activities to a lower-cost country. Now, imagine that this wish has become reality.

- Imagine that this corporate offshoring is highly debated. Which processes of institutionalization must have taken place so that offshoring is considered illegitimate (make sure to consider relevant stakeholders and environmental sectors)?
- Imagine that this corporate offshoring is generally accepted. Which processes of institutionalization must have taken place so that offshoring is considered legitimate (make sure to consider relevant stakeholders and environmental sectors)?

Write down your assumptions and discuss with fellow students.

From this perspective, an organization is effective and efficient if it manages the conflicting demands of stability and change, and if it succeeds in doing so within numerous stakeholder networks and international environments, all of which influence the organization and demand for even further learning and change. For achieving this, several factors need to be considered, such as a suitable organizational technology or physical layout, the right kind of organizational social structure, a favourable organizational culture and climate, and the fostering of the organizational ability to learn, adapt and change. These key challenges are highlighted in the following.

Link to Practice: Stellantis

What is Stellantis?

Stellantis is an automotive Original Equipment Manufacturer (OEM) and mobility provider that came into existence through the merger of Peugeot SA and Fiat Chrysler Automobiles NV which was announced on 16 January

(Continued)

2021 (Stellantis, 2021a). The holding includes 14 automotive brands including brands manufacturing passenger cars and light commercial vehicles, as well as mobility service providers (Stellantis, 2022a).

The Stellantis self-image: Global and diverse

Stellantis names diversity and inclusion (D&I) as one of its CSR targets and takes pride in diversity being one of its main strategic and organizational pillars (Stellantis, 2022b). In its operations and outlook, the holding seeks to combine local and global requirements (Stellantis, 2021b). The following quotes exemplify these core values:

> Formed from the combination of two groups with strong track records and sound finances, Stellantis is a truly global company of 400,000 diverse, highly talented and experienced employees who design, develop, manufacture, distribute, and sell vehicles and mobility solutions around the world while remaining deeply rooted in the communities in which they live and work. (Stellantis, 2021b)

> The driving force behind us is the diverse and talented group of men and women around the world who bring their passion and experience to their work every day. (Stellantis, 2022a)

> Our commitment to Diversity and Inclusion (D&I) is in our DNA, where the Stellantis community represents 170 nationalities across six regions of the world, contributing their unique perspectives and experiences. (Stellantis, 2022c)

> The three approaches for addressing D&I at Stellantis are: 'Respect for human values, respect for local traditions, culture and context, and finding global common ground considering regional specificities.' (Stellantis, 2022c)

This corporate self-representation exemplifies how organizations facing increasingly complex global and local environments try to meet the needs of their various stakeholders and achieve legitimacy. For doing so, they choose the networks they wish to contribute to, and make strategic decisions with regard to their organizational transformation processes and how they wish to achieve them.

Metaphors of Organization

Like CCM, organization studies (overview in Hatch, with Cunliffe, 2006) is a multi-paradigmatic field, involving functionalist, interpretive, postmodern (in the terminology of this book, critically interpretive) and critically functionalist perspectives. The idea is to look at the organizational challenge from different, complementing angles in light of each other, in order to gain the most complete picture of what organization is. Metaphors are a good way for doing so.

Metaphors work by establishing a link between two otherwise unrelated phenomena or terms. Via a fairly 'simple' analogy for a complex phenomenon, they generate ideas and make complex, abstract problems small and tangible.

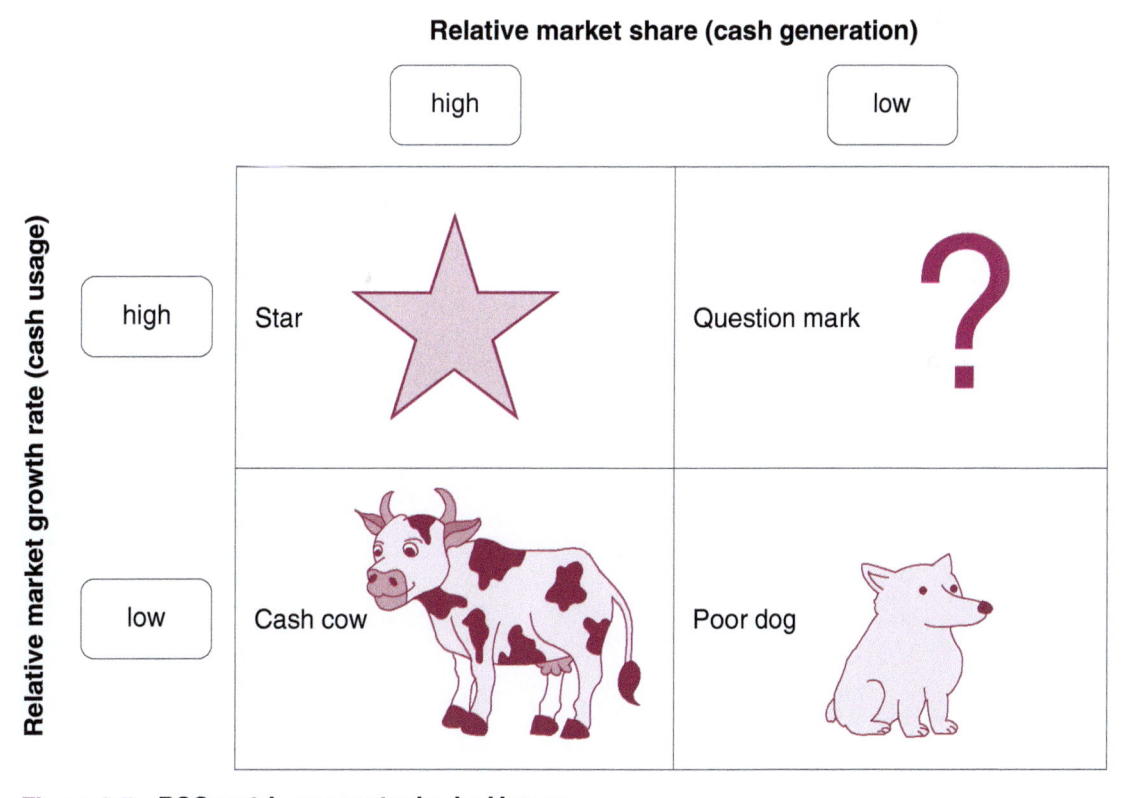

Figure 9.5 BCG matrix as a metaphorical image

Source: adapted from Henderson (2021)

CCM Applications

An example for the use of metaphors is the BCG (Boston Consulting Group) matrix (Henderson, 2021) which visualizes a product's relative market share compared to the leading competitor on this market (a projector for the product's ability to generate cash) and puts it in relation to the market growth rate (a projector for the product's need for using cash). The results are then classified into four categories which are labelled and visualized as: poor dogs, cash cows, question marks and stars (see Figure 9.5). Compared to the technical terminology underlying them, these four strong metaphors easily capture how a product is positioned on a market, what the product's potential on the market and the

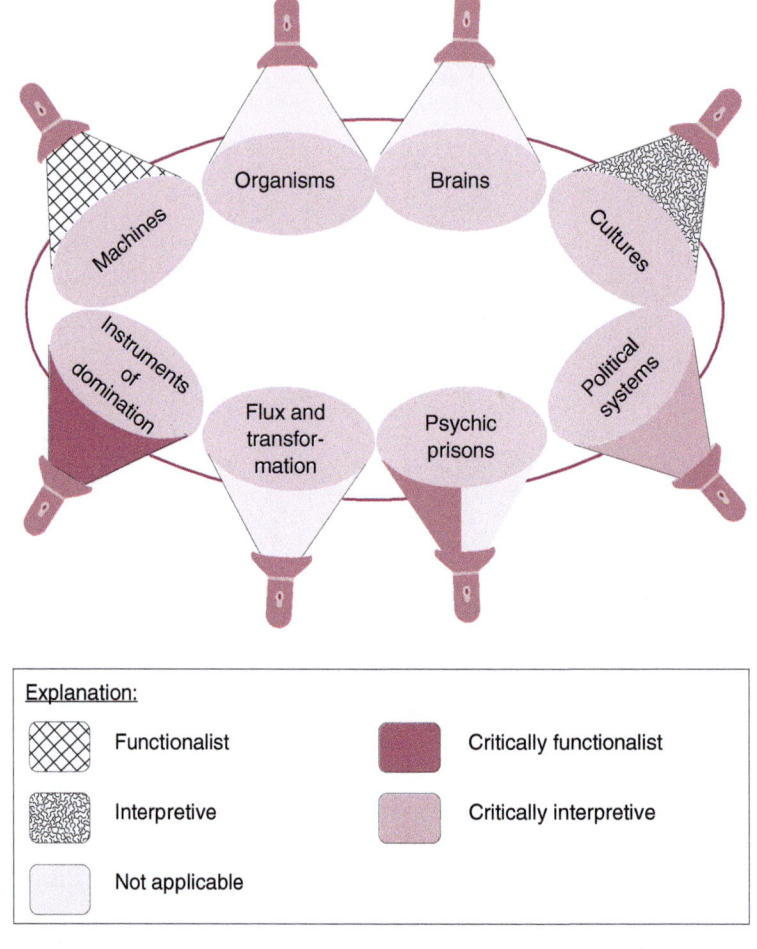

Figure 9.6 Metaphors of organization and their link to CCM paradigms

Source: adapted from Morgan (2006)

overall market potential is, and whether and how a product contributes to overall corporate profits or requires investment. Thus, the metaphors enable managers to make strategic decisions more easily; for example, to verify that enough products are on 'cash cow' stage to finance their 'questions marks' in order to develop them towards 'stars'. Or, they can identify 'poor dogs' and divest them, and forecast a product's potential lifecycle.

Metaphors are thus a way to generate ideas and insights in a simple and imaginative way. When related to organization, metaphors help managers, for example, to move beyond their respective cultural blind-spots concerning what they deem to be 'good organization' and how it should be achieved.

As an organizational tool, metaphors were first suggested by Gareth Morgan (2006). Figure 9.6 provides an overview, leading to a more differentiated discussion.

Morgan (2006) highlights how each metaphor generates unique insights, yet also hides certain, other and equally relevant aspects: For example, comparing a person with a lion might create the image of a person who is brave and ferocious, but it does not represent the whole of the person; metaphors evoke certain attributes, but omit others. Similarly, a certain idea of 'good organization' or implementing a certain concept for achieving it, might provide managers with some key solutions, but not with the whole picture. By adopting a certain structure, a certain management style, etc., an organization puts into effect certain advantages while missing out on others.

For example, one can certainly identify aspects of organization which are 'machine-like' (one of Morgan's initial metaphors). For example, a fast-food restaurant, which uses the same ingredients and offers the same dishes based on a standardized recipe, certainly 'works like a machine'. There are also advantages to be exploited if one designs organizations like a machine, such as efficiency, costs savings and reliability. However, an organization doesn't operate in a vacuum, and it should always adapt to and relate to its environment. For understanding these properties, the machine metaphor, focusing on internal workings, proves to be inconclusive. Consequently, another metaphor needs to be employed – organization as organisms.

If one perspective on organization prevails, other perspectives might fade away. 'Think "structure" and you'll see "structure". Think "culture", and you'll see all kinds of cultural dimensions. Think "politics" and you'll find "politics"' (Morgan, 2006: 339). Morgan's advice is therefore to search for and combine the insights brought by the different metaphors, being aware that 'In creating ways of seeing they [the metaphors] tend to create ways of *not* seeing' (Morgan, 2006: 338, emphasis in original). Table 9.3 provides an overview of these considerations.

Table 9.3 Metaphors of organization

Metaphor	Focuses on	Is associated with	Neglects, e.g.
Machine	How to organize the parts of the organizational machine the best possible; internal organizational workings	Efficiency, maintenance, production, order, clockwork, standardisation, measurement, control	Stakeholders, the environment, the human factor of organization, change, learning
Organism	How the organizational organism (system) is more than the sum of its parts (sub-system), and how the organization 'lives'	Adaptation, evolution, survival of the fittest, environmental conditions, prosperity and illness, life cycles, birth, life, death, growth, maturity, decline	What glues the parts of the organism together (culture), how organization and environment are indispensable (flux)
Culture	How organization is socially constructed, what makes people believe in an organization; what holds the organization together or divides people	Values, beliefs, motivations, implicit assumptions, iceberg, cultural glasses, rituals, ideology, traditions, sense of belonging, diversity	Mechanistic aspects of organization (machine), dark side of culture (psychic prison), change and fragmentation, power
Psychic prison	Negative effects of culture, how organizations control the sub-conscious and lead people to self-exploit	Cultural control, cult, subconscious, self-exploitation, repression, manipulation	Power aspects beyond culture, mechanistic aspects of organization, learning
Instrument of domination	Organization by force, how charismatic leaders are uncontrolled in their claim to power and 'hijack' organization; how workers are alienated	Alienation, silent followers, charisma, dictatorship, claim to power, force, exploitation, divide and rule, discrimination	How people are producers of power via their actions, how power is a constant relation of forces (political system)
Brain	How the neural nodes of organization are connected, process and spread information, and how organizational learning takes place	Learning, collaborative organizing, mindsets, intelligence, knowledge, networks, nodes, crowd, parallel innovation, distributed control	Power structures, culture, learning primate as a psychic prison
Political system	How organization emerges from acts of positioning (control versus resistance); how people promote interests and mobilize others	Control and resistance, (hidden) agendas, interests, mobilization, alliances, gatekeepers, informal power, networks, political deals	How power is also systemic and institutionalized (instrument of domination)
Flux and transformation	Organizing as ever-changing systems, how there is no identifiable border between the organization, networks and environment	Flow, change, organizing, dynamics, emergence, fuzzy borders, networks, self-organization, chaos, complexity, cause and effect	Organization as a closed system (machine), as entity (organism), as impacted on by power-effects

Source: adapted from Morgan (2006)

The task of the cross-cultural manager is thus to reflect upon their implicit assumptions of what constitutes 'good organization' and how it should be achieved, to entertain and consider alternatives (for which metaphors are a good way), to learn from alternative approaches, and, thus, to come to a more complex understanding and practice of organizing and organization. As Morgan (1997: 55–56) writes: 'The challenge facing the modern manager is to become accomplished in the art of using metaphor to find appropriate ways of seeing, understanding, and shaping the situations with which they have to deal.'

STUDENT ACTIVITY 9.10

Making the Link – Metaphors and CCM

You have now familiarized yourself with metaphors of organization. This tasks help you link them to CCM theory.

Task

Go back to Chapter 5 and consider the cultural dimensions presented there.

- Which cultural orientation (e.g. high or low context, high or low power distance) might be more linked to or neglected by a certain metaphor?

For example, high humane orientation – that is, the degree to which individuals are rewarded for being fair, caring and altruistic at work (GLOBE, 2020) – does not seem to fit the machine metaphor. It seems to fit the culture metaphor.

Organizational Learning and Change

Because the organizational environment and stakeholders change, organizations also need to change. One can observe that some organizations seem more able to change than others, which implies that they 'learn' more or in better ways. One can thus understand 'learning' as the process underlying successful organizational change.

Lewin (1951, 1958) suggests that organizational change involves three phases: *unfreeze, move* and *refreeze*. The idea is that managers initiate the change process (unfreeze), then move the organization to the desired new state, and then refreeze it again. This simplified and mechanistic approach never represents the complex reality of change; however, it can help managers to structure the task at hand. It makes change a reliable and planned process, and organizational stakeholders might be better able to handle it.

Lewin's model asks the manager to identify promoters and opponents to change. In the unfreeze phase, managers are asked to take advantage of existing stress or dissatisfaction amongst organizational stakeholders to turn them into active promotors. Resistance to change can be reduced via education or other measures directed at potential opponents which then, ideally, will not work against change actively but acquiesce to it. In a cross-cultural context, it is thus essential to map existing cross-cultural differences prior to entering the unfreeze phase. This way, the organization learns how culture impacts stakeholders' positions towards the intended change.

In the movement phase, managers should influence the direction of change by redesigning organizational structures and by steering organizational processes into the desired direction. For example, reporting structures might be altered, or team rituals might be changed. The change process should be ended as soon as a new balance is achieved. Changes are then institutionalized and turned into now formal rules and regulations. For example, the new reporting structures are then made manifest in a manual.

When using Lewin's model, managers should be aware of the fact that the model presents change as a top-down process, to be controlled by management, which does not meet current organizational realities. Therefore, they should use the idea of the phases to integrate organizational stakeholders in a joint change effort and view themselves as mediators or facilitators of this process and not as the ones controlling it.

What is learning? Two perspectives

Learning is the process that accompanies and underlies change. Or, in other words, organizations can only change if they learn. James March (1991) differentiates two modes of learning, namely exploitation and exploration.

- *Exploitation* means to use existing knowledge and resources to obtain value from what is already known. An example is budgeting – developing fine procedures in order to do the same things more efficiently.
- *Exploration* means to use knowledge and resources in unforeseen ways. An example for this is cross-cultural learning, such as embracing alternative leadership styles or to search for benefits in previously unknown practices.

March considers an exploration-focused organization to be a *learning organization*. There is a trade-off between the two modes, because you might, for example, refine the technologies in use in your organization (exploitation) or search for new technologies (exploration). Exploitation can be linked to more mechanistic designs whereas exploration suggests a more organic approach to change.

Learning can also be understood by means of its output. To this end, Chris Argyris and Donald Schön (1978) have suggested the concepts of single- and double-loop learning.

- *Single-loop learning* means to observe the consequences of previous actions in order to adjust behaviour in the future and to prevent similar mistakes. Single-loop learning thus solves problems as they manifest, yet cannot explain why these problems occurred in the first place.
- *Double-loop learning* means to learn from the outcomes of a previous learning cycle which then becomes an input for the next learning cycle. Organizations thus learn out of themselves, as immanent, for example, in organizational networks.

The next activity lets you apply these concepts.

Link to Practice: COVID-19 and Entrepreneurship

Starting one's own business – entrepreneurship – is another way of organizing. The amount of people who terminated their business because of the COVID-19 pandemic is significantly higher than the amount of people who became new entrepreneurs during the same period of time (Global Entrepreneurship Monitor (GEM), 2021: 30). However, in some countries the number of businesses being started is almost as high as the number of businesses being stopped (e.g. Indonesia, India or Chile). In Panama and Colombia, the number of new businesses even exceeded the number of the terminated ones (ibid.).

When asked about the opportunity to start a business (which is an important indicator for a country's entrepreneurial spirit) under COVID-19 conditions, entrepreneurs' answers varied widely, especially compared to 2019 (GEM, 2021: 33). In most European countries and Northern America, the opportunity perception fell (except for Italy – where it increased significantly – Russia, Slovak Republic and Latvia); yet in other regions, it did not (ibid.). In Saudi Arabia and Brazil, there was even a significant increase in opportunity perception.

This suggests that, whenever there is a new reality, there is not only hardship. People also need to re-invent their lives and themselves, and adapt to the new circumstances. Via this need, opportunity arises (GEM, 2021: 43–52). What is notable according to the Global Entrepreneurship Monitor 2020/2021 (ibid.) is that perceived opportunity is highest in Latin American

(Continued)

and the Caribbean, and in Middle Eastern and African economies; it is the lowest in the comparably well-off economies of Western Europe and North America. This suggests that the need to organize is the highest if people's needs are not met at present. This way, a crisis, such as the COVID-19 pandemic, can become a trigger for seeking out new opportunities, in particular in those economies that were not that well off prior to it (and which additionally provide the boundary conditions for entrepreneurship).

STUDENT ACTIVITY 9.11

Organizational Learning and Leadership Styles

Revisit the leadership styles identified by project GLOBE (www.globeproject.com); also see Table 4.2. These leadership styles depict characteristics of outstanding leadership as prevalent in a certain societal culture. Or, in other words, they provide you with indicators regarding the managerial mindsets underlying organizational design choices.

- Which leadership styles seem more indicative of exploration, which ones more of exploitation?
- Which leadership styles seem to lean towards single-loop learning, which ones towards double-loop learning?

Do organizations know what they learn?

There is also the question of whether organizations know what they learn. Barbara Leavitt and James March (1988) show that one can measure learning by means of *learning curves*. The more of an item is produced, the more is learned about how to produce it, and, consequently, production costs per item decrease not only because of economies of scale, but also because of the learning process accompanying increased production.

However, even though *something* is learned, organizational members might still not be able to say *what* was learned. Michael Polanyi (1967) thus suggested differentiating between explicit knowledge (what to do) and tacit knowledge (how to do). Tacit knowledge, such as how to ride a bike or brush one's teeth, emerges from experience and the 'doing' of things; it cannot be transferred by means of a rule book, and it is particularly difficult to exchange across distance or virtually. These types of knowledge can be visualized by means of an iceberg (Figure 9.7).

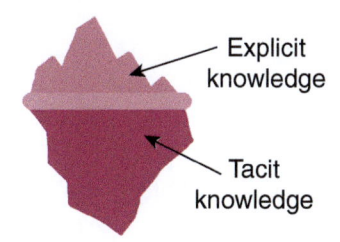

Figure 9.7 Knowledge as an iceberg

Knowledge management and exploring hidden knowledge is a key contemporary management challenge, in particular, if organizing is team-based and if distributed leadership is required (Zander et al., 2015).

In order to utilize existing tacit knowledge reserves for organizational learning, Ikojiro Nonaka and Hirotaka Takeuchi (1995) proposed the repeated employment of a four steps process, involving *socialization, externalization, combination* and *internalization*, which has become known as the *SECI Spiral*.

In the first step, *socialization*, knowledge is empathized; the 'feeling' for a task (how to do) is transferred. For example, a worker might show another worker how to operate a machine. Tacit knowledge is thus transferred into new tacit knowledge as another worker gets the same 'feel' for the machine. However, this approach is flawed as it can only work in small teams, it is rooted in the individual and it does not work well across distance. Furthermore, the organization does not know what it knows and has learned. For making learning explicit to those involved and available to the organization, three other steps are required.

During the second step, *externalization*, knowledge is articulated. For example, all machine operators might be asked to put their tacit knowledge into words by, for example, writing a manual. This way, tacit knowledge (how to do) is transferred into explicit knowledge (what to do). However, this externalization of knowledge will remain incomplete because each person cannot be fully aware of what they individually know.

The third step, *combination*, aims at closing this gap. Via the combination of all manuals, the bits and pieces of the individually available explicit knowledge are connected and made available collectively. Incomplete individual explicit knowledge is transferred into (hopefully complete) collective explicit knowledge. This way, the whole range of individual tacit knowledge is made collectively available to the organization.

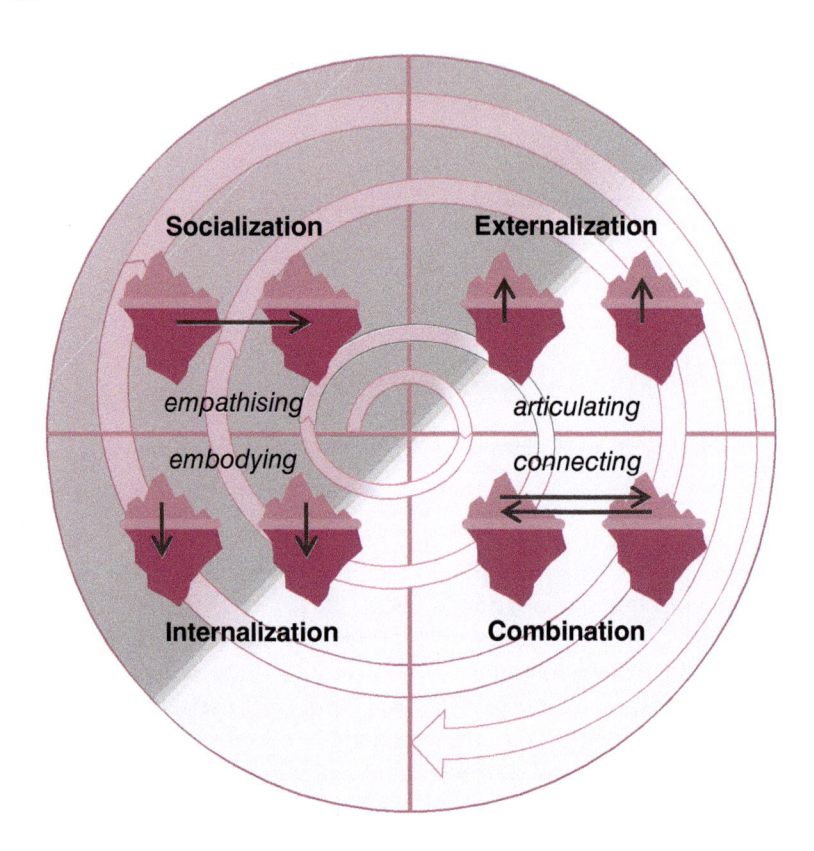

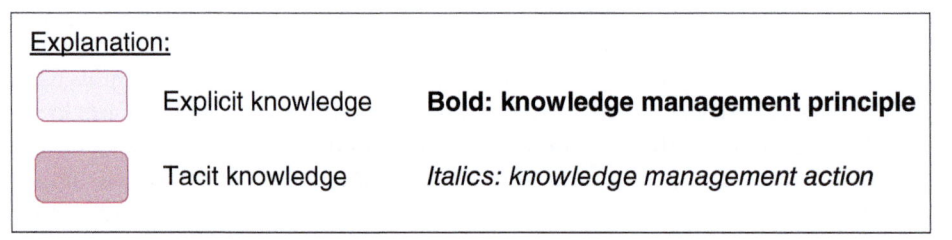

Figure 9.8 SECI Spiral

Source: adapted from Nonaka and Takeuchi (1995)

The fourth step is the *internalization* of the thus gathered explicit knowledge, for example by machine operators at another corporate site. They now read the combined manual and embody knowledge by putting it into practice. The transfer is thus back from explicit to tacit knowledge.

All steps need to be repeated, if inconclusive, and for an ongoing learning process. As a CCM tool, the SECI Spiral helps managers reflect upon their own tacit knowledge, such as ideas of 'good management' and how to implement these ideas. It also highlights that no single individual has the full understanding of a situation or task, and that it might be the combination of perspectives which delivers the highest outcome. It is thus particularly helpful for transferring knowledge across distance and cultures.

STUDENT ACTIVITY 9.12

Making the Link – SECI Across Cultures

Revisit the GLOBE leadership styles. Which tacit assumptions of 'good leadership' underlie each of them? How might a cross-cultural organization try to utilize the tacit knowledge associated with each leadership style? Work together in groups of students and make suggestions for how to socialize, externalize, combine and internalize tacit leadership knowledge across cultures.

Link to Practice: How to Diffuse Tacit Knowledge

Diffusing tacit knowledge is considered essential to organization. Yet, the process bears difficulties and dangers as related to perception and language (in the externalization stage), as related to time (in the internalization stage), and generally as related to value and distance (overview in Haldin-Herrgard, 2000).

Perception means that people are not aware of what they know, and even if they are, it is difficult to put this knowledge into words, as tacit knowledge is held non-verbally. Externalization is impacted by both effects. The internalization of tacit knowledge takes time – time that organizations might not dedicate to it. The 'value problem' refers to the insight that it is not only valuable tacit knowledge which is diffused but bad habits might be as well and, once spread, they might be impossible to get rid of. Finally, tacit knowledge is difficult to transfer across distance – a serious obstacle to successful global organization, or potentially also an opportunity, as bad habits spread less globally.

The cross-cultural challenge of organizational integration

In a cross-cultural context, learning and change begins with questions such as which change is desired, and by whom? Is what seems to be the best solution to a certain group or person the best organizational direction for all, or is it just the culturally biased perception of some? Reflexivity regarding the culturally learned premises and ways of 'how to normally do things' (Deal and Kennedy, 1982) is thus the starting and end point of any act of organization. The purpose is to create an organizational map of which ideas and practices are prevalent in an organization, and to come up with how these could be integrated for the best possible organizational performance.

Organizational theorist Mary Parker Follett suggested a way in which organizations can utilize synergies and complementarities of difference. She describes the following example (overview in Hatch, 2011: 79–80):

> Imagine you are studying in the library. You are quite exhausted; the air is sticky and you'd like to open the adjacent window. However, the person at the working desk next to you is surrounded by piles of notes, manuscripts and open books: they are afraid that opening the window will result in a gust of wind, leaving their desk in disarray. What are the solutions here?
>
> Fight or Conflict: there is no solution
>
> Compromise: both give up half of their needs – a very unsatisfying organizational outcome from Follett's perspective

Follett suggests a third alternative which satisfies everyone: integration (Héon et al., 2017). With this concept, she asks people and organizations to consider the abstract need or motivation that is behind a specific request or action. For example, the person who wishes to open the window actually desires fresh air, not the opening of the window. The person who objects to opening the window actually desires an orderly desk, not a closed window. Therefore, the presumed conflict of interests isn't one, and no one needs to give up their needs. Rather, the abstract requirements at hand – fresh air and no wind – can lead to new, innovative solutions, such as to open another window, in an adjacent room, an act of freshening up the air without any gusts of wind. With this core idea, Follett anticipates key concepts of CCM, such as the need to seek out difference, to change perspective and to learn from alternative styles and practices.

Integration is particularly difficult, yet indispensable in novel, unforeseen and challenging situations, such as the COVID-19 pandemic or any cross-cultural collaboration in general. For such situations, Follett recommends following what she calls the 'law of the situation'.

- With 'situation', Follett refers to a whole complex of reciprocal, changing and evolving interactions which require but also present opportunities for 'continual efforts to keep the process healthy' (Fox, 1968: 520).

- Integration (see previous) is Follett's definition of such a 'healthy process'.
- The 'law' of the situation means to act 'in accord with present integrations and anticipating those that still need to be made' (Fox, 1968: 520). It requires a circular response which considers both the present and the future needs of all.

Therefore, Follett proposes a very different understanding of change than Lewin (1951, 1958), with his mechanistic idea of how to plan and implement change. Her idea is that any collective or organizational response to 'problems' requires not a linear, but a circular process to involve all and to establish common purpose. Therefore, also 'leadership' only exists if it is accepted as such by others, and as emerging from the situation (Héon et al., 2017). This implies an organizational focus on 'power with', that is the collaborative dimension of power, and not on 'power over', the formerly held hierarchical idea of power according to which managers direct employees. This then calls for more collaborative approaches to organization, such as networks.

STUDENT ACTIVITY 9.13

Organizational Change and Learning, and Leadership Styles

Revisit the leadership styles identified by project GLOBE (www.globeproject.com); also see Table 4.2. These leadership styles depict characteristics of outstanding leadership as prevalent in a certain societal culture. Or, in other words, they provide you with indicators regarding the managerial mindsets underlying organizational design choices.

- Which leadership styles seem to lean more towards a mechanistic and hierarchical approach to change (Lewin), and which ones seem to lean more towards an organic and collaborative approach to change (Follett)?

Chapter Summary

People organize to meet needs related to many aspects of their lives. If processes of organizing are repeated and formalized, organization and organizations emerge. Organizations transform input to create a certain output, in relation to the organizational environment and relevant organizational stakeholders. Building blocks of organization are collaboration, coordination and differentiation, all of which can be further differentiated and categorized. Managers in the role as organizational designers need to shape organization in such a way that it is effective and efficient, as well as responsible and sustainable. For this, they need to manage the conflicting needs for stability and change in light of their corporate citizenship and the sustainability needs of a circular economy. Managers can choose between more mechanistic and organic designs, and can also contribute to virtual and non-virtual organizational networks. Bureaucracy is an inevitable outcome of every organization, and contemporary organizations need to balance its effects in order to organize for change *and* stability under complex and often changing boundary conditions. Managers need to consider how to transform the organization and to facilitate learning. Tacit knowledge may be a key source to organizational excellency, yet it is difficult to transfer and diffuse. Metaphors of organization and a focus on organizational role enactment are helpful angles for a more holistic understanding of what organization involves and how it is put into practice. For the best possible organizational outcome, managers need to carefully consider and balance the available organizational concepts and tools in light of their stakeholder networks, the organizational environment, and overarching requirements such as sustainability and corporate citizenship in a circular economy. Employing a cross-cultural management perspective on organization, this chapter provided you with initial and structured insights on the aforementioned matters.

Key Points

- People organize to meet needs.
- Acts of organizing made permanent are referred to as organization(s) and described via roles, functions and organizational social structures.
- Organization involves balancing cooperation and competition, and differentiation and integration by means of organizational design choices.
- All organizations develop bureaucracy as they grow – to positive and negative effects.
- Cultural dimensions, leadership preferences and cultural perceptions are part of the organizational fabric and need to be considered by the cross-cultural manager.
- Organizational learning, change and integration are essential for securing, improving upon or re-establishing the link between the organizational transformation process, the organizational stakeholder networks and the organizational environment, in particular in times of crisis and change.
- Tacit knowledge is a key source for organizational competitiveness and excellency, yet it is also difficult to transfer and diffuse.

- Managers play organizational roles on various stages.
- Metaphors of organization are helpful for understanding how an organization 'ticks', also in terms of culture, and for making more informed managerial choices.

Review Questions

1. Why do people organize?
2. How can organization be further classified and categorized?
3. What are indicators of acts of organizing having become permanent?
4. What are the main building blocks of organization, and which organizational design choices are associated with them?
5. What is bureaucracy, and is it good or bad from an organizational perspective?
6. How do managers enact organizational roles, and why is it relevant to pay attention to how organizational roles are enacted?
7. What are metaphors of organization, and how can metaphors be a helpful tool for the cross-cultural manager in the role of organizational designer?
8. How can cross-cultural management theory shed further light on organization?
9. What are ways in which organizational learning and change can be achieved, why is learning and change an organizational requirement, and why and how is it difficult to implement both?
10. Why and how are stakeholders relevant to organization, also from a cross-cultural management perspective?

Opening Case Revisited

Culture permeates organization, and micro, meso and macro levels of culture and organization are interrelated. The ways in which people, organizations and countries react to fundamental changes in the global environment, such as the ones induced by the COVID-19 pandemic, are thus also a CCM phenomenon. Figure 9.9 summarizes the contours of organization, including culture.

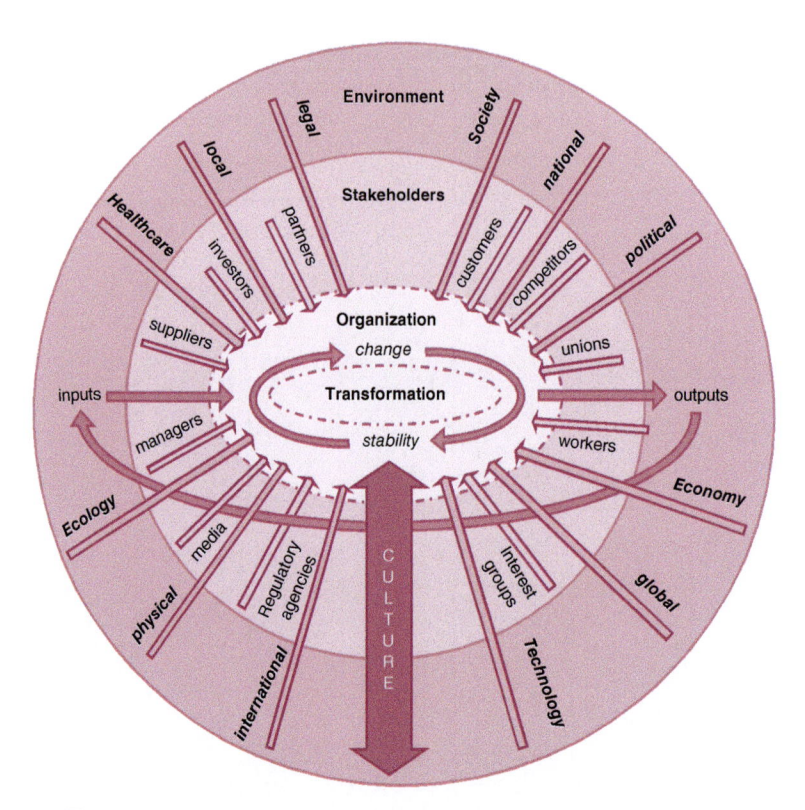

Figure 9.9 The contours of organization, including culture

Closing Activity

When the German automotive multinational BMW took over Rover from British Aerospace, this resulted in a 'culture clash' between the two organizations (Fuller-Love, 2008). Prior to the takeover, Rover had won design awards and was making profits. Six years later, the company was sold at a substantial loss by BMW, and BMW only retained the new successful Mini car (ibid.). The open access case study by Nerys Fuller-Love (2008) explains how certain environmental aspects were out of the company's control and how 'the culture clash certainly exacerbated the problem' (p. 93). All influencing factors of organizational integration, including culture, are thus highlighted by the BMW–Rover case. For a structured analysis, apply your full knowledge of this to it. The guiding questions of the student activities of this chapter provide you with the sub-questions to be asked to the case. If required, search the internet for more information. Write a detailed report, using visual aids such as the ones provided in this chapter. The case study is available at:

Further Reading

The Sage Handbook of Organization Studies (Clegg et al., 2006) provides an overview on this field of research and practice. An overview on Organization Theory, with a focus on modern, symbolic and postmodern perspectives, can be found in Hatch, with Cunliffe (2006). Meta-metaphors of organization, as well as a discussion of Morgan's metaphors and their usefulness for developing organization theory, can be found in Örtenblad et al. (2016). Gannon and Pillai (2010) have applied the idea of metaphors to national culture, in an attempt to integrate functionalist and interpretive approaches to CCM. The original ideas of a 'scientific management' as proposed by early industrial theorists Taylor and Fayol, are highlighted by Hendry (2013) who also provides a very concise and easily accessible discussion of key organizational themes such as bureaucracy, leadership or change. Hendry's (2013) chapter on CCM, though, does not move beyond a basic overview of comparative and functionalist CCM.

References

Argyris, C. and Schön, D. (1978) *Organizational Learning: A Theory of Action Perspective*. Reading: Addison-Wesley.

Brodbeck, F., Frese, M. and Javidan, M. (2002) 'Leadership made in Germany: Low on compassion, high on performance', *Academy of Management Executive*, 16(1): 16–29.

Clegg, S.R., Hardy, C., Lawrence, T. and Nord, W.R. (2006) *The Sage Handbook of Organization Studies*. London: Sage.

Deal, T.E. and Kennedy, A.A. (1982) *Corporate Culture: The Rites and Rituals of Corporate Life*. Boston: Addison-Wesley.

Fox, E.M. (1968) 'Mary Parker Follett: The enduring contribution', *Public Administration Review*, 28(6): 520–529.

Fuller-Love, N. (2008) 'Culture clash: A case study of Rover and BMW', *International Business Research*, 1(1): 93–100. Available at: https://ccsenet.org/journal/index.php/ibr/article/download/1021/39411 [last accessed 31 July 2022].

Gannon, M.J. and Pillai, R. (2010) *Understanding Global Cultures – Metaphorical Journeys Through 29 Nations, Clusters of Nations, Continents and Diversity*. Los Angeles: Sage. (1st edn, 2009.)

Global Entrepreneurship Monitor (GEM) (2021) *2020/2021 Global Report*. Available at: www.gemconsortium.org/file/open?fileId=50691 [last accessed 31 July 2022].

GLOBE (2020) *An Overview of the 2004 Study: Understanding the Relationship Between National Culture, Societal Effectiveness and Desirable Leadership Attributes*. Available at: https://globeproject.com/study_2004_2007?page_id=data#data) [last accessed 31 July 2022].

Goffman, E. (1956) *The Presentation of Self in Everyday Life*. Edinburgh: University of Edinburgh. Social Sciences Research Centre. Monograph No. 2.

Haldin-Herrgard, T. (2000) 'Difficulties in diffusion of tacit knowledge in organizations', *Journal of Intellectual Capital*, 1(4): 357–365.

Hatch, M.J. (2011) *Organizations: A Very Short Introduction*. Oxford: Oxford University Press.

Hatch, M.J., with Cunliffe, A. (2006) *Organization Theory – Modern, Symbolic and Postmodern Perspectives*. Oxford: Oxford University Press. (1st edn, 1996.)

Henderson, B. (2021 [1970]) *The Product Portfolio*. Available at: www.bcg.com/de-de/publications/1970/strategy-the-product-portfolio [last accessed 1 June 2021].

Hendry, J. (2013) *Management: A Very Short Introduction*. Oxford: University Press.

Héon, F.H., Damart, S. and Nelson, L.A.T. (2017) 'Mary Parker Follett: Change in the paradigm of integration', in D.B. Szabla, W.A. Pasmore, M.A. Barnes and A.N. Gipson (eds), *The Palgrave Handbook of Organizational Change Thinkers*. Frankfurt: Springer International. pp. 1–22.

Hofstede, G. (1980) *Culture's Consequences: International Differences in Work Related Values*. Beverly Hills: Sage.

Hofstede, G. (2001) *Culture's Consequences: Comparing Values, Behaviors, Institutions and Organizations across Nations*. London: Sage.

House, R., Hanges, P., Javidan, M. and Gupta, V. (2004) *Culture, Leadership, and Organizations: The GLOBE Study of 62 Societies*. Thousand Oaks: Sage.

Leavitt, B. and March, J. (1988) 'Organizational learning', *Annual Review of Sociology*, 14: 319–340.

Lewin, K. (1951) *Field Theory in Social Science*. New York: Harper & Row.

Lewin, K. (1958) 'Group decisions and social change', in E.E. Maccobby, T.M. Newcomb and E.L. Hartley (eds), *Readings in Social Psychology*. New York: Holt, Rinehart Winston. pp. 459–473.

March, J.G. (1991) 'Exploration and exploitation in organizational learning', *Organization Science*, 2(1): 71–87.

Meyer, E. (2017) 'Being the boss in Brussels, Boston and Beijing', *Harvard Business Review*, July–August: 70–77.

Morgan, G. (1997) *Imaginization*. Newbury Park: Sage.

Morgan, G. (2006) *Images of Organization*. Newbury Park: Sage. (1st edn, 1986.)

Nonaka, I. and Takeuchi, H. (1995) *The Knowledge-Creating Company: How Japanese Companies Create the Dynamics of Innovation*. Oxford: Oxford University Press.

Örtenblad, A., Putnam, L. and Trehan, K. (2016) 'Beyond Morgan's eight metaphors: Adding to and developing organization theory', *Human Relations*, 69(4): 875–889.

Pfeffer, J. and Salancik, G.R. (2003) *The External Control of Organizations: A Resource Dependence Perspective*. Stanford: Stanford University Press.

Polanyi, M. (1967) *The Tacit Dimension*. New York: Anchor Books.

Selznick, P. (1957) *Leadership in Administration*. New York: Harper & Row.

Stellantis (2021a) The Merger of FCA and Groupe PSA has been Completed, press release, 16 January. Available at: www.stellantis.com/en/news/press-releases/2021/january/the-merger-of-fca-and-groupe-psa-has-been-completed?adobe_mc_ref= [last accessed 31 July 2022].

Stellantis (2021b) Stellantis: Building a World Leader in Sustainable Mobility, press release, 19 January. Available at: www.stellantis.com/en/news/press-releases/2021/january/stellantis-building-a-world-leader-in-sustainable-mobility [last accessed 31 July 2022].

Stellantis (2022a) About Us. Available at: www.stellantis.com/en/company/about-us [last accessed 31 July 2022].

Stellantis (2022b) Dare Forward: Stellantis Long-Term Strategic Plan. Available at: www.stellantis.com/en/investors/events/strategic-plan [last accessed 31 July 2022].

Stellantis (2022c) Diversity and Inclusion. Available at: www.stellantis.com/en/responsibility/diversity-and-inclusion [last accessed 31 July 2022].

Szkudlarek, B. (2009) 'Through Western eyes: Insights into the corporate training field', *Organization Studies*, 30(9): 975–986.

Weber, M. (1947) *The Theory of Social and Economic Organization* (trans., A.M. Henderson and T. Parsons). London: Collier Macmillan Publishers.

Weick, K. (1995) *Sensemaking in Organizations*. Thousand Oaks: Sage.

WHO (2020) WHO Director-General's Opening Remarks at the Media Briefing on COVID-19 – 11 March 2020. Available at: www.who.int/dg/speeches/detail/who-director-general-s-opening-remarks-at-the-media-briefing-on-covid-19---11-march-2020 [last accessed 3 September 2020].

Wiles, J. (2020) With Coronavirus in Mind, is Your Organization Ready for Remote Work? Available at: www.gartner.com/smarterwithgartner/with-coronavirus-in-mind-are-you-ready-for-remote-work/ [last accessed 4 September 2020].

Zander, L., Butler, C.L., Mockaitis, A.I., Herbert, K., Lauring, J., Mäkelä, K., Paunova, M., Umans, T. and Zetting, P. (2015) 'Team-based global organizations: The future of global organizing', in R. van Tulder, A. Verbeke and R. Drogendijk (eds), *The Future of Global Organizing. Progress in International Business Research*. Bingley: Emerald Group Publishing Limited. pp. 227–243.

CCM, and Technology and Social Media 10

Learning Objectives

After reading this chapter, you should:

- have a detailed understanding of how technology and cross-cultural management are interrelated in multiple, sometimes contradicting ways
- be aware of what 'technology' involves from an organizational perspective, and how technology can be classified in terms of its cross-cultural implications
- be familiar with key technological applications of cross-cultural management, such as user interface design or usability engineering
- know how social media, and information and communications technology have changed people's cross-cultural encounters
- be able to assess the cross-cultural dimension of technology via key concepts such as the cultural variance.

Reading Requirements

- You should have read the chapters on CCM and international business (Chapter 8) and on CCM and organization (Chapter 9), as well as Part I of this book.

Introduction

The previous chapter highlighted how contemporary CCM is interrelated with international business and organization. Complementing this perspective, this chapter considers how technology and social media are relevant to CCM today in multiple, often contradicting ways. For example, technology and social media bear the danger of an ethnocentric enculturation into a single network of people that is not representative of the whole of a person's potential cultural connections. This can result in cultural myopia and segregation. On the other hand, technology and social media allow access to cultural contexts otherwise beyond a person's reach. This way, technology might democratize and diversify CCM. Focusing on technology and CCM, this chapter analyses their interrelations on three intersecting levels, namely on the level of societies and international business (macro), on the level of organizations (meso) and on the level of individuals and their interpersonal interactions (micro).

Opening Case

Frugal and *Jugaad* Innovation

Frugal innovation, reverse innovation, frugal engineering, Gandhian innovation, low-cost innovation – these are but some of the terms that describe a contemporary technological phenomenon which tries to address the combination of two issues: limited resources and meeting the needs of a huge mass of low-income customers.

> **Frugal innovation** A sustainable and value-for-money approach to innovation under resource-constrained boundary conditions

India, the 'epicentre of frugal innovation' (Hossain, 2021: 1), has its own name for it: '*jugaad*', which means coming up with a (innovative) solution using the means one has at hand. *Jugaad* is 'the gutsy art of spotting opportunities in the most adverse circumstances and resourcefully improvising solutions using simple means' (Radjou et al., 2012a: 4).

Carlos Ghosn, who is said to first have used the expression 'frugal engineering' in 2006, states that companies must learn 'a whole new mindset' from their presence in emerging markets (Radjou et al., 2012b). This new approach to developing new products and services focuses not only on cutting costs (low-cost innovation), but also on value; it is not about coming up with cheap products, but rather about making '"good enough" offerings that deliver significant value for money to cost-conscious consumers' (Radjou et al., 2012b). Moreover, sustainability plays an important role as these products and services are often born out of and are intended for

(Continued)

> 'resource constrained situations' (Ploeg et al., 2021). The Mitticool refrigerator which is made of clay and does not need electricity to keep one's groceries cool is one such example that fulfils both sustainability and innovation requirements (Radjou et al., 2012a: 2).
>
> Frugal innovations can be found in a wide range of industries, such as automotive (Tata Nano, the tractors from Mahindra and Mahindra, etc.), information and communication technology (see, for example, the initiative 'One Laptop per Child'), banking (money transfer via mobile phone, such as M-Pesa in Kenya), and healthcare (the Jaipur leg, named after a city in Southwest India, a rubber-based prosthetic leg for people with below-knee amputations).
>
> Sometimes, frugal innovation results in reverse innovation. The term 'reverse innovation' firstly involves the frugal process of creating a product or a service in an emerging market that is tailored to the needs of the customers on that market (often translated into giving up fancy, unnecessary features), and, secondly, the successful introduction of that product or service to customers from so-called developed markets (Govindarajan, 2012). Therefore, frugal innovation's potential impact reaches out beyond the markets and cultures from which it originates.

Technology and International Business

Jugaad and frugal innovation is an example of how technology and international business interrelate in the contemporary world. Key questions to be considered are the extent to which technology is culture-free or culture-bound (for example, how 'Indian' is an approach such as *jugaad*?) and as to whether technology is able to mediate hierarchies and inequalities of international business (for example, does the internet provide more people with access to more knowledge, products and services?). These aspects of technology will be highlighted in the following section.

Technology as culture-free and culture-bound

Whereas some technologies are culture-free (universal or global), others are culture-bound (specific to a cultural context). For example, it has been argued that younger generations use social media differently to older ones; a behavioural difference in generational cultures. Also, the languages spoken (and written) differ across countries – an objective difference in societal cultures that influences technology design and usage.

STUDENT ACTIVITY 10.1

The Culture of Technology

Choose a technology which you use in daily life (e.g. an object such as a mobile phone or a communications technology such as e-mail). Observe its features and how you use them over the course of a week.

- Which groups do you share the usage of this device with? Who uses it in similar ways? Give this 'culture' a name tag, such as generational culture, student culture, etc.
- Is the technology or technical product which you interact with universal (free of culture) or culture-specific (tailored to the specific needs a user with your cultural experiences might have)?
- Based on your analysis, to what extent is this technology culture-bound and culture-free? Which features of the technology of your choice seem more culture-bound than others?
- Exchange with fellow students and figure out the differences and commonalities in your findings, and how they are relevant to managing across cultures today.

Does technology flatten international business?

Technology enables people to 'travel' to other cultures, even if they never actually change place, and it exposes them to a variety of cultural influences wherever they are. Technology also facilitates organizing across distance and cultures. For example, technological change has enabled job profiles such as global supply chain management and has facilitated the conditions for global virtual team collaboration. This means that less people need to be sent abroad across cultures, but nonetheless work cross-culturally, and that companies and countries require less investment in physical infrastructure to 'be' international. Out of this arise new organizational and individual opportunities.

In 2005, US-American journalist Thomas L. Friedman thus enthusiastically wrote *The World Is Flat*. With this book title, he referred to the argument that, due to globalization and technological progress, more individuals, companies and countries than ever before can now pursue developmental opportunities without following the historical industrialization patterns of the developed world. Friedman thus predicted a more equal – that is, a 'flattened' – international business environment.

Link to Practice: Overcoming the Digital Divide

ICT Information and communications technology, such as e-mail

Digital divide Cross-country or cross-group inequalities in technological access

E-literacy People's versatility in understanding and/or using technologies, e.g. ICT

The **digital divide** refers to the insight that, in any given country, not everyone has equal access to communication and information technology (**ICT**), in particular in the Global South (ITU, 2019). This is understood as a major obstacle to further economic advancement. To tackle this problem and to increase people's **e-literacy**, many governments issue educational programmes and invest in digital infrastructure. For example, in a much-promoted move, the Indian government distributed a '500 Rupee (£7/USD10) laptop' in 2009 (Ramesh, 2009). Moreover, there is the *gender digital divide*, which refers to the condition of more men than women having access to ICT. In terms of internet users by gender, the gender digital divide has increased throughout the Arab States, Asia and the Pacific, and Africa (ITU, 2019). Gender equality in internet usage can be found in just over a quarter of all countries worldwide, and the proportion of women using the internet is higher than that of men in a mere 8 per cent of countries (ibid.). In terms of people's development opportunities, this is a problematic finding.

Observations to this end are, for example, that many so-called 'developing' countries of the Global South skipped a landline telecommunications system, jumping directly to the next stage and often surpassing the so-called 'developed' countries of the Global North in terms of technological opportunities. Mobile phone penetration rate in Kenya, for example, was reported to be 95.1 per cent in 2018 (*APA News*, 2020), and the country has instantaneously embraced new solutions such as mobile phone banking, which are not yet widespread in – and also not easily adaptable to – many of those countries who are presently considered the 'industrialized' and 'developed' world (Kao et al., 2020).

One can also observe the development of global hubs for highly specialized services that are supported by technology. An example is the Indian city of Bangalore (Bengaluru). It has come to be known as India's Silicon Valley, yet it actually hosts a variety of knowledge-intensive industries such as the long-distance provision of medical services such as x-ray analyses, tax accounting services, aeronautics research and development, and call centre operations. What these industries have in common is that they could only emerge for an international customer-base *because of* technology, the international advantage of the Indian market being the combination of knowledge at comparably low cost.

Also, whereas it was more common in the early stages of Western corporate internationalization that foreign direct investment (FDI), as well as managerial and organizational knowledge, tended to flow from industrialized to developed countries, 'reverse' FDI, from developing to developed countries is now increasingly common. In the process, the old international business categories 'developed' and 'developing'/'emerging' become blurred. For example, Chinese companies now invest heavily in Central and South Asian and African countries, often winning local governmental bids against companies from Western Europe, North America or Australia.

However, as a more critical CCM points out (see Chapter 7), the hierarchies of CCM and IB, as brought about by certain historical developments, such as colonialism, and established corporate internationalization paths, e.g. from Western to non-Western countries, have not just magically vanished. Still, technology seems to have democratizing effects on IB and, potentially, CCM.

STUDENT ACTIVITY 10.2

Is the World Flat?

It is said that technology democratizes organizations and management. However, it might be that some people do not have access to a certain technology, such as information and communications technology (ICT), or to the infrastructure enabling cooperation via ICT, such as high-speed internet. This is called the 'digital divide'. Please gather more information about the digital divide in your own country and in another country of your own choice (note that, for some countries, depending on the language-in-use, e.g. in your own country, you will have to find the appropriate translation of the term 'digital divide').

Take note of the ICT which you use to conduct this research. Reflect upon how you and your country of residence/origin are placed in terms of

(Continued)

> the 'digital divide'. Are you favoured or disadvantaged in terms of ICT? Is the access to ICT taken for granted from your own perspective and in your country of origin/residence? Is the access to ICT something which you or people in your country of origin/residence normally lack? Are there internal differences in your country of origin/residence that favour some locations or some groups over others (e.g. differences in income, living in rural versus urban areas)?
>
> After you have gathered information on two countries and have reflected upon how you are placed in terms of the digital divide in relation to other people, visualize your findings in an appropriate manner. Your visualization should include (1) the inner-country differences for both countries, (2) the comparison of the two countries, (3) your own standpoint in comparison to different groups of people in your own country, and (4) your own standpoint in comparison to similar groups in the other country. Finally, use your visualization to answer the question: *Is the world flat?*

Technology and Organization

Core technology The tools, machines and other equipment devised for doing work, *and* the craft or knowledge it takes to produce and operate them

Socio-technical system Systems, such as organizations, in which humans and technology closely interact

From an organizational perspective, technology, understood as the 'core' by which organizations convert input to output, spans much more than the mere 'tools' and 'technologies' used by people, such as information and communication technology, high technology or service technology. Rather, '**core technology**' involves the tools, machines and other equipment devised for doing work, *and* the craft or knowledge it takes to produce and operate them. The term 'technology', as used in such a way, thus refers to all means which organizations use to convert raw inputs into finished outputs, and to deliver products and services to customers and clients; it integrates the social (human) and the object-related (technological) dimension of work. In that sense, organizations are systems employing socio-technical means to achieve their goals – they are **socio-technological systems** (Trist and Bamforth, 1951). The technologies employed and how people interact with them thus shape meso-level organizational culture.

> **STUDENT ACTIVITY 10.3**
>
> **The Technology of Organizing and Organization**
>
> Re-read Chapter 9 on Organization and CCM. Keep your learnings for the further reading of this chapter.

Organizations are open systems which are linked to their environment in multiple ways: they draw input from the environment, they deliver output to the environment, and their task is to do so in an effective, efficient and responsible manner. The organization and the environment are interrelated via relevant stakeholders and networks, to be managed by the organization.

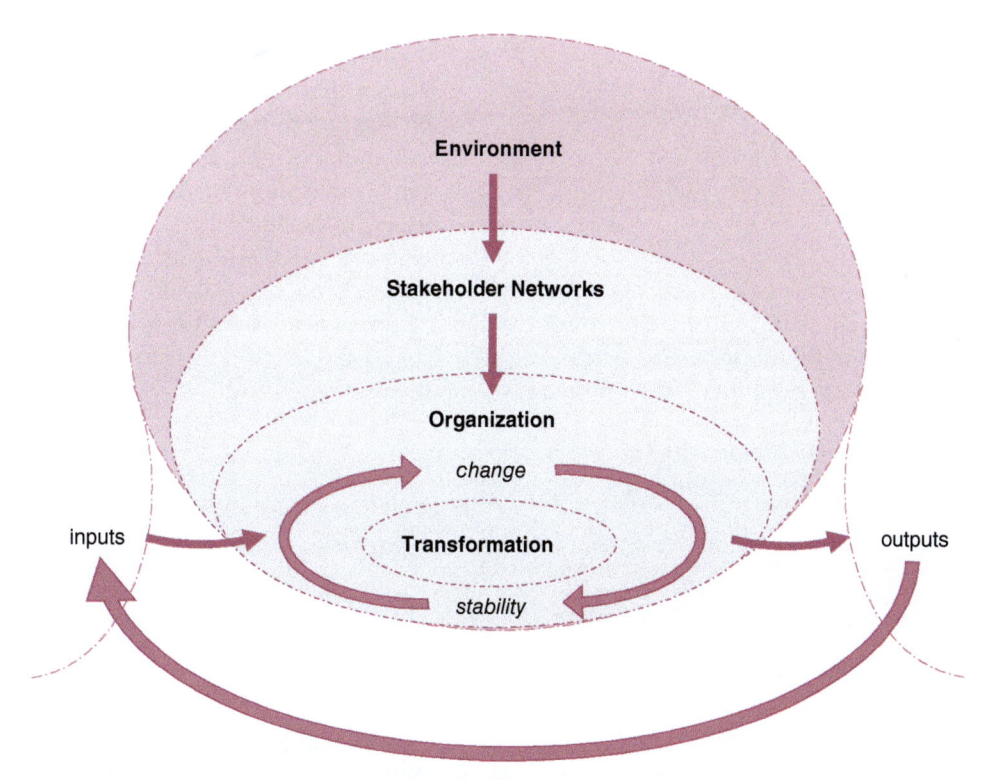

Figure 10.1 Organizational transformation and the environment

In this sense, hospitals can be regarded as technologies that are concerned with people's health, and universities are technologies for achieving education. Across cultures, this then implies that key elements of organizational technology, such as work flows, human–machine interaction, the usage of software systems, or 'culture' diverge and need to be integrated by the cross-cultural manager.

For managing the interrelations between the internal organizational transformation process and the organizational environment, two main principles have been proposed:

> **Technological imperative** The idea that organizational technology is what determines organization and needs to be kept stable

> **Contingency theory** The idea that organizations are embedded in and dependent upon their environment and thus need to change, adapt and transform

- The **technological imperative** refers to the idea that technology determines certain structural features such as centralization, span of control, formalization, roles and responsibilities, and communication channels. Organizations should therefore try to keep technology as stable as possible – an incentive not to change.
- **Contingency theory** refers to the insight that an organization cannot be designed independently of its stakeholders and its environment. The environment involves, for example, political, economic, socio-cultural, geographical, legal and technological aspects, and often poses new demands on organizations – a clear argument in favour of the need for change. The main goal of contingency theory is thus to figure out a best way to organize that considers both the requirements of the organizational environment *and* the technology in use.

Together, this explains why there is a difference in organizational cultures even in the same societal environment.

STUDENT ACTIVITY 10.4

Technology and Contingency Theory

Whenever companies are active internationally, they face the need to meet new environmental and stakeholder demands when transforming input into output.

Select a company or organization of your choice. Then consider the specifics of this company's national environment(s).

- What is the core transformation process in which this company or organization is engaged? Define technology in the aforementioned organizational sense.
- To what extent has the company adapted its transformation process and/or its stakeholder management to culture-specific local conditions? For answering this question, look up corporate or media reports.

Manufacturing technologies and their cultural impact

Joan Woodward (1965), one of the first organizational sociologists to draw attention to technology, surveyed 100 English manufacturing organizations. She differentiated organizational technology in relation to what is produced, and how, and drew implications for the best organizational design as befitting the mode of production from there. Design refers to the managerial choices made in order to ensure organizational performance (for details, see Chapter 9), or, in other words: to achieve the best possible transformation.

Unit or small batch technologies produce one item (unit) at a time, or small batches at the most. People employing them work creatively, perform a variety of tasks and often use discretion. Examples are custom-made clothes, engineering prototypes or designer products.

Unit, mass and continuous process Three main manufacturing technologies

Large batch or mass technologies produce a large batch or a 'mass' of identical goods or products by means of standardized and often mechanized procedures. The whole production process is broken down into discrete and sequential tasks, performed either by humans or by machines. Each worker or machine engages in a repetitive task of small scope, and adjacent steps of the production process are usually performed in close vicinity. The classic example is the automotive production line.

Continuous process technologies cannot be broken into discrete parts and involve the continuous processes of a certain input, such as raw materials like oil. Those operating the technology do not work alongside it (as is the case for mass-based technologies) but only tend to it, while the technology in use (e.g. refinement processes) enables the transformation.

CCM Applications

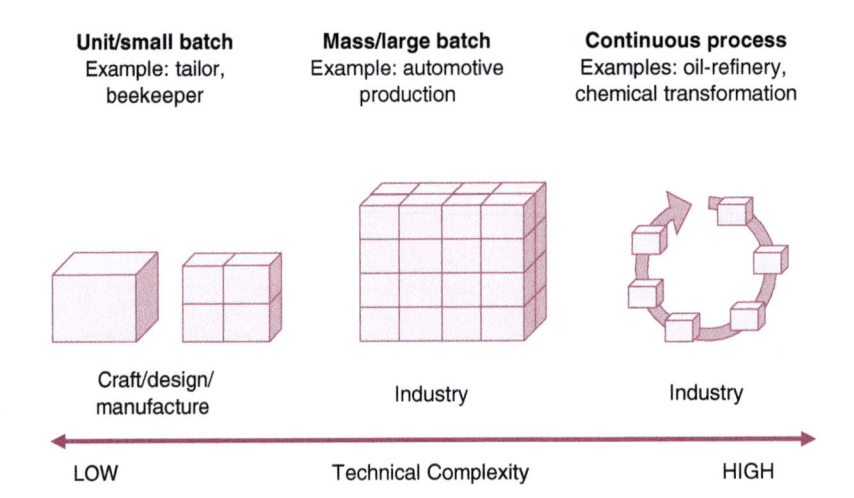

Figure 10.2 Production technology in the manufacturing organization: Three types

Source: adapted from Woodward (1965)

As Figure 10.2 shows, technological complexity increases from one level to the next. Centralized and large spans of managerial control, as well as mechanistic (formalized, rule-oriented) organizational structures, are preferred for mass production, whereas the other two have more decentralized ways of decision-making and small spans of managerial control. Continuous process technologies require decision-making that is decentralized the most, and unit-based technologies fit best to more flexible and less formalized (so-called 'organic') organizational designs that are conducive of change.

STUDENT ACTIVITY 10.5

Three Types of Technology and Their Leadership Implications

The GLOBE study (GLOBE, 2020) has identified six largely culturally contingent leadership styles.

Table 10.1 GLOBE leadership styles

Leadership style	Explanation
Charismatic	The ability to inspire, to motivate and to expect high performance outcomes from others based on firmly held core values.
Team-oriented	The ability to effectively build teams and implement a common purpose or goal among team members.
Participative	The degree to which managers involve others in making and implementing decisions
Humane-oriented	The degree to which leaders are supportive and considerate but also include compassion and generosity
Autonomous	The degree to which leaders are independent and individualistic
Self-protective	The degree to which leadership focuses on ensuring the safety and security of the individual and group through status enhancement and face saving

Source: adapted from GLOBE (2020)

Consider these styles in relation to the three aforementioned technologies. Which technology seems more conducive of which leadership style? Which one does not seem to fit to a certain style? Compile a table with your insights and exchange your findings with fellow students to refine them.

Further typologies of technology in organizations

With his differentiation into long-linked, mediating and intensive technologies, James Thompson (1967) moved beyond the industrial sector. This classification will be presented and discussed below in light of CCM.

Long-linked technologies

Long-linked technologies are the processes underlying large-scale or mass production; they structure people's tasks in a sequential manner. The overall production is split into discrete, repetitive tasks of small range, and people work hand in hand with technology (e.g. robots). The classic example for this technology is the assembly line of an automotive plant.

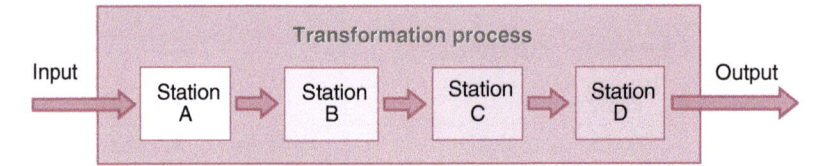

Figure 10.3 Long-linked technologies

Source: adapted from Thompson (1967); Hatch (2011: 44)

Tasks are performed in a fixed sequence, which means that there is a linear interdependence of tasks (C builds upon B, which builds upon A). Inputs, outputs and the transformation process itself are standardized. Long-linked technologies thus require coordination via scheduling tasks and workers, and time-planning is imperative. An example for such a coordination mechanism is Kanban.

Link to Practice: Kanban

Kanban is a lean workflow management method ('technology'), first introduced in the Japanese automotive industry, that is intended to visualize the work process via Kanban Cards or Kanban Boards, maximize efficiency via reducing stock and improving timing, and to improve continuously via reflexive learning cycles.

STUDENT ACTIVITY 10.6

Kanban and Lean Production

Do some research on the concept of lean production, in particular Kanban. Answer the following questions:

- How does Kanban work?
- Who invented it and when, and in light of which boundary conditions (industry, global competition, etc.)?
- How has Kanban improved manufacturing, e.g. in the automotive and the automotive supplier industry?
- What kind of organizational 'culture' does Kanban promote?
- Which global organizational or industrial need does Kanban fulfil?

Next, research and note the cultural dimension score of Japan (Hofstede scores and GLOBE study scores).

> **Kanban** A lean production and workflow method

- How 'Japanese' is Kanban?

Answer in writing. Next, discuss with fellow students.

Mediating technologies

Mediating technologies facilitate an exchange between otherwise independent parties, such as buyers and sellers or borrowers and lenders. They pool people and tasks together. For example, bankers use funds provided by savers to make loans to borrowers, and an internet marketplace brings together buyers and sellers. Inputs and outputs are not standardized, but the transformation process is. The coordination effort for mediating technologies is limited, however; they require rules and standard procedures to make it clear how the parties should interact and make decisions. For example, there are common terms of usage for those interacting on an e-marketplace. Still, each customer may 'walk' through the shop at their own leisure and via their own path – there is no fixed sequence of neither the clients' inputs nor of the tasks required for generating the desired output.

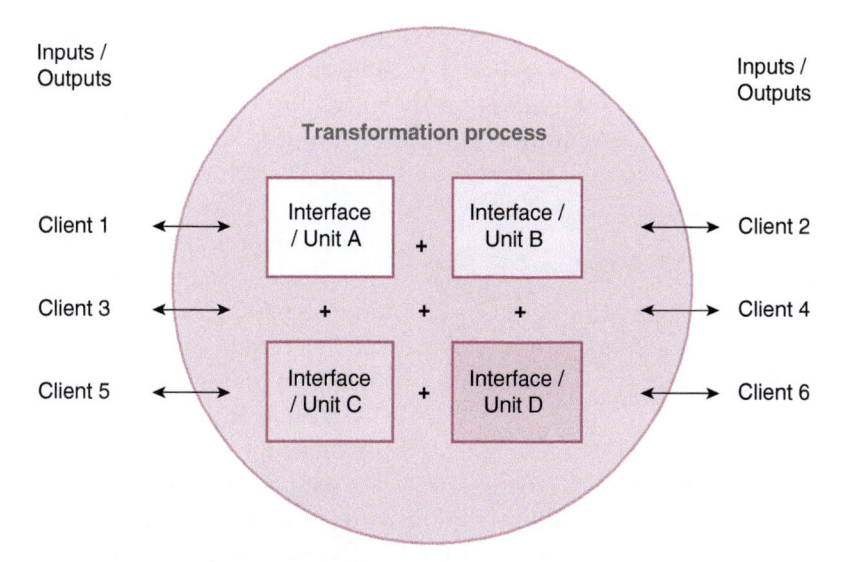

Figure 10.4 Mediating technologies

Source: adapted from Thompson (1967); Hatch (2011: 44)

> **Link to Practice: Comments on the New Samsung Mobile on Facebook – A Cross-Cultural Case Study**
>
> Facebook is a social media platform connecting people across the globe; it is a mediating technology. In an empirical study, Moro et al. (2020) analysed how users from Australia, India and South Africa commented on a new Samsung mobile phone on Facebook. They found that the users highlighted different features of the phone and also assessed the same features differently. For both aspects, national cultural dimensions (see Chapter 5) were found to be an explanatory variable. The study thus underscores the assumption that technologies, such as the hardware–software combinations found in mobile phones, interrelate with people in culture-specific ways. On a second level, the study highlights how social media, as a global mediating technology, enables cross-cultural communication on a common interest (in this case the new Samsung mobile phone) and thus integrates national–cultural difference in ways which would have been impossible without technology.

Intensive technologies

Intensive technologies require the greatest degree of mutual cooperation and communication across people and tasks. There is a high task interdependence, which is also a reciprocal task; each person and task is dependent upon all others. In contrast to long-linked technologies with their unidirectional workflow, intensive technologies result in reciprocal and multidirectional workflows. Teamwork is required, and for ensuring it, individuals need to use discretion, give and receive feedback, and adjust to each other, as each unique situation requires.

> **Long-linked, mediating and intensive** Three main organizational technologies

Any organization that uses intensive technology uses long-linked and mediating technologies as well. It is just that, in a certain situation, the intended outcome requires intensive technology and cannot be reached solely by the means of the other two. For example, a hospital employs mediating and long-linked technologies to care for people. Yet, if a patient crashes in the emergency room, a team of specialists need to work in parallel and in interaction to save the patient's life. At this point, intensive technology is employed.

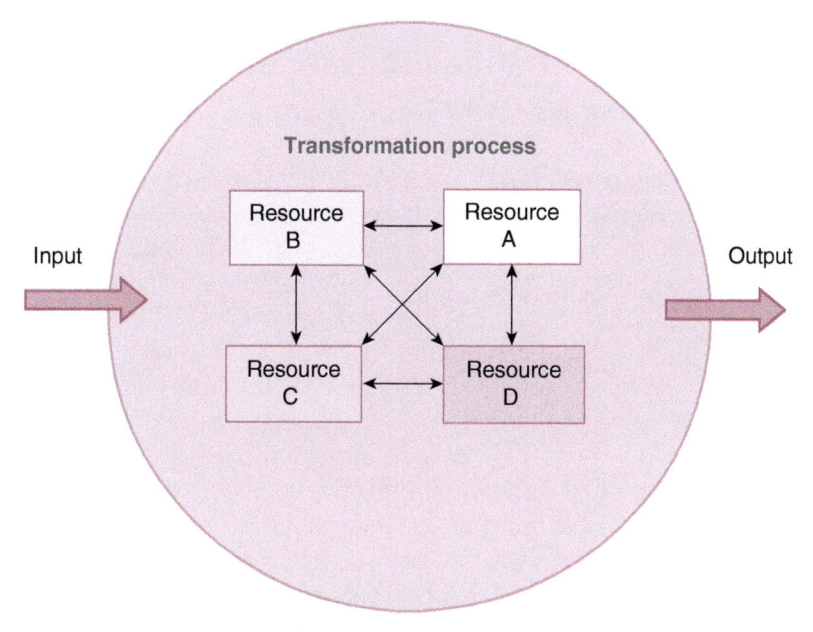

Figure 10.5 Intensive technologies

Source: adapted from Thompson (1967); Hatch (2011: 45)

Link to Practice:
Addressing the Patient Cultural Divide

When treating people by means of intensive technologies, medical personnel must assume that patients will react to these technologies and describe their condition in different, culture specific ways (Tirell, 2001). This phenomenon is referred to as the *patient cultural divide*. For effective treatment and a better patient compliance, it needs to be addressed by medical providers.

Table 10.2 summarizes the types of technology, the types of input and transformation process underlying them, the task interdependence established and the coordination mechanisms required and draws implications for CCM from there. As Table 10.2 shows, pooled interdependence only requires rules and procedures, but sequential interdependence uses rules, procedures and scheduling, while reciprocal interdependence uses all these forms of coordination plus mutual adjustment.

Making the link – Cultural variance of technology and its CCM implications

The previous considerations have highlighted that not all technologies predict human behaviour exactly. Rather, there is an associated **cultural variance** (CV). The higher the variance, the less culturally predictive the technology. Table 10.2 highlights the degree of CV in relation to inputs and outputs, the transformation process, and the nature of inner-organizational interdependence of tasks and resources. If input/output-related, task-related, or transformation-related CV is high, this suggests a higher degree of cultural complexity and, thus, higher CCM demands on the cross-cultural manager. Also, the higher the CV, the higher the likelihood that organizational reality deviates from macro-comparative cultural dimension scores. This then provides cross-cultural managers with recommendations of which CCM perspective to employ and how to proceed for managing the situation.

> **Cultural variance** The variations associated with technology's cultural impact

Table 10.2 Organizational technologies and their cross-cultural management implications

Type of Technology	Inputs/Outputs: Type and CV	Organizational transformation: Type and CV	Task interdependence: Type and CV	Major/minor means of coordination	Degree of cultural complexity
Long-linked	Standardized (low I/O CV)	Standardized (low Tr CV)	Sequential (low Ta CV)	Schedules, Rules and procedures	Low
Mediating	Non-standardized (high I/O CV)	Standardized (low Tr CV)	Pooled (medium Ta CV)	Rules and procedures	Medium
Intensive	Non-standardized (high I/O CV)	Non-standardized (high Tr CV)	Reciprocal (high Ta CV)	Mutual adjustment, Schedules, Rules and procedures	High

CV = Cultural variance
Tr CV = Transformation-related cultural variance
I/O CV = Input/output-related cultural variance
Ta CV = task-related cultural variance
Source: adapted from Hatch (2011: 167)

STUDENT ACTIVITY 10.7

The Technological Imperative, Organizational Design and CCM

Managers need to design organizations, and for doing so, they can choose between mechanistic, more organic and network-oriented organizational designs (Chapter 9). As preparation for this task, re-read the section on organizational design in Chapter 9 and make sure to understand Figure 9.2.

Next, apply new knowledge from this chapter to the CCM task of organizational design. For doing so, revisit Table 9.2 which provides you with an overview on key design decisions. Now, consider the technological imperative – which type of technology calls for what type of organizational design? What does this then imply for cultural variance? Add these considerations to Table 9.2. For example, transformation by means of long-linked technologies requires centralized control mechanisms. Thus, control should be centralized, which then reduces the cultural variance of control.

Write down your findings and be prepared to discuss them in class.

Tasks and technology

Another aspect to be considered when classifying organizational technology is the degree of **task variability** and **task analysability**. For visualizing this aspect of organizational technology, Charles Perrow (1967) has suggested a two-by-two matrix (see Figure 10.6).

If the idea of routine and non-routine work is mapped onto Woodward's idea of unit, mass and continuous process technologies, large batch/mass production is characterized by a high amount of routine work.

Task variability and analysability Two main dimensions for classifying work

Conversely, unit production ('craft'), due to its small batch size, continuous process technologies and high level of technological complexity, are characterized by a high amount of non-routine work. This then also implies that organizations which wish to make use of the unique potential of non-routine, non-analysable work (e.g. graphic design) or of analytical non-routine work (e.g. research and development engineering) need to make sure that these groups are not fully subjected to technologies which will force them into routine work, such as long-linked technology.

CCM Applications

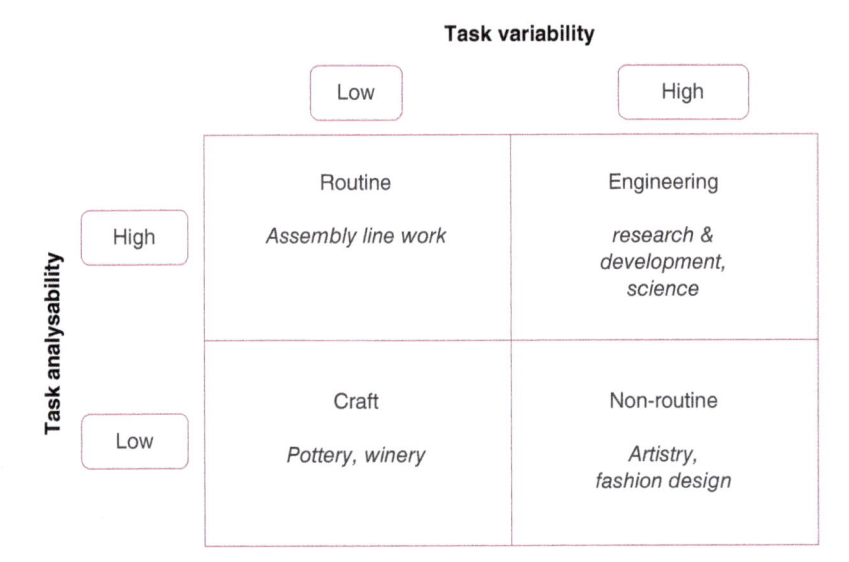

		Task variability	
		Low	High
Task analysability	High	Routine *Assembly line work*	Engineering *research & development, science*
	Low	Craft *Pottery, winery*	Non-routine *Artistry, fashion design*

Figure 10.6 Organizational technologies in relation to task variability and analysability Based on: Perrow (1967)

Link to Practice: How to Make your Software Developers Happy (and Avoid Burnout)

Software developers are the classic example of employees who perform analytical non-routine work and who should therefore not be subjected to too mechanistic and bureaucratic organizational structures and strict managerial control. Software developers are key to corporate innovation and hard to recruit and retain (Kelly, 2022). Due to the industry's high turnover rates, 'how to keep software developers happy' has become a key human resource management issue (ibid.). However, the question is also coupled with another dilemma, namely, how to avoid developers 'burning out'. Due to the nature of their work and their intrinsic commitment to it, there is also the danger of developers exhausting themselves at work – simply because work is 'so intriguing and fulfilling' and because there are no control mechanisms (such as managerial control, organizational structures or routine technologies) preventing that. Recent strategies to free developers of mundane tasks and less intensive technological work even more (Kelly, 2022) might thus further increase work intensity – with potential negative side-effects on the individual.

The Cross-Cultural Implications of Organizational Technology

Organizational technology influences how people work together, what kind of leadership and management proves best to solve the problem at hand, and how organization is designed and structured.

This insight that organizational structure, and human sensemaking and interaction are mutually constitutive of each other is also referred to as **structuration theory** (Giddens, 1979). Translated to technology, this means that technology shapes how people use it, and at the same time people also adapt technology to their needs and cultural requirements (Orlikowski, 2000). For example, graphic artists will use the same software program differently than accountants or research engineers.

> **Structuration theory** Here, the insight that technology structures how humans use it and that humans create the meanings of technology via their doings

Cultural dimensions are a helpful tool for assessing and managing the cross-cultural challenge of technology. The next activity focuses on making this link.

STUDENT ACTIVITY 10.8

Making the Link – The Cross-Cultural Implications of Technology

Revisit the concept of cultural dimensions (Chapter 5, Tables 5.4 to 5.6). Consider which type of organizational technology seems more conducive to a high or low orientation of a certain cultural dimension. Visualize your hypotheses by means of a table.

For example, long-linked technologies require standardized inputs to generate standardized outputs; a sequential work flow needs to be regulated and scheduled. Its technological imperative will most likely encourage an organizational design and individual behaviour which is characterized by comparably high uncertainty avoidance. If the type of

(Continued)

long-linked technology is furthermore characterized by a high task analysability and a low task variability, it is even more conducive to high uncertainty avoidance. The effect will be further supported if the purpose of employing long-linked technology is mass production. See Table 10.3 for a visualization of this example.

Table 10.3 Organizational technologies in relation to cultural dimensions

Type of technology	Task variability	Task analysability	Production output	Conducive to
Long-linked	low	high	mass	High uncertainty avoidance

The purpose is not to prove that a certain technology must cause a certain cultural orientation or that the prevalence of certain cultural dimensions must result in a certain technology but to come to plausible hypotheses as to their underlying interrelations.

Actors, Things and CCM

As the previous considerations suggest, it is not only that people *use* technology, but technology and humans also interact. For example, at the assembly line, one work station might be staffed with a person and another one might be staffed with a production robot, and both are linked via the sequence of long-linked technology and via the joint output goal of mass production. Humans also develop feelings for and tacit knowledge ('how to interact with and use technology') regarding technology. The term Socio-Technical System (STS) (Trist and Bamforth, 1951) describes such close human–technology interlinkages. These are systems, such as the healthcare system, wherein technical and social dimensions are interrelated. From an STS perspective, the degree to which both factors (social and technical system) fit, complement and shape each other is relevant to how well the system functions. Another, more recent approach to the same question is **Actor–Network Theory** (ANT, see Spotlight). For CCM,

Actor–Network Theory (ANT) Here, the idea that cross-cultural contexts are shaped by human and technological actors alike the implication of both is that cross-cultural managers cannot take social action independently of technology.

> ### Spotlight: Actor-Network Theory
>
> Developed first at Centre de Sociologie de l'Innovation of the École Nationale Supérieur de Mines and often associated with the names of Madeleine Ackrich, Michel Callon, John Law and Bruno Latour, the Actor–Network Theory (ANT), which understands society and nature as equal actors in their own right is both a popular and controversial social theory (for overview, see Latour, 1996, and for a critical review, see Collier, 2009).
>
> The main premise of ANT is that the world is constituted by networks of actors (Law, 1992). A network contains not only humans but also machines, animals, books, buildings, etc. or, as Law (1992) put it, 'heterogeneous materials' (p. 381). This perspective has two implications. Firstly, an actor is anything 'that acts, or to which activity is granted by others' (Latour, 1996: 373). Secondly, any actor can only act in relation to and in combination with other actors; it is they who give the actor its space and time for action (Latour, 1996). The result is a web of interrelations between society and technology, in which different actors (be they human or non-human) interact and constantly negotiate their space (and power) of manoeuvring (Callon, 1984). From this perspective, technology is thus not an external force that impacts upon people. Rather, it is an 'acting' part of the social networks of actors (Latour, 1996) and needs to be considered as such.

User interface design from a cross-cultural perspective

Technology is often characterized by a combination of hardware and software. For example, a computer is a combination of mechanical and electrical components (hardware) and programs and code which enable its functionality (software). A key aspect here is the question of how to translate human input into something which the computer can directly execute. For this, four steps have to be completed:

- A user instructs a computer; for example, press the 'bold' button in word.
- A computer program is executed which describes the underlying functionality in a certain program language (source code).

- The computer program is translated into machine code, that is the translation of the source code into a machine-processable form.
- The computer hardware executes the instructions.

As this list suggests, technology in itself is already cross-cultural and requires multiple acts of interpretation and translation, e.g. between source code and machine code.

Most people interact with computers on a daily basis, a phenomenon referred to as human–computer interaction (HCI). However, most of these people are not technologically literate. For example, those using a word processing program do not even need to possess basic knowledge of how this program functions in technological terms – they simply press a button. The field addressing the question of how to make technology accessible, is referred to as **User-Interface (UI)** Design. Examples of human–machine interaction involving user interfaces (UIs) are: accessing bank accounts and withdrawing money from the ATM (automated teller machine), purchasing online flight tickets from various websites, or using language-learning apps.

> **User interface** The part of a technology with which a user interacts

> **Usability engineering** The art and craft of designing user interfaces

To make sense to a non-tech user, UIs need to be 'readily comprehended, quickly learned, and reliably operated' (Butler, 1996: 53). Moreover, there are also international standards (such as ISO 9241 or ISO 13407), which provide guidelines and information on design principles and ergonomic requirements.

Usability engineering, the art and craft of designing UIs, needs to consider a combination of universal, cultural and individual factors, as well as objective regulations and subjective interpretations, to let users interact with technology intuitively, efficiently and effectively (Marcus, 2006).

Link to Practice: Culture in the Computer Game Industry

When designing computer games, designers need to bridge the need for a potentially global product or service (a computer game), and the need for being close to the culturally diverse buyers and users of this product or service. This requires assessing and integrating culture-bound and culture-free HCI elements in the best possible way (see Heimgärtner, 2019). Crucial elements to be considered for such an integrated UI design are, for example, people's mental models, navigation, interaction and appearance (Marcus, 2006). For example, Arabic is written and read from right to left, which then means that the whole layout of a webpage needs to be changed so that users can navigate it intuitively. Cultural orientations such as individualism and collectivism influence gamers' preferences (Chakraborty and Norcio, 2009). Furthermore, high-context and low-context ways of how to process knowledge differ considerably (ibid.). Whereas low-context knowledge is acquired 'verbally, explicitly, directly, at high speed and to the point', high-context knowledge is acquired 'experientially, implicitly, indirectly, slowly and within the circumstances'. When designing computer games, this would then imply fewer pictures, more and more precise information and a clear and linear structure of the argument (low-context) or more pictures, emotional associations, less written messages and a more holistic layout of the whole of the page (high-context). Colour schemes and divergent perceptions of icons are another, relevant aspect to be considered (Callahan, 2005), as are language and translation issues (Chakraborty and Norcio, 2009).

Making the Link: Cross-Cultural Differences in Technological Requirements – Two Studies

Considering Japan, Nicaragua and the Arab world, Schoper and Heimgärtner (2013) highlight the challenges of designing a UI for navigation systems. Firstly, there are country-specific differences in the objective user requirements. For example, most streets in Japan have no names. Secondly, users interpret technology differently, and expect different functionalities of it – a difference in subjective culture. For example, due to a high context orientation in Japan, a navigation system might offer information on alternative romantic routes (which would provide drivers with a more holistic and 'high-context' driving experience). A navigation system designed for Arab countries might exhibit a Mecca compass, which is considered an important feature for observant Muslims (Schoper and Heimgärtner, 2013: 97).

(Continued)

Taking a comparative approach to the same question, Lachner et al. (2018) focus on one cultural dimension (power distance, according to the Hofstede scores) and two countries: Germany (Hofstede score 35) and Vietnam (Hofstede score 70). They consider the effects of this dimension on UI design, for example, in relation to navigation structure, visual presentation and language usage. Based on their insights, they then designed two website prototypes designed for lower and higher power distance. They found that their study participants (14 Germans and 14 Vietnamese) favoured the prototype which included UI design principles based on the lower or higher power distance orientation of respective countries of origin.

STUDENT ACTIVITY 10.9

User Interface Design and CCM

Imagine that you wish to set up a global marketplace which functions by means of mediating technology. This implies that each client or customer will enter the marketplace via a central webpage. On this webpage, the client should find:

- a search function
- customized offers of interest
- general information on the marketplace
- login option for returning users.

The only information which you have at this point is the location of the user, i.e. the specific GPS coordinates from which the user is logging in. This means that you can infer country culture from there. Select three countries of your choice and consider which parts of the UI design you should check for their potentially culturally contingent characteristics. When doing so, differentiate between objective differences in functionality and hypotheses regarding potential differences. For example, some languages are written top-down, left-to-right or right-to-left – this is an objective difference between the countries of your choice. Users might prefer more or less written information, based on a lower or higher context orientation, as prevalent in their country of residence (this is a hypothesis to be tested – it *might* be relevant for UI design – not an objective difference).

- Find one objective difference and one hypothesis to be tested for each country.
- Based on these findings, sketch an entry page to your website for each of the three countries, taking into consideration the benefits of standardization, as well as the need for cultural adaptation.
- Show and explain your visualization to other students.

Towards an Internet of Things?

Sometimes, single devices, such as a computer, are embedded into wider functionalities. For example, a computer might serve the purpose of steering a nuclear power plant. These systems are then referred to as **embedded systems**. A further development of embedded systems are so called **cyber-physical systems**. These are embedded systems which are also connected via information and communications technology, for example in a cloud. For example, it is now possible to steer production elsewhere from a central production unit at a specific location. Ultimately, this means that objects are connected via technology, without any human interference. For example, there are fridges that inform you of which items to restore, autonomous driving systems for vehicles, and buildings or entire cities that use so-called 'smart objects and technologies' to optimize energy consumption or to address public safety issues or transportation problems. The proliferation of such phenomena is referred to as the **Internet of Things (IoT)**. A frequently voiced idea is that the IoT started from the moment the number of 'things or objects' surpassed the number of persons connected to the internet, and this is supposed to have happened somewhere between 2008 and 2009 (Evans, 2011: 2–3).

Embedded systems Systems, such as software, which are part of larger systems

Cyber-physical systems Embedded systems which are connected, e.g. via the internet

Internet of Things The phenomenon that more 'things' than humans are connected via the internet

On a global scale, the IoT implies that there are cross-cultural interactions without any human contribution, and also an increasing number of interactions of humans with technology. Its promoters stress the usefulness of the IoT for humans. For example, some enjoy the comfort of no longer having to order food, as their smart fridges can do that for them, others preheat their ovens shortly before arriving at home using their mobile phones (Zolfagharifard, 2016). Smart leak sensors, smart bulbs and smart thermostats are some of the devices now on the market, which are aimed at saving energy and money (Cericola, 2019). Companies may cut costs and enhance manufacturing productivity with the help of smart adaptable assembly lines (ElMaraghy and ElMaraghy, 2016). The advances in sensor technology might simplify the monitoring of air and water quality, or radiation (Ullo and Sinha, 2020), while satellite technology and thermal alert systems can detect volcanic activity before eruption (Schmidt, 2020). Consequently, based on real-time information as well as on historical data, authorities and policy makers can look for optimal solutions or react faster to environmental challenges. From the perspective of Dave Evans, former chief technologist and chief futurist of Cisco, the IoT 'will change everything – including ourselves' (2011: 2) for the better. Cisco (2013) even proposed the expression Internet of Everything (IoE), which includes not only things, but also people, processes and data, and there is also the expression of a Social Internet of Things (SIoT) (Firouzi et al., 2020). Critical voices highlight the threats which the IoT might pose to the users' privacy, such as tracking, localization, profiling or inventory attacks (Ziegeldorf et al., 2013). There is also the question of the consequences of technology, for example as in the case of dual- or multiple-use goods and services. A 3D-printer, for example, can also be used to print weaponry.

Pause and Reflect: How Technologically Literate Should CCM Be?

Whether technology will bring the 'end of the future' as Bridle's (2019) book title suggests, can be doubted, but this statement of his might deserve attention: 'We know more and more about the world, while being less and less able to do anything about it' (p. 186). Based on this statement, please reflect on how technologically literate CCM is, and how technologically literate CCM - and you yourself - *should* be. What role does and should technology play in achieving key CCM goals, such as utilizing the benefits of diversity, and achieving complementarities and synergies? What are the technological responsibilities of the cross-cultural manager, and of CCM as a discipline?

First, draw conclusions of your own. Next, discuss with fellow students.

Link to Practice: Cortana by Microsoft

When developing the intelligent assistant Cortana, Microsoft's developers used cultural dimensions in programming the artificial intelligence (AI) that provides Cortana with a perceived 'personality' (overview in Ash, 2015). Depending on the language of the user, the assistant will, for example, phrase questions in a more direct (low context) or more indirect (high context) manner. Cortana will, for example, use self-deprecating humour in the UK, and 'smile with her voice' in China. From this perspective, technology's interrelations with culture are positive, resulting in better products. However, there are also critical voices asking the question of why the default setting of all AI assistants is a female voice (Stewart, 2018). As humans are likely to humanize technology and as this technology is also programmed in such ways that it seems to have a culturally suitable personality, this might reinforce perceptions of female subservience across culture (ibid.) – clearly a negative interrelation between technology and culture.

Social Media and CCM

Social media is a relevant facet of how people today experience and walk through the world. It is also increasingly used for business-related purposes. For example, corporate HR departments outsource the management of their employees' work-related profiles to the employees' own social media account. Ultimately, this means that the employee takes care of updating their own competencies, skills and work-related experiences, and HR simply access them via a social media interface. Social media is also an opportunity for quick recruitment and career management, and it enables the HR manager to link themselves with people across distances, locations and cultures.

At the same time, there are social and cross-cultural dangers associated with social media. Users tend to only surround themselves with those who are similar, and the algorithms underlying the respective social media platforms will only suggest confirmatory or associated input, based on previous user behaviour and search patterns. This way, a social media environment can easily become a closed and culturally limited bubble, without the user being aware of this happening or having any idea of what they miss. The dangers of these effects are outlined by German journalist Hans Demmel (with Friedrich Küppersbusch, 2021) in their book *Anderswelt* [Otherworld]. In this book, which was published in September 2021, Demmel describes how he informed himself only by means of right-wing (social) media for half a year and how this experience changed his perception and presumptions of 'reality and truth' in drastic, often appalling ways. What he particularly noted was that he was not exposed to a variety of standpoints anymore and, consequently, lost his sense of the 'social, political and cultural middle' regarding burning topics such as ongoing politics and election campaigns, economics, the management of the COVID-19 pandemic, or migration and social integration.

> ### STUDENT ACTIVITY 10.10
>
> ### Social Media and Cross-Cultural Challenges
>
> Imagine that you are about to move to another country for a certain purpose. Imagine both the country and what you are about to do there. Now, consider how you will use social media, and which social media you will use, to familiarize yourself with your new cultural surroundings and to make yourself at home there. How will you use social media to remain connected with those whom you left at home? To what extent will social media enlarge your cultural horizon, to what extent might it limit it, and what should you consider in your social media usage to make sure that the cross-cultural advantages of social media overweigh its potential dangers?
>
> If you have actually moved to another country recently, then please reflect upon this real-life experience for this activity.

Link to Practice: 'Do Africans Have Cars?' (Ajala, 2022)

Blogger and 'TikTok star' Charity Ekezie from Nigeria noticed that many people outside the African continent seem to hold stereotypical views about it (Ajala, 2022). She took matters in her own hands and greeted questions such as 'Do African have cars?' with sarcastic videos and posts on the social media platform TikTok. She explains in mock-seriousness that poorer Africans swing from liana to liana to work whereas richer Africans ride on camels (in North Africa) or baboons (in West African). All this she states while standing in front of local scenery with a car in the background.

Chapter Summary

Technology and cross-cultural management are interrelated in multiple, sometimes contradicting ways. To assess technology's impact on culture, managers need to consider how technology may contribute to existing inequalities but at the same time may also 'flatten' the world. On an organizational level, technologies influence how 'things are normally done'. Cross-cultural managers working in multinational or global organizations or networks thus need to carefully balance the cultural requirements of the internal transformation process and the demands of the organizational environment and stakeholder networks. In some aspects, technology has furthermore become a cross-cultural actor of its own, as also AI assistants or videos 'travel across cultures', and much may be learned from these cross-cultural experiences and interactions. On a very personal level, most people nowadays use some degree of social media by which they are exposed to cross-cultural interactions but also contribute to them. It is thus part of the cross-cultural manager's responsibility to contribute to technology in CCM in a 'good way'.

Key Points

- Technology and social media are part of today's cross-cultural management.
- Via technology, people 'travel' to other countries without ever changing place.
- On a global level, technologies might contribute to existing inequalities but also democratize business.
- On an organizational level, technology refers to the technology, tools and machines used for transformation *and* the craft, knowledge and skill of using them.
- Several typologies of organizational technologies enable the cross-cultural manager to consider how the organization is shaped by its technology *and* contingent upon its environment.
- Cultural variance is a key concept for assessing technology's impact on managers and organizations.
- Via the Internet of Things, technology has become a cross-cultural actor of its own.
- Humans and technologies are mutually constitutive; together, they shape sociotechnical systems and actor networks.
- Cross-cultural interface design is a key cross-cultural management application.
- Social media enables new cross-cultural interactions.
- It is the cross-cultural manager's responsibility to shape technology responsibly.

Review Questions

1. Which international business conditions facilitated frugal or *jugaad* innovation? What can be learned from the rise of frugal innovation about technology's impact on business and organizations?
2. What are the effects which information and communications technology have upon people, societies and organizations? How would you rate these effects?
3. Is technology culture-free or culture-bound? Use the example of computer gaming to make your point. What does this imply for cross-cultural management?
4. What are user interfaces and how is their design relevant from a cross-cultural management perspective?
5. How and to what extent does technology shape organizational culture? Use examples and refer to different types of technology to make your point.
6. How and to what extent does technology shape organizational leadership requirements? Use examples and refer to different types of technology to make your point.
7. What are the spaces (e.g. socio-technological systems) in which humans and technology interact and which they shape together? Name them and explain their main features.
8. How has social media changed people's cross-cultural exposures?
9. Will technology make people more cross-culturally competent? Why (not)?
10. Will social media make people more cross-culturally competent? Why (not)?

Opening Case Revisited

The Opening Case presented a specific approach to innovation (frugal innovation), which, in its Indian context, is referred to as *jugaad* innovation. It describes an innovation that meets most (but not all) of customers' needs via good enough functionality at comparably low prices and by means of the least resources.

As a phenomenon, frugal innovation is most widespread in India. Is *jugaad* specifically 'Indian' and, if so, how exactly, and in which aspects? To answer this question, do the following:

- Check the cultural dimension scores for India. Do they seem conducive to a *jugaad* approach to innovation?
- Consider meaning and sense-making. How is *jugaad* interpreted in Indian media and public? Do some research on the internet to identify sources which tell you something about whether people *believe* (who? for what purposes?) that *jugaad* is culturally Indian.
- Reflect upon your findings critically. There is also the concept of Hindutva ('Hindu-ness') in India, a movement which constructs India as a Hindu nation, united and spurred by 'Hindu values'. Do some research on the internet. Is *jugaad* an objective success story of how a certain history or cultural disposition of a country are more conducive to higher innovation, or is it also used by some to promote nationalist ideas of 'Indianness' as a superior cultural root?

Closing Activity: Technologies and Cultural Code-Switching in CCM

The cross-cultural management of technology often involves the mediation between global and culturally contingent elements. For example, a keyboard or a touchscreen with keyboard functionality is a global technology used by virtually everyone who has access to a smartphone, tablet, laptop or personal computer. Its purpose is to connect a user input with a certain hardware device. However, languages – as potentially culture-specific ways of transmitting meaning and putting thought into action – function differently. Some languages are letter-based, such as the Latin or Cyrillic alphabet; others, such as Indian languages (e.g. Devanagari or Dravidian scripts) or Japanese (e.g. Hiragana and Katakana script) are syllable-based; in some languages, it is customary not to write down vowels (e.g. Hebrew, Arabic); and in even others, each word is represented by a pictogram of its own (e.g. Mandarin Chinese).

Therefore, how *can* a keyboard mediate between the culturally contingent user inputs and the global hardware used? Obviously, one way of going about this problem would be to use a culture-specific keyboard. The most frequent alphabet on a keyboard is the Latin one, yet there are also other keyboards in use, e.g. for Arabic or Cyrillic. However, some input requirements simply don't fit the physical design of a keyboard as there is no way that it could ever depict approximately 300 syllables, let alone the thousands of Chinese pictograms in existence. Furthermore, because the world is increasingly glocalized (characterized by numerous combinations of global and culturally contingent local influences and requirements), keyboard users often need to manage a variety of requirements. Sometimes they might need to input an URL, using the Latin alphabet, and sometimes they might need to write a message in, let's say, Mandarin Chinese. Thus, there is a high requirement of

CCM Applications

> **Cultural code-switching** Moving back and forth between different cultural codes

cultural code-switching; that is, the frequent need to change the cultural code in use. Depending on where you stand on this matter, choose between Option 1 and Option 2 of the following activity.

Option 1

If you have never used a non-Latin alphabet keyboard, research the internet on the various options in existence for converting a non-Latin alphabet into a format that can be processed by a letter-based keyboard design. Consider, in particular, scripts which are based on the unit of syllabi or words, and the need for cultural code-switching, that is, ways to input non-Latin alphabet-based script and Latin letters interchangeably. Answer the following questions:

- How does technology mediate between different language requirements?
- What are the strengths of technology in enabling cultural translation and combination?
- Imagine the skillset of those using technology for cultural code-switching. Which cross-cultural competencies and skills do people develop this way, beyond the actual practice of inputting one script by means of another script's letters?

Option 2

If you are a frequent speaker of a language that is not Latin-alphabet based and if you also use this language in your daily technology-based communication, reflect upon the following:

- Which technologies enable you to mediate between different language requirements, and how exactly do these technologies function?
- What have you learned about cultural code-switching via using these technologies? Or, in other words, how has technology contributed to your abilities to switch between different language-based codes and combine them to a higher outcome?
- Which of these cultural code-switching abilities are also useful in real life, without technology and beyond the actual practice of inputting one script by means of another script's letters?

For both of these options, afterwards discuss with fellow students and draw implications for CCM in general. How does cultural code-switching, not only regarding technology, move your CCM skills to a higher level? What are the organizational benefits of cultural code-switching, and how can this ability be trained and further developed?

Further Reading

Orr's (1996) ethnography of Xerox machine technicians is still brilliant in how it describes in detail how humans give meaning to the technical objects which they interact with via cultural routines of their own. Friedman's (2005) popular book *The World Is Flat*, provides intriguing insights into a time when the 'flattening of the world' via technology had just begun. Focusing on the negative effects of technology, Bridle (2019) paints a 'New Dark Age' associated with information technologies – make up your own mind whether you agree with this outlook.

References

Ajala, H. (2022) '"Do Africans have cars"? How a TikTok star breaks stereotypes about Africa', Media Diversity Institute, 24 May. Available at: www.media-diversity.org/do-africans-have-cars-how-a-tiktok-star-breaks-stereotypes-about-africa/ [last accessed 31 July 2022].

APA News (2020) Mobile Phone Penetration Rate in Kenya. Available at: https://apanews.net/en/news/kenya-mobile-phone-penetration-at-951-percent-report [last accessed 1 September 2020].

Ash, M. (2015) 'Cortana brings cultural savviness to new markets', Windows Experience Blog, 20 July. Available at: https://blogs.windows.com/windowsexperience/2015/07/20/cortana-brings-cultural-savviness-to-new-markets/ [last accessed 31 July 2022].

Bridle, J. (2019) *New Dark Age. Technology and the End of the Future.* London: Verso.

Butler, K.A. (1996) 'Usability engineering turns 10', *Interactions*, 3(1): 58–75.

Callahan, E. (2005) 'Interface design and culture', *Annual Review of Information Science and Technology*, 39(1): 255–310.

Callon, M. (1984) 'Some elements of a sociology of translation: Domestication of the scallops and the fisherman of St Brieuc Bay', *The Sociological Review*, 32(S1): 196–233.

Cericola, R. (2019) 'How to save money and energy with smart home devices', *New York Times, Wirecutter*, 6 January. Available at: www.nytimes.com/wirecutter/blog/smart-home-devices-save-money-energy/ [last accessed 23 June 2021].

Chakraborty, J. and Norcio, A.F. (2009) 'Cross cultural computer gaming', in N. Aykin (ed.), *Internationalization, Design and Global Development*. Berlin, Heidelberg: Springer. pp. 13–18.

Cisco (2013) The Internet of Everything. Cisco IoE Value Index Study. Available at: www.cisco.com/c/dam/en_us/about/business-insights/docs/ioe-value-index-faq.pdf [last accessed 23 June 2021].

Collier, S. J. (2009) 'Review: Reassembling the social: An introduction to Actor Network Theory by Bruno Latour', *Contemporary Sociology*, 38(1): 81–83.

Demmel, H. (2021) *Anderswelt: Ein Selbstversuch mit rechten Medien*. München: Antje Kunstmann.

ElMaraghy, H. and ElMaraghy, W. (2016) 'Smart adaptable assembly lines', *Procedia CIRP*, 44: 4–13.

Evans, D. (2011) 'The Internet of Things. How the next evolution of the internet is changing everything'. Available at: www.cisco.com/c/dam/en_us/about/ac79/docs/innov/IoT_IBSG_0411FINAL.pdf [last accessed 21 June 2021].

Firouzi, F., Farahani, B., Weinberger, M., DePace, G. and Aliee, F.S. (2020) 'IoT fundamentals: Definitions, architectures, challenges, and promises', in F. Firouzi, K. Chakrabarty and S. Nassif (eds), *Intelligent Internet of Things. From Device to Fog and Cloud*. Cham: Springer. pp. 3–50.

Friedman, T.L. (2005) *The World is Flat: A Brief History of the Twenty-First Century*. Stuttgart: Holtzbrinck Publishers.

Giddens, A. (1979) *Central Problems in Social Theory: Action, Structure and Contradiction in Social Analysis*. Berkeley: University of California Press.

GLOBE (2020) *An Overview of the 2004 Study: Understanding the Relationship Between National Culture, Societal Effectiveness and Desirable Leadership Attributes*. Available at: https://globeproject.com/study_2004_2007?page_id=data#data [last accessed 3 August 2021].

Govindarajan, V. (2012) 'A reverse-innovation playbook', *Harvard Business Review*, 90(4): 120–125.

Hatch, M.J. (2011) *Organizations: A Very Short Introduction*. Oxford: Oxford University Press.

Heimgärtner, R. (2019) 'Towards a toolbox for intercultural user interface design', *Proceedings of the 3rd International Conference on Computer–Human Interaction Research and Applications*. pp. 156–163. Available at: www.scitepress.org/Papers/2019/83452/83452.pdf [last accessed 31 July 2021].

Hossain, M. (2021) 'Frugal innovation and sustainable business models', *Technology in Society*, 64: 1–7.

ITU (2019) *The Digital Gender Gap is Growing Fast in Developing Countries*. Available at: https://itu.foleon.com/itu/measuring-digital-development/gender-gap [last accessed 31 July 2022].

Kao, G., Honh, J., Perusse, M. and Sheng, W. (2020) *Turning Silicon into Gold: The Strategies, Failures, and Evolution of the Tech Industry*. New York: Apress, Springer Nature.

Kelly, J. (2022) 'How to make software developers happy and avoid burnout', *Forbes Magazine*, 1 June. Available at: www.forbes.com/sites/jackkelly/2022/06/01/how-to-make-software-developers-happy-and-avoid-burnout/ [last accessed 31 July 2022].

Lachner, F., Nguyen, M.-A. and Butz, A. (2018) 'Culturally sensitive user interface design: A case study with German and Vietnamese users', *Proceedings of the Second African Conference for Human–Computer Interaction: Thriving Communities*. Available at: www.medien.ifi.lmu.de/pubdb/publications/pub/lachner2018africhi/lachner2018africhi.pdf [last accessed 31 July 2022].

Latour, B. (1996) 'On actor-network theory: A few clarifications', *Soziale Welt*, 47(4): 369–381.

Law, J. (1992) 'Notes on the theory of the Actor-Network: Ordering, strategy and heterogeneity', *Systems Practice*, 5(4): 379–393.

Marcus, A. (2006) 'Cross-cultural user-experience design', in D. Barker-Plummer, R. Cox and N. Swoboda (eds), *Diagrammatic Representation and Inference*. Berlin, Heidelberg: Springer. pp. 16–24.

Moro S., Pires G., Rita P. and Cortez, P. (2020) A Cross-Cultural Case Study of consumers' communications about a New Technological Product. Available at: https://repositorium.sdum.uminho.pt/bitstream/1822/73578/3/RBIRS-17-451-Manuscript-R2.pdf [last accessed 31 July 2022].

Orlikowski, W. (2000) 'Using technology and constituting structures: A practice lens for studying technology in organization', *Organisation Science*, 11(4): 404–428.

Orr, J. (1996) *Talking about Machines: An Ethnography of a Modern Job*. Ithaca: Cornell University Press.

Perrow, C. (1967) 'A framework for comparative organizational analysis', *American Sociological Review*, 32(2): 194–208.

Ploeg, M., Knoben, J., Vermeulen, P. and van Beers, C. (2021) 'Rare gems or mundane practice? Resource constraints as drivers of frugal innovation', *Innovation: Organization & Management*, 23(1): 93–126.

Radjou, N., Prabhu, J. and Ahuja, S. (2012a) *Jugaad Innovation. Think Frugal, Be Flexible, Generate Breakthrough Growth*. San Francisco: Jossey-Bass.

Radjou, N., Prabhu, J. and Ahuja, S. (2012b) 'Frugal innovation: Lessons from Carlos Ghosn, CEO, Renault-Nissan', *Harvard Business Review*. Available at: https://hbr.org/2012/07/frugal-innovation-lessons-from [last accessed 31 July 2022].

Ramesh, R. (2009) 'India to unveil the £7 laptop', *The Guardian*, 2 February. Available at: www.theguardian.com/world/2009/feb/02/india-computer-cheapest [last accessed 31 July 2022].

Schmidt, L.J. (2020) Sensing Remote Volcanos. Available at: https://earthdata.nasa.gov/learn/sensing-our-planet/sensing-remote-volcanoes [last accessed 31 July 2022].

Schoper, Y. and Heimgärtner, R. (2013) 'Lessons from intercultural project management for the intercultural HCI design process', in A. Marcus (ed.), *Design, User Experience, and Usability. Health, Learning, Playing, Cultural and Cross-Cultural User Experience*. Berlin, Heidelberg: Springer. pp. 95–104.

Stewart, R. (2018) 'AI gender: Whose default is it?', *The Drum*, 24 October. Available at: www.thedrum.com/news/2018/10/24/all-mouth-no-trousers-do-ai-assistants-have-gender-problem [last accessed 31 July 2022].

Thompson, J. (1967) *Organization in Action*. New York: McGraw-Hill.

Tirell, S.E. (2001) 'The cultural divide between medical providers and their patients – aligning two world views', *Bioethics Forum*, 17(3–4): 24–30.

Trist, E. and Bamforth, K. (1951) 'Some social and psychological consequences of the long wall method of coal getting', *Human Relations*, 4: 3–38.

Ullo, S.L. and Sinha, G.R. (2020) 'Advances in smart environment monitoring systems using IoT and sensors', *Sensors (Basel)*, 20(11): 3113.

Woodward, J. (1965) *Industrial Organization*. London: Oxford University Press.

Ziegeldorf, J.H., Morchon, O.G. and Wehrle, K. (2013) 'Privacy in the Internet of Things: Threats and challenges', *Security and Communication Networks*, 7: 2728–2742.

Zolfagharifard, E. (2016) 'Smarter than the average appliance: Samsung reveals "Family Hub" fridge that orders food, plays films and even lets you see INSIDE IT remotely', *Daily Mail*, 6 January. Available at: www.dailymail.co.uk/sciencetech/article-3386204/Smarter-average-appliance-Samsung-reveals-Family-Hub-fridge-orders-food-plays-films-lets-INSIDE-remotely.html [last accessed 30 June 2022].

PART IV
CCM SKILLSET

The previous parts of this book have guided you from overarching CCM concepts and their underpinnings to smaller application areas of cross-cultural management. Part IV brings your CCM skillset to the point by highlighting key aspects of how to develop your cross-cultural management competencies and of how to design your cross-cultural management research. The chapters in Part IV are not intended as an exhaustive manual but rather as orientation guidelines which help you navigate CCM in theory (research) and practice.

Chapter 11 is rooted in an experiential learning approach; that is, the idea that CCM competencies are built from experience and that intercultural simulations may approximate such experiences. It introduces key tools for learning from experience, such as models of cross-cultural adjustment and intercultural learning, or the circle of intercultural interactions. It also helps you apply CCM concepts to the situation at hand, and to use them for further learning.

Chapter 12 introduces three key debates in CCM studies which help you position your own research project in these terms. These are: the question as to whether culture should be considered holistically or in its causality; whether CCM research is about emics ('insider research') or etics ('outsider research'); and whether one should study culture in its subjectivity or objectivity. The discussion of these questions provides a more pragmatic approach to designing CCM research than potential alternatives such as paradigmatic considerations. Further methodological choices follow from there. The purpose of this chapter is thus to enable you to make your own CCM research design choices – and not to make them for you.

Developing Your Cross-Cultural Management Competencies

11

Learning Objectives

After reading this chapter, you should:

- know key models of cross-cultural learning
- be aware of how intercultural learning is facilitated
- have experienced or informed yourself about experiential learning methods
- know ways of how to develop the cross-cultural management competencies of yourself and others.

Reading Requirements

- You should have read Part I of this book

Introduction

A person is generally understood to be interculturally competent if they are able to influence a cross-cultural (management) situation appropriately and effectively (Spitzberg and Changnon, 2009). Developing such intercultural competencies requires knowledge and skills, and they need to be built from experience that is reflected upon.

> **Intercultural learning** The cognitive, affective and conative processes by which cross-cultural (management) competencies are built

> **Experiential learning** A learning method that simulates 'real-life' experience

The process of building cross-cultural competencies is referred to as **intercultural learning**. Intercultural learning involves thought (cognitive mental processes), emotion (affective mental processes) and action (conative mental processes) (Gudykunst et al., 1977), and the degree to which individuals engage – or do not engage – in this ongoing process influences its progression and outcome (see Figure 11.1). Cross-cultural management competencies are thus also built from the motivation to acquire them (Spitzberg, 2000).

Because culture and cross-cultural differences are experienced in a situation and in interaction with others, **experiential learning** is the main didactical means for supporting the development of cross-cultural (management) competencies (Kolb, 1984). Experiential learning involves activities which simulate an intercultural interaction or key aspects of it, and this chapter is based on this approach. You can either read through the experiential learning activities of this chapter or you can experience them in class. Throughout the chapter, the opening simulation will be debriefed with the help of models and theories of intercultural learning and cross-cultural competencies.

Developing intercultural competencies requires key personal and interpersonal skills such as empathy, ambiguity and uncertainty tolerance, personal strength and resilience, reflexivity and motivation. Influencing factors are those in interaction (self and others), the situation itself and its wider boundary conditions (see Figure 11.1).

As Figure 11.1 visualizes, intercultural learning is a non-linear and multi-layered process which involves multiple intersections and dependencies. For example, how people experience a certain context – as beneficial, threatening, rewarding and so on – depends on how motivated they are to understand, feel and act upon the situation, and also on their degree of motivation to develop their abilities and skills across all three sides of the intercultural learning triangle (doing, feeling, understanding). Humans are producers of culture and how (well) they experience it.

Nonetheless, intercultural learning loops are not only self-chosen but also influenced by others, the situation and the wider boundary conditions. Humans are products of culture and dependent upon existing social structures and practices and those involved.

Moreover, cross-cultural management competencies require more than just knowledge and rational thought. They require situations which are acted upon

Developing Your CCM Competencies

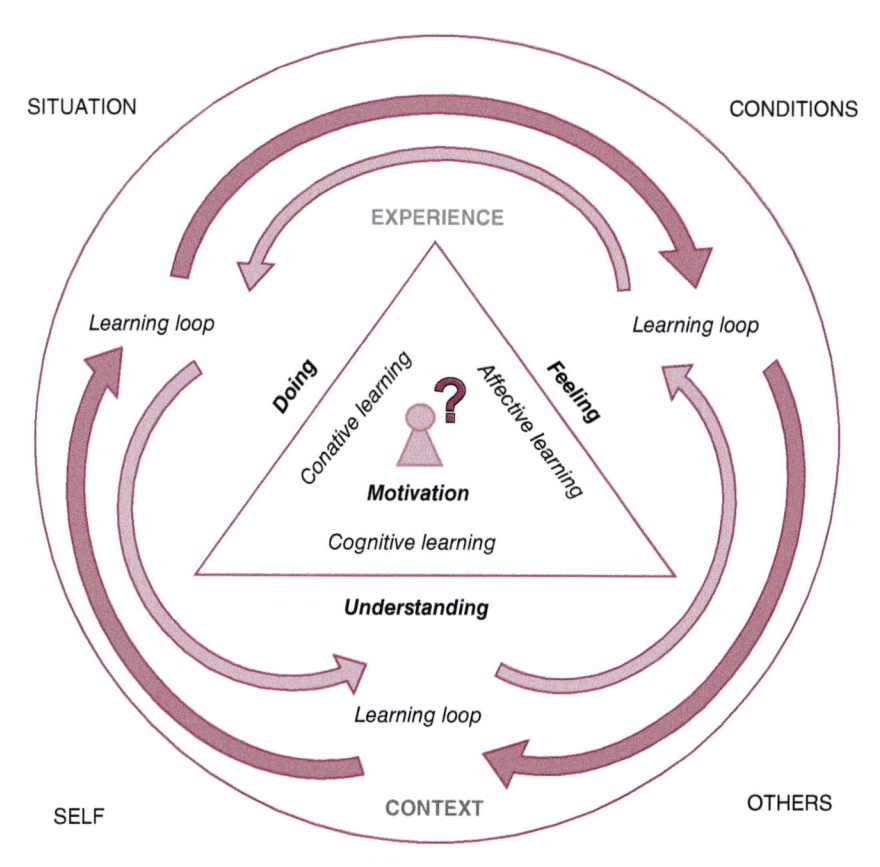

Figure 11.1 Intercultural learning in context

Source: adapted from Mahadevan and Kilian-Yasin (2013)

and experiences which are 'felt', acknowledged and reflected upon with the help of models and theories of intercultural learning and cross-cultural competency development.

To approximate processes of intercultural learning, this chapter is rooted in experiential learning methods. After having worked through it, you will have gained more holistic insights into what it takes to develop cross-cultural management competencies beyond rational thought and as involving feelings and actions in a situation. If you have not only read through, but have also participated in the opening simulation, you will additionally have experienced an intercultural learning process. In any case, you will have the opportunity to initiate the next intercultural learning loop by means of the closing activity.

In a Nutshell: Intercultural Competence and Cultural Intelligence

Two terms – intercultural or cross-cultural competence, and cultural intelligence – have been proposed by scholars to describe and assess what makes people succeed in intercultural interactions.

> **Intercultural competence**
> The ability to influence a situation effectively and appropriately

Intercultural competence has been defined as the ability to interact effectively and appropriately with members of other cultures and/or to influence an intercultural interactional context in an effective and appropriate manner (Spitzberg, 2000: 379–380). Effectiveness refers to the ability to reach one's goals. Appropriateness requires not losing sight of the other person's interests and the requirements of the situation when doing so. For example, dominance over others is effective, but it is not appropriate.

Most theories agree that intercultural competence involves a complex set of abilities and/or dispositions. Often-stated components are affective (emotional), behavioural (conative) and cognitive elements (Gudykunst et al., 1977), or, in later conceptualizations (Deardorff, 2006; Spitzberg, 2000), motivation (involving emotion and affection), knowledge (rooted in cognitive processes), attitudes and skills (related to behaviour and action). Intercultural competence is partly acquired and partly possessed, and in order to develop it, one needs to experience cross-cultural situations and reflect upon them. This requires managers to venture beyond their respective comfort zones.

Cultural intelligence, also referred to as 'cultural quotient' (CQ), is another, related concept. It describes 'a person's capability to adapt effectively to new cultural contexts' (Earley and Ang, 2003: 59). This capability is assumed to have a combined cognitive, motivational and behavioural basis, and '[w]ithout all these facets acting in concert, a person does not display cultural intelligence' (Earley and Ang, 2003: 59). Again, there is a complex interrelation of traits and experiences, of knowledge and action, and of multiple factors contributing to behaviour in context.

> **Cultural intelligence** A person's capability to adapt effectively to new cultural contexts

Opening Activity: Building Bridges on Eybeceenia

This is an experiential learning activity (an intercultural simulation) that can be either read or experienced. Throughout the chapter, you will encounter models which will help you understand the situation described in the simulation.

If the activity is conducted, it requires an atmosphere of trust, and the facilitator should have some knowledge in facilitating experiential learning activities. Should you agree to participate in the activity, the experience might bring you out of your comfort zone, and you might feel stressed out during and after the activity. Afterwards, the activity will be debriefed with the help of models of cross-cultural and intercultural competencies. Critical and power-related aspects of the activity (see below) will be debriefed as well.

Some aspects of the activity, such as gender roles, might be perceived as stereotypical. The activity is also related to inequalities on systemic levels, such as privileges, disadvantages and inequalities related to the **Global North** and **Global South**. If experienced, these aspects of the activity may cause negative feelings and distress and might result in discriminatory actions on the part of some participants, including yourself. These consequences will be debriefed after the activity.

Global North Denomination for the richer and more industrialized countries, which are mainly located in the northern hemisphere. From a critical perspective, also a questionable term as the current status quo is assumed to be rooted in historic inequalities such as colonialism and imperialism (which made certain regions 'richer' and shaped how they are perceived, namely as 'more developed').

Global South Denomination for the poorer and less industrialized countries, which are mainly located in the southern hemisphere. From a critical perspective, also a questionable term as the current status quo is assumed to be rooted in historic inequalities such as colonialism and imperialism (which made certain regions 'poorer' and shaped how they are perceived, namely as 'less developed').

(Continued)

Facilitator's instructions

The purpose of the activity is that a group of engineers visit the island of Eybeceenia to learn from the Eybeceenias how to build earthquake-resistant and ecologically friendly bridges. Facilitators should first read both manuals (engineers and Eybeceenian), then read through the facilitator's instructions, and, with this knowledge in mind, re-read the participants' manuals with a focus on 'how to facilitate'.

- If the simulation *is facilitated*, participants in the simulation may *not* read the facilitator's instructions.
- If the simulation *is not facilitated*, then students should read the facilitator's instructions after they have read both manuals, and then re-read the manuals with an awareness of the facilitator's role.

Technicalities

- The following facilities are required: two rooms, ideally adjacent rooms, or one room and a work station, e.g. in the aisle, near to it. If this is the first time you are facilitating an experiential learning activity, two facilitators (to support participants at each location) are recommended.
- The following material is required: numerous sheets of paper (old papers may be re-used), two glue-sticks, two pairs of scissors, two rulers, two pencils, two toy cars, multiple pens or pencils (as tokens, see below), red sticky dots, post-it notes.

Preparing the simulation

- The facilitator needs to arrange the main room with two tables. These tables need to be placed approximately 40 centimetres/15 inches apart. The tables symbolize mountains, with a river running between them, on the island of 'Eybeceenia'. Across this ravine, a prototype bridge shall be built. There needs to be enough space in this room for participants to move freely and to engage in this activity.
- The adjacent, smaller room or work space will be the engineers' work station and should be arranged as a meeting space.
- Prior to facilitating the simulation, the facilitator should have provided the participants with an introduction to experiential learning, and its purposes and consequences for those participating. Kolb (1984) is a good experiential learning source for facilitators, in particular his idea of the 'experiential learning cycle' which will be implemented by

means of this activity and which may also be visualized to the participants during the debriefing of the simulation.

Facilitating the simulation

- Participants gather in the main room.
- This is one way in which the activity may be introduced by the facilitator:

    Welcome to the island of Eybeceenia. Eybeceenia is one of the most developed and environmentally friendly countries on the globe, and its citizens live in harmony with nature. The island is hilly, with numerous rivers cutting across the mountainside, and earthquakes are common. Due to the topography of the island, Eybeceenian companies have become global leaders in how to build earthquake-resistant and ecologically friendly bridges. Engineers from all over the globe travel to Eybeceenia to acquire this knowledge and skills.

- The facilitator also needs to point out to the participants that engineers are willing to learn and that Eybeceenians are willing to share and transfer their knowledge.
- The facilitator then needs to place participants in two groups of equal size, to be named 'engineers' and 'Eybeceenians'. For creating groups, playful activities such as drawing role cards and so on might be employed.
- Both groups then gather together and are given their respective manuals.
- Engineers are then escorted to their work station by a facilitator. At that work station, they will find numerous sheets of paper (old papers may be re-used), one glue-stick, one pair of scissors, one ruler, one pencil. They may use this equipment for preparation, and may also take it to Eybeceenia.
- Eybeceenians remain in the room and are asked to read their instructions and to allocate roles to each other (men, women, wise/non-binary persons). Afterwards, they may start to practise Eybeceenian culture. If participants ask *how exactly* they shall play their respective roles, the facilitator shall encourage them to remain authentic and to imagine how they, personally, would live a certain role. This means that participants have the freedom to create 'real-life Eybeceenian culture' beyond the given cultural script, in line with the insight that humans are both products and producers of culture.

(Continued)

- During the simulation, the facilitator(s) need to keep track of time, move between the rooms, answer questions and also introduce the respective next steps of the activity, such as escorting the technical project leader and the financial control expert from the engineering team to Eybeceenia and back. They should do so in an unobtrusive manner. If asked by participants what exactly the task is, etc., facilitators shall not provide solutions but answer vaguely such as 'I am not even here anymore' or non-verbally with a shrug, etc., so that participants take ownership of the simulation. During the activity, the facilitator needs to take notes which are shared with the participants during the debriefing.
- When taking notes, pay attention to misunderstandings or 'missing links' in interaction and to expressions of emotions such as anxiety or confusion (as, for example, indicated by laughter or jokes), and to note observations ('person xy speaks loudly'), and not own interpretations ('person xy is aggressive').
- Crucial interactions in the simulation are a) the first encounter between the two engineering delegates and the Eybeceenian community, b) how Eybeceenian culture is 'reported back' to the engineers by the two delegates, c) the first encounter of all participants, d) how knowledge transfer is managed – for example, who takes control of the situation, which strategies are employed, and by whom, etc.
- Facilitators need to inform participants about the facilitator's role in advance. Participants need to consent. If a participant cannot continue with the simulation or feels uncomfortable during it, they are free to stop participating at any time.
- Facilitators should consider this activity to be an experiential learning opportunity for themselves as well. Try to find a way of facilitating which is effective and appropriate, and which feels 'authentic'. This way, experience in living the role is built. A little playfulness, if not overdone, it helps. For example, facilitators might assume the role of a 'flight attendant' when escorting engineers to Eybeceenia, e.g., by saying, 'last call for the flight to Eybeceenia', etc.
- Recording the activity increases reflexive learning, yet this option must be used with care and has to be agreed upon by all. Ethical and legal aspects must be clarified in advance.
- This activity requires participants of more than one gender. In a single-gender group, roles of 'men' and 'women' need to be renamed, e.g., into 'left' and 'right' of the ravine.

Instructions for engineers

Situation

You are a group of engineers who are experts in bridge-building and who are accompanied by management and financial control experts. Together, you travel to the island of Eybeceenia. Your task is to learn from the inhabitants of Eybeceenia – the Eybeceenians – how to build earthquake-resistant and ecologically friendly bridges. This technique has been invented on Eybeceenia, which is considered one of the most developed and ecologically friendly nations in terms of living standard, healthcare and sustainability. You will travel to Eybeceenia on a field trip in order to acquire this know-how. Your superiors expect a manual of how to build such bridges from you. For compiling this manual, you don't have much time after your field trip, therefore it is essential that you keep proper notes during the exercise and develop a process of how to document your learning when being on the island.

Construction plan

- For constructing the bridge, the following technical equipment is available: sheets of paper; one glue-stick, one pair of scissors, one ruler, one pencil.
- You know how to use this material; however, the special Eybeceenian way of construction is unknown to you.
- You will have to build the prototype yourself. You may only use the technical equipment that has been given to you.
- The bridge has to support two Eybeceenian cars for the duration of 1 minute. The cars need to be able to pass each other without the danger of collision.

Your corporate culture

- Your group consists of line management, technical experts (including a technical project manager) and financial control experts.

(Continued)

- Your company is a large, hierarchical multinational enterprise. Beyond assigning people to projects, there is no real encouragement of teamwork.
- Within the organization, everyone is assigned a specific task and will be measured against whether and to what degree they were successful in completing this task.
- Those managers who market their skills most expertly seem to move up the ladder the quickest; however, amongst engineers, it is the technical expertise that counts, and engineers tend to mistrust too much self-advertising.
- Technical expertise is highly valued; however, engineers are often frustrated by being asked to develop cost-efficient solutions by the financial control experts – they would prefer to go for real technological excellence instead.
- Proper process management and documentation of tasks are highly valued.

Instructions

- You have *20 minutes* to read the instructions and to develop an approach to (1) learning how to build bridges Eybeceenian style and (2) documenting your learning during the simulation for your final manual.
- Next, you will send your technical project leader and your financial control expert to Eybeceenia for *5 minutes*. Please mark them with a red dot.
- After the return of the experts, you have another *5 minutes* for planning.
- Afterwards, construction will begin. Construction time on Eybeceenia is *30 minutes*.

After construction, please reflect upon (1) your experiences and (2) on how you perceived the Eybeceenians in their ability to work, in their way of working, in their behavioural patterns and in their attitudes towards engineers.

Instructions for Eybeceenians

Situation

You are an inhabitant of the island of Eybeceenia which is considered one of the most developed nations in terms of education, living standard, healthcare and sustainability. Your task is to teach a group of foreign engineers how to build earthquake-resistant and ecologically friendly bridges across a ravine which is in the middle of your island (symbolized by the gap between the two central tables). The material for constructing earthquake-resistant and ecologically friendly bridges is: numerous sheets of paper (old papers may be re-used), one glue-stick, one pair of scissors, one ruler, one pencil.

Bridges are considered earthquake-resistant and ecologically friendly if they can support two toy cars for 1 minute. The best way to reach this goal is to roll several sheets of paper, to align these rolls, and then to pave them with flat sheets of papers (see Figure 11.2).

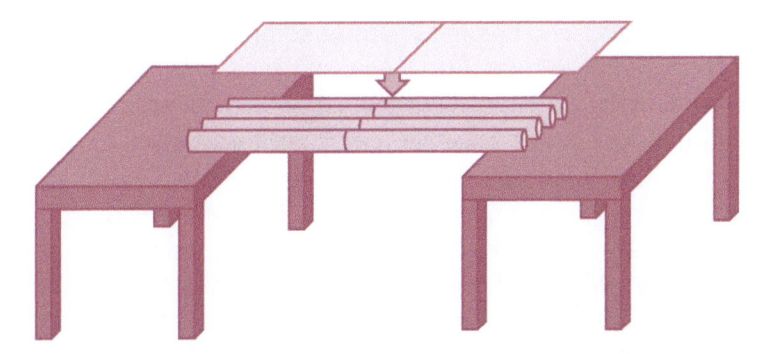

Figure 11.2 How to build earthquake-resistant and ecologically friendly bridges

The aforementioned bridge-building technique has been invented on Eybeceenia, based on Eybeceenian philosophy that one needs to live in harmony with nature and should not industrialize the country in violation of this harmony. Therefore, on Eybeceenia, those who are well educated and care for the community are the most appreciated; earning money and making a career are secondary.

Your work ethos

- Most companies on Eybeceenia are small and medium-sized enterprises with informal organizational structures and flexible teams.

(Continued)

Co-workers know each other on a personal level; hierarchy, material gain or competition are not that valued.
- Eybeceenian society consists of three distinct groups: *women, men* and *wise persons*. Please split your group into these three roles. It is customary for women to put a red dot on their outfit, and those of you in the role of women should do so now.
- Wise persons can be of any gender; the differentiation into male and female does not apply to them. Wise persons are recognized by a post-it note on their chest. The post-it note signals that they have meditated and have thus acquired wisdom.
- In Eybeceenian society, *individuals care for each other during work*. Hence, it is common to exchange tokens of appreciation constantly. During the simulation, these tokens are symbolized by pens which are given back and forth (*also while working*). If one does not keep exchanging tokens of appreciation, this is rude and simply impolite. To keep the circulation going, all Eybeceenians need to keep track of who has given tokens of appreciation and who needs to receive some.
- *Wise persons* usually don't work manually; they are the ones who are approached in times of conflict or when the community requires guidance.
   - For their services to the community, wise persons are given tokens of appreciation, and their basic needs are being cared for by the community (for example, they receive food and drink).
   - Upon calling a community gathering, wise persons usually give back the tokens of appreciation to the community.
   - This is why regular community gatherings are important; otherwise the tokens of appreciation will not continue to circulate, and this might destabilize the relationship patterns amongst people.
- *Greetings* are of no big importance on Eybeceenia – people know each other anyway. The only exception is paying respects to wise persons during prayer time or when receiving their help and guidance.
- On Eybeceenia, one tries to find a solution to every problem and for that one might need more time. Therefore, instead of an explicit 'no', one tends to say phrases such as, 'Please ask again tomorrow' or 'I will consider it and get back to you', in the hope that the other person will understand that one is working on the solution and will ask again. Unfortunately, if one has not found the solution by then, one will need to say such phrases again, and in this way the expression might come to mean 'no' ultimately. It is expected that others are able to decipher this.

Construction plan

- For constructing the bridge, the following technical equipment is available: paper, one glue-stick, one pair of scissors, one ruler, one pencil. All of these are natural Eybeceenian resources. They can be used, bent, etc., as context requires. There is no single way of how to construct a bridge. The only requirement is that the bridge needs to pass the earthquake-resistance test.
- A bridge is earthquake-resistant when it supports two cars for 1 minute. The cars need to be able to pass each other without the danger of collision. Prior to construction, the cars are parked near the ravine.

Instructions

- Please familiarize yourself with Eybeceenian behavioural patterns and practice how to do things the Eybeceenian way and design a suitable bridge (*20 minutes*).
    - For this, it would be best to divide the group into male/female and wise persons. The first group can work on working patterns and bridge building; the second group can work on the rituals of prayer and giving guidance.
    - Both groups should not forget the tokens of appreciation and practising a problem-solving attitude in communication, as symbolized by the phrase 'please come back tomorrow'.
- After *20 minutes*, two foreigners will visit you for *5 minutes*. During this time, please act like an Eybeceenian. Afterwards, you have *5 minutes* to reflect upon this experience, interact within the community and practise Eybeceenian behaviour.
- Afterwards, construction time will begin. You have *30 minutes*.

After construction, please reflect (1) upon your own experiences and (2) on how you perceived the engineers in their ability to work, in their way of working, in their behavioural patterns, and in their attitudes towards Eybeceenians.

Experiencing Intercultural Learning in Context

The purpose of culture as 'the way in which we normally do things around here (but not there)' (based on Deal and Kennedy, 1982) is to structure behaviour and to interpret experience. Cross-cultural situations are those situations in which people's expectation of 'how to normally do things' is not met and in which one's behavioural and interpretive repertoire remains insufficient. Usually, there is more than one perspective involved; two or more ways and ideas of 'how to do things' and 'what things mean' meet. The task is thus to bride these differences and to build new, *inter*cultural interpretations and ways of doing things. However, this poses a challenge, because venturing out of 'what seems normal' might bring people out of their comfort zone, and, if the Opening Activity was facilitated, you have experienced these challenges during the simulation.

Cross-cultural situations, such as the one simulated by the Opening Activity, are trigger points for further intercultural learning. People experience difference beyond 'what seems normal' and, if they dig deeper into what these differences mean, why and how they manifest and what can be learned from the experience, they will extend the scope of their ways of doing things. It is this phenomenon which makes CCM hugely rewarding. There is learning beyond one's fear zone, and exploring experiences of person–situation 'mis-fit', for example, in intercultural interactions, triggers this learning. Figure 11.3 visualizes CCM as a process of personal growth by which one's comfort zone is enlarged.

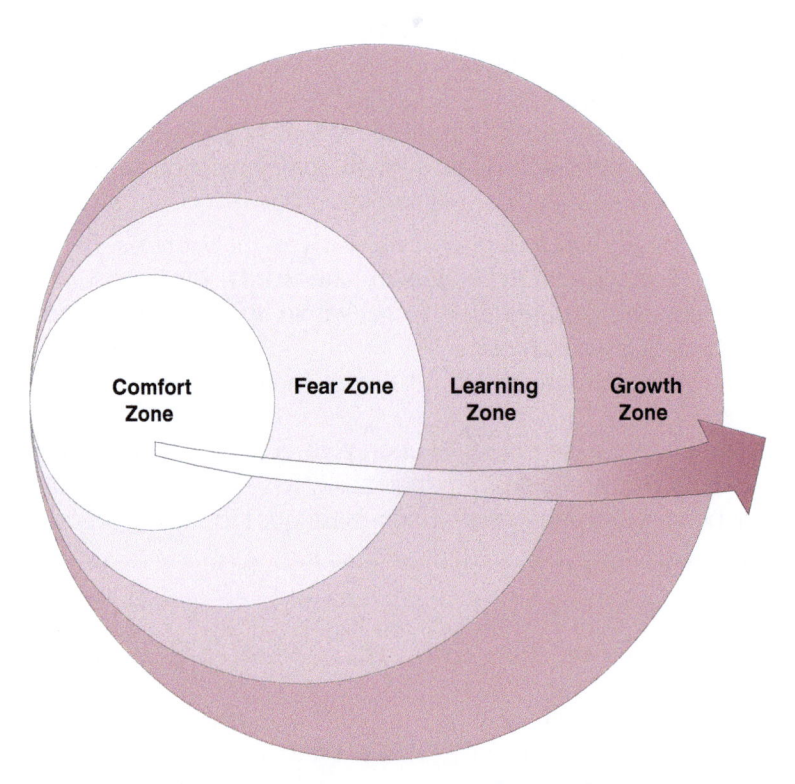

Figure 11.3 **Cross-cultural management as a process of individual growth**

STUDENT ACTIVITY 11.1

Learning Beyond One's Fear Zone

Consider how there is learning beyond one's fear zone in CCM (Figure 11.3). Now, apply this model to yourself:

- What is it that you feel comfortable doing in cross-cultural management?
- What is it that you aspire via engaging in cross-cultural management? What will your cross-cultural management experiences do for you?
- What will it take to reach this outcome? What do you need from others, and what kind of situations will support this process?
- What is it that you fear about entering or being in cross-cultural management?
- What will it take to overcome these fears? What do you need from others, and what kind of situations will support this process?

Find a fellow student whom you trust and exchange your considerations with them.

People and culture in intercultural interactions

People are products and producers of culture. In the opening situation, this is represented by the cultural scripts given to the participants. The manuals describe how Eybeceenians and engineers 'normally do things' (*given culture*). At the same time, people engage in a process of cultural creation when interacting. For example, those playing the roles of engineers and Eybeceenians are the ones making the script evolve. Each group of people will find slightly different solutions, based on the situation and what they bring to it, e.g. their previous socialization and cultural experiences (*cultural creation*).

Culture is also both 'real' and imagined. For example, there are real, objective differences between Eybeceenian companies and the corporate culture of the visiting engineers. On the other hand, this structure is interpreted by those interacting. Again, *cultural realities* and *cultural interpretations* never fully overlap.

STUDENT ACTIVITY 11.2

Culture and Leadership in the Opening Activity

Revisit Table 4.2 which depicts the GLOBE leadership dimensions. If required, revisit the GLOBE study (GLOBE, 2020) to fully understand these leadership styles. Please consider leadership to be a *collective*, not an individual task. With this background knowledge in mind, read through the instructions of the opening simulation (both groups).

1. Which leadership styles are 'normal' to each group? Which styles will be experienced and interpreted as problematic or as indicative of 'bad leadership' by each group? Which potential conflicts originating from given differences in leadership style across the two groups might manifest during the activity?

2. Version a) – if the Opening Activity is facilitated

    - How would you describe the leadership style which evolved in your respective group? How did you experience the leadership style of the respective other group? Can you classify each in terms of the GLOBE study leadership styles?
    - What happened in terms of leadership conflicts or leadership styles when the two groups met? Did the differences in leadership style play out as expected (based on the group manuals)? How (not) so? Which solutions or innovative and integrative approaches were found by those interacting?
    - Did the joint group manage to find a new, *inter*cultural leadership approach? Was this approach balanced or did one group dominate the other, and how do you interpret this?

3. Version b) – if you read through the activity

    - Which solutions do you propose to manage and overcome the differences in leadership style across the two groups?
    - Which intercultural leadership style do you recommend for inter-group collaboration? What will it take from the perspective of each group to adjust to and implement this style?
    - How shall domination of one group over the other be avoided?

Culture as glasses, backpack, iceberg and water

Because intercultural interactions require more than cognitive analyses, metaphors of culture – such as culture as an iceberg, backpack, glasses and water – are helpful tools for learning more about the situation.

During intercultural interactions, culture is like an *iceberg* in the following sense: what happens is visible to everyone, but why this is happening and what it means (and to whom) remains invisible to outsiders. Moreover, even those acting in certain ways are often not aware of *why* they are doing so. Culture is largely tacit (it cannot be put into words), and we ourselves might not be aware of why we are doing things this way.

In relation to people, culture is also like a *backpack*. People bring ideas and behavioural styles to the situation, they can make decisions what to unpack or not, and they can also decide to pack new things and take them to future interactions. Enlarging the content of one's cultural backpack requires reflexivity and motivation; one needs to investigate its content to become aware of it, and to engage with others to learn more about what they bring to the situation.

Culture also provides people with perspectivity. Groups of people wear *cultural glasses* tinted in slightly different ways. Therefore, they tend to interpret a situation differently, which means that the same situation might *mean* different things, depending upon the specific shape of the cultural iceberg upon which the interpretation rests.

Etic and emic perspective

In any intercultural interaction, there will be an inside (emic) perspective – the one of the cultural 'expert' who experiences culture from the inside – and an outside (etic) perspective – the one of a newcomer and learner of culture who experiences culture from the outside. It has thus been said that culture relates to humans like water to fish, as only when taken outside of the water will the fish realize that they need water to survive. For example, it is only in light of 'how Eybeceenians normally do things' that 'engineering culture' takes shape and vice versa. Finding oneself in another cultural context is thus disorientating and confusing. What things mean and how things are done is not a certainty anymore; rather, it becomes a question mark and a challenge. Consequently, there is the requirement to readjust one's glasses and repack one's backpack. Figure 11.4 visualizes these ideas.

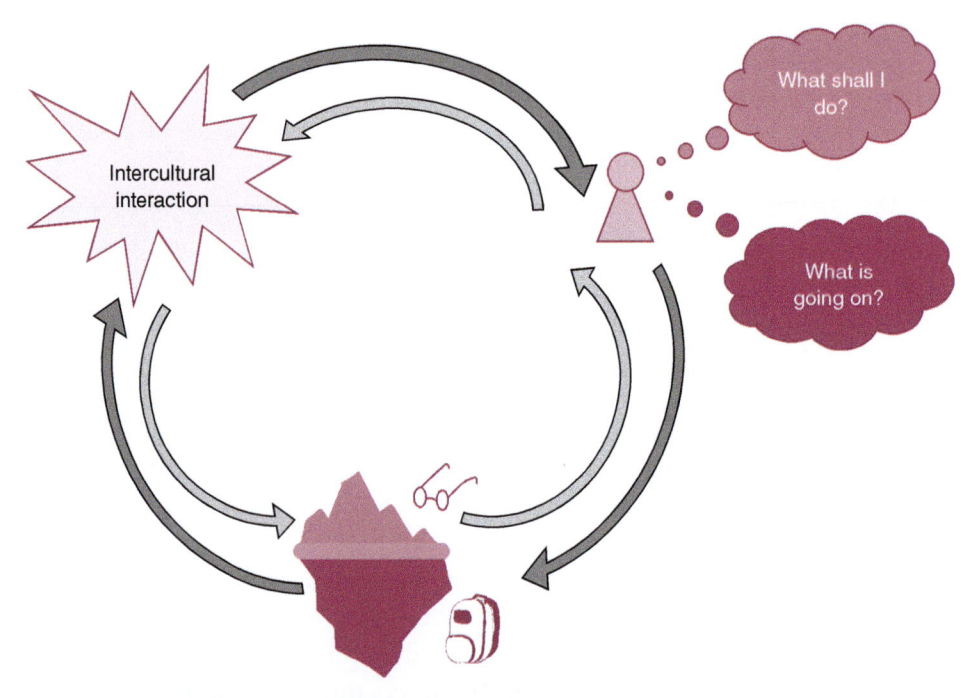

Figure 11.4 Individuals, and their cultural resources, in interaction

STUDENT ACTIVITY 11.3

Emic and Etic in Interaction

Re-read the Opening Activity. If you participated in it, then re-visit your experiences.

- How would you describe each group's cultural backpack? What do they bring to the interaction?
- How might each group perceive the other cultural group? Or, in other words, with which cultural glasses might they look upon them?
- What might be challenging for each group when interacting with the others? Or, in other words, what kind of 'water' will this 'type of fish' miss?
- For each group, identify key tacit elements of culture that are 'below the surface'. For this task, you need to view the manual for each group in light of the respective other group to bring relative differences to the surface.

Answer in writing and exchange your findings with fellow students to refine them. When doing so, provide reasons, e.g. own simulation experiences and/or information from the cultural manuals. Make sure that your answers move beyond etic perspectives.

Integrating the cycle of intercultural interaction

The emic meanings of others are invisible to outsiders to a certain culture (they are below the surface). Rather, outsiders tend to base their interpretations on what they bring to the situation (their own cultural backpack) and how they have learned to interpret it (their own cultural glasses). Perceptions of difference are thus filtered by one's own cultural orientations. Moreover, perceptions of difference are influenced by what one seeks to take away from the situation and the personal resources one is able to mobilize. This then implies, for example, that the way in which the engineers *perceive* the Eybeceenians has to do more with what the engineers bring to the situation than with how the Eybeceenians *really* are, and vice versa. Figure 11.5 visualizes this understanding for interaction parties A and B. For simplicity reasons, only one interpretive process (A's options of interpreting B) has been visualized. B's interpretive options would be exactly the opposite.

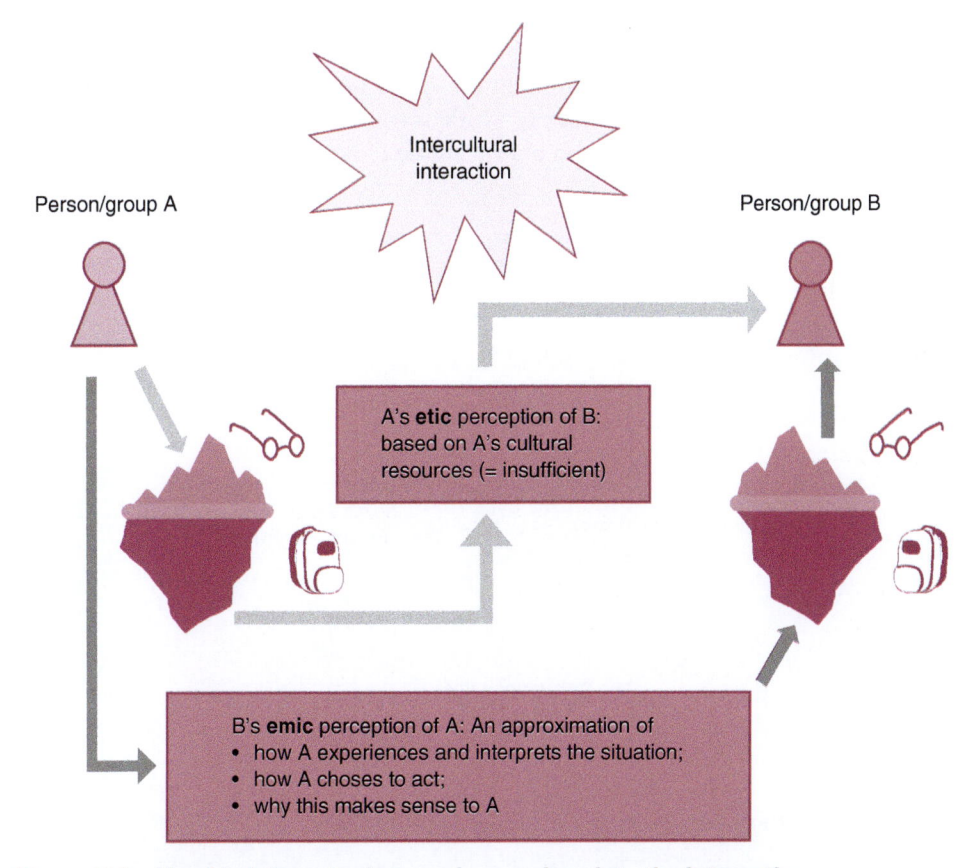

Figure 11.5 **Need to integrate deep emic meanings into the interaction**

At first sight, both parties base their interpretation and actions on their outside ('etic') perceptions of the respective other group or person. For example, due to their habit of calling frequent community meetings (a practice unknown in engineering corporate culture), the engineers might perceive the Eybeceenians as distracted and non-cooperative (an etic perspective). Likewise, the Eybeceenians might fail to understand that engineers, too, are interested in relationships, but live them differently, namely via an elaborated corporate network of functions and responsibilities at work. Consequently, Eybeceenians might perceive engineers as non-cooperative as well. This implies that a cross-cultural situation is difficult to everyone involved.

The key insight here is that both groups develop negative perceptions of each other – sometimes the exact same ones! If those involved base their further actions on etic perceptions and interpretations, difference is further affirmed by everyone's consecutive actions. Ultimately, this then leads to two divergent interpretive cycles – Group A and B. In this case, engineers and Eybeceenians grow further apart by further interacting.

However, Figure 11.5 also suggests a solution to this dilemma, namely, to try to approximate the meanings, interpretations and motivations underlying an action *from the other person's or group's perspective*. If the goal of an action – e.g. the need for collaboration – is understood and exchanged, then both parties might realize that there is common ground to be explored. In the case of engineers and Eybeceenians, both wish to transfer knowledge and to work towards a more sustainable future. Via this thought, interpretive cycles might be aligned and, ultimately, integrated (see Figure 11.6)

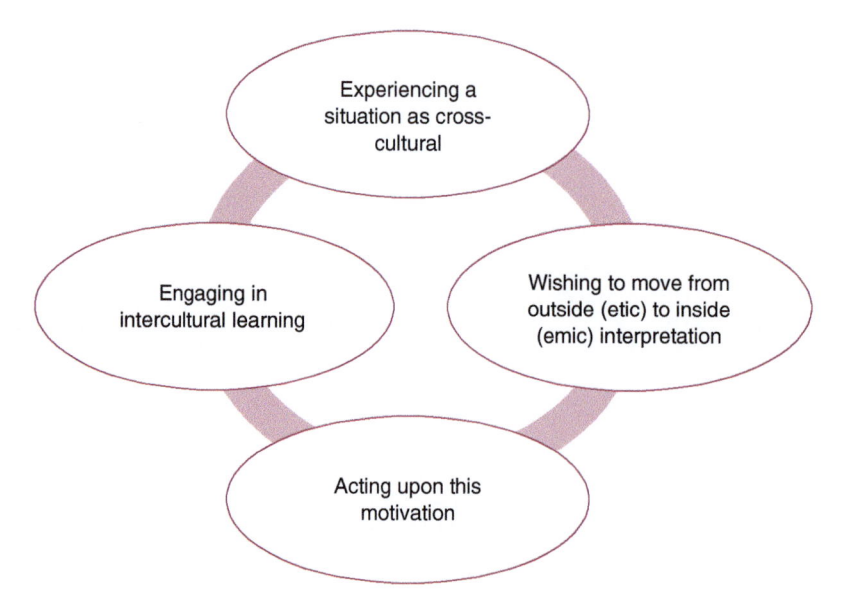

Figure 11.6 An integrative cycle of intercultural interaction

STUDENT ACTIVITY 11.4

Perceptions of Difference in Intercultural Interactions

Form groups of four to five students. If the opening activity was facilitated, each group should consist of two to three engineers and two to three Eybeceenians (ideally with different roles, e.g. male, female, wise person). Reflect and discuss the following.

Task, version a) – if the Opening Activity is facilitated

Puzzling with culture

- Which aspects of how the respective other group did things are still puzzling to you? Write down one good example by each group member.
- Ask the members of the respective other group to explain their motivations or the scripts underlying this behaviour. Write down this explanation in such a way that future engineers visiting Eybeceenia will better understand Eybeceenian behaviour, and vice versa.

Changing and integrating perspectives

- Which aspects of the respective other group's behaviour did you perceive as annoying, uncooperative, wrong, unnecessary or simply stupid? (Describe what is 'above the surface' but do not blame or judge.) Write down one good example by each group member.
- Which aspects of your own role and/or cultural script caused this perception to emerge? Or, in other words, how did your own cultural glasses and backpack shape your perceptions of the other group? Add this to your description.
- Finally, rewrite the situation in such a way that it brings the underlying motivation of those displaying a certain behaviour to the surface. Add this to your description.

Task, version b) – if you read through the Opening Activity

- Focus on the 'red dot'. What does it mean from an engineering perspective? What does it mean from an Eybeceenian perspective? Write this down.

(Continued)

- Do you expect engineers and Eybeceenians to become aware of the respective alternative meaning of the 'red dot', or do you expect them to draw wrong conclusions based on what the 'red dot' means to them? Why so?
- The red dot is a crucial aspect of culture in the opening simulation because it 'means' deeper things for each group; it is a cultural symbol that represents more than can be seen. Beyond the simulation, how should managers identify and become aware of the meanings of cultural symbols in intercultural interactions? How will *you* try to identify those aspects of culture that 'mean more' when finding yourself in a cross-cultural situation?

Learning Culture from Surface to Depth

Cultural patterns Repetitive and systematic ways in which culture and cultural norms manifest across individuals

Cultural norms Standards which are accepted as 'normal' in a cultural group

To overcome feelings of distress, but also to remain able to act upon a situation (or to reclaim this ability), managers need to structure their experiences. A helpful way of doing so lies in identifying norms and patterns. A **cultural pattern** is a certain regularity of how to do things: it points to those aspects of culture which are repetitive. Even if managers do not yet know what these patterns *mean*, they can still identify *what they are and how they look* on the level of *surface culture*.

On a deeper level, patterns deliver insights into **cultural norms**. Cultural norms encompass those aspects of culture to which a person who wishes to qualify as a group member (in this case, as a good manager) needs to adhere more or less. Neither cultural norms nor cultural patterns are clear-cut rules. Rather, they provide people with a measuring rod for the acceptable bandwidth in a situation or context (see Figure 11.7). For example, imagine that you are going to participate in a meeting in another country and want to be perceived as a 'good manager'. What you need to do is not to do 'everything right' but rather to learn how 'things are normally done' and then locate yourself within the commonly accepted normality. This means that cultural norms and patterns always imply internal heterogeneity; no two individuals do things exactly the same way.

Developing Your CCM Competencies

Cultural group A

(Perceived) violation of cultural norm

Bandwidth of cultural norm

(Perceived) violation of cultural norm

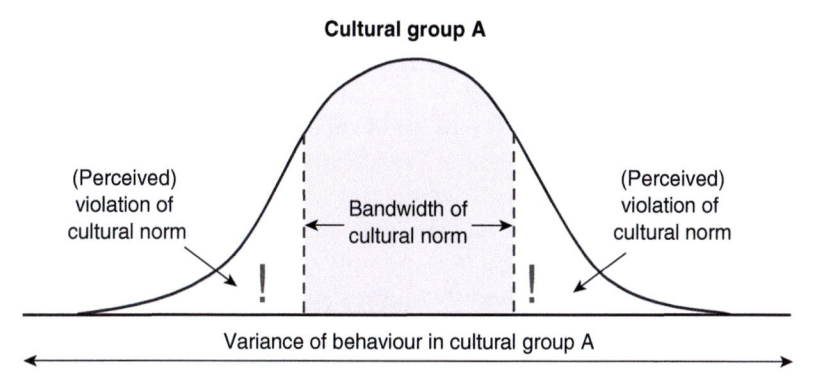

Variance of behaviour in cultural group A

Figure 11.7 Cultural norms – the intra-cultural view

Patterns are the most insightful when applied to repetitive events such as meetings. For repetitive events, people develop **routines**, standardized ways of doing things. In other words, when facing a comparable situation, people work from a cultural template. This way, they are – or at least feel – more prepared and oriented. Unfortunately, if the template is not shared, for example, in a cross-cultural situation, disorientation for all increases.

> **Routines** Shared standardized ways of doing things during repetitive cultural events

Cross-culturally, norms and patterns are thus also homogeneous enough to be identified as such on a collective level (see Figure 11.8). When representatives of cultural groups 'A' and 'B' meet, it is thus likely that they will experience the representative of the other group as 'culturally different'. This is why engineers and Eybeceenians, despite their internal diversity, are perceived as a 'single group' by the respective other group,

Cultural group A   **Cultural group B**

(Perceived) violation of cultural norm

Cultural norm A

Cultural norm B

(Perceived) violation of cultural norm

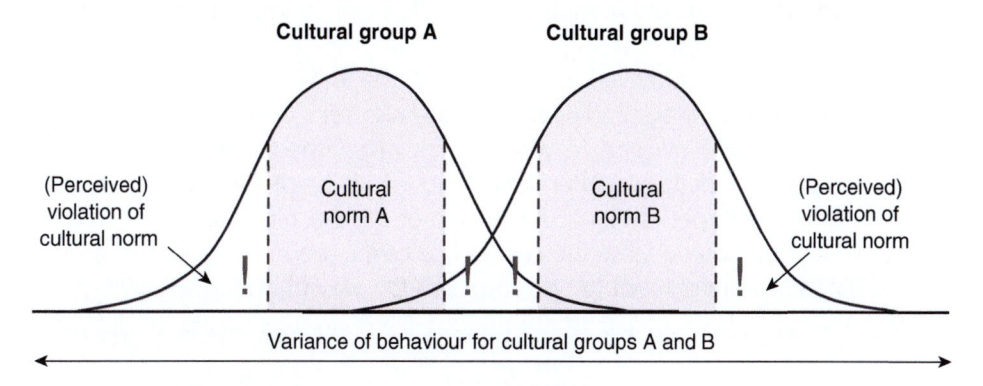

Variance of behaviour for cultural groups A and B

Figure 11.8 Cultural norms – the cross-cultural view

Cultural dimensions or cultural value orientations (see Chapter 5) acknowledge this patterned quality of culture. They are thus a useful tool for making first sense out of an intercultural interaction, in particular, when it comes to routines. To recap, cultural dimensions are selected universal aspects of culture by means of which relative differences across cultures can be approximated. For example, the cultural dimension collectivism versus individualism (Hofstede, 1980) describes people's degree of group- versus self-orientation, or, in other words, their relatively different answers to the question: 'How much "I" comes into the "We"?' When looking at the Opening Activity, one can see that the answer to this question differs across engineers and Eybeceenians. For example, roles and functions are allocated in different ways to individuals, and there are also specific ways in which community becomes relevant (if at all).

STUDENT ACTIVITY 11.5

Cultural Dimensions in the Opening Activity

Form groups of four to five students. If the Opening Activity was facilitated, each group should consist of two to three engineers and two to three Eybeceenians (ideally with different roles, e.g. male, female, wise person). Sit together and revisit Tables 5.1 to 5.6, and Figures 5.1 and 5.2, depicting cultural dimensions.

1. Apply cultural dimensions to the respective cultural scripts of each group. Which relative differences can you identify?
2. Version a) – if the Opening Activity is facilitated

    - Reflect upon the simulation. How did these expected differences across the groups manifest during the simulation? How and in which aspects did participants deviate from the given norms of your cultural group?
    - Reflect on negative perceptions of the other group and cross-group misunderstandings, missing links and conflicts during the simulation. How and to what extent might these be explained by means of cultural dimensions? How is it helpful to reflect upon negative experiences with the help of cultural dimensions?
    - How could you view the respective other group's orientation as a positive enrichment to your own group's way of doing things?

3. Version b) – if you read through the Opening Activity
   - Which conflicts do you expect to arise from these given differences?
   - What would be required to overcome them?
   - How could both cultural styles enrich each other, and how would you propose to combine and integrate them (give examples)?

If managers start investigating culture by means of cultural dimensions, they will certainly find regularities. However, understanding *deep culture* requires seeking for exceptions from the rule. For example, if you reflect on the Opening Activity, is it *really* like this that all engineers/Eybeceenians behave the same, or can you identify smaller categories (sub-groups) within both? To learn culture from surface to depth, managers should therefore always seek exceptions to newly found cultural patterns. Any idea of 'this is how Eybeceenians/engineers are' should thus be understood as a first hypothesis that needs to be falsified via experience ('this is how a certain Eybeceenian sub-group is', and 'this is how another Eybeceenian sub-group is').

CCM as a Process of Personal Growth

Being taken outside of one's own culture and of what is familiar (the idea of culture as water to fish) may trigger disorientation, anxiety and distress. Managers don't experience themselves as effective and efficient anymore; rather, they realize that what they have learned to represent and do (their identity and behavioural styles as managers) does not fit the situation anymore. Their further managerial development, as well as corporate success, then depends on how they react to this personal and task-related challenge. Figure 11.9 visualizes this situation and the further process of managerial growth.

If utilized as an intercultural learning trigger, the experience of being a mis-fit to the situation will lead managers to reconsider their current managerial style and identity in light of the novel contextual requirements. The requirement is that they engage reflexively with the link between themselves and the current situation. Next follows a process in which the manager puzzles with current and provisional managerial styles. What could they do and who could they be? This abstract conceptualization takes place in the manager's head; they play around with possibilities, build hypotheses and fathom what they might do. Next, the manager tries out elements of these thus conceptualized new managerial styles and identities. They act upon what they have conceptualized, and they test the effect of their actions upon

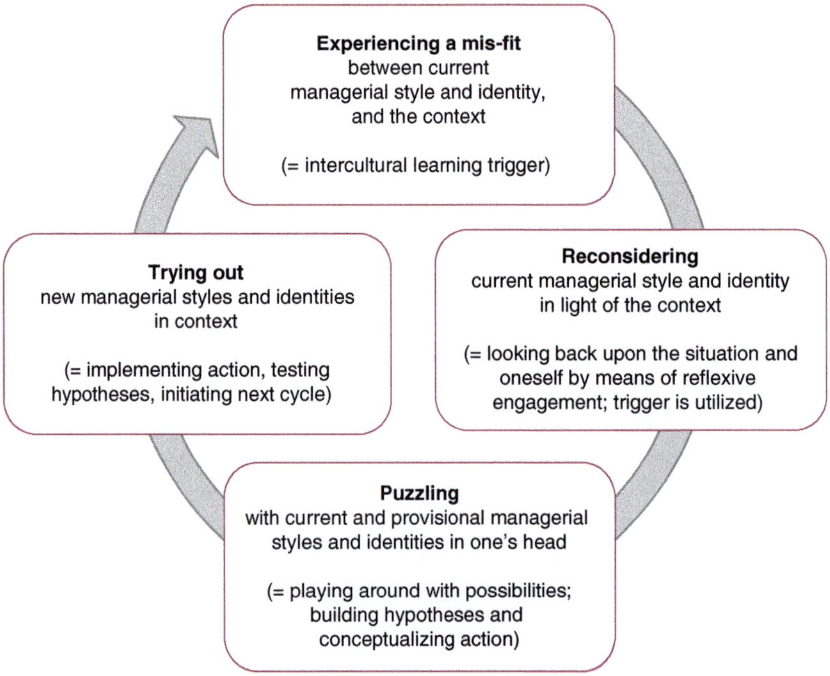

CCM Skillset

Experiencing a mis-fit
between current managerial style and identity, and the context

(= intercultural learning trigger)

Reconsidering
current managerial style and identity in light of the context

(= looking back upon the situation and oneself by means of reflexive engagement; trigger is utilized)

Puzzling
with current and provisional managerial styles and identities in one's head

(= playing around with possibilities; building hypotheses and conceptualizing action)

Trying out
new managerial styles and identities in context

(= implementing action, testing hypotheses, initiating next cycle)

Figure 11.9 Managerial growth via experiential intercultural learning

Source: adapted from Kolb (1984)

the situation. Ideally, they have then improved upon the manager–situation fit. Or, their initial hypotheses proved to be wrong. In any case, the experiential learning cycle starts anew. This way, the manager does not only learn how to influence the situation more appropriately and effectively – they also enlarge their managerial repertoire. By viewing themselves in light of a novel situation, they discover more possibilities of who they could be and what they could do.

STUDENT ACTIVITY 11.6

Culture as Communication in Interaction

Re-read the section 'The "culture as communication" approach: Dimensions by Hall' in Chapter 5. In this section, you will find cultural dimensions related to communication in the wider sense, namely as related to language, social relations, distance and perceptions of time. These dimensions are part of the opening simulation. For example, work is more circular (polychronic) on Eybeceenia, and more linear (monochronic) amongst engineers. Likewise, communications and social relations on Eybeceenia indicate high-context orientation (consider how a 'no' comes into being on Eybeceenia) whereas building and maintaining engineering relations is no further specified (which indicates low-context orientation). In light of these examples, now work together in groups. If the activity was facilitated, the groups should include representatives of both groups and all roles.

- First, apply the cultural dimensions by Hall to the opening simulation and find all aspects in the manual which are indicative of them.
- Secondly, if the opening activity is facilitated, reflect on the interaction. When and how did you experience or observe a difference that might have been rooted in Hall's cultural dimensions?

Write down the cultural dimensions and your examples (ideally, compile a table) and be prepared to exchange your findings. Tables 5.2 and 5.3 are helpful to your task.

CCM as Multiple Cross-Cultural Adjustments

In intercultural interactions, people and context interrelate. Several models are helpful for understanding structuring this sometimes overwhelming experience.

Stages of intercultural learning

Bennett (1986) proposed that managers facing an unfamiliar cultural context go through six stages of intercultural learning. These stages are classified as ethnocentric or ethnorelative. An *ethnocentric* perspective judges others from the outside and is based on the outsider's cultural orientations – it is an insufficient 'etic' viewpoint. An *ethnorelative* perspective approximates the 'emic' meanings of others and views them in their own terms. Figure 11.10 visualizes Bennett's (1986) model of intercultural learning.

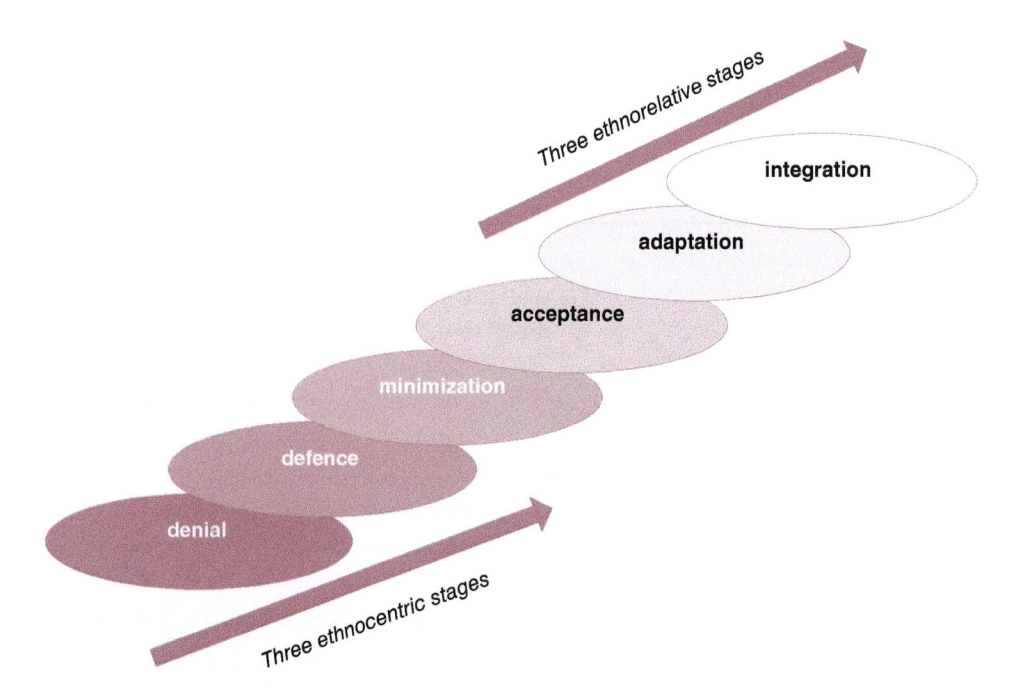

Figure 11.10 Stages of intercultural learning

Source: adapted from Bennett (1986)

The three ethnocentric stages of experiencing difference are:

- *Denial* – 'my cultural perspective is the only one that exists'. Example: 'This is the only way in which to manage.'
- *Defence* – 'my culture is better than theirs' or – if reversed by a process of 'over-adaptation' – 'their culture is better than mine'. Example: 'Our style of managing is better than/inferior to theirs.'
- *Minimization* – 'their culture is different, but it's actually only a – lesser – variant of our/my culture'. Example: 'Their management methods are not yet as sophisticated as ours, but they will get there.'

After having overcome the last ethnocentric stage of *minimization*, individuals might move through three ethnorelative stages of experiencing difference.

- *Acceptance* – 'cultural differences exist'. Example: 'Their way of managing is different than ours.'
- *Adaptation* – 'maybe I change my ways of doing things to be more like their way of doing things'. Example: 'I could try to manage like this.'
- *Integration* – 'I want to combine their and my way of doing things'. Example: 'I would like to choose the best of both managerial styles.'

STUDENT ACTIVITY 11.7

Integrating Managerial Styles

Work together in a team of four students. Re-read the Opening Activity. If you participated in it, your group should consist of engineers and Eybeceenians.

Version a) – if the Opening Activity is facilitated

- Individually, reflect upon yourself and your perspective on the respective other group. Which stage of intercultural learning did you perceive yourself to be on? Which stage of intercultural learning did you perceive the other group to be on?
- Exchange your perceptions with others and ask their opinion on the matter.
- As a group, identify three relevant aspects of how Eybeceenian and engineering ways of managing work-related activities differ.
- Individually, suggest how you could personally act based on an ethnorelative stage of integration regarding these aspects and specify what kind of support you would need from others for achieving this goal.
- Together, consider how it would benefit the situation and all involved if more or all of those interacting had based their actions on the ethnorelative stage of integration.

If the whole of your group has thoroughly considered these questions and *still* believes that all or most of them acted on the integrative stage, then please explain why and how you were able to put such high intercultural competencies into practice.

Version b) – if you read through the Opening Activity

- Choose three relevant aspects of how Eybeceenian and engineering ways of managing work-related activities differ. How would a managerial style that integrates these differences look like? What would an integrative manager do?

Integration does not equal compromise. The task is not to choose half of each group's managerial style (= compromise), nor should you discard one style as inferior. When discussing solutions in your team, pursue an integrative style as well. Find a solution which acknowledges all team members.

Culture shock as a trigger for intercultural learning

> **Culture shock** A phase model of how cultural differences are experienced and dealt with by individuals.

The model of **culture shock** (Oberg, 1960) suggests that finding oneself in an unfamiliar cultural context can lead to crisis and, ideally, recovery via re-adjustment. For example, when meeting for the first time, engineers and Eybeceenians might strongly experience how different they are, and they need to come to terms with this experience and adjust. This process has been visualized by means of a *U-curve* (Lysgaard, 1955; Figure 11.11).

The underlying idea of culture shock theory is that individuals often enter another cultural context with a positive attitude (they are on top of one side of the 'U-curve'), at least if they have self-chosen or agreed to the experience. This is called the 'honeymoon phase' during which individuals are highly satisfied, yet might also not yet have a realistic picture of the other culture and of themselves as adjusting to it. In the host culture, they then face cultural adjustment challenges, making them 'slide down' the U-curve until they reach middle bottom. In the process, they experience crisis and culture shock, and need to find coping strategies to recover, and to adjust and adapt. This way, they climb up the other side of the U-curve, until they reach the top at the far end via 'mastering'

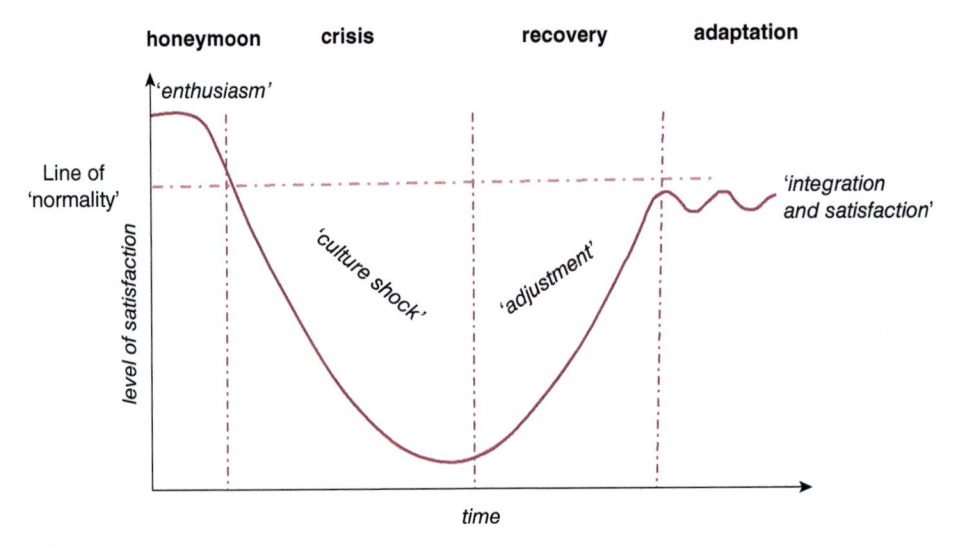

Figure 11.11 **Culture shock (U-curve)**

Source: adapted from Lysgaard (1955); Oberg (1960)

the other culture on a more profound level. Depending on the model, the focus of the cross-cultural adjustment process is, for example, on individual satisfaction, performance or psychological aspects of adaptation. The models also differ as to whether individuals reach a higher or lower satisfaction or adjustment after having recovered from culture shock, as compared to the initial 'honeymoon' level (it is debated whether the two sides of the U are balanced or not, and, if not, into what direction the U leans). Empirical studies furthermore suggest a time variance in phases.

In its varieties, the U-curve model depicts how, at first, individuals might merely grasp the surface aspects of another culture which leads to them experiencing high adjustment and/or satisfaction, and how an in-depth realization of 'difference' and of the difficulties involved requires time to sink in, decreasing adjustment over time. This means that cross-cultural difficulties that seem more profound than before can signify a successful intercultural learning process – and, hence, increased intercultural competency.

STUDENT ACTIVITY 11.8

Culture Shock in the Opening Activity

You need to have participated in the Opening Activity for this activity.

Work together in a team of four students, re-read both manuals and re-visit your experiences. Your group should consist of both engineers and Eybeceenians.

- Reflect upon the first meeting and the bridge-building activity. How did the engineers experience the Eybeceenians, and vice versa?
- Which stages of the U-curve model can you identify in how people, including yourself, experienced the respective other group?
- To what extent and how did this change during the simulation?
- What did the engineering visitors report back to the engineers? Which stages of the U-curve model can you identify in these statements?

Discuss in class and complement your insights with the facilitators' observations.

STUDENT ACTIVITY 11.8

(Alternative Version): Culture Shock in Real Life

When and how did you experience culture shock in real life? Visualize your experiences of cultural adjustment, and its stages, by means of a U-curve. Reflect upon the degree to which you successfully adjusted and, with your current CCM knowledge, suggest improvements. Present and discuss in class.

Reverse culture shock Re-adjustment challenges as experienced by individuals returning from a successful adaptation to another cultural context

Re-entering a formerly familiar cultural context might cause re-adjustment challenges as well, because a successful adjustment 'elsewhere' can make a person a foreigner to the cultural context which they had left behind. If this is the case, then the required process of cultural adjustment, potentially involving culture shock, starts anew – two successive U-curves which form a *W-curve* in the so-called **reverse culture shock** model (Gullahorn and Gullahorn, 1963; Figure 11.12).

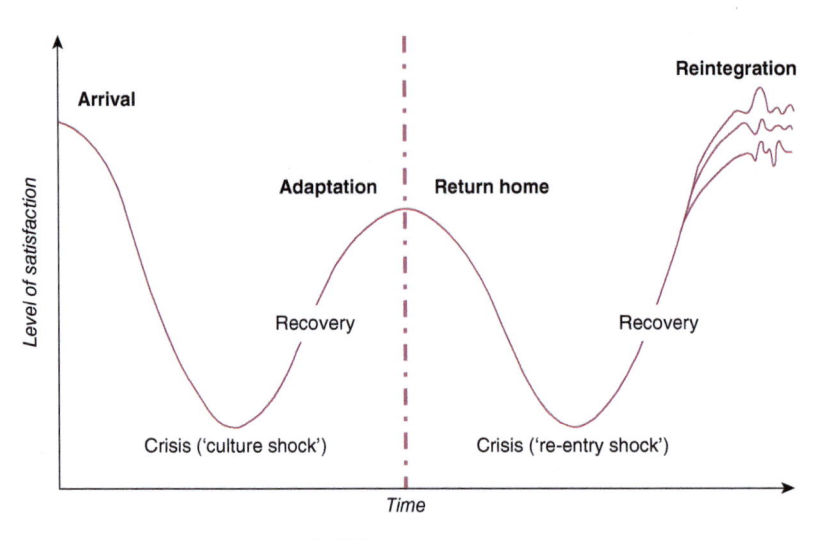

Figure 11.12 **Reverse culture shock (W-curve)**

Source: adapted from Gullahorn and Gullahorn (1963)

As a term, culture *shock* is linked to the underlying idea of difference as being negative, uprooting or challenging. Contemporary CCM scholars thus have replaced it by terms such as 'cross-cultural adjustment'. This is to make the point that any experience of low adjustment is neither pathological nor to be avoided. Rather, it should be embraced as an indispensable stepping stone for triggering deeper intercultural learning and for facilitating intercultural competency development. Cross-cultural adjustment thus stresses the long-term positive aspects of any presumed 'culture shock' over the immediate negative ones. It also focuses on the 'normality' of experiencing difference on many levels as an inevitable component of our social and organizational lives.

The goal is that individuals (and organizations) achieve a sense of a realistic 'normality' when dealing with cultural complexity and multiple cultures. In this sense, neither 'honeymoon' (potentially unrealistic euphoria regarding difference) nor 'culture shock' (a potentially exaggerated sense of crisis regarding difference) are to be trusted. If viewed from this angle, the relevance of phase models of cultural adjustment such as 'culture shock theory' lies in making individuals aware of which cultural differences they experience and what (the experience of) cultural difference actually *does* to them.

STUDENT ACTIVITY 11.9

Cross-Cultural Adjustment

- Reflect upon situations in which you needed to adjust to an unfamiliar cultural context. Which skills did you develop in the process and how might these be useful when having to act in an unfamiliar situation such as the one described by the opening activity?
- Write your findings down and exchange with a fellow student to identify complementarities in the competencies and skills which you bring to the interaction. Complementarity means that the other person may have strengths that could counterweigh a potential weakness which you bring to the interaction, and vice versa.

Contemporary cross-cultural management as ongoing adjustment

'Going to Eybeceenia' is a classic CCM scenario: a person or team goes abroad to encounter a single, distinct and unfamiliar culture. While this might still happen today, contemporary CCM is moreover characterized, amongst other factors, by cultural complexity, multiple cultures, diverse identities, new organizational forms, complex international business environments, and the impact of technology and social media. Both Eybeceenians and engineers must have done a quick internet search about each other, and they might have met on social media before.

Under such conditions, it is likely that managers will experience fewer all-encompassing 'first contact' culture shocks and more partially different situations to which to adjust in their everyday managerial lives. For example, every new team and project might trigger differences, for example, in generational, gender, regional, professional, technological, organizational, societal, and so on, cultures. However, because these triggers are potentially less all-encompassing than 'meeting engineers' or 'going to Eybeceenia', they might go unnoticed – an intercultural learning opportunity lost.

The contemporary challenge is thus to recognize and to experience these trigger points to the fullest, in order to develop one's intercultural competencies. Also, what is new under contemporary CCM conditions, is that the required multiple cross-cultural adjustments and their timelines are not aligned across individuals: one person's familiarity with a certain generational culture is another team member's culture shock (see Figure 11.13). If utilized for collective intercultural learning, then these multiple individual cross-cultural adjustments signify an increasing 'growing together' of all involved.

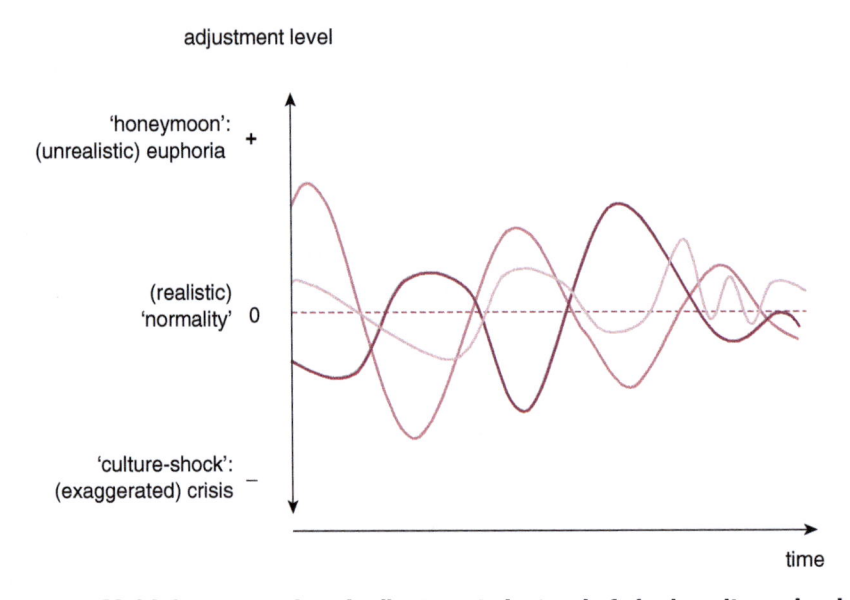

Figure 11.13 **Multiple cross-cultural adjustments instead of single culture shocks**

STUDENT ACTIVITY 11.10

The Impact of Organizational Cultures in Intercultural Interactions

There are ways in which Eybeceenian and engineers' work are also influenced by differences in organizational cultures. Some of these aspects are structural (in the manual), some of them are behavioural (how people live their roles and functions).

Step 1

Individually, re-read Chapter 9 on CCM and organization and identify all links to the opening activity of this chapter. Consider, in particular, cross-group differences in:

- building blocks of organization
- organizational design, roles and role enactment
- relevance and degree of bureaucracy
- organizational networks and stakeholders
- metaphors of organization underlying each group's strategies and actions
- organizational ability and motivation concerning learning and change

If the activity has been facilitated, differentiate between what the manuals specified (organization) and how the manuals were put into effect during the interaction (organizing).

Step 2

Exchange your findings with fellow students to refine them. If the activity is facilitated, then seek out students from both groups and in all roles.

Link to Practice: Corporate Intercultural Human Resource Development

Companies try to minimize managers' low cross-cultural adjustment, based on the rationale that a poorly adjusted manager will underperform.

(Continued)

For example, a company does get a return on their investment in international assignments for the duration of the low adjustment period (Black and Mendenhall, 1991).

A specific tool for maximizing cross-cultural adjustment is intercultural training. The term refers to a one- or two-day group activity by which participants are trained for working together with representatives of another national culture or are being prepared for moving to this culture. This culture is referred to as the 'target culture' of the intercultural training, and intercultural trainers – those facilitating this activity – tend to be specialized on target cultures. Intercultural training activities are usually commissioned by the corporate Human Resource (HR) department or function. HR often employs freelance intercultural trainers to conduct the activity.

The underlying idea of intercultural training is that intercultural competencies can be trained and are crucial to managerial effectiveness (Leeds-Hurwitz, 1990; Szkudlarek, 2009). To speed up the learning process, intercultural training often works with simplified models of culture, based on the idea that it is sufficient to focus on selected aspects which will then manifest themselves in interactions across national cultures (Leeds-Hurwitz, 1990). Thirdly, intercultural training tends to employ experiential methods. Experiential learning (Kolb, 1984) places people into a situation, for example, by means of role plays or simulations. Basically, it means to work with 'what if?' scenarios, so that participants do not only develop theoretical knowledge but also the tools for how to apply this knowledge to a situation, in a way that works for the individual person. The opening and closing activities of this chapter exemplify this approach. Evaluating the quality and effects of such activities is a key HR issue in practice.

In addition, there are attempts to assess people's potential intercultural competencies or, in other words, cultural intelligence (CQ) (Earley and Ang, 2003) in advance. The tricky aspect here is that it is difficult to figure out which inherent, invisible motivations and traits might cause a certain observable behaviour which can then be deemed more or less interculturally competent. Furthermore, it is difficult to conceptualize and assess how the different factors interrelate and contribute to each other. Finally, also the action of others and the context of the situation influence how interculturally competent a person may or may not behave (see discussion on intercultural competence in Deardorff, 2009; Spitzberg and Changnon, 2009; and a scale for measuring CQ in Earley and Ang, 2003).

STUDENT ACTIVITY 11.11

Human Resource Development in Practice

Work together in groups of four to five students. Read the box on Corporate Intercultural Human Resource Development above and imagine that you are members of the HR department of the engineering company in the opening simulation. Your task is to select and prepare – as far as possible – the team which will acquire the knowledge of building bridges in the opening simulation.

- How would you select the members of the team going to Eybeceenia?
- Which personal traits, skills, attitudes, motivation and knowledges do you deem indispensable? Which of these can be acquired and developed, which ones cannot?
- How can you support people in the adequate competency development, before, during and after the simulation?
- How, if anyhow, will you measure people's intercultural competencies and their contribution to the success of the intercultural interaction?
- After these considerations, which HR challenges and problems remain unsolved?

Chapter Summary

Cross-cultural management is not a logical, neutral and rational discipline, but a deeply human one. It requires that cross-cultural managers *act, think* and *feel* in a situation, and *reflect* upon what they experience. Unfamiliar situations such as the one simulated by the Opening Activity require managers to actively engage with their cultural backpack, to reconsider its content, and to find ways to enlarge their managerial repertoire. Figure 11.14 summarizes this process.

As Figure 11.14 suggests, building CCM competencies is an ongoing circular process. First, a situation is experienced as cross-cultural. Next, the situation has to be interpreted in such a way that one can influence it effectively and appropriately. The interpretation thus has to be 'tested' upon the situation via acting upon it. Ideally, this can influence the situation to some extent and in a desired way. After reflecting upon the outcome of one's actions, one probably needs to refine one's hypothesis again.

This idea of CCM as an ongoing process of learning and adjustment suggests that experiences of difference ('culture shocks') are enriching to individuals because they trigger new interpretations and facilitate building new hypotheses to be tested

CCM Skillset

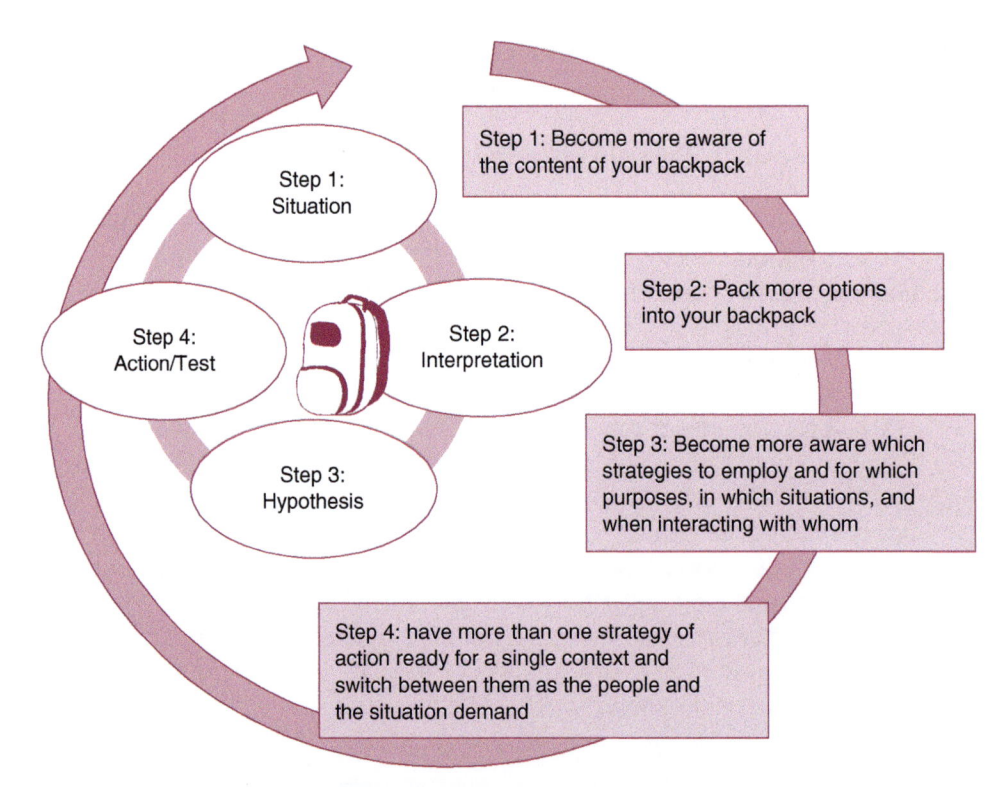

Figure 11.14 (Re-)packing your cultural backpack to enlarge your managerial repertoire

Step 1: Situation
Step 2: Interpretation
Step 3: Hypothesis
Step 4: Action/Test

Step 1: Become more aware of the content of your backpack
Step 2: Pack more options into your backpack
Step 3: Become more aware which strategies to employ and for which purposes, in which situations, and when interacting with whom
Step 4: have more than one strategy of action ready for a single context and switch between them as the people and the situation demand

upon and tried out in a situation. The requirement is that managers venture outside of their comfort zones, and this is what makes CCM so daunting. However, this is also the exact same phenomenon which makes CCM hugely rewarding. There is learning beyond one's fear zone, and experiencing intercultural interactions helps you discover this. For initiating a process of personal growth, managers need to train themselves in identifying culture's impact upon themselves and others, and to conceptualize and experiment with new managerial styles and identities. Ideally, this will enable them to switch between multiple inside (emic) and outside (etic) perspectives and enrich and diversify 'who they are' and 'what they can do'. Organizations support this process by means of intercultural training or further human resource development measures.

Key Points

- A popular definition describes intercultural competency as the ability to influence a (cross-cultural) situation effectively and appropriately.
- Intercultural learning involves moving from ethnocentrist to ethnorelative perspectives.

- Building cross-cultural management competencies requires knowledge, skills, motivation and experience which is reflected upon.
- Well-designed experiential learning methods such as intercultural simulations approximate CCM experiences and trigger intercultural learning processes.
- Acknowledging the impact of culture as glasses, backpack, iceberg and water helps managers to identify and reflect upon culture's impact on them.
- The circle of intercultural interactions is a helpful model for understanding how to build first hypotheses to be tested against the situation.
- When interacting across cultures, managers need to refine their cultural categories, thus learning culture from surface to depth.
- Culture shock is commonly experienced when finding oneself in an unfamiliar cultural context. If utilized, it may trigger further intercultural learning and processes of cross-cultural adjustment.
- Reverse culture-shock is experienced after returning to a formerly familiar cultural context after a successful adjustment elsewhere – if utilized, it may trigger even higher cross-cultural competencies.
- Contemporary cross-cultural management is characterized by every person's constant need to adjust and thus also implies a potential for offering deeper and more profound intercultural learning experiences to those involved.

Review Questions

1. What are experiential learning methods and when and how are they useful for developing cross-cultural management competencies?
2. How are cultural dimensions useful for learning culture from surface to depth?
3. Why and how shall managers change from etic to emic perspectives in intercultural interactions?
4. What are cultural norms and patterns, and how shall managers in intercultural interactions consider them?
5. How can considering culture as glasses, backpack, iceberg and water help managers in their intercultural learning processes?
6. What is meant by culture shock, and how has the culture-shock model been refined and extended to meet contemporary CCM requirements and conditions?
7. What is intercultural learning and by means of which criteria may 'successful' intercultural learning be identified?
8. What is meant by the circle of intercultural interactions and how can understanding their experiences in terms of this model help managers to enlarge their repertoire?

(Continued)

> 9. How do companies try to facilitate the development of cross-cultural competencies amongst their employees?
> 10. What differentiates a cross-culturally competent manager from others?

Opening Activity Revisited: Reflexive Thoughts

For revisiting the Opening Activity, please read Chapter 7 on a critical CCM. Then, consider the following: The manuals of the Opening Activity provide the impression that it is the 'engineers' who are 'modern' in the sense of a 'Western rationality and modernity'. Conversely, the Eybeceenians seem to be a 'far away', 'non-Western' people living a traditional, potentially more spiritual life.

During the simulation, it often happens that participants in the engineering role treat those in the Eybeceenian role in a condescending manner. Sometimes, it is assumed that the Eybeceenians' English is rudimentary or that they might not possess or know the tools, equipment and facilities required for knowledge transfer. Sometimes, it emerges from the simulation that the engineers are 'White' and the Eybeceenians are 'non-White'. None of the latter assumptions are part of the manual – how can they emerge?

They emerge because the simulation triggers hidden, critical inequalities by evoking historically learned stereotypes, images and cultural delineations. For example, there is the implicit idea that 'Western' corporate life is 'rational', whereas 'non-Western' corporate life is less so, assuming a higher performance orientation in a thus constructed 'rational West'. There is also the idea that gender equality is a 'Western' phenomenon and that 'non-Western' peoples need to be 'developed' in this aspect. By differentiating Eybeceenian society into gender roles, such as 'male' and 'female', an image of 'non-Western gender inequality' might be evoked. Likewise, the community gathering might evoke feelings of 'non-Western religiosity' and lead to power differential in the interaction. Contrary to the instructions, the engineers will then claim superiority, even though they are supposed to be the 'learners of culture'. However, as the pieces of the Opening Case in Chapter 7 suggest, all of these are historically and systemic inequalities to be challenged, not a global reality. It might still be that a certain 'non-Western culture' is 'traditional' and 'religious' – but this needs to be figured out empirically, and in relation to the individuals experiencing this cultural context. It may not be presupposed *in general*.

Thus, if negative power effects emerged when you participated in the opening simulation, make sure to reflect. The simulation introduces an alternative worldview, namely a reality beyond binaries in which people ('Eybeceenian') could be spiritual *and* modern, and community-oriented *and* technologically advanced *at the same time*. Out of this, new options emerge. For example, Eybeceenian society seems to easily acknowledge non-binary or third genders (represented by wise persons) – a 'hidden' category amongst engineers.

For bringing your CCM competencies to this next level, apply the models and tools of a critical CCM to the opening simulation and, if facilitated, to your experiences of it. Identify critical aspects of the simulation and their root causes (e.g. habitus, discourse, power) and devise ways for overcoming them and, generally, for moving beyond dominance in intercultural interactions.

Closing Activity: Building Bridges Across Cultures

Building bridges across cultures is a metaphor for the cross-cultural manager's task. For the Closing Activity, work together in a group of students (if the Opening Activity was facilitated, make sure to include diverse roles and both groups).

First, reflect:

- What, if any, are the dangers of intercultural simulations? To what extent do they enable learning and to what extent might they perpetuate stereotypes?
- What is the advantage of using artificial cultures – such as engineers and Eybeceenians – instead of 'real cultures' in experiential learning activities?
- Related to such activities, what is the responsibility of those designing and facilitating intercultural simulations?
- Related to such activities, what is the learners' responsibility or the responsibility of those engaging in intercultural simulations?
- Why is it relevant to debrief an intercultural simulation, and which elements (such as change of perspective) does such debriefing require?

Next, imagine that you need to compile a manual based on the Opening Activity and how it has been debriefed throughout this chapter. The manual is intended for a friend, fellow student or colleague who is going to interact across cultures for the first time. When compiling the manual, use examples (also your own experiences) from the opening simulation and add visualizations, if helpful. Make sure to consider:

- What does your friend need to know about intercultural learning processes?
- What should your friend pay attention to when interacting across cultures?
- Which feelings and emotions is your friend likely to experience, and how should they deal with these?
- How can your friend know that they are in 'culture-shock', and in which processes should they engage (and how?) to recover?
- Why and how should your friend try to identify cultural patterns and norms, and how can they learn culture from surface to depth?

- How can your friend *experience* what is written in your manual? Which activity could they pursue that could simulate the required cross-cultural experience?
- How can you make sure that you have done justice to your responsibility as the person compiling an intercultural training manual?

Be prepared to exchange your findings in class.

Facilitator's reflexive instructions

After the Opening Activity has been revisited, the following aspects are worth discussing:

1. The introduction clearly portrays Eybeceenia as an advanced, sustainable, 'modern' country – how can it nonetheless happen that Eybeceenians are thought of as traditional, and in what ways is this effect transferrable to real-live situations, practices and systems? What needs to be done (and who needs to do it) to change reality to the better?
2. On Eybeceenia, gender in the sense of 'having a gender' is relevant. Men and women are supposed to differ in how they dress, and binary and non-binary individuals differ in terms of occupation. Is such interdependency coupled with differentiation 'modern' or 'traditional'? What would happen if male and female ideas of 'what kind of job to do' (e.g. 'only men work with scissors because they are a martial tool') differed? From there, implications for real life and other identity categories emerge. The important aspect is to not presuppose that inter-group equity (full inclusion and participation) can only be reached via full equality (everyone behaves and 'is' the same). However, it should also be considered how a *systemic* differentiation between group identities is problematic (e.g. a law system allocating different rights to binary and non-binary individuals), and that all practices of interdependency/complementarity tend to favour one group over others or might be complied with only reluctantly by some.

Further Reading

Kolb (1984) is one of the foundational sources for experiential learning; there are numerous publications building upon his 'experiential learning cycle'. The *Sage Handbook of Intercultural Competence* (Darla Deardorff, 2009), particularly the chapter by Brian Spitzberg and Gabrielle Changnon, provides an in-depth overview on intercultural competence. Part VI of *The Sage Handbook of Contemporary Cross-Cultural Management*

(Szkudlarek et al., 2020) is dedicated to the development of cross-cultural management competencies, also with a focus on higher education. Joyce Osland and Alan Bird (2000) provide advice on how to use cultural dimensions for learning cultures from surface to depth. Barnga (Thiagarajan and Thiagarajan, 2006), a card game, and Ecotonos (Hofner-Saphiere, 1997), a problem-solving simulation, are two well-known intercultural experiential learning games. There are also learning activities involving 'synthetic cultures' that facilitate cross-cultural competency development by means of artificial cultures (Pedersen, 2022).

References

Bennett, M.J. (1986) 'A developmental model approach to training for intercultural sensitivity', *International Journal of Intercultural Relations*, 10(2): 179–186.

Black, J.S. and Mendenhall, M. (1991) 'The U-Curve adjustment hypothesis revisited: A review and theoretical framework', *Journal of International Business Studies*, 22(2): 225–247.

Deal, T.E. and Kennedy, A.A. (1982) *Corporate Culture: The Rites and Rituals of Corporate Life*. Boston: Addison-Wesley.

Deardorff, D.K. (2006) 'Identification and assessment of intercultural competence as a Student outcome of internationalization', *Journal of Studies in International Education*, 10(3): 241–266.

Earley, P.C. and Ang. S. (2003) *Cultural Intelligence: Individual Interactions across Cultures*. Palo Alto: Stanford University Press.

GLOBE (2020) *An Overview of the 2004 Study: Understanding the Relationship Between National Culture, Societal Effectiveness and Desirable Leadership Attributes*. Available at: https://globeproject.com/study_2004_2007?page_id=data#data [last accessed 3 August 2021].

Gudykunst, W.B., Wiseman, R.L. and Hammer, M.R. (1977) 'Determinants of a sojourner's attitudinal satisfaction: A path model', in B. Ruben (ed.), *Communication Yearbook*. New York: Brunswick. pp. 415–425.

Gullahorn, J.T. and Gullahorn, J.E. (1963) 'An extension of the U-curve hypothesis', *Journal of Social Issues*, 19(3): 33–47.

Hofner-Saphiere, D. (1997) *Ecotonos – A Multicultural Problem-Solving Simulation*. Yarmouth: Intercultural Press.

Hofstede, G. (1980) *Culture's Consequences: International Differences in Work Related Values*. Beverly Hills: Sage.

Kolb, D. (1984) *Experiential Learning: Experience as the Source of Learning and Development*. Upper Saddle River: Prentice Hall.

Leeds-Hurwitz, W. (1990) 'Notes in the history of intercultural communication: The foreign service institute and the mandate for intercultural training', *Quarterly Journal of Speech*, 76(3): 262–281.

Lysgaard, S. (1955) 'Adjustment in a foreign society: Norwegian Fulbright grantees visiting the United States', *International Social Science Bulletin*, 7: 45–58.

Mahadevan, J. and Kilian-Yasin, K. (2013) 'Interkulturelles Lernen im berufsbezogenen Kontext: Ein beispielhaftes Modell zur kombinierten und integrierten Kompetenzentwicklung' *[Intercultural learning in applied professional contexts: an exemplatory model for developing combined and integrating competencies]*, in G. Berkenbusch, K. von Helmolt and W. Jia (eds), *Interkulturelle Lernsettings: Konzepte – Formate – Verfahren*. Stuttgart: ibidem Press. pp. 151–174.

Oberg, K. (1960) 'Culture shock and the problem of adjustment to new cultural environments', *Practical Anthropology*, 7: 177–182.

Osland, J. and Bird, A. (2000) 'Beyond sophisticated stereotyping – understanding cultural sensemaking in context', *Academy of Management Executive*, 14(1): 65–79.

Pedersen, P. (2022) *A Synthetic Culture Laboratory*. Available at: www2.hawaii.edu › ~barkai › PEDERSEN [last accessed 31 July 2022].

Spitzberg, B.H. (2000) 'A model of intercultural communication competence', in L.A. Samovar and R.E. Porter (eds), *Intercultural Communication - A Reader*. Belmont: Wadsworth. pp. 375–387.

Spitzberg, B.H. and Changnon, G. (2009) 'Conceptualizing intercultural competence', in D.K. Deardorff (ed.), *The Sage Handbook of Intercultural Competence*. Thousand Oaks: Sage. pp. 2–52.

Szkudlarek, B. (2009) 'Through Western eyes: Insights into the corporate training field', *Organization Studies*, 30(9): 975–986.

Szkudlarek, B., Romani, L., Caprar, D.V. and Osland, J.S. (eds) (2020) *The Sage Handbook of Contemporary Cross-Cultural Management*. London: Sage.

Thiagarajan, S. and Thiagarajan, R. (2006) *Barnga: A Simulation Game on Cultural Clashes – 25th Anniversary Edition*. Yarmouth: Intercultural Press.

Designing Your Cross-Cultural Management Research

12

Learning Objectives

After reading this chapter, you should:

- be able to differentiate emic and etic, subjective and objective, and causal and holistic approaches to culture
- understand for which scenario which of these approaches is applicable or not
- know which questions to ask in order to position and design your CCM research.

Reading Requirements

- You should have read Chapter 2 of this book

Introduction

Cross-cultural management studies is a multidisciplinary field; it encompasses a variety of ideas of how culture is part of management. For future and present cross-cultural managers, this is relevant because every concept of culture enlarges the scope of analysis and action. Multiple approaches to culture provide you with more opportunities to gain insights into CCM realities, and to manage a CCM situation effectively and appropriately.

Chapter 2 traced how the concept of culture in CCM has evolved, namely from the idea of distinct national cultures to a more nested understanding of multiple cultures, and towards cultural complexity, multiple cultural flows and contextualized identities 'at home'. It shed light onto how cultures – defined in various ways – interrelate in more complex, differentiated and de-localized ways with management and organizations.

Building upon these insights, Chapter 12 provides you with a variety of approaches to culture in CCM. In particular, it differentiates between holistic and causal, between emic and etic, and between subjective and objective culture, and discusses which of these approaches is applicable to which situations and for which purposes.

After having read Chapter 12, you should have acquired the knowledge and skills to identify culture and its impact on contemporary CCM. In particular, you should be able to make managerial decisions about which approach to culture (not) to apply to which situation, based on your understanding of when and how which approach is useful or not.

Opening Case

A Customized CCM Scenario

In this chapter, you will work with your own customized Opening Case. The first Student Activity leads you through it. Before engaging in this activity, read the adjacent Spotlight.

STUDENT ACTIVITY 12.1

A Meeting I Have Participated In

For developing this case, refer back to an actual meeting you have participated in or observe a meeting in which you are about to participate. Ideally, choose a meeting which you attend on a regular basis, e.g. a student work group or team meeting. Examples could be a weekly corporate meeting, a student work project for a specific course or your sports team grouping together regularly prior to the next match.

Write down your experiences of the situation. Describe the situation and its boundary conditions clearly. Who is present and in what roles (e.g. student, intern, manager, professor)? What is the relation between people (e.g. have you (not) met before)? What is the meeting about? Where does it take place?

Next, take a look at the Spotlight box on the basic variations of culture. Review your writing and structure it according to these basic elements, such as typical–not typical, or bad–normal–good.

When doing so, make sure to pay attention to the following sub-questions:

- How would this meeting typically start?
- How would a good meeting, a 'normal' meeting and a bad meeting unfold? Differentiate between these three basic types.
- What would be a good or a bad outcome of this meeting (and for whom)?
- How would this meeting typically end?

Be prepared to use your notes again for the next activities.

Spotlight: Business Meetings and the Basic Variations of Culture

Repetitive events such as meetings often follow a certain script from which people seldom deviate. Conflict arises if people follow different scripts, that is, ideas and practices of how the event should be shaped and develop, and if they also interpret what happens differently based on culture-specific guidelines of what certain things 'mean'. Basic variations of culture are, for example, whether a meeting is *typical* or *not typical*. You will also have ideas of whether, for example, how a meeting is conducted is *good*, *bad* or *'normal'*. Every cultural interaction furthermore has a *beginning*, a *middle* and an *end*, and it involves both *process* and *outcome*. Uncovering these basic variations thus provides people with a guideline of how to act in a (cross-)cultural interaction, such as a meeting.

Culture in Cross-Cultural Management Studies

Cross-cultural management studies is the academic discipline that wishes to shed light onto how exactly culture interrelates with management, business and organization. Whilst it is generally agreed that culture is a complex phenomenon that might involve virtually 'everything', it is heavily debated in contemporary CCM studies how culture should be conceptualized and studied. Key debates involve:

- the causal versus the holistic approach to culture
- emics versus etics, which is linked to
- subjective versus objective culture.

For CCM practice, these debates are relevant, because managers and researchers require a structured understanding of the available options for making informed choices which CCM tools to use in which situation and for which purposes.

Debate 1: Causal versus holistic culture

Causal approach to culture An approach to culture that focuses on how selected aspects of culture *cause* a certain situation, behaviour or motivation

Holistic approach to culture An approach to culture that studies it in its entirety to discover complex configurations and patterns beyond simple cause and effect

The first decision to be made when conceptualizing culture is whether culture is considered in its entirety or only as involving selected traits. Leung and van de Vijver (2008) have labelled this a **holistic approach to culture** (entirety) versus a **causal approach to culture** (selected traits). Due to methodological dilemmas (*how* to study the whole of culture?) most CCM texts conclude that, for the sake of operationalization (Brannen et al., 2004: 33; House and Javidan, 2004: 15) or measurability (Minkov, 2011: 5), researchers should focus on selected cultural traits (House and Javidan, 2004: 17; Nardon and Steers, 2009: 3), such as values.

However, in practice, both approaches have their advantages and disadvantages, and, therefore, the individual challenge is to choose the right approach for the right task at hand. Ultimately, this means that there is no 'right' or 'wrong' conceptualization of culture in CCM theory and practice, but rather that the choice needs to fit the purpose.

The following section provides you with two examples for each approach, namely **participant observation** in cultural anthropology (holistic approach) and the *study of values* as selected cultural traits – in this case, *individualism and collectivism* – in cross-cultural psychology (causal approach). Both disciplines have contributed to CCM studies; they exemplify the conceptual and methodological richness and diversity of CCM today on which managers and researchers can draw.

Culture as 'that complex whole': The holistic approach

Cultural or social **anthropology** is the discipline focusing on a holistic study of culture – not necessarily across cultures. It has put forward one of the broadest definitions of culture, namely culture as,

> **Anthropology** The discipline focusing on studying people's social dimension holistically

> that complex whole which includes knowledge, belief, arts, morals, law, custom, and any other capabilities and habits acquired by man as a member of society. (Tylor, 1871: 1)

Approaching culture holistically requires longitudinal and in-depth methods, such as **participant observation**, also known as **fieldwork** or **ethnography**. It requires the researcher's longitudinal immersion into the culture of those studied (overview in Spradley, 1980). In contrast to detached observation, where the researcher is present but not involved, participant observation demands for (inter-)action. The researcher should, for example, learn the language of those studied, engage in their day-to-day activities and participate in social events (see Spotlight).

> **Participant observation** Gaining cultural insights via deep immersion and reflecting upon this experience with the help of theory

> **Fieldwork or ethnography** Uncovering holistic culture from the point of those studied

Spotlight: How the In-Depth Study of Culture Came into Being

Participant observation was first put forward by social anthropologist Bronislaw Malinowski (1922), partly out of sheer necessity and specific circumstances. In 1914, Malinowski was accompanying an anthropologist to the

(Continued)

> island of New Guinea, the southern part of which was annexed by Australia as part of the British Commonwealth. At this point, World War I broke out, and as an Austrian subject and enemy of the British Commonwealth, Malinowski should have been detained. However, he managed to obtain permission from the Australian government to undertake ethnographic research in their territories. He ended up staying on the Trobriand Islands in Melanesia for two years, and it is from this experience that he developed the method of participant observation.

When employing the holistic approach, one can never grasp 'the whole of culture' at a time. One therefore needs to split culture up into its interrelated facets, in order to make its complexity small and manageable (as depicted by Figure 12.1).

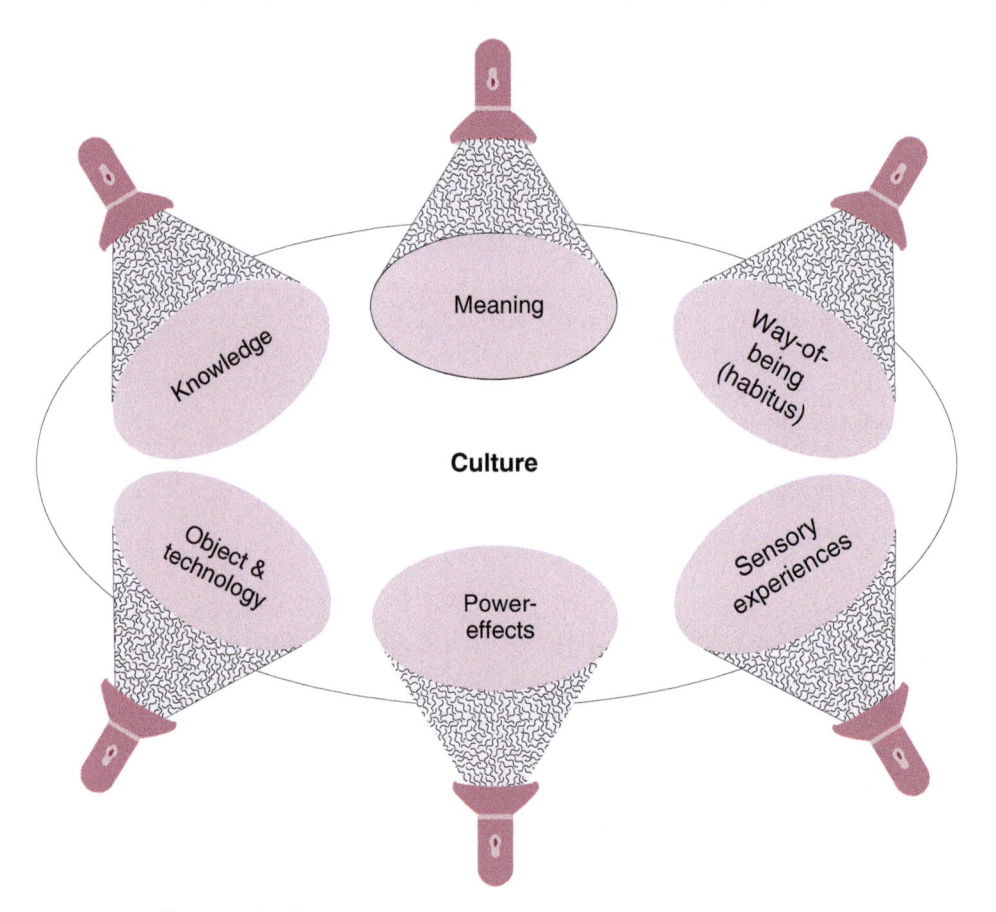

Figure 12.1 **Facets of culture**

The recommendation is thus that cross-cultural managers and researchers should focus on one facet of culture at a time, gain insights on it, and then move to the next one, in order to complement the picture. This way, a holistic overview on culture emerges. The following section summarizes the key aspects of each facet (shown in Figure 12.1) and how to identify them.

> *Cultural knowledge* is mostly tacit; it cannot be put into words (Polanyi, 1967). For example, you (like everyone) have learned ways of 'how to normally conduct a meeting', and you share these with people who are 'similar' to you in a certain context, such as members of the same corporate department or fellow students. Nonetheless, it might be impossible to put this knowledge into words – a meeting just 'feels right' or doesn't.

> *Cultural meaning* refers to the invisible, yet culturally learned link between visible and invisible aspects of culture. If you picture culture as an iceberg, then 'meaning' is the link between its above-the-surface and below-the-surface parts. For example, the degree to which managers are expected to express compassion for others varies considerably across societal cultures (Chhokar et al., 2007). This suggests that, in some professional or organizational cultures, a caring and emotional manager is seen as contributing to the good outcome of a meeting whereas in others the same behaviour is viewed as irrational or overly emotional and, thus, incompetent.

Fine distinctions between groups of people are also made via **habitus** (Bourdieu, 1977); that is, how people behave, dress and carry their bodies. For example, when observing employees in the canteen, you might be able to make a guess as to what kind of department or profession they belong to simply by how they dress, with whom they group, and potentially even by what they eat for lunch.

People furthermore 'learn' and transmit culture also via *sensory experiences*; that is, their *being-in-the-world* (Merleau-Ponty, 1965). For example, how a room 'smells' is part of how you experience a meeting. Also, space 'feels' in certain ways – it may, for example, suffocate people or isolate them.

> **Habitus** The 'fine distinctions' by which markers of social difference are reproduced, often pre-reflexively (Bourdieu, 1977)

Additionally, any contemporary CCM contexts, such as multicultural and dispersed teams are unthinkable without *objects*, such as smartphones, laptops and other equipment, and *technology*, such as the world wide web, shared server spaces and 'clouds' (see Chapter 10). Sometimes, objects and technologies might even be the key actors, for example, in the case of a virtual meeting there can be no human interaction that bypasses them.

> **Privilege** An advantage not personally earned by a person

Power effects as a facet of culture are related to the **privilege**–disadvantage ratios that manifest in specific cultural contexts (also see Chapter 7). For example, as the GLOBE study (House et al., 2004) suggests, gender equality, whilst varying across societal cultures, is not yet (fully) achieved in any of them, at least not at the time when the data was collected and analysed. This inequality might show up in any given meeting, for example, it could be that men are given more time for their arguments compared to women or non-binary leaders, because it is more culturally established that men lead.

The strength of the holistic approach to culture is that it delivers in-depth insights into the whole of culture. Its major weakness is that, if you describe the whole of culture, you can only do this for small and local cultures – a village, a single corporate site, a single team of employees – otherwise, the mere amount and richness of the data will overwhelm you. Therefore, this method is not suitable for a cross-cultural management that wishes to compare more than one level or aggregate culture on a larger scale (see next section).

STUDENT ACTIVITY 12.2

The Facets of Culture of the Meetings I Am In

Refer back to your description of a meeting you have participated in (Student Activity 12.1).

Restructure and expand your description to make sure that you consider all facets of culture in this context. Provide descriptive examples for each facet.

Cultural value orientations: The selective (causal) approach

Large-scale comparative CCM, also known as *quantitative societal culture research* (QSCR, Peterson and Søndergaard, 2011), requires a causal approach to culture. The focus of this CCM sub-field lies in comparing national or societal macro-cultures (sometimes with an additional focus on organizational cultures, e.g. House et al., 2004) by means of quantitative methods, and with regard to certain selected aspects of culture, so-called *cultural dimensions* (Hofstede, 1980) or *cultural value orientations* (Schwartz, 1992). You have encountered this approach in Chapter 5. The Schwartz Value Survey (see Spotlight) is another example.

The specific cultural value orientations to be discussed in this section are *individualism* and *collectivism*. Studies on individualism and collectivism are a prominent theme in cross-cultural psychology (Berry et al., 2002; Shweder and Sullivan, 1993; Triandis, 1980), another main contributor to CCM knowledge. Cross-cultural psychology refers to the comparative study of the ways in which culture and psyche make each other up and also relate to other variables such as economy or environment. Individualism and collectivism are also assumed to be the most studied cultural value orientation in the history of CCM (Thomas, 2020), which is why these orientations are presented here to exemplify the causal approach to culture.

Spotlight: The Schwartz Value Survey

In 1992, Shalom H. Schwartz published the article 'Universals in the content and structure of values: Theory and empirical tests in 20 countries' in which he developed what then became known as 'the theory of basic human values'.

> **Values** Criteria by which people judge a situation

Values are understood as criteria by which people judge a situation (Schwartz, 1992: 1). They are:

(1) concepts or beliefs, (2) pertain to desirable end states or behaviors, (3) transcend specific situations, (4) guide selection or evaluation of behavior and events, and (5) are ordered by relative importance. (1992: 4)

Building on previous work with Wolfgang Bilsky, Schwartz identified ten values as 'near universal' (1992: 37) in the sense that they contain all values 'to which individuals attribute at least moderate importance' (p. 59) and which have the same meaning across the 20 countries in which the survey was conducted. These ten near universal values are: Power, Achievement, Tradition, Hedonism, Self-Direction, Universalism, Security, Stimulation, Benevolence and Conformity.

In the 1992 study's design, participants in the survey were asked to rate their own value preferences on a nine-point scale from 'opposed to my value' up to 'of supreme importance', with the help of value items such as

(Continued)

'helpful', 'honest', 'forgiving' 'loyal', etc. For example, the value type 'Self-Direction' contained six value items which had to be rated: freedom, creativity, independent, choosing own goals, curious and self-respect.

Twenty years later, Schwartz et al. (2012) refined the theory of basic individual values, including a set of 19 values and a new measure scale. The key insight here was: 'Values form a circular motivational continuum' (p. 2), and the 19 values are ordered 'on the continuum based on their compatible and conflicting motivations, expression of self-protection vs. growth, and personal vs. social focus' (p. 2).

Thus, whereas the 1992 study tested the extent to which individuals are influenced by universal values, the 2012 study rather asked how individual motivations and available sets of values are interrelated. This mirrors advancements in CCM studies in the sense that the discipline now understands the interrelations between individual and culture not as a one-way causality (culture shapes the individual) but as a two-way process (humans are products and producers of culture) (see Chapter 2).

The initial ten values are still present in the 2012 study, but some of them have now been sub-divided and described further. The value type 'Power', for example, is split into 'Power–Dominance' defined as 'Power through exercising control over people' and 'Power–Resources' defined as 'Power through control of material and social resources' (p. 60). The authors conclude that 'the refined values theory provides greater precision of prediction and explanation for a diverse set of attitudes and beliefs than the original theory' (p. 49). Again, this is in line with the trend towards more contextualized CCM studies, in which power aspects play an increasingly relevant role.

The causal approach to culture rests on three premises. First, the idea is finding aspects of culture which can be assumed to be universal to all cultures; it is this assumption that makes them comparable. For example, it can be assumed that individuals in every cultural context need to figure out 'how much "I" is in the "We"?'; that is, to what extent do they understand themselves as individuals and to what extent do they understand themselves as members of a group, and what does this interrelation mean to them? This is thus a universal cultural orientation, named *individualism versus collectivism*.

Second, the idea is to investigate how these selected aspects *cause* cross-cultural differences. Compared to the anthropological approach to culture, it is thus only a tiny aspect of culture which is studied, yet because of this exact quality of the approach, culture becomes quantifiable and comparable, and causalities can be established, for example, by means of quantitative investigations. For example, one could try to collect data on people's dispositions regarding individualism and collectivism in numerous cultures, aggregate this data and then establish patterns in the sense of which culture is more or less individualistic than the other.

Thirdly, the causal approach rests on the assumption that one can study a collective phenomenon, culture, on an individual level if one finds individual indicators for it. For example, it is argued that a sense of an intergroup self is indicative of collectivism, and that a sense of an interpersonal self is indicative of individualism, with individual-level indicators for both (Triandis, 1995). Table 12.1 summarizes this assumption.

Table 12.1 Individual-level indicators of collectivism and individualism

Cultural orientation	Sense of self	Individual indicators
Collectivism	Intergroup	Individuals value group goals above their personal goals
		In-group (one group to which the individual belongs above all) provides support and security
		People and the relationship between them (e.g. cooperation) matter most
		Vertical relationships (parent–child) are more important than horizontal relationships (friend–friend)
Individualism	Interpersonal	Individuals value personal goals over group goals
		An individual belongs to many groups; no specific in-group which is relevant above all others
		The connection to a particular group is not necessarily strong
		Therefore, the influence of any group on the individual is weaker

Source: adapted from Triandis (1980)

A major methodological goal of studies promoting a causal approach to culture is to refine the link between collective and individual level; that is, culture and the individual. For example, it has been argued that the concepts of collectivism and individualism are too broad in order to grasp the multi-dimensional character of individuals' sense of self (Singelis et al., 1995). Out of this followed the differentiation between vertical and horizontal collectivism and individualism, based on the construals of independent and interdependent self (Markus and Kitayama, 1991) which are a refinement of intergroup and interpersonal self.

- An independent view on the self implies that 'individuals seek to maintain their independence from others by attending to the self, and by discovering and expressing their unique inner attributes' (Markus and Kitayama, 1991: 224). It is indicative of individualism.

- An interdependent view on the self stresses the interrelatedness of individuals: 'Experiencing interdependence entails seeing oneself as part of an encompassing social relationship and recognizing that one's behavior is determined, contingent on, and to a large extent organized by what the actor perceives to be the thoughts, feelings and actions of *others* in the relationship' (Markus and Kitayama, 1991: 227, emphasis in the original). It is indicative of collectivism.

Horizontal individualism and collectivism refer to the idea that both independent and interdependent selves are equal with the selves of others, whereas vertical individualism and collectivism involve the idea that both independent and interdependent selves are different to the selves of others. Table 12.2 summarizes these considerations.

Table 12.2 Horizontal and vertical collectivism and individualism and their indicators

	Individualism		Collectivism	
	Horizontal	Vertical	Horizontal	Vertical
Independent self	✓	✓		
Interdependent self			✓	✓
Individuals are more or less equal in status	✓		✓	
Inequality accepted/expected		✓		✓

Source: adapted from Singelis et al. (1995)

STUDENT ACTIVITY 12.3

The Cultural Orientations Underlying the Meetings I Am In

Refer back to your description of a meeting you have participated in.

Task 1

Consider collectivism and individualism (Table 12.1).

- Which sense of self characterizes yourself more (intergroup or interpersonal)?

Task 2

Consider horizontal and vertical collectivism and individualism (Table 12.2).

- Find aspects of your meeting description which are indicative of one or more of these underlying orientations.
- Now, consider other meetings you have participated in. Which of the four cultural orientations seem(s) to underlie them? You can choose more than one.
- Reach a conclusion beyond specific meeting contexts. Which cultural orientation is the most indicative of the meetings you are in *across* contexts such as university, work, gatherings amongst family and friends? You can only choose one.
- Would you say that there cultural value orientations in how meetings are normally conducted in the country wherein you live?

Debate 2: Emics versus etics

Another way of classifying how culture is conceptualized in CCM studies is the differentiation between emics and etics. The terms 'emic' and 'etic' originate from linguistic anthropology (Pike, 1967). They are distinct, yet, complementary research paradigms. To describe them, Kenneth Pike (1967) offers the example of 'how to study a car's functioning': if the car is described as a whole and its parts are presented in relation to each other, then this is considered to be an emic analysis (internal or insider view). If the car is presented as a sum of parts and these parts had been categorized in advance according to some general criteria, then this is an etic analysis (external or outsider view). Researchers or practitioners investigating a particular subject, such as culture, can thus proceed from an etic, an emic, or a combined viewpoint.

The classification of a certain research approach as emic or etic is never fully exhaustive; however, there are strong tendencies associated with certain disciplinary angles. For example, cross-cultural psychologists Triandis et al. (1971) posit that emics simply doesn't fit cross-cultural research (of the aforementioned QSCR-kind). On the other hand, fieldwork and ethnography in CCM studies are deeply rooted in emics (Moore and Mahadevan, 2020). There is also an academic tradition which implies that both of them are equally 'valid'.

The terms emic and etic were coined later than the studies applying them. Behavioural psychologist Burrhus Frederic Skinner (1938) was one of the first to formulate and test laws on operant behaviour – an etic approach. The emic perspective can be traced back to cultural anthropologist Bronislaw Malinovski (2002 [1922]), who argued for understanding culture from 'the native's point of view' (p. 19). Neither of them characterized their research in the terms 'etic' and 'emic'.

Both approaches have also met critique in CCM studies. For example, Triandis et al. (1971), whilst promoting etics, warn against what they call 'pseudoetics', an approach which implies transferring a concept (usually a Western/American one) to another culture and using it there even though it does not apply. Offering a critique of emics, Barnard (2002) points out that anything that is considered 'emic' is actually created by the researcher based on their observations (and not by those studied) – it remains open whether the researcher's perspective truly is 'the native's point of view'. Therefore, a better description of emics would be the understanding that emics require the researcher to constantly oscillate between inside (emic) and outside (etic) viewpoints. This then requires high involvement and reflexivity on part of the cross-cultural manager and researcher, as, for example, postulated by Moore and Mahadevan (2020).

Furthermore, an increasing number of scholars argue that it is the synthesis or combination of emics and etics which is 'partly able to counteract one another's theoretical weaknesses in describing culture' (Morris et al., 1999: 789). The idea is that this will lead to synergies (Maznevsky, 2013), and to further theoretical and methodological developments (Romani et al., 2011). For the cross-cultural manager and researcher, it is therefore relevant to choose their approaches to culture as the circumstances and the problem at hand demand.

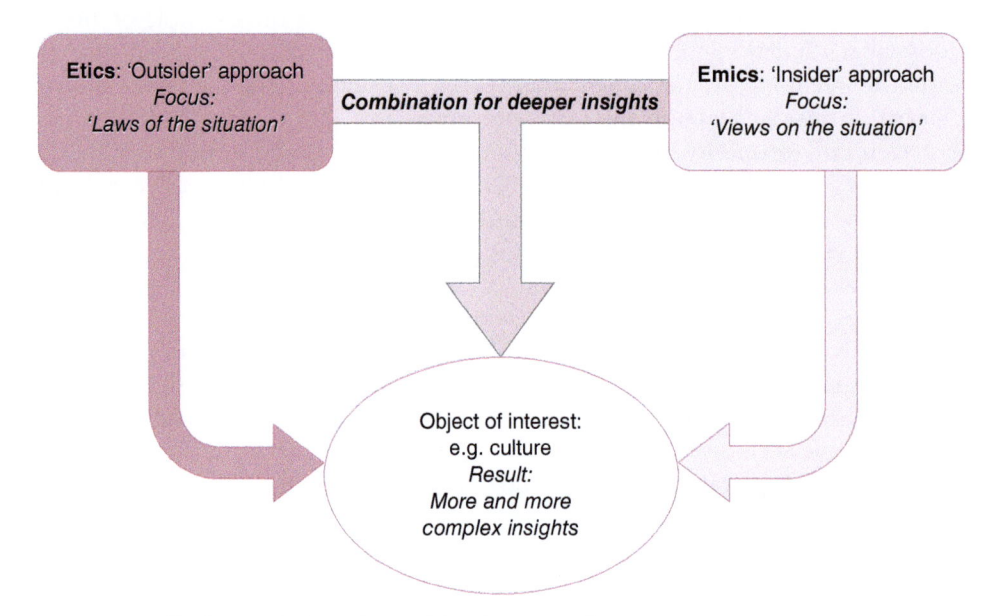

Figure 12.2 **Emics and etics: A combined approach**

Link to Practice: Metaphors of National Culture

There are several approaches that combine emics and etics in CCM research. For example, Gannon and Pillai (2010) suggest that one can approach the etic realities of national cultures by means of metaphors. Metaphors, an emic approach to culture, work by establishing a link between two otherwise unrelated phenomena or terms; they involve interpretation and 'making sense' of a situation. Via a fairly 'simple' analogy for a complex phenomenon, metaphors may thus generate ideas and make complex, abstract problems small and tangible. Gannon and Pillai (2010) propose, for example, the Japanese Garden, the Swedish Stuga, French Wine, Estonian Singing, American Football, the Italian Opera, the Turkish Coffeehouse, the Spanish Bullfight, Argentine Tango or the Sub-Saharan African Bush Taxi as metaphorical entry points to national or wider regional cultures. Their idea is that the whole of a national or wider regional culture unfolds from these objects, activities or phenomena.

Dangers of this approach – like with any macro-level classification of culture – are stereotyping, presenting culture as unchanging and timeless, and overstressing the homogeneity and relevance of national or wider regional cultures. There are also global knowledge imbalances within the study itself (like in all large-scale macro-cultural investigations); for example, the whole of Sub-Saharan Africa is dealt with by means of one chapter, whereas Western Europe is awarded with numerous chapters. Furthermore, the interests and agenda of those using this knowledge need to be considered. For example, every macro-level categorization of difference involves the possibility that people at work *use* national cultural stereotypes to exaggerate the differences which they experience and thus to alienate others. Nonetheless, metaphors might stimulate further thoughts and imagination beyond cultural dimensions.

STUDENT ACTIVITY 12.4

Approaches in Light of Each Other

In your previous activities, you have applied the holistic and the selective (causal) approach to culture, respectively. Now, compare the outcome of both approaches with each other. What are the strengths and weaknesses of each approach? How can the emic and etic approaches to culture complement each other?

Debate 3: Subjective versus objective culture

The differentiation between *objective* culture and *subjective* culture (Berger and Luckmann, 1995) is another decision to be made when dealing with culture in CCM.

- **Objective culture** refers to factual aspects of certain systems, such as institutions, structures, laws or regulations. These influences and subsequent cross-cultural differences – e.g. between countries, between industries and between professions – are objective because they are often laid out in writing or are clearly visible, for example, whether the language of business *is* different or the same across certain countries.
- **Subjective culture** refers to how culture shapes the ways in which people experience the world and behave towards others, and what they expect from themselves and others. These influences and subsequent cross-cultural differences are subjective because they emerge in people's minds; that is, how they interpret (give meaning) to the world, and how they then structure what they experience – for example, the pictures in mind which you hold about people in other countries.

Simply speaking, objective culture can be assumed to be 'just there' (an accounting procedure in a company or a taxation system of a country simply exists). They key question from this perspective is: How does culture *work*?

Conversely, subjective culture involves perspectivity and positionality as different people view the same reality from different positions. Their ideas and actions about it are subjective and rooted in a certain perspective, and therefore one needs to ask: What does culture *mean* (and to whom)?

Subjective culture How culture is perceived

Objective culture How culture *is*

Objective culture (the irrefutable 'facts' about a situation) can be more easily unified than subjective culture (the perspectives regarding what a situation 'means'). They also tend to be more stable than subjective meanings. Cultural value orientations and the selective approach to culture are thus more suitable for assessing objective culture than for providing conclusive insights into what shapes subjective culture. For example, countries differ regarding their insurance laws – a relative difference in value orientations might be deduced on a macro level. Also, corporate practice regarding insurances differ – an objective relative difference on a meso level.

Differentiating between subjective and objective culture is tricky. For example, people attach meaning even to objective cultural facts such as national laws or an established corporate procedure. They might agree to it or not, or they might like it or not. This then influences their actions. They might follow it actively or try to deviate from it. Ultimately, if a sufficiently large number of people believes in the same version of what a certain law 'means', they might choose to establish alternatives. The result is a change in objective culture. Likewise, companies interpret objective national insurance laws when making their respective insurance decisions: divergent meso-level interpretations of objective macro-culture result in objective meso-level differences. Therefore, like emics and etics, a combined approach to objective and subjective culture might deliver the most insights.

> **STUDENT ACTIVITY 12.5**
>
> ### Are Cross-Cultural Differences Imagined or Real?
>
> Select one country which you are very familiar with, based on own experiences, and one country which you don't know much about and have never visited
>
> **Task 1**
>
> Think about 'pictures in mind' which you might have regarding these two countries. What comes to your mind? Write this down.
>
> - Find five aspects of objective cross-cultural differences between these two countries. Prove the objective differences by means of sources.
>
> **Task 2**
>
> Answer the following questions:
>
> - How are your subjective pictures in mind different from the objective differences which you have identified?
> - How do the pictures differ for a country you are familiar with and a country you are unfamiliar with?
> - What can be learned from this exercise for how cross-cultural researchers and managers should reflect upon and approach cross-cultural differences in theory and practice?
>
> Exchange with fellow students and/or be prepared to present in class.

Chapter Summary

The holistic and the causal approach to culture are the extreme poles from which to conceptualize culture in CCM studies. The holistic approach is rooted in the idea that cross-cultural managers need to immerse themselves into the situation and conduct their own cultural exploration in the sense of practical 'fieldwork' or 'participant observation'. This way, they will learn from the experience and be enabled to move beyond the comfort zone of their 'own ways of doing things'. However, because culture as 'that complex whole' is so complex, its exploration is only possible in small and often local cultural contexts. Even then, culture has to be split up into facets, in order to make it manageable. Therefore, the purpose of this method lies in enabling the cross-cultural manager and researcher to uncover deep culture in all its richness, or, in other words, to formulate questions which no one knew to ask in the first place, and to find answers to previously unknown questions.

A causal approach to culture investigates only selected aspects of culture which are assumed to be universal. It aims at finding indicators for culture on an individual level in order to collect data on a collective construct (culture). Out of this emerge insights which can be aggregated on larger levels, such as nations and societies. Thus the strength of this method is that it provides the cross-cultural manager and researcher with first hypotheses of what underlies the behaviour of a person or what shapes a context. For example, the principle of individualism or collectivism might explain much of the behaviour, motivation, communication, values, aspirations, reactions and so on which a person or a group of people exhibit, not only in a single cultural context but across many situations. Therefore, with this knowledge in mind, the cross-cultural manager and researcher can investigate individual and group behaviour for the principles which underlie them on a much larger level.

In practice, cross-cultural managers and researchers need both – a holistic and a causal approach to culture – and they need to choose the approach that fits their purposes and a certain situation the best. The cross-cultural insights gathered, as well as the process gaining them, will naturally differ. A holistic approach lets the cross-cultural researcher and manager uncover the emic viewpoints of those encountered, and this requires high involvement. Cross-cultural insights emerge from how the cross-cultural researcher or manager reflects upon differences encountered in a specific culture, and how they are perceived by others in return – empirical material which is qualitative in nature. Conversely, a selective approach (etics) does not require personal involvement, and cross-cultural insights emerge from the causalities apparent in the mostly quantitative data. This implies that a causal and selective approach is more suited to deliver insights into objective culture and that a holistic approach to culture is applicable to uncovering subjective culture. Table 12.3 summarizes these considerations.

Table 12.3 How to design your cross-cultural management research – a structured summary

	Holistic approach	Selective approach
Underlying perspective	Emic	Etic
Own involvement requirement	High	Low/none
Own reflexivity requirement	Medium/high	Low/none
Scope of investigation	Small cultural contexts	Large cultural units
Cross-cultural insights	Emerge from the reflections of how emic and etic viewpoints are different in this context	Emerge from comparison of the data gathered
Time requirement	Longitudinal	No requirement
Typical qualities of data	Qualitative	Quantitative
Objective: gain insights on	'that complex whole'	Selected causalities

The differentiation and structured summary proposed in Table 12.3 differs from how CCM research is commonly delineated; for example, along the lines of specific CCM paradigms (Chapter 4). The reason for this choice is that this book considers research to be a practical endeavour. When engaging in it, students, researchers and managers need to make many small decisions with the purpose of improving upon what is known (also see Bell and Thorpe, 2013). When viewed from this perspective, designing CCM research is not (only) about doctoral or postdoctoral research projects but rather about the constant question of how to *use* the available CCM concepts and tools for understanding and impacting upon practice. Managers as reflexive practitioners and students as reflexive learners are involved in this endeavour, too, based on the interrelated insights that 'nothing is as practical as a good theory' (Greenwood and Levin, 1998: 19) and that 'the best way to understand something is to try and change it' (ibid.).

The three debates chosen are central to making such practical, change-driven CCM research choices and to identifying areas of knowledge- and skills-creation that are relevant to CCM academia and practice. Therefore, this chapter has concentrated on them. What this chapter has *not* done is outline 'how to do' CCM research in detail, for example how to design a valid questionnaire or how to analyse data, based on the assumption that such knowledge and skills come later in the process. They can be obtained via other sources once the big decisions concerning 'what do I believe is culture', and 'how shall it be studied', and for what purposes, have been made. For making such big decisions, this chapter has offered a structured, yet not exhaustive approach to understanding how and where to start when designing your CCM research.

Key Points

- Designing your CCM research starts with positioning it in terms of current academic debates on how to conceptualize and study culture.
- Further methodological choices follow from the broad decisions on whether to study holistic or causal culture, emics or etics, and subjective or objective culture.
- The positioning decisions made are associated with distinct strengths and weaknesses, and bring about distinct risks and opportunities.
- The research choices made need to fit the problem or task at hand.
- Paradigmatic delineations are another, more meta-level way of how to position your CCM research.

Review Questions

1. What are the main characteristics of a holistic and a causal approach to culture, respectively?
2. What are the main characteristics of approaching CCM as emics and etics, respectively?
3. What are the main characteristics of a subjective and an objective approach to culture, respectively?
4. What are the strengths and weaknesses, and the risks and opportunities, of gaining insights on holistic and causal culture, respectively?
5. What are the strengths and weaknesses, and the risks and opportunities, of studying emics and etics, respectively?
6. What are the strengths and weaknesses, and the risks and opportunities, of gaining insights into subjective and objective culture, respectively?
7. Assume that a manager needs to lead a newly formed global virtual team. Which approach to cross-cultural research do you propose for figuring out cultural diversity in the team?
8. Assume that a company wishes to enter new global markets. Which approach to cross-cultural research do you propose for figuring out whether consumer behaviour on the new market is similar to the home market?
9. Assume that a start-up company and a multinational company from two different countries are about to engage in a corporate partnership. Which approach to cross-cultural research do you propose for assessing and integrating both corporate cultures?
10. Assume that you, as a manager, need to prepare for expatriation. Which approach to cross-cultural research will you pursue during the preparation phase abroad? Which approach to cross-cultural research will you employ for learning culture from surface to depth while being abroad?

Opening Case Revisited

In Chapter 12, you have encountered key debates of contemporary CCM studies. Throughout, you have used these concepts to reflect upon the Opening Case; that is, your own meeting description. This enables you to design your own CCM research along three differentiating lines: holistic versus causal/selective, emics versus etics, and subjective versus objective, or to pursue a combination of these elements. With the full understanding of this chapter, you may now revise and improve upon your first approximation of 'how meetings are normally done'. To deepen your learning, choose another cultural phenomenon and describe it in sufficient depth and complexity.

Closing Activity

The closing activity is differentiated into several interrelated steps, such as:

- building a research foundation
- drafting a research proposal
- peer-reviewing the research proposal of others, and
- revising your own research proposal.

These circular steps are the building-blocks of every (student) research, also in CCM.

Trying them out yourself will deepen your understanding of how to design CCM research, and you will furthermore test this understanding in practice. Thereby, this activity closes the loop regarding your understanding of what CCM studies involve and how to do CCM research in practice, and it also brings the content of this book to a closure.

Step 1: Building a research foundation

For generating more informed ideas of how to design CCM research in practical ways, re-read Chapter 4 on the worldviews (or paradigms) informing CCM studies. Consider:

- What is culture from the perspective of each paradigm?
- How are the four paradigms linked to and interrelated with the three key debates covered in this chapter?

Next, read Chapters 5 to 7 in detail (these focus on one paradigm each). Consider:

- What detailed advice for designing and conducting CCM research emerges when you add paradigmatic considerations to the debates?

- What kind of methods should be used from the perspective of each paradigm?
- Which paradigm is useful for solving which CCM problem?
- How can a combined approach deliver higher insights, for example concerning questions such as emics and etics, causal and holistic culture, and objective and subjective culture?

Finally, write a summary for each chapter that summarizes what you have learned ('What am I taking with me?'), how and when you will use this learning, and who might profit from this learning as well.

Step 2: Drafting a research proposal

Choose one cultural phenomenon or problem area and write a draft research proposal. This proposal needs to include:

- a few sentences about *what is known* (state of the art in theory and/or practice)
- a few sentences about *what is not known* (the 'gap' in research and/or practice)
- a few sentences about *what should be learned* (proposed research outcome)
- a few sentences about *why what should be learned is relevant*, and *for whom* (answer the 'So, what?' question which a potential reader has in mind)
- a few sentences about *how this will be learned* (research design), differentiated into *how to study* this phenomenon or problem area (data collection), and *how to analyse* the empirical material collected (data analysis)
    - particularly in case of quantitative/functionalist research on causal culture, a research question and first hypotheses/propositions regarding the assumed causalities of culture
    - particularly in case of subjective/interpretive research on holistic culture, a few sentences about who the researcher is and how they are positioned in relation to the phenomenon/problem area studied (perspectivity)
- if you can, a proposed draft schedule, differentiated into research stages such as literature review, data collection, data analysis, writing, proof-reading, etc.
- a preliminary list of key sources upon which research approach and relevance, as outlined and identified by you, are based
- a few sentences about what is still unclear to you; for example, concrete methodologies, 'how-to-do' knowledge concerning methods
- a few sentences about how you plan to close these gaps and which guidance you require by your lecturer in the process.

Write approximately two pages.

Step 3: Engaging in peer review

Hand in your proposal to another student for peer review, and be prepared to peer review their proposal as well. For conducting the peer review, proceed as follows:

- Read the other student's proposal carefully, summarize the key ideas in a few sentences and look at what you have written. Is the text coherent? If not, where are the gaps? What shall be done to close these gaps?
- Have a look at the source list. Does it look convincing? Are the sources sufficient and adequate for what is going to be studied?
- Is what is going to be studied relevant? (Is there an answer to the 'So, what?' question?)
- Are the ways in which the phenomenon/problem area are going to be studied (methodology and methods) feasible and adequate? Do they fit the worldview underlying the research?
- Does the student have a good understanding of what they do (not yet) know, and are the ways in which the student wishes to close their knowledge and skills gap outlined convincingly? Can you provide further advice on how to close the other person's knowledge and skills gap?
- Based on the status quo of this research proposal, what is still missing to make it 'excellent'? Provide the student with key avenues for further improvement that are rooted in the existing research proposal (do *not* project your own ideas upon the other person's project but rather *follow them in their own research design* – your task is to make *their* research better).

A good review acknowledges the existing approach and adds to it.

Step 4: Revise and submit

After having conducted a peer review yourself, you now know the criteria which your lecturer, supervisor or tutor will use to evaluate your own proposal. Furthermore, you will have received concrete advice by a fellow student by now. Improve upon your own proposal in this light and hand it in to your lecturer, supervisor or tutor for feedback.

Step 5 onwards: Initiate and engage in the next learning and peer-discussion loops

After having received your research proposal back, consider the feedback which you have been offered:

- How has your lecturer understood your proposal? Did they understand the proposal in the way you intended it to be understood or were there

misunderstandings? If so, in what aspects? How will you revise your proposal in order to clarify and explicate your proposed approach more and to minimize the risk of misunderstanding?
- Does the feedback make sense to you? If not, what will you need to ask your lecturer to understand their feedback?
- Which avenues for further improvement does your lecturer propose? How does this advice improve upon your existing proposal? What will you do to implement this advice? If you have the feeling that the advice does not do your proposal justice or cannot be implemented, how do you now proceed?
- Which suggestions help you close existing gaps? Are your expectations met? If not, what is still missing?

Revise your proposal accordingly and resubmit.

Research is a personal process, and one's research proposal being evaluated by others is a situation not easily handled. You might even feel offended, frustrated, etc., when facing the feedback you have received. Overcome this feeling by understanding that the purpose of peer reviews is to make *your* research better. Therefore, assume that the reviewer has a point. Try to find this point. Only then assume that the reviewer is wrong or has conducted a bad review. If you were misunderstood, ask yourself why has this been so? If the review is not helpful, ask yourself what kind of review would you have wished for? Learn from asking both questions. Additionally, train yourself in conducting reviews – the more you do so, the better you become at working with the feedback of others. In these small, practical ways, you will then become better at designing CCM research.

Further Reading

The *Very Short, Fairly Interesting and Reasonably Cheap Book about Management Research* by Emma Bell and Richard Thorpe provides an overview on current management research perspectives (Bell and Thorpe, 2013). It understands research as a managerial tool in practice and asks reflexive questions such as: What kind of researcher do you want to be? Luciara Nardon and Richard Steers discuss another key debate in CCM studies, namely the question as to whether national cultures converge, for example because of globalization effects, or whether they diverge, for example because of localization effects (Nardon and Steers, 2009). This debate is another fruitful starting point for designing your CCM research. If you want to learn more about quantitative societal culture research, you will find an academic overview in Peterson and Søndergaard (2011). McCurdy et al. (2005) outline one way of how to conduct ethnography on undergraduate level, namely an ethnographic interview which is then analysed by means of cognitive anthropology. This is a rather 'quantitative' and 'functionalist' approach to ethnography and might thus have boundary-spanning qualities for CCM research as related to management or engineering. Berry et al. (2002) provide a good overview on cross-cultural psychology and value-based research.

An overview on and advice regarding quantitative and qualitative methods for business students can be found in Saunders et al. (2009). Part II of *The Sage Handbook of Contemporary Cross-Cultural Management* (Szkudlarek et al., 2020) introduces the key CCM research methods of survey, experiment and ethnography, and also highlights methods of a critical CCM. If you want to contextualize your CCM research within organizations, then *The Sage Handbook of Organizational Research Methods* (Buchanan and Bryman, 2011) is a good first entry point for further learning. Qualitative comparative analysis (QCA) is an approach that integrates key CCM debates via a cross-cutting methodology – it seems to gain momentum particularly in International Business Studies (Fainshmidt et al., 2020).

References

Barnard, A. (2002) 'Emic and etic', in A. Barnard and J. Spencer (eds), *Encyclopedia of Social and Cultural Anthropology*. London: Routledge. pp. 275–279.

Bell, E. and Thorpe, R. (2013) *A Very Short, Fairly Interesting and Reasonably Cheap Book about Management Research*. London: Sage.

Berger, P. and Luckmann, T. (1995) *Modernity, Pluralism and the Crisis of Meaning*. Gütersloh: Bertelsmann Foundation.

Berry, J.W., Poortinga, Y.H., Segall, M.H. and Dasen, P.R. (2002) *Cross-Cultural Psychology: Research and Applications*. Cambridge: Cambridge University Press.

Bourdieu, P. (1977) *Outline of a Theory of Practice*. Cambridge: Cambridge University Press.

Brannen, M.Y., Gómez, G., Peterson, M.F., Romani, L., Sagiv, L. and Wu, P.-C. (2004) 'People in global organizations: Culture, personality and social dynamics', in H.W. Lane, M.L. Maznevski and M.E. Mendenhall (eds), *The Blackwell Handbook of Global Management: A Guide to Managing Complexity*. Hoboken: Wiley Blackwell. pp. 26–54.

Buchanan, D.A. and Bryman, A. (2011) *The Sage Handbook of Organizational Research Methods*. London: Sage. (1st edition, 2009.)

Chhokar, J.S., Brodbeck, F.C. and House, R.J. (eds) (2007) *Culture and Leadership across the World: The GLOBE Book of In-Depth Studies of 25 Societies*. Mahwah: Erlbaum.

Fainshmidt, S., Witt, M.A., Aguilera, R.V. and Verbeke, A. (2020) 'The contributions of qualitative comparative analysis (QCA) to international business research', *Journal of International Business Studies*, 51(5): 455–466.

Gannon, M.J. and Pillai, R. (2010) *Understanding Global Cultures – Metaphorical Journeys through 29 Nations, Clusters of Nations, Continents and Diversity*. Los Angeles: Sage. (1st edn, 2009.)

Greenwood, D.J. and Levin, M. (1998) *Introduction to Action Research: Social Research for Social Change*. Thousand Oaks: Sage.

Hofstede, G. (1980) *Culture's Consequences: International Differences in Work Related Values*. Beverly Hills: Sage.

House, R. and Javidan, M. (2004) 'Overview of GLOBE', in R. House, P. Hanges, M. Javidan and V. Gupta (eds), *Culture, Leadership, and Organizations – The GLOBE Study of 62 Societies*. Thousand Oaks: Sage. pp. 9–28.

House, R., Hanges, P., Javidan, M. and Gupta, V. (2004) *Culture, Leadership, and Organizations: The GLOBE Study of 62 Societies*. Thousand Oaks: Sage.

Leung, K. and van de Vijver, F.J.R. (2008) 'Strategies for strengthening causal inferences in cross-cultural research: The consilience approach', *International Journal of Cross-Cultural Management*, 8(2): 145–169.

Malinovski, B. (2002) *Argonauts of the Western Pacific: An Account of Native Enterprise and Adventures in the Archipelagoes of Melanesian New Guinea*. London: Routledge. (1st edn, 1922.)

Markus, H.R. and Kitayama, S. (1991) 'Culture and the self: Implications for cognition, emotion, and motivation', *Psychological Review*, 98(2): 224–253.

Maznevsky, M. (2013) 'Comments on the interview: Best approaches and practices to increase cultural awareness and prepare managers for working in a culturally diverse environment', *Academy of Management Learning and Education*, 12(3): 509–511.

McCurdy, D.W., Spradley, J.P. and Shandy, D.J. (2005) *The Cultural Experience – Ethnography in Complex Society*. Long Grove: Waveland Press.

Merleau-Ponty, M. (1965) *Phenomenology of Perception*. London: Routledge & Kegan Paul.

Minkov, M. (2011) *Cultural Differences in a Globalizing World*. Bingley: Emerald.

Moore, F. and Mahadevan, J. (2020) 'Ethnography and cross-cultural management', in B. Szkudlarek, L. Romani, D.V. Caprar and J.S. Osland (eds), *The Sage Handbook of Contemporary Cross-Cultural Management*. London: Sage. pp. 127–140.

Morris, M.W., Leung, K., Ames, D. and Lickel, B. (1999) 'Views from inside and outside: Integrating emic and etic insights about culture and justice judgement', *Academy of Management Review*, 24(4): 781–796.

Nardon, L. and Steers, R.M. (2009) 'The culture theory jungle: Divergence and convergence in models of national culture', in R.S. Bhagat and R.M. Steers (eds), *Cambridge Handbook of Culture, Organizations and Work*. Cambridge: Cambridge University Press. pp. 3–22.

Peterson, M.F. and Søndergaard, M. (2011) 'Traditions and transitions in quantitative societal culture research in Organization Studies', *Organization Studies*, 32(11): 1539–1558.

Pike, K.L. (1967) *Language in Relation to a Unified Theory of the Structures of Human Behavior*. The Hague: Mouton & Co. (1st edn, 1954.)

Polanyi, M. (1967) *The Tacit Dimension*. New York: Anchor Books.

Romani, L., Primecz, H. and Topçu, K. (2011) 'Paradigm interplay for theory development: A methodological example with the Kulturstandard Method', *Organizational Research Methods*, 14(3): 432–455.

Saunders, M., Lewis, P. and Thornhill, A. (2009) *Research Methods for Business Students*. Harlow: Pearson Education. (1st edn, 1997.)

Schwartz, S.H. (1992) 'Universals in the content and structure of values: Theoretical advances and empirical tests in 20 countries', *Advances in Experimental Social Psychology*, 25: 1–65.

Schwartz, S.H., Cieciuch, J., Vecchione, M., Davidov, E., Fischer, D., Beierlein, C., Ramos, A., Verkasalo, M., Lönnkvist, J.-E., Demirutku, K., Dirilen-Gumus, O. and Konty, M. (2012) *Refining the Theory of Basic Individual Values*. Available at: www.zora.uzh.ch/id/eprint/66833/1/Schwartz_etal_in_press_JPSP.pdf [last accessed 16 September 2020].

Shweder, R.A. and Sullivan, M. (1993) 'Cultural psychology: Who needs it?', *Annual Review of Psychology*, 44: 497–523.
Singelis, T.M., Triandis, H.C., Bhawuk, D.P.S. and Gelfand, M.J. (1995) 'Horizontal and vertical dimensions of individualism and collectivism: A theoretical and measurement refinement', *Cross-Cultural Research*, 29(3): 240–275.
Skinner, B.F. (1938) *The Behavior of Organisms*. New York: Appleton-Century Co.
Spradley, J.P. (1980) *Participant Observation*. Belmont: Wadsworth.
Szkudlarek, B., Romani, L., Caprar, D.V. and Osland, J.S. (eds) (2020) *The Sage Handbook of Contemporary Cross-Cultural Management*. London: Sage.
Thomas, D.C. (2020) 'Reflexive Chapter: Some thoughts on cross-cultural management research', in B. Szkudlarek, L. Romani, D.V. Caprar and J.S. Osland (eds), *The Sage Handbook of Contemporary Cross-Cultural Management*. London: Sage. pp. 393–405.
Triandis, H.C. (1980) 'Reflections on trends in cross-cultural research', *Journal of Cross-Cultural Psychology*, 11(1): 35–58.
Triandis, H.C. (1995) *Individualism & Collectivism*. Oxford: Westview Press.
Triandis, H.C., Malpass, R.S. and Davidson, A.R. (1971) 'Cross-cultural psychology', *Biennial Review of Anthropology*, 7: 1–84.
Tylor, E.B. (1871) *Primitive Culture: Researches into the Development of Mythology*. London: John Murray.

Index

Page numbers in *italics* refer to figures and tables.

achieved vs ascribed status *155*
actor-network theory (ANT) 338–9
adaptation
   in negotiation of meaning 192
   and standardization, trade-offs between 247–51
Adler, N. 43
administration
   troubleshooting and leadership 57–8
   see also bureaucracy
affectiveness vs neutrality *155*
anthropology 405–6
Argyris, C. and Schön, D. 305
Aristotle 267
arranged marriages 173
artificial intelligence (AI)
   Cortana by Microsoft 345
   Internet of Things (IoT) 343–4
assimilation and multiculturalism 123–4

backpack, culture as 27–8, 166, 373, *374*
Barnard, A. 414
Bartlett, C.A. and Ghoshal, S. 249, 253
being-in-the-world 176–7, 407
   language and technology 175–6
Bennett, M.J. 383–4
Berger, P. and Luckmann, T. 172, 416
Bhabha, H.K. 224
bicultural identities
   halfies and hypenated selves 83–4
   hidden potentials 81–2
   high and low integration (BII) 78–9
   and third cultural identities 74–6, 77, 84
'born global' company 259, 260
Boston Consulting Group (BCG) *299*, *300*
Bourdieu, P. 202, 209, 407
Brannen, M.Y. 179
   and Thomas, D.C. 74

'bull-whip effect' 46–7
bureaucracy
   organizational design and 287–8
   see also administration
burnout, software developers avoiding 336

Cairns, G. and Śliwa, M. 267
capital, types of 57, 210–11
categorical imperative 265–6
causal vs holistic culture 404–13
child labour 219, 281
Christmas/seasonal greetings 213
chronemics 145–6
circuits of power 215–19
circular economy 264, 265, 295
Clegg, S. 215
closure effect, definition of 209
collaboration and coordination 281–3
colonialism 221–2
   see also postcolonial approaches to power
combination (SECI Spiral of organizational learning) 307, *308*
communication, culture as 142–50, 382–3
comparative approach *see* functionalist CCM
competence development 357–9, 393–6
   in context 369–78
   learning from surface to depth 378–81
   managerial status 155–6
   motivation 20–2
   opening and closing activities 361–9, 396–8
competition and cooperation 282
competitive advantage 254
compromise, in negotiation of meaning 192
computer game industry, UI design in 340–1
Confucian work dynamism/long-term vs short-term orientation 151, *152*
context/situation
   categories of difference 191

and communication 146–7, *148*
competence development 369–78
intercultural competencies 5, 6
'law of the situation' 310–11
meaning and experience in *see* interpretive CCM
contingency theory 326–7
continuous process technologies 327, 328
control and resistance in circuits of power 215–16
convergent and divergent processes, in global virtual teams 55–6
core technology, definition of 324
corporate citizenship 264
corporate internationalization, philosophies and aims underlying 252–4
corporate social performance 264
corporate social responsibility 263–8
corporate–start-up partnerships 32
Cortana by Microsoft 345
cosmopolitanism and multi-cultural rootedness 84–5
COVID-19 pandemic 60–1
 and entrepreneurship 305–6
 as organizational challenge 277–8, 313, *314*
critical CCM 198–9, 231–3
 functionalist and interpretive approaches, compared 110–11, 113–15
 international business (IB) 263
 moving beyond accepted normality 229–31
 opening case and closing activity 199–201, 233–4
 power 109–10, 114
  effects of ethnicity 121–6
  of history 219–29
  managing circuits of 215–19
  multidimensional approach 202–5
  multifaceted kaleidoscopic practice 206–14
critical discourse analysis (CDA) 208, 209
cross-cultural management (CCM) (overview) 3–4, 33–4
 changing realities of 6–14
 contemporary 4–6
 contemporary challenges 29–32
 definitions of 14–15
 'good' vs 'bad' 22–6
 opening case and closing activity 4–5, 34–5
 pyramid-building model 18–21
 triangle model 15–18
cultural assimilation 123–4
cultural capital 210

cultural complexity framework 45–50
cultural dimensions 23–6, 380–1
 see also cultural value orientations; functionalist CCM, comparative approach
cultural distance 257–8
cultural diversity, definition of 23
cultural flows
 and interconnectedness 51–3
 mimicry and hybridity 223–4, *225*
cultural glasses 26, 166, 373, *374*
cultural identities
 definition of 45
 switched 'on' and 'off' 45, 46, 47
 see also bicultural identities; identities of managers; identity; identity work
cultural intelligence and intercultural competencies 360
cultural knowledge and meaning 407
cultural norms 378–9
cultural patterns 378–80
cultural schemes 74
cultural universalism
 definition of 135
 vs particularism *154*
cultural value orientations 138–9, 140–2, 408–13
 see also cultural dimensions
cultural variance (CV) of technology 334
culture
 definition and management of 22–6
 metaphors of 26–9
culture effects, in global virtual teams 55
culture shock as trigger for intercultural learning 386–9
culture-free vs culture-bound technology 320–1
cyber-physical systems, definition of 343

Deal, T.E. and Kennedy, A.A. 22, 310, 369
deconstruction 230–1
deep culture 381
Demmel, H. with Küppersbusch, F. 345–6
denaturalization 229–30
differentiation and integration 281–3
digital divide, overcoming 322
discourse 206–9
dispersion and diversity, in global virtual teams 55–6
divergent and convergent processes, in global virtual teams 55–6
doxa, definition of 211

economic capital 210
efficiency and effectivity, trade-offs between 247–8

El-Mafaalani, A. 71
embedded systems, definition of 343
emic (inside) and etic (outside) perspectives 166–7, *168*, 181, 373, 374
　approximating emic meanings 186–90
　ethnocentric and ethnorelative perspectives in intercultural learning 383–4
　etic shortcomings 182–6
　integration of 375–6
　research approach 413–15
'empty signifiers' 218
enculturation, definition of 23
English language fluency 207–9
entrepreneurship
　and COVID-19 pandemic 305–6
　gender gaps in 158–9
epistemology, definition of 107
Erasmus + programme, EU 21–2
ethical imperialism 265
ethical relativism 265
ethical universalism 265
ethics and sustainability 263–8
ethnicity, power effects of 121–6
ethnocentric company 253
ethnocentrism 182–3, 383–4
ethnography, definition of 405
ethnorelativism 186, 383–4
European Union (EU/EC) 21–2, 61, 124, 245
Evans, D. 344
expatriate
　definition of 7
　monocultural vs student sojourner 70–2
experiential learning 358–9, *382*
explicit and tacit knowledge 306–9
exploitation and exploration modes of learning 304
externalization (SECI Spiral of organizational learning) 307, *308*

Facebook, new Samsung mobile on 332
fact and discourse 206–9
facts about ethnicity 125
Fang, T. 27
fear zone and personal growth process *370*, 371
field
　definition of 202
　and habitus 209–12
fieldwork, definition of 405
Finish–Spanish communicative norms 143
Fisher-Tiné, H. 226

'flattened' international business environment 321–4
Flyvjerg, B. 231, 268
Follett, M.P. 310–11
Foucault, M. 224
Fox, E.M. 57, 310, 311
framing and frames of reference 178–9
Friedman, T.L. 321
frontstage, backstage and offstage roles 289–90
functionalist CCM 108, 135, 159–61
　comparative approach formation of 137–50
　large-scale studies 150–9
　leadership styles 116–18
　international business (IB) 243
　interpretive and critical CCM, compared 109, 110–11, 113–14
　opening case and closing activity 136–7, 161–2
future perspective 59–60
　identity and mobility 85–7, 90–1

gender culture 18
gender gaps in entrepreneurship 158–9
Generation Z 9–10
generational culture 18
geocentric company 253
Giddens, A. 337
global company 249
global cultures 47
global leadership 57–8
global and local exposure of people and companies 245–53
global nomads 84
Global North and Global South
　definitions of 12, 221–2, 361
　influence of technology 322–3
global and virtual cultures 45–6
global and virtual teams
　differentiating between 54–6
　increasing relevance of 53–4
globalization and glocalization 245–7
GLOBE study 116–18, 157–8, 159, 280–1
Goffman, E. 175, 289–90
going and being international 254–5

habitus
　definition of 209, 407
　and fields 209–12
halfies and hyphenated selves 83–4
Hall, E.T. 142–50, 382–3

Index

Hatch, M.J. 279, 310
   with Cunliffe, A. 285, 295, 299
   Schultz, M. and 104
hegemonic discourse 207–9
Hendry, J. 29, 57–8
Héon, F.H. et al. 310, 311
hermeneutics and phenomenology 176–7
Hidegh, A. and Primecz, H. 229
history
   of ethnicity 122–5
   power of 219–29
Hofstede, G. 26, 151–5, 158, 243, 258, 280–1, 380
holistic vs causal culture 404–13
House, R. et al. *see* GLOBE study
human resource (HR) development 391–2, 393
human–computer interaction (HCI) *see* user interface (UI) design
hybridity and mimicry 223–4, *225*
hyphenated selves 83–4
hypotheses
   building 187–8
   testing 191

iceberg
   culture as 28–9, *119*, *174*, 373, *374*
   knowledge as *307*
identities of managers 68, 69–79, 87–9, 92–5
   mobility and migration 79–91
   opening case and closing activity 68–9, 95–7
identity
   culture as identity tree 27
   and identification 69, *70*
   negotiation 76
   and power 48–9
   social identity theory 184–5
identity work 77, 79
   definition of 76
   integrated model of 91–2, *93*
IKEA
   ethical dilemma 266–7
   pathway to internationalization 260–1
imaginative geographies and Orientalism 227–9
imperialism, definition of 221
inclusive and multicultural leadership 49–50
inclusive workplace: 'where are you from?' issue 89–90
individualism vs collectivism/communitarianism *151*, *155*, 409–13

indulgence vs restraint *152*, 243
innovation
   Jugaad 319–20, 348–9
   in negotiation of meaning 192
inside and outside perspectives *see* emic (inside) and etic (outside) perspectives
inside-out view of biculturalism 83–4
institutionalization 295–6, 297
institutions and principles of international business (IB) 244–5
integration
   bicultural identities 78–9
   challenge of 310–11
   cycle of intercultural action 375–8
   definition of 124
   and differentiation: building blocks of organization 281–3
   emic (inside) and etic (outside) perspectives 375–6
   identity work 91–2, *93*
   management styles 385
   regional economic 245
   and regulation in international business (IB) 244–5
intellectual capital 57
intensive technologies 332–3
inter-subjective reality 172–3
interconnectedness 51–3
intercultural competencies 5–6
   and cultural intelligence 360
   see also competence development
intercultural interactions 180–92
intercultural learning 358–9, *382*
   culture shock as trigger for 386–9
   stages of 383–4
intercultural management 15–16
intercultural perspective 17–18
intercultural training, definition of 7, 143
internal vs external control *155*
internalization (SECI Spiral of organizational learning) 308
international business (IB) 240, 269–71
   local and global exposure of people and companies 245–54
   opening case and closing activity 240–1, 271–3
   purpose and process of internationalization 254–61
   responsible stakeholder management 262–8
   and technology 320–4
   underpinnings of 242–5
international company 249

International Labour Organization (ILO):
    World Day against Child Labour 219
International Organization for Migration (IOM):
    definition of migrant 228–9
Internet of Things (IoT) 343–4
interpretive CCM 109, 166, 192–4
    functionalist and critical approaches,
        compared 110–11, 113, 114–15
    intercultural interactions 180–92
    locating and overcoming meaning-making
        gaps 119–20
    meaning and experience in context
        culture in context 177–80
        meaning beyond understanding 176–7
        starting point 182
        symbolic meaning 173–5
        transmission of meaning 175–6
    opening case and closing activity 168–72,
        194–5
    social construction of reality 172–3
    see also emic (inside) and etic (outside)
        perspectives

Javidan, M. 57
    et al. 158
Johanson, J. and Vahlne, J.-E. 257, 258–9, 260
Jugaad innovation 319–20, 348–9

Kanban and lean production 330–1
Kant, I. 265
Kipling, R. 221
Kluckhohn, C. and Strodtbeck, F. 138,
    140–1, 142
knowledge
    cultural 407
    learning and types of 306–9
    and power 224, *225*
Kogut, B. and Singh, H. 258

language
    anthropology and linguistics 138
    and communicative media 178
    discourse 206–9
    and technology
        being-in-the-world 175–6
        cultural code-switching 349–51
large batch/mass technologies 327, 328
'law of the situation' 310–11
leadership
    global 57–8
    GLOBE study 116–18, 157–8, 159, 280–1
    multicultural and inclusive 49–50
    roles across cultures 291–2
    styles 116–18
lean production and Kanban 330–1
learning *see* competence development;
    intercultural learning; organization,
    learning and change
Leavitt, B. and March, J. 306
Lewin, K. 303–4
liability of foreignness 257
local and global exposure of people and
    companies 245–53
local identity 84, 85
long-linked technologies 329–31
long-term vs short-term orientation 151, *152*

McCurdy, D.W. et al. 185
macro-cultures, definition of 42–3, 135, 277
Malinowski, B. 405–6, 414
manufacturing technologies and their cultural
    impact 327–8
March, J. 304
market entry and cultivation 256–9
markets 242–3
Markus, H.R. and Kitayama, S. 411–12
Martins, L.L. and Schilpzand, M.C. 54
masculinity vs femininity dimension *152*
mass/large batch technologies 327, 328
Maznevski, M. 18, 19, 55, 56
meaning
    cultural 407
    of ethnicity 121–2
    and meaning-making *see* interpretive CCM
mechanistic and organic organizational
    designs 285–6
mediating technologies 331–2
meetings 402–3, 421
    culture as communication 149
Merleau-Ponty, M. 407
meso-cultures, definition of 43–4, 277
metaphors
    of culture 26–9, 373, *374*
    of national culture 415
    of organizations 299–303
method and methodology, definitions of 107
micro-cultures, definition of 42–3, 277
microaggression 90
migrant, definitions of 81, 228–9
migration 80–1
    mobility and 79–91
mimicry and hybridity 223–4, *225*
monocultural expatriate vs
    student sojourner 70–2

monocultural identities 72–3, 75
Moore, F. and Mahadevan, J. 413, 414
Morgan, G. 301, *302*, 303
Morris, M.W. et al. 414
motivation and skills development 20–2
multi-paradigmatic approach and interplay 104
multicultural and inclusive leadership 49–50
multiculturalism and cultural assimilation 123–4
multinational companies, typology of 249–50
multiple cross-cultural adjustments 383–93
multiple cultures 50–1
   flows and interconnectedness 51–3
   nested 43–5

N-cultural individuals/interactions 18, 19, 30–1
N-cultural intercultural competencies 5
naïve realism 185
national culture
   metaphors of 415
   organizational politics of 296
   to global virtual teams 40–63
native categories 185–6
navigation systems, UI design in 341–2
neo-colonialism 221
networks and stakeholders 292–8, *325*
niche market 259
nodes
   and networks 292
   of power 215
non-paradigmatic approach 112
non-verbal communication 143
Nonaka, I. and Takeuchi, H. 307
'normalities', different 23–6
normalization, definition of 229

objective vs subjective culture 416–17
oceans and waves, culture as 27
onion, culture as 26
ontology, definition of 107
organic and mechanistic organizational designs 285–6
organization 277, 311–13
   design and roles 284–92
   learning and change 278, 303–11
   metaphors of 299–303
   opening case and closing activity 277–8, 313, *314*
   principles of organizing and 279–84
   see also under technology
organizational transformation
   definition of 278
   networks, stakeholders and environment 292–8, *325*
Orientalism and imaginative geographies 227–9
othering and saming 183–4

para-verbal communication 143
paradigms 103–5, 126–8
   contrasts and connections between 112–16
   definition of 104
   opening case and closing activity 105–6, 128–30
   paradigmapping 107–12
   in practice 116–26
participant observation 405–6
performance
   corporate social 264
   organizational 285
   role enactment 289–90
   team 54
personal growth process *370*, 371, 381–2
perspectivity and positionality 166
phenomenology and hermeneutics 176–7
Phillips, M. and Sackman, S. 50–1, 70
philosophies and aims underlying corporate internationalization 252–4
phronēsis 267–8
Pike, K. 413
Polanyi, M. 306, 407
polycentric company 253
polychronic time orientation (P-time) 146
positionality and perspectivity 166
'post-millennials' *see* Generation Z
postcolonial approaches to power 220–3
   creative potential 223–5
   and subalternity 226–7
power
   configurations of 12
   global virtual teams 55
   identity-related factors 48–9
   power distance *151*
   privilege–disadvantage ratios 408
   see also critical CCM; postcolonial approaches to power
price of wine 212
principles
   and institutions of international business (IB) 244–5
   of organizing and organizations 279–84
privilege, definition of 408
problematization and deconstruction 230–1
professional culture 18

professional global cultures 47
proxemics 144–5
psychic difference 257
psychological capital 57
pyramid-building model 18–21

Ravishankar, R.A. 89–90
reconstruction 230
recontextualization 179
refugee, definition of 81
regiocentric company 253
regional economic integration 245
regulation and integration 244–5
repatriation 70–2
research design 401–2, 418–20
    debate 1: causal vs holistic culture 404–13
    debate 2: emic vs etic perspectives 413–15
    debate 3: subjective vs objective culture 416–17
    opening case and closing activity 402, 421–4
resistance in circuits of power 215
responsible stakeholder management 262–8
reverse culture shock (W-curve) 388
rooted cosmopolitanism 84–5
Rotterdam, port of 53
routines 379
rules of practice 213–14

Said, E. 227–8
salience: cultural and social identities 46
saming and othering 183–4
Samsung mobile on Facebook 332
Schultz, M. and Hatch, M.J. 104
Schwartz, S.H. 139, 409–10
seasonal greetings 213
SECI Spiral of organizational learning 307–9
segregation, definition of 123
self-colonization 226
sensory experience *see* being-in-the-world
separation in negotiation of meaning 192
sequential vs synchronic time *155*
similarity-attraction phenomenon 185
single- and double-loop learning 305
situation *see* context/situation
skills *see* competence development; intercultural competencies
Skinner, B.F. 414
small batch/unit technologies 327, 328
small talk 146
smart technologies 343–4
Smith, A. 243
social capital 57, 210

social construction of reality 172–3
social distinctions *see* habitus
social identity theory 184–5
social legitimacy of organizations 295–6, 297
social media 345–6
socialization (SECI Spiral of organizational learning) 307, *308*
socio-technical systems (STS) 324–6, 338
software developers avoiding burnout 336
'software of the mind', culture as 26
sojourners 71
space bubbles (proxemics) 144–5
specificity vs diffuseness *155*
sprinkler strategy 257, 258
stakeholder analysis 262–3
stakeholder management, responsible 262–8
stakeholders
    networks and organizational environment 292–8, *325*
    and shareholders 262
standardization and adaptation, trade-offs between 247–51
Stellantis 297–8
structuration theory 337
structure vs agency 212–13
    rules of practice 213–14
    see also circuits of power
student sojourner vs monocultural expatriate 70–2
subalternity 226–7
subjective vs objective culture 416–17
successful cross-cultural management 31
Sumner, W.G. 182
sustainability
    ethics and 263–8
    3Ps of 264–5, 294, 295
symbolic capital 210–12
symbolic interactionism 174–5
symbolic meaning 173–5
    and meaning-making gaps 119–20

tacit and explicit knowledge 306–9
target marketing 259
task interdependence in global virtual teams 56
task variability and analysability 335, *336*
teams *see* global and virtual teams
technological imperative
    definition of 326
    and organizational design 335
technology 318–19, 347–8
    advances in 11

and international business (IB) 320–4
objects 407
opening case and closing activity 319–20, 348–51
and organization 324–36
   cross-cultural implications of 337–45
   social media 345–6
   transmission of meaning 175–6
   see also global and virtual cultures; global and virtual teams
third culture identities 75–6, 77, 84
Thompson, J. 329
3Ps of sustainable business 264–5, 294, 295
time-orientation (chronemics) 145–6
timing of market entry and cultivation 257–9
trade as positive-sum game 242–3
transnational company 250
transnational market segment 259
Triandis, H.C. 413, 414
triangle model 15–18
Trompenaars, F. and Hampden-Turner, 154–7
troubleshooting 57–8
trust in global virtual teams 56

U-curve model of culture shock 386–8
uncertainty avoidance *152*
unfreeze, move and refreeze phases of organizational change 303–4
unit/small batch technologies 327, 328

United Nations: IOM definition of migrant 228–9
universalism *see* cultural universalism; ethical universalism
Upsala model of corporate internationalization 258–9, 260–1
user interface (UI) design 339–43
utilitarianism 266

values
   cultural value orientations 138–9, 140–2, 408–13
   definition of 139
VIPs, psychology of space 145
virtual cultures 46
virtual interactions 178
virtual organizations 293
virtual teams *see* global and virtual teams

waterfall strategy 257, 258
Weber, M. 287
Westocentrism 263
'where are you from?' issue 89–90
whistleblowing 205
Woodward, J. 327
World Day against Child Labour 219
World Trade Organization (WTO) 11, 244–5

Zander, L. et al. 58, 307